RECAP

APPLY

REVIEW

SUCCEED

REVISION GUIDE

AQA GCSE

Religious Studies B (9 – 1)

Catholic Christianity

with Islam and Judaism

Harriet Power
David Worden

OXFORD
UNIVERSITY PRESS

OXFORD
UNIVERSITY PRESS

Great Clarendon Street, Oxford, OX2 6DP, United Kingdom

Oxford University Press is a department of the University of Oxford. It furthers the University's objective of excellence in research, scholarship, and education by publishing worldwide. Oxford is a registered trade mark of Oxford University Press in the UK and in certain other countries

© Oxford University Press 2018

British Library Cataloguing in Publication Data
Data available

978-0-19-842287-7

10 9 8 7 6 5 4 3 2 1

Paper used in the production of this book is a natural, recyclable product made from wood grown in sustainable forests. The manufacturing process conforms to the environmental regulations of the country of origin.

Printed in Italy by L.E.G.O. SpA

Links to third party websites are provided by Oxford in good faith and for information only. Oxford disclaims any responsibility for the materials contained in any third party website referenced in this work.

Please note that the Practice Questions in this book allow students a genuine attempt at practising exam skills, but they are not intended to replicate examination papers.

ACKNOWLEDGEMENTS

The publishers would like to thank the following for permissions to use their photographs:

Cover: Hands of God and Adam, detail from The Creation of Adam, from the Sistine Ceiling, 1511 (fresco) (pre restoration), Buonarroti, Michelangelo (1475-1564)/Vatican Museums and Galleries, Vatican City/Bridgeman Images

Artworks: QBS Learning, Jason Ramasami

Photos: p14: Cosmin-Constantin Sava/123RF; **p15:** Godong/UIG via Getty Images; **p16:** patrimonio designs ltd/Shutterstock; **p17:** Olan/Shutterstock; **p35:** Catherine Leblanc/Godong/Getty Images; **p52:** Adam Jan Figel/Shutterstock; **p56 (T):** Aldo Murillo/iStock; **p56 (B):** drbimages/iStock; **p66:** Zvonimir Atletic/Shutterstock; **p67:** Thoom/Shutterstock; **p86:** giulio napolitano/Shutterstock; **p95:** World History Archive/Alamy Stock Photo; **p102:** sedmak/iStock; **p110:** MuMuV/iStock; **p117:** afby71/iStock; **p128:** JOAT/Shutterstock; **p138:** Ira Berger/Alamy Stock Photo; **p140:** Gapper/Alamy Stock Photo; **p154:** Oleksandr Rupeta/Alamy Stock Photo; **p157:** Rhonda Roth/Shutterstock; **p160:** Design Pics Inc/Alamy Stock Photo; **p176:** Jes2u.photo/Shutterstock; **p205:** David Worden; **p208:** David Worden.

We are grateful to the authors and publishers for use of extracts from their titles and in particular for the following:

The Scripture quotations contained herein are from the **New Revised Standard Version Bible**, copyright © 1989, Division of Christian Education of the National Council of Churches of Christ in the U.S.A. Used by permission. All rights reserved. The New Revised Standard Version Catholic Edition of the Bible, Harper Catholic Bibles - a division of Harper Collins.; Excerpts from **The Qur'an OWC** translated by M. A. S. Abdel Haleem (Oxford University Press, 2008). © M. A. S. Abdel Haleem 2004, 2005. Reproduced with permission from Oxford University Press.; Excerpts from **Catechism of the Catholic Church**, http://www.vatican.va/archive/ccc_css/archive/catechism/ccc_toc.htm (Strathfield, NSW: St Pauls, 2000). © Libreria Editrice Vaticana. Reproduced with permission from The Vatican.; **Pope Benedict XVI:** *Deus Caritas Est*, December 25th 2005 (The Vatican, 2005). © Libreria Editrice Vaticana. Reproduced with permission from The Vatican.; **Pope Benedict XVI:** *World Day of Peace*, speech 2006, https://w2.vatican.va/content/benedict- (The Vatican, 2006). © Libreria Editrice Vaticana. Reproduced with permission from The Vatican.; **Pope Benedict XVI:** *Verbum Domini*, On the Word of God in the Life and Mission of the Church, September 30th 2010 (The Vatican, 2010). © Libreria Editrice Vaticana. Reproduced with permission from The Vatican.; **Pope Benedict XVI:** *Message for the World Day of Peace*, January 1st 2012 (The Vatican, 2012). © Libreria Editrice Vaticana. Reproduced with permission from The Vatican.; **Pope Francis:** Speech, June 7th 2013, (The Vatican, 2013). © Libreria Editrice Vaticana. Reproduced with permission from The Vatican.; **Pope Francis:** Speech to the 38th Conference of the FAO, June 20th 2013, (The Vatican, 2013). © Libreria Editrice Vaticana. Reproduced with permission from The Vatican.; **Pope Francis:** Speaking at a meeting with Italian President Giorgio Napolitano, June 8th 2013, (The Vatican, 2013). © Libreria Editrice Vaticana. Reproduced with permission from The Vatican.; **Pope Francis:** Twitter post, September 2nd 2013, https://twitter.com/pontifex/status/374466943312330753 (The Vatican, 2013). © Libreria Editrice Vaticana. Reproduced with permission from The Vatican.; **Pope Francis:** Speech, September 29th 2013, (The Vatican, 2013). © Libreria Editrice Vaticana. Reproduced with permission from The Vatican.; **Pope Francis:** *Evangelii Gaudium*, On the Proclamation of the Gospel in Today's World, November 24th 2013, (The Vatican, 2013). © Libreria Editrice Vaticana. Reproduced with permission from The Vatican.; **Pope Francis:** *Homily*, Mass at the Military Memorial of Redipuglia, September 13th 2014, (The Vatican, 2014). © Libreria Editrice Vaticana. Reproduced with permission from The Vatican.; **Pope Francis:** Speech at the Pontifical Academy of Sciences, October 27th 2014, (The Vatican, 2014). © Libreria Editrice Vaticana. Reproduced with permission from The Vatican.; **Pope Francis:** *Laudato Si*, May 24th 2015, (The Vatican, 2015). © Libreria Editrice Vaticana. Reproduced with permission from The Vatican.; **Pope John XXIII:** *Pacem in Terris*, On Establishing Universal Peace in Truth, April 11th 1963 (The Vatican, 1993). © Libreria Editrice Vaticana. Reproduced with permission from The Vatican.; **Pope John Paul II:** *Message for the World Day of Peace*, January 1st 2001 (The Vatican, 2001). © Libreria Editrice Vaticana. Reproduced with permission from The Vatican.; **Pope Paul VI:** *Sacrosanctum Concilium*, Constitution on the Sacred Liturgy, December 4th 1963 (The Vatican, 1963). © Libreria Editrice Vaticana. Reproduced with permission from The Vatican.; **Pope Paul VI:** *Dei Verbum*, Dogmatic Constitution on Divine Revelation, November 18th 1965 (The Vatican, 1965). © Libreria Editrice Vaticana. Reproduced with permission from The Vatican.; **Pope Paul VI:** *Inter Mirifica*, Decree on the Media of Social Communications, December 4th 1963 (The Vatican, 1963). © Libreria Editrice Vaticana. Reproduced with permission from The Vatican.; **Pope Paul VI:** *Dignitatis Humanae*, On the Right of the Person and of Communities to Social and Civil Freedom in Matters Religious, December 7th, 1965 (The Vatican, 1965). © Libreria Editrice Vaticana. Reproduced with permission from The Vatican.; **Pope Paul VI:** *Gaudium et Spes*, Pastoral Constitution on the Church in the Modern World, December 7th, 1965 (The Vatican, 1965). © Libreria Editrice Vaticana. Reproduced with permission from The Vatican.; **YOUCAT:** *YOUCAT*, (Ignatius Press, 2011). Reproduced with permission from Ignatius Press.

We have made every effort to trace and contact all copyright holders before publication, but if notified of any errors or omissions, the publisher will be happy to rectify these at the earliest opportunity.

Contents

PART ONE: CATHOLIC CHRISTIANITY 14

Introduction

What will the exam be like?

For your GCSE Religious Studies exam, you will sit two papers.

- **Paper 1 will cover Catholic Christianity.** Chapters 1 to 6 of this guide will cover six topics related to Catholic Christianity – creation, incarnation, the Triune God, redemption, church and eschatology. Paper 1 will feature questions on four of these topics. You will need to answer all four questions.

- **Paper 2 will cover Islam, Judaism and themes.**
  You will need to answer two questions on your chosen religion – either Islam or Judaism, not both. Chapters 7 and 8 of this guide will help you to answer the questions on Islam. Chapters 9 and 10 will help you to answer the questions on Judaism.

  You will also need to answer two questions chosen from three themes. Chapters 11 to 13 of this guide will cover the three themes – religion, relationships and families; religion, peace and conflict; and religion, human rights and social justice.

If you are studying **St Mark's Gospel**, Paper 2 section B will have **two questions on St Mark's Gospel** and you will need to answer both, as well as two questions on either Islam or Judaism from section A.

> **TIP**
>
> Each paper is 1 hour and 45 minutes long, and you'll need to answer four full questions. Aim to spend 25 minutes on each question.

What kind of questions will be on the exam?

Each question on the exam will be split into five parts, worth 1, 2, 4, 5 and 12 marks.

The 1 mark question

The 1 mark question tests knowledge and understanding.

It is always a **multiple-choice question** with four answers to choose from. It will usually include the command words: '**Which one of the following…**'

Which **one** of the following is the idea that God is three-in-one?

Put a tick (✔) in the box next to the correct answer.

A Atonement ☐

B Incarnation ☐

C Salvation ☐

D Trinity ☐

[1 mark]

How is it marked?

1 mark is awarded for a correct answer.

The 2 mark question

The 2 mark question tests knowledge and understanding.

It always begins with the command words 'Give two...' or 'Name two...'

Give **two** ways in which religious believers help victims of war.

[2 marks]

How is it marked?
1 mark is awarded for 1 correct point.
2 marks are awarded for 2 correct points.

TIP

The examiner is expecting two simple points, not detailed explanations. You would get 2 marks if you answered "1) praying for victims; 2) providing food and shelter". You don't need to waste time by writing in full sentences and giving long explanations.

The 4 mark question

The 4 mark question tests knowledge and understanding.

It always begins with the command words '**Explain two...**'

Explain **two** ways in which music influences Catholic worship.

[4 marks]

How is it marked?
For the first way or belief:

- 1 mark is awarded for a simple explanation
- 2 marks are awarded for a detailed explanation.

For the second way or belief:

- 1 mark is awarded for a simple explanation
- 2 marks are awarded for a detailed explanation.

So for the full 4 marks, the examiner is looking for two ways/beliefs and for you to give detailed explanations of both. The examiner is expecting you to write in full sentences.

What is a detailed explanation?
An easy way to remember what you need to do for the four mark question is:

Make one point ➤ Develop it

Make a second point ➤ Develop it

TIP

One point you might make to answer this question is to say "Music increases the beauty of worship." This would get you 1 mark. For a second mark you could develop the point by giving further information: "Sacred music can make a service more joyful and lift people's hearts to God." There is more you could probably say, but as you'd get 2 marks for this, it would be better to turn your attention to thinking about a second way in which music influences Catholic worship, for example by getting people more fully involved in worship, and then developing that second point.

But how do you develop a point? You might do this by:

- giving more information
- giving an example
- referring to a religious teaching or quotation.

The 'Great Britain' question

In the questions on Islam and Judaism, there may sometimes be additional wording to the 4 mark question, asking you to explain contrasting or similar beliefs between Islam/Judaism and '**the main religious tradition of Great Britain.**'

> Explain **two** ways in which the beliefs of Islam/Judaism and the main religious tradition of Great Britain about abortion are similar.
>
> **[4 marks]**

The main religious tradition of Great Britain is Christianity, so in your answer **you must refer to Christianity and either Islam or Judaism.**

The 5 mark question

The 5 mark question tests knowledge and understanding.

Like the 4 mark question, it always begins with the command words '**Explain two…**' In addition it will also ask you to '**Refer to scripture or another source of Christian/Muslim/Jewish belief and teaching in your answer.**'

> Explain **two** ways in which Jesus is the fulfillment of the law.
>
> Refer to scripture or another source of Christian belief and teaching in your answer.
>
> **[5 marks]**

How is it marked?

For the first reason/teaching/belief:

- 1 mark is awarded for a simple explanation
- 2 marks are awarded for a detailed explanation.

For the second reason/teaching/belief:

- 1 mark is awarded for a simple explanation
- 2 marks are awarded for a detailed explanation.

PLUS 1 mark for a relevant reference to sacred writings or another source of religious belief.

So for the full 5 marks, the examiner is looking for two reasons/teachings/beliefs and for you to give detailed explanations of both, just like the 4 mark question. **For the fifth mark, you need to make reference to a writing or teaching that is considered holy or authoritative by a religion.** The examiner is expecting you to write in full sentences. You might aim to write five sentences.

> ## TIP
>
> If you can quote exact phrases this will impress the examiner, but if you can't then it's fine to paraphrase. You do not need to know the chapter and verse of the quotation, but it would be helpful to name the holy book, for example, to specify that it is a teaching from the Bible.

What counts as 'scripture or another source of religious belief and teaching'?

Scripture and religious beliefs or teachings might include:

- a quotation from a holy book, for example the Bible or the Qur'an
- a statement of religious belief such as the Apostles' Creed or the Shahadah
- a prayer such as the Lord's prayer or the Shema
- a statement made by a religious leader, for example the Pope or Chief rabbi
- a quotation from a religious text such as the Catechism of the Catholic Church or Hadith.

The 12 mark question

The 12 mark question tests analytical and evaluative skills. It will always begin with a statement, and then ask you to **evaluate the statement.** There will be bullet points guiding you through what the examiner expects you to provide in your answer.

From Paper 1 and Paper 2 section A (Islam or Judaism):

'The Bible tells Christians all they need to know about God's creation.'

Evaluate this statement. In your answer you should:
- give reasoned arguments to support this statement
- give reasoned arguments to support a different point of view
- refer to Christian teaching
- reach a justified conclusion.

[12 marks]
[+3 SPaG marks]

TIP

The examiners are not just giving marks for what you know, but for your ability to weigh up different sides of an argument, making judgements on how convincing or weak you think they are. The examiner will also be looking for your ability to connect your argument logically.

From Paper 2 section B (themes):

'War is never right'

Evaluate this statement. In your answer you:

- should give reasoned arguments in support of this statement
- should give reasoned arguments to support a different point of view
- should refer to Christian arguments
- may refer to non-religious arguments
- should reach a justified conclusion.

[12 marks]
[+3 SPaG marks]

TIP

For Paper 2, on thematic issues, you can use different views from within Christianity, and you can also use non-religious views

How is it marked?

Level	What the examiner is looking for	Marks
4	A well-argued response with two different points of view, both developed to show a logical chain of reasoning that leads to judgements supported by relevant knowledge and understanding. ***References to religion applied to the issue.***	10–12 marks
3	Two different points of view, both developed through a logical chain of reasoning that draws on relevant knowledge and understanding. ***Clear reference to religion.***	7–9 marks
2	One point of view developed through a logical chain of reasoning that draws on relevant knowledge and understanding. OR Two different points of view with supporting reasons. ***Students cannot move above Level 2 if they don't include a reference to religion, or only give one view point.***	4–6 marks
1	One point of view with supporting reasons. OR Two different points of view, simply expressed.	1–3 marks

Tips for answering the 12 mark question

- **Remember to focus your answer on the statement you've been given**, for example 'War is never right.'

- **Include different viewpoints, one supporting the statement, one arguing against it** – for example one viewpoint to support the idea that war is *never* right, and an alternative viewpoint to suggest that war is sometimes necessary.

- **Develop both arguments showing a logical chain of reasoning** – draw widely on your knowledge and understanding of the subject of war, try to make **connections** between ideas. Write a detailed answer and use evidence to support your arguments.

- **Be sure to include religious arguments** – a top level answer will explain how religious teaching is relevant to the argument.

- **Include evaluation** – you can make judgements on the strength of arguments throughout, and you should finish with a justified conclusion. If you want to, you can give your own opinion.

- **Write persuasively - use a minimum of three paragraphs** (one giving arguments for the statement, one for a different point of view and a final conclusion). The examiner will expect to see extended writing and full sentences.

Spelling, Punctuation and Grammar

Additional marks for **SPaG – spelling, punctuation and grammar** will be awarded on the 12 mark question.

A maximum of 3 marks will be awarded if:

- your spelling and punctuation are consistently accurate

- you use grammar properly to control the meaning of what you are trying to say

- you use specialist and religious terminology appropriately. For example, the examiner will be impressed if you use appropriately the term 'resurrection' rather than just 'rising from the dead'.

> **TIP**
>
> This question is worth the same amount of marks as the 1, 2, 4 and 5 mark questions combined. Try to aim for at least a full page of writing, and spend 12 minutes or more on this question.

> **TIP**
>
> Always try to use your best written English in the long 12 mark questions. It could be a chance to pick up extra marks for SPaG.

In Paper 1, SPaG will be assessed on each 12 mark question, and the examiner will pick your best mark to add to the total.

In Paper 2, SPaG will be awarded on both 12 mark questions for Islam or Judaism.

How to revise using this book

This Revision Guide takes a three step approach to help with your revision.

RECAP	This is an overview of the key information. It is not a substitute for the full student book, or your class notes. It should prompt you to recall more in-depth information. Diagrams and images are included to help make the information more memorable.
APPLY	Once you've recapped the key information, you can practise applying it to help embed the information. There are two questions after each Recap section. The first question will help you rehearse some key skills that you need for the questions on the exam that test your knowledge (the 1, 2, 4 and 5 mark questions). The second question will help you rehearse some key skills that you will need for the 12 mark question, which tests your evaluative skills. There are suggested answers to the Apply activities at the back of the book.
REVIEW	At the end of each chapter you will then have a chance to review what you've revised. The exam practice pages contain exam-style questions for each question type. For the 4, 5 and 12 mark questions, there are writing frames that you can use to structure your answer, and to remind yourself of what it is that the examiner is looking for. When you've answered the questions you can use the mark schemes at the back of the book to see how you've done. You might identify some areas that you need to revise in more detail. And you can turn back to the pages here for guidance on how to answer the exam questions.

The revision guide is designed so that alongside revising *what* you need to know, you can practise *how* to apply this knowledge in your exam. There are regular opportunities to try out exam practice questions, and mark schemes so you can see how you are doing. Keep recapping, applying and reviewing, particularly going over those areas that you feel unsure about, and hopefully you will build in skills and confidence for the final exam.

Good luck!

1.1 Michelangelo's *Creation of Adam*

RECAP

Essential information:

☐ *Creation of Adam* is a painting by Michelangelo that shows God bringing Adam to life.

☐ The painting reflects a number of important Christian beliefs about God's nature and his role as the creator of humanity.

How does *Creation of Adam* reflect Catholic beliefs?

Creation of Adam was painted by Michelangelo on the ceiling of the Sistine Chapel in Rome in the sixteenth century. It is one of the most famous works of Christian art on the theme of creation.

Creation is the act through which God made the universe. The story of creation is told in **Genesis**, the first book in the Bible. Genesis provides the foundation for Christian beliefs about creation, and about God's nature as the creator. These beliefs are reflected in *Creation of Adam* in the following ways.

- Adam is not yet fully alive, he is waiting for God's touch to bring him to life
- Shows that humanity depends on God for life

- God and Adam both look powerful and muscular, they are lying in similar positions
- Reflects the teaching that humanity is made in the image of God (Genesis 1:27)

- God looks much older than Adam
- Shows that God is ancient and eternal, while humanity is not

- Adam is shown as the perfect man, full of strength and potential
- Reflects the teaching that God made everything 'very good' (Genesis 1:31 (NRSV))

- God is carried through the air by a group of angels
- Shows that God is **transcendent** (beyond and outside life on earth and the universe)

- God is shown bringing a human to life rather than any other species
- Reflects the teaching that humans are unique, as they are specially created by God and are in close contact with him

- God and Adam are reaching out their hands to each other
- Reflects the idea that there is a longing for a close relationship between God and humanity

Paintings allow artists to express ideas that can be hard to convey in words. They can inspire people and help them understand their faith. But paintings are also limited in what they can show. It can be difficult to present complex spiritual ideas or teachings in a work of art. For example, here are two ways in which *Creation of Adam* doesn't reflect Catholic beliefs:

- Genesis 2:7 says that God brought Adam to life by breathing into his nostrils, rather than touching him.
- In the painting God and Adam are nearly the same size, suggesting that humans and God are equal. This goes against Catholic teachings.

APPLY

A Give two ways in which *Creation of Adam* reflects the belief that God made everything to be good.

B '*Creation of Adam* illustrates important Christian beliefs about the relationship between God and humanity.'

Give three arguments to support this statement, and one argument against it.

TIP

Always read the statement carefully. Here your arguments need to be about how God and humanity relate to each other. Considering Christian beliefs that are just about God, or just about humanity, is not enough.

RECAP

Essential information:

☐ Hildreth Meière's mosaic in New York's St Bartholomew's Church shows the hand of God in the act of creation.

☐ Like *Creation of Adam*, the mosaic shows that God is powerful and eternal.

☐ Whereas *Creation of Adam* focuses in on the creation of humanity, the mosaic conveys a sense that God is always creating everything.

How does Meière's mosaic reflect Catholic beliefs?

In the early twentieth century, the American artist Hildreth Meière created a number of mosaics for St Bartholomew's Church in New York, USA. This one shows the hand of God in the act of creation.

- Lines extend from God's hand to the edge of the circle (which depicts the edge of the universe)
- Reflects the idea that God created everything in the universe, and that his influence and power touch all things

- God's hand is large compared to the size of the cloud above it
- Helps to show God's greatness and power

TIP

If you are asked about works of art in your exam, you won't be given any pictures for reference – so make sure you can describe the art in words.

Comparing Meière's mosaic and *Creation of Adam*

	Creation of Adam	Meière's mosaic
God's nature	Both show God is the creator Both show God is powerful and eternal	
How God is shown	God is shown as an old man. Some Christians object to this as they think an eternal God should not be shown as an ageing man	Only God's hand is shown. Some Christians think this symbol of God's creative power is a more acceptable way of showing God, as God is infinite
God's role in creation	*Creation of Adam* focuses on the act of God creating humanity, so it conveys more about the relationship between God and humanity	Meière's mosaic is more abstract. It conveys a greater sense that God is always creating everything, but shows less about God's relationship with humanity

APPLY

A Give two ways in which Meière's mosaic shows that God is powerful.

B 'Meière's mosaic gives a better idea about God's role as the creator than *Creation of Adam*'.

Do you agree with this statement? Explain your reasoning.

Why might someone else have a different point of view?

TIP

For your exam you should be able to compare *Creation of Adam* with one other work of art that also shows a Christian understanding of creation. You can choose Meière's mosaic or another work of art such as the stained-glass window depicting Adam and Eve by Jean-Baptiste Capronnier, or the fresco depicting the creation of the sun and moon by John of Kastav.

RECAP

Essential information:

☐ The creation story in Genesis 1 shows that God is the creator of everything, and that he created humanity in his own image.

☐ It shows that God is **transcendent** (beyond and outside life on earth and the universe), as he is able to create solely through the power of his own word.

☐ It also shows that God is **omnipotent** (all-powerful), as he is able to create anything he wants.

Creation in Genesis 1

Genesis 1 describes God's creation of the universe. It tells how God created it over six days, using the power of his word to bring things into being.

Unlike some Christians, Catholics do not think that Genesis 1 is meant to be a scientific account of creation (see page 21). However, they do believe Genesis 1 teaches important truths about God's nature and his role in creation.

What does Genesis 1 teach about the nature of God?

God is creator

- **God is the only creator, who has created everything.** This is significant for Christians because it means they should worship only this one God.
- All of creation is special, because all of it has been created by God. Therefore it should be cared for and looked after (see page 18).
- Genesis 1:27 shows that God created humans in his own image, which means that **humans share qualities with God** (like love and compassion). These qualities allow humans to have a close relationship with God.

God is omnipotent

> ❝God saw everything that he had made, and indeed, it was very good. ❞
> *Genesis 1:31* (NRSV)

- **God has the power to do whatever he wants**; he can even create things from nothing.
- Genesis 1:31 says everything God made is 'very good'; God is so powerful he can make everything exactly the way he wants it.
- Belief in God's omnipotence inspires Christians to trust in God, as they know he has the power to do or change anything.

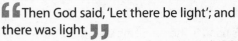

The nature of God

God is transcendent

> ❝Then God said, 'Let there be light'; and there was light. ❞
> *Genesis 1:3* (NRSV)

- **God only needs his own word in order to create**; when he says 'Let there be ...', that thing immediately comes into being. God is completely above and beyond the created world – he is transcendent.
- The idea of transcendence also means **God is beyond human understanding.** Christians believe God cannot fully be described in human words, or fully understood by human minds; God's transcendence inspires awe.

APPLY

A Explain two ways in which Genesis 1 shows that God is omnipotent.

B 'The most important lesson that Genesis 1 teaches Catholics is to trust in God.'

Evaluate this statement.

TIP

To 'evaluate' this statement, explain whether you think it's true or not, and why. Consider whether there are other beliefs supported by Genesis 1 that are more important for Catholics.

Essential information:

☐ Genesis 2 shows that humans share the Spirit of God.

☐ Genesis 2 shows that God has given humans **free will** (the ability to make decisions and think for themselves).

Humans share the Spirit of God

> **"** … then the Lord God formed man from the dust of the ground, and breathed into his nostrils the breath of life; and the man became a living being. **"**
>
> *Genesis 2:7* (NRSV)

- Genesis 2:8 explains how God made humans in his image.
- God created Adam, the first man, by breathing into him.
- The Hebrew word for 'breath' is *ru'ach*, which is also translated as 'spirit'.
- This shows that **humans share the Spirit of God**; God's spirit gives humans some of his qualities.

Humans are given the gift of free will

Christians believe Genesis 2 shows that God has given humans free will.

- It describes how God made the garden of Eden for Adam to live in.
- God tells Adam that he may eat from any tree in the garden except for the tree of the knowledge of good and evil.
- Although God 'commands' Adam not to eat from the tree, he doesn't actively prevent Adam from doing so. He gives Adam a choice: the free will to decide for himself whether or not to eat from the tree.

Free will doesn't mean that humans can do whatever they like without any consequences. Christians believe that using free will to sin results in turning away from God, and this is why evil exists in the world. Using free will to live in a way that pleases God brings humans closer to God.

A Give two examples in the Genesis creation stories that show that God has given humans free will.

B 'The idea that humans have free will is the teaching in the Genesis creation stories that has the greatest influence on how Catholics live their lives today.'

Give arguments to support this view. Then give arguments against it.

TIP

To help answer this question, you could make a list of the main beliefs in the Genesis creation stories, and then write down a few sentences to say how each belief influences the way Catholics live today. Your knowledge from the rest of the course will help here.

1.5 The significance of the creation stories for Catholics

Essential information:

☐ The Genesis creation stories teach Christians that the idea of **stewardship** is important: God expects them to look after the world and take care of it on his behalf.

☐ The creation stories also teach that humans have **dignity** (they are worthy of honour and respect), and that the **sanctity of life** is important (life is holy and sacred).

Stewardship

- In Genesis 1:28, God tells Adam and Eve to 'subdue' the earth and 'have dominion' over every living thing. This suggests that humans have been given **power and authority to rule over all other creatures**.
- In Genesis 2:15, God puts Adam in the garden of Eden to 'till it and keep it'. This suggests **looking after the world with care and love**.
- These two verses teach Christians that they have a duty to look after the environment on behalf of God.
- Christians believe the world is a gift from God, but God expects them to protect and care for the world in return.

TIP
Page 24 describes some of the ways that Catholics try to act as good stewards of the earth.

> **"**This responsibility for God's earth means that human beings … must respect the laws of nature and the delicate [balance] existing between the creatures of this world.**"**
>
> *Laudato Si 68*

TIP
This belief means Catholics are against practices that do not respect people's dignity, such as exploiting the poor (see page 206) and racial discrimination (see page 211).

The dignity of human beings

- Genesis 1 states that God made humans 'in his image' (Genesis 1:27).
- **All humans are equal** because they have all been created by God and share in the qualities of God.
- For Catholics, this means that **all people have dignity** – they are worthy of honour and respect.
- Catholics believe that everyone should respect their own dignity and the dignity of other people.

The sanctity of life

- In Genesis 1, God blesses humans after he creates them (Genesis 1:28).
- Catholics believe that **all creation is holy** because it has been created and blessed by God.
- This idea that life is holy and sacred – particularly human life – is known as the sanctity of life.
- For Catholics, belief in the sanctity of life means that every stage of life should be treated with care and respect. This is an important reason why Catholics are against euthanasia (see page 105) and abortion (see page 41).

APPLY

A Give two ways that belief in the sanctity of life influences Catholics today.

B 'The teachings in the Genesis creation stories mean that humans can do what they like with the world's resources.'

Give arguments for and against this view.

Would the majority of Christians agree with this view? Explain your answer.

TIP
Page 23 will help you to answer this question.

1.6 The origins and structure of the Bible

Essential information:

☐ The Bible is the sacred book of Christianity. It contains different types of writing (literary forms) such as historical accounts, poems and letters, which were written for different audiences and purposes.

☐ The first part of the Bible is the Old Testament. It tells of God's relationship with the Jews during the years before Jesus was born.

☐ The second part of the Bible is the New Testament, written by followers of Jesus in the century after his death. It tells of his life and teachings.

The Old Testament

The Old Testament describes how God guided the Jews throughout their early history, before the arrival of Jesus. It contains four main sections.

Law

The first five books, telling how the Jews became the people of God. Also contain the 'laws' or guidelines that God wanted the Jews to follow (including the Ten Commandments).

History

These show how God guided the Jews and how they often refused to listen. These stories were included to help later generations avoid making the same mistakes.

Wisdom

Include a mixture of prayers, psalms, poems and books of advice. These help people understand their faith and live in a way that pleases God.

Prophecy

The books of the prophets whose inspired words challenged the people to remain faithful to God and taught them that God is active in the world.

The New Testament

The New Testament deals with the life and teachings of Jesus and his **apostles** (Jesus' closest followers, who became leaders of the early Church). It can be split into four main sections.

The Gospels

Cover the actions and teachings of Jesus.

The Acts of the Apostles

Tell of some of the events in the early Church (up to about 60CE).

The Epistles

Letters that were written by the apostles and discuss how to follow Jesus' teachings in everyday life.

The Book of Revelation

Written by the apostle John. It includes his own mystical visions, which some Christians believe describe the end of the world.

These books were not the only early Christian writings, but they were accepted into the New Testament because they passed four important criteria:

- They were backed by the authority of one of the apostles, or someone close to the apostles.
- They were written early on (mostly before the end of the first century).
- They agreed with other teachings and accounts of Christian beliefs.
- They were accepted by all Christian Churches at the time.

A Name two of the main sections in the Old Testament and describe what they contain.

B 'The New Testament is the only part of the Bible that Christians need to read.'

Explain why most Christians would disagree with this statement. Give examples in your answer.

TIP

When you answer the 12 mark question it is always a good idea to back up your arguments by giving specific examples. Here you can refer to specific books from the Bible in your answer.

1.7 Inspiration and the Bible as the word of God

Essential information:

☐ The Bible is the word of God; it reveals God to humans and teaches them about God and what he wants for humanity.

☐ The writers of the Bible were inspired (or guided) by the **Holy Spirit**, who is the Third Person of the Trinity (see page 49).

☐ The Bible should be interpreted through the teachings of the **Magisterium** (the teaching authority of the Catholic Church).

How is the Bible the word of God?

The Bible is called the word of God because Christians believe that throughout the Bible, God speaks to his people. This happens in a number of ways:

- **God guided the writing of the Bible through the Holy Spirit.** The Holy Spirit is God's presence and love in the world, who guides people to do the right thing and to know the will of God. Christians call this guidance **inspiration**. They believe that the writers of the Bible were inspired – or guided – by the Holy Spirit.
- **The Bible contains the word of God given by the prophets.** These were people inspired by God. As they warned and guided people to remain faithful to God, they passed on God's word and message.
- **The Bible tells of the actions and teachings of Jesus in the Gospels.** Jesus is the Word of God made flesh (see page 31). Through Jesus, God speaks directly to all people.
- **The Bible contains the writings of the apostles in the Epistles.** The apostles were Jesus' closest followers and were filled with the Holy Spirit. This inspired them to preach and teach God's word.

Interpreting the Bible today through the Magisterium

The Bible was written a long time ago, by people living in a very different time and society. Catholics need guidance on how to interpret the Bible today, and how to apply its teachings to their everyday lives.

Catholics are guided in their interpretation of the Bible by the Magisterium. This is the teaching authority of the Catholic Church, which comes from the Pope and the bishops. They have the authority to shape and confirm the Church's teachings (see page 54).

Catholics believe that the **Magisterium is continually inspired and guided by the Holy Spirit**. This means they can trust the Magisterium to correctly interpret the meaning of the Bible.

TIP

You can use this quote in your exam to show that Catholics believe the Bible is the word of God. They also believe it should be interpreted by the Magisterium to make the word of God relevant to the modern world.

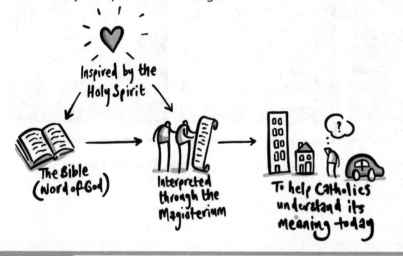

Inspired by the Holy Spirit

The Bible (Word of God)

Interpreted through the Magisterium

To help Catholics understand its meaning today

❝ Sacred Scripture is the word of God … while sacred tradition takes the word of God … and hands it on to their successors in its full purity ❞

Dei Verbum 9

Ⓐ Explain two ways in which the Bible is the word of God.

Ⓑ 'Christians do not need the Church. They can learn everything about how to be a good Christian from the Bible alone.'

Explain why Catholics would disagree with this statement.

Why might some other Christians agree with it?

RECAP

Essential information:

☐ The Catholic Church teaches that the Genesis creation stories should not be interpreted literally. This means that Catholics can accept scientific explanations for how the universe was created.

☐ Some Christians (fundamentalists) believe the Genesis creation stories should be interpreted literally, and that the universe was created in six days.

Catholic interpretations of the Genesis creation stories

The Genesis creation stories tell how God created the universe and humanity (see pages 16–17). The Catholic Church teaches that these creation stories are **myths**. This means that:

- they are stories that intend to convey deep or complex spiritual truths
- they are not meant to be taken literally.

Catholics believe the creation stories are not meant to be scientific explanations of how creation happened. For example, Genesis 1 tells how God created the universe and everything in it in six days. The Catholic Church teaches that 'day' in this context means a much longer period of time.

This means that Catholics can accept the creation stories alongside the Big Bang theory and the theory of evolution.

For Catholics, the main messages of the creation stories are that:

1 God made everything.
2 Everything that God made was good.
3 Humans are the high point of God's creation.

> **Example of a creation story as a myth**
> In Genesis 2, God creates the first woman from the rib of the first man. Catholics do not think that this actually happened. Instead, this is meant to show that humanity is divided into two complementary halves that complete each other.

> ❝ The Big Bang … does not contradict the divine act of creating, but rather requires it. The evolution of nature does not contrast with the notion of Creation ❞
> *Pope Francis, 27 October 2014*

Fundamentalist interpretations of the Genesis creation stories

Fundamentalists are Christians who interpret the Bible more literally. Many believe that the Bible is a factual record which describes events exactly as they happened. This is because:

- The Bible is the word of God so it must be accurate in all respects.
- God loves humans so wouldn't mislead them by giving them incorrect information.
- Humans have no right to prefer their own interpretations to the actual words of God.

This means that **many fundamentalists believe the universe and all life in it were literally created in six days**, as described in Genesis 1. They would therefore disagree with the theory of evolution.

However, not all fundamentalists hold the same views. For example, some are happy to accept that the universe might be as old as scientists suggest. But they still disagree with the theory of evolution, believing instead that God made humans separately (rather than them evolving from other species), as indicated in the Genesis creation stories.

APPLY

(A) Give two messages of the creation stories for Catholics.

(B) 'The universe must have been created in six days because that is what the Bible says happened.'

Explain why fundamentalists agree with this view.

Now explain why Catholics disagree with this view. What do Catholics believe instead?

Essential information:

- [ ] **Natural law** refers to the moral principles and values (or 'laws') that are thought to be inherent to all humans.

- [ ] Natural law states that Catholics should do good and avoid evil. They should also respect the sanctity of life.

- [ ] The Catholic Church teaches that science and religion need to support and work with each other.

What is natural law?

Natural law refers to the idea that **humans are born with an understanding of what is right and wrong**. This understanding is 'natural'; it is a part of human nature.

The Catholic Church teaches that humans are born with the ability to know what is good and what isn't because:

- **God made all of creation good** (Genesis 1). Humans are part of this creation.
- **Humans are made in the image of God** (Genesis 1:27). They share in his qualities, including the quality of being good.

For the Catholic Church this means that:

- **Following natural law is important because it is part of God's will for humans**. God created humans with this in-built moral code, so humans should follow it.
- **Humans should not need rules to tell them what is right**. Natural law states that humans should know right from wrong intuitively.

The most basic natural law is to **do good and avoid evil**. But there are other moral principles that are also associated with natural law, for example to **protect and preserve life**. This is related to the idea of the sanctity of life (see page 18), which teaches that all life is holy and sacred, so it should be protected.

The Catholic Church and science

Between 1962 and 1965, the Pope and the bishops held a series of meetings to talk about important issues and update the Catholic Church's teachings on a number of topics. These meetings are known as the **Second Vatican Council**.

> **"**if methodical investigation … is carried out in a genuinely scientific manner … it never truly conflicts with faith **"**
>
> *Gaudium et Spes 36*

TIP

This quote can be used in your exam to show that the Catholic Church believes religion and science do not have to oppose each other.

The Second Vatican Council stressed that **religion and science support each other**. It confirmed the following teachings:

Teaching	Example
• Religion and science do not have to contradict each other • The Catholic Church is very supportive of advances in science that help people to understand God's creation • Religion and science might come up with slightly different answers, but this is because they are asking slightly different questions	• If the Genesis creation stories are read as myths rather than literally, they do not contradict the theory of evolution • Georges Lemaitre was a Catholic priest who first proposed the Big Bang theory, which explains how the universe began • Religion tries to explain *why* things happen while science tries to explain *how* things happen

 A Give two reasons why Catholics believe people are born with an understanding of natural law.

 B 'It is not possible to believe in the Big Bang theory and in the Christian faith.'

Give two reasons why the Catholic Church disagrees with this statement.

Why might some other Christians agree with this statement?

TIP

The information on page 21 will help you to answer this question.

1.10 Caring for the environment

Essential information:

☐ Christians should care for the environment because the whole of creation is God's gift, and therefore holy because it comes from God.

☐ Christians show their love of God by treating other people, animals and the environment with love and respect.

☐ Jesus taught Christians to 'love your neighbour as yourself'. For Christians, this means caring for the environment in which their neighbour lives.

Reasons to care for the environment

Why do Catholics believe they should care for the environment?

Reason 1	Reason 2	Reason 3
All of creation is special because it was made by God to be good (Genesis 1).	God made humans stewards of the earth (Genesis 2).	Jesus taught Christians to 'love your neighbour as yourself' (Mark 12:31).
This means that every part of it should be valued.	This means that humans have been given a responsibility by God to look after the earth (see page 18).	For Christians, the word 'neighbour' includes all the people they share the world with.
Catholics can show their love for God by taking care of the world that he has created.		So Christians are expected to understand how pollution and littering will affect all human life, including future generations.

The Church's teachings on caring for the environment

The Catholic Church teaches that there is a delicate balance within creation. Damaging one aspect of the environment may affect other elements too. **Natural resources** – materials found in nature and used by humans to make more complex things – should be used carefully to preserve them for future generations. Catholics should think about how their actions will affect the world in the centuries to come.

> **Example of the Church helping to protect the environment**
> In 2008, the Vatican installed thousands of solar panels on the roof of one of its main halls. These help to light and regulate the temperature of a number of buildings in the Vatican. They have reduced the Vatican's carbon emissions by about 200 tonnes each year.

A Give two religious reasons why Catholics believe it is important to care for the environment.

B 'The best way for Catholics to show love for their neighbour is to protect the environment.'

Read this response which argues against the statement:

There are more direct ways that Catholics can show love for their neighbour. For example, Catholics can show love by helping people directly – such as by giving them food or clothes – rather than just helping to protect the environment they live in. This is a better way to show love for your neighbour as it more closely follows Jesus' advice for how to care for people in the parable of the Sheep and the Goats.

Write a paragraph in reply to this response, which supports the statement above.

Then write a concluding paragraph where you weigh up both sides of the argument and decide whether you think the statement is true or not.

TIP
The parable of the Sheep and the Goats is discussed on page 36.

Essential information:

☐ The idea that Christians have a duty to look after the environment on God's behalf is known as stewardship (see page 18).

☐ Catholics can help to protect the environment at local, national and global levels.

☐ Ways that Catholics might do this include living in a way that has less impact on the environment, educating others about how to care for the environment, and campaigning against policies or laws that damage the environment.

Ways that Catholics can care for the environment

Catholics believe that God expects them to care for the environment on his behalf. This can be done on three levels:

1 At a local level:
- throw away less waste
- recycle more
- walk, cycle or use public transport instead of driving
- take part in local environmental projects
- encourage churches to reduce their carbon footprints (e.g. by installing solar panels)
- educate others about the importance of protecting the environment.

2 At a national level:
- put pressure on politicians to support laws that protect the environment
- support and buy products from environment-friendly businesses
- put pressure on companies to ensure they follow environment-friendly policies.

3 At a global level:
- put pressure on governments to implement policies agreed at international meetings (such as Rio +20)
- boycott or help to expose international companies that threaten the environment.

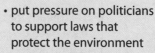

TIP

You can use this quote in your exam to show that the Catholic Church teaches that everyone should actively help to protect the environment.

The Catholic Church teaches that it is not enough just to think or talk about being environmentally friendly – it is important for all Catholics to take real actions to help protect the environment. Although one person might not be able to make much of a difference, the actions of many people all working towards the same goal will add up to make noticeable progress.

> ❝ Everyone's talents and involvement are needed to redress the damage caused by human abuse of God's creation. ❞
> *Pope Francis quoting the bishops of South Africa, Laudato Si 14*

A Give two examples of ways that Catholics can show stewardship of the environment.

B 'For an individual Catholic, there is no point in trying to save the environment because one person cannot make a difference.'

Explain what the Catholic Church's response to this view is.

Do you agree with the Catholic Church's response? Why or why not?

TIP

Remember that it is useful to give specific examples to back up your arguments. Here you could give examples of what an individual person can do to help save the environment.

RECAP

Essential information:

☐ **Sustainability** means living in a way that respects the environment and its natural resources in order to keep everything in balance and harmony.

☐ For Catholics, living sustainably respects God's creation and helps them to be good stewards of the earth.

☐ CAFOD is a Catholic charity that supports sustainability, mainly through helping those in poverty to improve the quality of their lives in a sustainable way.

How sustainability links to Catholic beliefs

- Much of the world's energy and many of the products we use come from natural resources. Sustainability involves only using natural resources at a rate at which they can be replaced, in order to reduce long-term damage to the environment.
- Sustainability links to the Catholic belief that God made every part of creation good, so all of creation is important and valuable.
- Catholics believe that promoting sustainable living helps to respect the goodness of all of God's creation.

CAFOD's work on sustainability

CAFOD is the official aid agency for the Catholic Church in England and Wales. It aims to help people living in poverty, in order to create a more balanced (and therefore sustainable) world. CAFOD supports projects that promote sustainable living and help to protect the environment.

Examples of the ways that CAFOD supports sustainability include:

> Encouraging people in England and Wales to live more simply and use fewer natural resources. For example, CAFOD gives *livesimply* awards to communities that are taking concrete steps to live in a simpler, more sustainable way.

> Helping to found the Beyond 2015 campaign, which supported the creation of the UN Sustainable Development Goals in 2015. Many governments have agreed to try to achieve these goals by 2030 to improve people's quality of life and make the world more sustainable.

> Working with groups like MONLAR in Sri Lanka, which helps farmers to adopt sustainable, effective and inexpensive farming methods (such as the use of natural fertilisers).

> Supporting or setting up projects that use renewable energy (such as solar panels).

TIP
You need to know about CAFOD's work on sustainability for your exam. Learning specific examples of the work they do will help you to develop your answers.

APPLY

Ⓐ Give two examples of ways in which CAFOD encourages sustainability.

Ⓑ 'By promoting sustainability, CAFOD is expressing Catholic beliefs.'

List arguments to support this statement. Use examples of CAFOD's work in your answer.

TIP
Learning specific examples of the work of Christian charities can help you to develop and add more detail to your answers.

REVIEW

Test the 1 mark question

1 Which **one** of the following terms means that God is beyond and outside life on earth and the universe?

A Omnipotent ☐ B Stewardship ☐ Ⓒ Transcendent ☑ D Magisterium ☐ **[1 mark]**

2 Which **one** of the following describes the basic natural law?

Ⓐ Do good and ☑ avoid evil ☐ B Do not murder ☐ C Honour your father and mother ☐ D Obey the Ten Commandments ☐ **[1 mark]**

Test the 2 mark question

3 Give **two** ways in which the Genesis creation stories show that God is omnipotent. **[2 marks]**

1) Created everything from nothing (ex nihilo).

2) Everything he created was 'good' and how He wanted it.

4 Give **two** reasons why Christians can accept the authority of the New Testament. **[2 marks]**

1) Written by people who lived alongside Jesus.

2)

Test the 4 mark question

5 Explain **two** ways in which the idea of stewardship influences the work of CAFOD. **[4 marks]**

● **Explain one way.**	One way in which the idea of stewardship influences the work of CAFOD is in their support of environment-friendly projects.
● Develop your explanation with more detail/an example/ reference to a religious teaching or quotation.	For example, they support projects that use renewable energy (such as solar panels).
● **Explain a second way.**	A second way in which the idea of stewardship influences the work of CAFOD is in their campaigns that encourage everyone to live more sustainably.
● Develop your explanation with more detail/an example/ reference to a religious teaching or quotation.	This means living in a way that cares for the environment in the long term, so the earth is left in a good state for future generations to enjoy.

6 Explain **two** ways in which the belief that humans are made in the image of God influences Catholic teachings about dignity and the sanctity of life. **[4 marks]**

● **Explain one way.**	
● Develop your explanation with more detail/an example/ reference to a religious teaching or quotation.	
● **Explain a second way.**	
● Develop your explanation with more detail/an example/ reference to a religious teaching or quotation.	

7 Explain **two** Christian beliefs about free will. **[4 marks]**

1 Exam practice

Test the 5 mark question

8 Explain **two** beliefs about the nature of God that are expressed in the creation stories of Genesis 1 and 2.

Refer to scripture or another source of Christian belief and teaching in your answer. **[5 marks]**

● **Explain one belief.**	*One belief about the nature of God that is expressed in the creation stories is that God is transcendent.*
● Develop your explanation with more detail/an example.	*The creation stories show that God only needs his own word in order to create, so he is completely above and outside the created world.*
● **Explain a second belief.**	*A second belief about the nature of God that is expressed in the creation stories is that God is omnipotent.*
● Develop your explanation with more detail/an example.	*God is powerful enough to create things from nothing and make them exactly the way he wants them to be.*
● Add a reference to scripture or another source of Christian belief. If you prefer, you can add this reference to your first belief instead.	*Genesis 1:31 says that everything God made is 'very good'.*

TIP

This question asks you to refer to scripture or another source of Christian belief and teaching in your answer. You only need to do this once to gain the fifth mark, either as part of your first point or as part of your second point.

9 Explain **two** ways that the Genesis creation stories are interpreted differently by different Christians.

Refer to scripture or another source of Christian belief and teaching in your answer. **[5 marks]**

● **Explain one way.**	
● Develop your explanation with more detail/an example.	
● **Explain a second way.**	
● Develop your explanation with more detail/an example.	
● Add a reference to scripture or another source of Christian belief. If you prefer, you can add this reference to your first belief instead.	

10 Explain **two** ways in which Catholics believe that science and religion can work together.

Refer to scripture or another source of Christian belief and teaching in your answer. **[5 marks]**

1 Exam practice

Test the 12 mark question

11 'The teachings about the nature of God expressed in Genesis 1 and 2 have no relevance for Catholics in the twenty-first century.'

Evaluate this statement. In your answer you should:

- give reasoned arguments to support this statement
- give reasoned arguments to support a different point of view
- refer to Christian teaching
- reach a justified conclusion.

[12 marks]
Plus SPaG 3 mark

REASONED ARGUMENTS IN SUPPORT OF THE STATEMENT ● **Explain why some people would agree with the statement.** ● Develop your explanation with more detail and examples. ● Refer to religious teaching. Use a quote or paraphrase or refer to a religious authority. ● **Evaluate the arguments.** Is this a good argument? Explain why you think this.	Some Catholics might agree with this statement because they think that Genesis 1 and 2 teach about God's nature in relation to the creation of the universe, not in relation to the world today. For example, Genesis 1 teaches that God is transcendent, because he is able to create using just the power of his word ('Then God said, "Let there be light"; and there was light'). But some Catholics might think this quality of God isn't relevant to them today, and it's more important to focus on his immanence (the fact that he is involved in life on earth, because this quality helps them to have a close relationship with God.
REASONED ARGUMENTS SUPPORTING A DIFFERENT VIEW ● **Explain why some people would support a different view.** ● Develop your explanation with more detail and examples. ● Refer to religious teaching. Use a quote or paraphrase or refer to a religious authority. ● **Evaluate the arguments.** Is this a good argument? Explain why you think this.	Many Catholics would disagree with this statement because they think that Genesis 1 and 2 teach eternal truths about God's nature that are still important today. For example, Genesis 1 teaches that God is the creator, who has created everything. This means the whole of creation is special. This is one of the reasons the Catholic Church teaches that Catholics today should care for the world and protect the environment. Genesis 1 also teaches that God is omnipotent. This is relevant for Catholics today because it gives them faith to trust in God, as they know he has the power to look after them and to do anything.
CONCLUSION ● **Give a justified conclusion.** ● This could include your own opinion together with your own reasoning. ● **Include evaluation.** Explain why you think one viewpoint is stronger than the other or why they are equally strong. ● Do not just repeat arguments you have already used without explaining how they apply to your reasoned opinion/conclusion.	The Genesis creation stories teach that God is the creator, omnipotent and transcendent. I understand why some Catholics might think there are other teachings about God's nature that are more relevant to the twenty-first century, such as his immanence. But these beliefs about the nature of God still influence the Catholic faith today and how Catholics live their everyday lives. So overall I disagree with the statement and think most Catholics would too.

TIP
The examiner will also be assessing your spelling, punctuation and grammar in this question — so write carefully using your best written English.

12 'The Church is important for Catholics because without it they would not know how to live in a way that pleases God.'

Evaluate this statement. In your answer you should:

- give reasoned arguments to support this statement
- give reasoned arguments to support a different point of view
- refer to Christian teaching
- reach a justified conclusion.

[12 marks]
Plus SPaG 3 marks

REASONED ARGUMENTS IN SUPPORT OF THE STATEMENT ● **Explain why some people would agree with the statement.** ● Develop your explanation with more detail and examples. ● Refer to religious teaching. Use a quote or paraphrase or refer to a religious authority. ● **Evaluate the arguments.** Is this a good argument? Explain why you think this.	
REASONED ARGUMENTS SUPPORTING A DIFFERENT VIEW ● **Explain why some people would support a different view.** ● Develop your explanation with more detail and examples. ● Refer to religious teaching. Use a quote or paraphrase or refer to a religious authority. ● **Evaluate the arguments.** Is this a good argument? Explain why you think this.	
CONCLUSION ● **Give a justified conclusion.** ● This could include your own opinion together with your own reasoning. ● **Include evaluation.** Explain why you think one viewpoint is stronger than the other or why they are equally strong. ● Do not just repeat arguments you have already used without explaining how they apply to your reasoned opinion/conclusion.	

13 '*Creation of Adam* is the work of art that best illustrates Christian beliefs about creation.'

Evaluate this statement. In your answer you should:

- give reasoned arguments to support this statement
- give reasoned arguments to support a different point of view
- refer to Christian teaching
- reach a justified conclusion.

[12 marks]
Plus SPaG 3 marks

Check your answers using the mark scheme on page 230. How did you do?
To feel more secure in the content you need to remember, re-read pages 14–25.
To remind yourself of what the examiner is looking for in your answers, go to pages 8–13.

2 Incarnation

2.1 Jesus as God incarnate *and*
2.2 God's message to Joseph

Essential information:

- The **incarnation** is when God took on the human condition to become Jesus.

- Luke 1:26–38 tells the story of the **annunciation**. This is when the angel Gabriel asked Mary to accept the role of the mother of the Son of God.

- Matthew 1:18–24 tells of the visit of the angel Gabriel to Joseph.

- Both Luke and Matthew's accounts teach that Jesus is the Son of God, conceived by the Holy Spirit.

The meaning of the incarnation

- For Christians, the fact that God was prepared to experience being human **shows how much God loves the human race**.
- God knows what it is like to be human, and this helps Christians to **value God's love**.

The incarnation is announced

In the Bible, Luke 1:26–38 and Matthew 1:18–24 tell the stories of the angel Gabriel's visits to Mary and to Joseph, to announce God's plan of sending his Son into the world.

Luke's account
- Focuses on Mary's role in the incarnation.
- Tells the story of when the angel Gabriel visited Mary.
- Gabriel tells Mary she will conceive and give birth to a son, named Jesus, who will be the Son of God.
- Jesus will be conceived through the power of the Holy Spirit.
- Because it is important to God that humans have free will, God gives Mary the choice of whether or not to be Jesus' mother. Mary gives her consent and agrees to God's wishes by saying 'let it be with me according to your word'.
- Gabriel's message is for all believers, as through Jesus' birth God is fulfilling his promises to the Jews.
- Jesus is fully human and fully God.

> ❝ He will be great, and will be called the Son of the Most High ❞
> *Luke 1:32* (NRSV)

Matthew's account
- Focuses on Joseph's part in the incarnation.
- Tells the story of how Joseph planned to break up with Mary because she was pregnant before they were married.
- But an angel visited Joseph in one of his dreams and told him it was right to marry Mary, because her child was conceived by the Holy Spirit.
- The angel confirms that Jesus (whose name means 'God saves') is being sent to earth by God to save humanity from its sins.
- The angel also calls Jesus by the name 'Emmanuel'. This is a Jewish name meaning 'God is with us', which confirms that Jesus is the Son of God.

> ❝ … for the child conceived in her is from the Holy Spirit. She will bear a son, and you are to name him Jesus, for he will save his people from their sins. ❞
> *Matthew 1:20b–21* (NRSV)

Although there are some differences between the accounts in Luke and Matthew's Gospels, they both make the same main points:

- Mary was a virgin.
- God worked through human beings to bring about his plan for humanity.
- Jesus was conceived by the power of the Holy Spirit.
- Jesus was the Son of God.
- The angel Gabriel announced Jesus' birth.

A   Give two reasons why the incarnation is important to Christians.

B   'For Christians, Luke 1:26–38 and Matthew 1:18–24 prove that Jesus was God.'

List arguments to support this statement.

TIP
If a question asks you to 'give two reasons', you don't need to explain the reasons in detail. Simply state what they are.

2.3 Jesus, the Word of God

Essential information:

☐ The **Word of God** is another name for the Son of God, who is both fully God and a separate person of the Trinity.

☐ John 1:14 tells how the Word of God became human in the form of Jesus.

☐ As the Word of God, Jesus is God's expression of his love for humans.

The relationship between the Word and God

- The Catholic Church teaches that God is **three Persons**: the Father, the Son and the Holy Spirit. Together these three Persons are referred to as the **Trinity**.
- The Son of God – the Second Person of the Trinity – is also known as the **Word of God**.
- The Word of God **became human** in the form of Jesus, which is why Jesus is sometimes called 'the Word of God made flesh'.

> **TIP**
> The Trinity is explained in more detail on pages 49–50.

In the Bible, John 1:1–4 teaches the following about the nature of the Word of God:

Teaching	Explanation	Phrase in John 1:1–4 that shows this
The Word of God is eternal.	Like God the Father, the Word of God has always existed.	'In the beginning was the Word'
The Word of God *is* God.	A word comes from inside a person and is an expression of what is inside that person. In the same way, the Word of God comes from inside God and is God's self-expression.	'the Word was God'
The Word of God is also distinct from God.	While the Word and God are united and co-exist, there is also a distinction between them.	'the Word was with God'
The Word of God is how God expresses his power and love.	The Word of God gives life, light and guidance to people.	'What has come into being in him was life, and the life was the light of all people'

Jesus as the Word of God

This verse confirms that Jesus is the Word (or Son) of God. The Word has always existed, but took on human nature to live on earth as Jesus.

The Word came to earth to guide people closer to God, and to teach them how to share in his love.

> ❝ And the Word became flesh and lived among us, and we have seen his glory, the glory as of a father's only son, full of grace and truth. ❞
>
> *John 1:14 (NRSV)*

The word '**grace**' means 'free gift' (see page 39). Jesus is God's free gift to the human race and is an expression of God's love for humans.

A Give two Christian beliefs about the Word of God given in John's Gospel.

B 'John 1:1–4 and 1:14 teach that God and the Word of God are exactly the same.'

Evaluate this statement.

> **TIP**
> To 'evaluate' this statement, start by giving arguments for and against the statement. Then use these arguments to explain whether you think the statement is true or not.

2.4 Jesus as both fully human and fully God

Essential information:

- [ ] Christians believe that Jesus is both fully human and fully God.
- [ ] During his lifetime, Jesus sometimes described himself as 'the **Son of Man**' to emphasise his humanity.
- [ ] At his trial before the Jewish Council, Jesus confirmed he was the **Son of God**. This indicated that he shared in God's divine nature and power.

Jesus as the Son of Man

Son of Man

Christians believe **Jesus was fully human**, as he lived a complete human life filled with human experiences and emotions. Jesus' human nature is emphasised in the phrase 'the Son of Man', which he sometimes used to talk about himself. This phrase has two different meanings. It can be used:

- as a general title that any person might use to refer to themselves; in this sense, it is a title that just refers to a normal human being
- as a title for someone who has been given power and authority by God.

Jesus used this phrase when he talked about the suffering he would have to endure during his crucifixion.

> **"**Then he began to teach them that the Son of Man must undergo great suffering, and be rejected by the elders, the chief priests, and the scribes, and be killed, and after three days rise again.**"**
>
> *Mark 8:31* (NRSV)

If Jesus were not fully human, he would not have been bothered by the pain and suffering of his crucifixion. But he knew that, as a human, his crucifixion would cause him great agony.

Jesus as the Son of God

Son of God

- When Jesus was arrested and brought before the Jewish Council, the high priest asked Jesus 'Are you the Messiah, the Son of the Blessed One?' (Mark 14:61 (NRSV)).
- Jesus replied by saying 'I am'. He **acknowledged he was the Son of God**.
- Jesus then went on to say 'you will see the Son of Man seated at the right hand of the Power' (Mark 14:62 (NRSV)). Here, Jesus used the title 'Son of Man' to emphasise his humanity, but he also said he had a share in God's power, emphasising his divinity.

God is eternal, so has no beginning or end. This means that Jesus could not *become* God after his death. So the resurrection proves that Jesus always *was* God, but during his life on earth he limited himself to the human condition.

A Give two different meanings of the phrase 'Son of Man'.

B 'Jesus could not possibly have been fully human and fully God at the same time'.

Explain why Christians would disagree with this statement. Use examples to support your argument.

TIP

Remember the difference between the terms 'give' and 'explain'. 'Give' just requires you to state a piece of information; 'explain' requires you to develop the information by going into more detail.

RECAP

Essential information:

☐ A symbol is a simple design that represents something more complex.

☐ Christians value symbols as a simple way of expressing deep religious beliefs.

☐ The **Ichthus** (fish), **Alpha and Omega**, and **Chi-Rho** are three important Christian symbols.

Ichthus (fish)

The Greek word *ichthus* means 'fish'. But Christians also use this word as a type of acronym, where the letters represent a series of Greek words that make up the following saying about Jesus: **Jesus Christ, Son of God, Saviour.**

- In the early days of Christianity, the Ichthus symbol was used by Christians as a **declaration of their faith**, as it showed they believed Jesus Christ was the Son of God and the Saviour.
- At a time when Christians could be persecuted for their faith, they could quickly draw and then erase the fish symbol to show they were Christians, or to indicate where Christian meetings were being held.

Alpha and Omega

- Alpha (A) is the first letter of the Greek alphabet. Omega (Ω) is the last letter.
- They are used to indicate that **God and Jesus are involved in everything from beginning to end**.
- They have been used in Christianity since at least the first century; they are referred to in the Book of Revelation.
- The symbols are used in many places in churches, vestments and Christian art. But they have a special place on the Paschal candle (the candle lit at the Easter Vigil to represent the Risen Christ – see page 94).

Chi-Rho

The Chi-Rho symbol is a monogram formed from the first two letters of the Greek word for Christ, when written in capitals.

- For Christians the symbol is a **reminder of the death of Jesus**.
- It reminds Christians that Jesus was sent by God to save humanity through his death (see page 65).
- Because of this, the symbol has great power to inspire Christians.
- Many Christians may wear the Chi-Rho as an alternative to the cross or crucifix, as an expression of their faith.

APPLY

(A) Give the names of the three symbols you have studied, making sure the spelling is correct.

(B) 'Religious beliefs are best expressed using words. There is no need for Christians to use symbols.'

List arguments against this point of view. Include at least two specific examples in your answer.

TIP
Remember that giving examples is a useful way to back up your arguments. Here you can use examples of specific symbols to help explain why they are sometimes more useful than words.

2.6 How the incarnation affects Catholic attitudes towards religious art

Essential information:

☐ In some religions, such as Judaism and Islam, it is an offence to show God in any form.

☐ Because God showed himself on earth as a human in the incarnation, the Catholic Church believes it is acceptable to use human images to depict God.

Reasons against religious art

Some religions are reluctant to portray God in art and some forbid it.
Reasons for this include the following:

Reason	Explanation
It isn't possible to portray God accurately.	An infinite God cannot be accurately represented using finite (limited) human means, such as paintings and sculptures.
Art can mislead people about what God is like.	Because art cannot portray God accurately, it can give people wrong ideas about what God is like.
Praying in front of an image or a statue may mislead people.	When people pray in front of an image or a statue, others may get the impression that the image or statue is being worshipped as a God.
It is against the second commandment.	Some people, such as Jews and some Christians, including Baptists and Methodists, believe the second commandment forbids people to make statues or paintings of God: 'You shall not make for yourself an idol' (Exodus 20:4 (NRSV)).

Catholic attitudes towards religious art

The Catholic Church approves of the use of religious art, including art that depicts God.
The Church teaches that religious art can:

- inspire people
- give people something to focus on as they pray
- help people to learn about aspects of God's work
- have a positive role in religious life.

Reasons why the Church approves of religious art include the following:

Reason	Explanation
Jesus was fully human.	This makes it acceptable to show Jesus in a human form. Although no one knows what Jesus looked like, the Bible teaches that he was a man with human qualities; therefore any work of art that captures these qualities has value.
Jesus was fully God.	This makes it acceptable to show God in a human form. Because God revealed himself on earth in the form of a human, it is fine to depict him in that form.
Jesus died to save all of humanity.	This means Jesus can be shown as a member of any ethnicity, because all people in the world were affected by his death and resurrection.

A Give two ways in which Catholics use religious art.

B 'Art that depicts God should be forbidden.'

Write a paragraph to support this statement. Include specific reasons and examples in your writing to strengthen your arguments.

Essential information:

- ☐ *Christ the Redeemer* in Rio de Janeiro, a Sacred Heart statue, and the crucifix are three different statues of Jesus.

- ☐ Christ the Redeemer is a statue of Jesus with outstretched arms, which represent his obedience to God the Father and love for all people.

- ☐ The **crucifix** is a reminder of the crucifixion of Jesus and God's act of love in freeing people from the power of sin and death.

The Sacred Heart

A Sacred Heart statue is a statue of Jesus that represents his total self-giving love for all people. It usually includes some or all of the following features:

> **TIP**
>
> For your exam, you are expected to be able to explain the meaning and significance for Catholics of one sculpture or statue of Jesus. You can choose any sculpture or statue of Jesus for this.

An expression of peace and love

Flames coming from the heart, which represent the burning love that Jesus has for all people

A hole or piercing through the heart to represent one of the soldiers piercing Jesus' side with a spear after he died

A crown of thorns surrounding the heart to represent the crown that was placed on Jesus' head when he was mocked by soldiers at his crucifixion

One of Jesus' hands pointing to his heart, to draw attention to it

Holes in the hands, from where Jesus was nailed to the cross

For Catholics, the Sacred Heart statue is a **reminder of the total love that Jesus has for all people**. This love was demonstrated in particular when Jesus accepted his death in order to save humanity, which is why the Sacred Heart statue includes symbols of Jesus' crucifixion.

Different Christian attitudes to art that portrays Jesus

Some Christians (including Catholics) approve of art that shows Jesus because it can help people to focus on aspects of his teachings and life. However, some Christians are against depicting Jesus in art because:

- the second commandment indicates it is wrong to worship images, and some people may believe that Christians are worshipping the statues (see page 34)
- depicting Jesus as a human could be misleading, because it ignores the fact he is also fully God
- no one knows what Jesus looked like, so it is wrong to try to depict him through art.

A Explain two ways in which statues can remind Catholics of Jesus' love for them. You may use examples to help you answer this question.

B 'Statues help Christians to worship God'.

Do you agree with this statement? Explain your view, using examples.

Then explain why someone else might have a different point of view.

> **TIP**
>
> When giving your opinion in an answer, always explain your reasoning, and refer to religious beliefs.

2.8 The moral teachings of Jesus

Essential information:

☐ Through his teachings, Jesus gave his followers a new and deeper understanding of the **law**: the commandments and rules that God gave to the Jews, which can be found in the Old Testament.

☐ In the Beatitudes and the parable of the Sheep and the Goats, Jesus teaches Christians how to live a moral life that is pleasing to God.

The Beatitudes

- Christians believe that Jesus 'fulfilled' the law. This means that he generally followed the law, but he also **developed the law to make it more perfect**.
- In the Old Testament, the law mainly focused on the actions people should or shouldn't do. Jesus taught that it is more important to **focus on people's attitudes**. If people start with the right attitude, then they will do the right thing.
- For example, Jesus taught that instead of just avoiding murder, people should have a loving attitude and should avoid getting angry with others.

Jesus' approach to the law is shown in the Beatitudes (Matthew 5:1–12), which form the first part of the **Sermon on the Mount**. This is a sermon (or talk) that Jesus gave to his followers to teach them how to live a life dedicated to pleasing God.

The Beatitudes are a series of statements in which **Jesus blessed certain attitudes or approaches to living**, and said how people with those attitudes would be rewarded. For example:

> 'Blessed are the meek, for they will inherit the earth.'

> 'Blessed are the pure in heart, for they will see God.'

> 'Blessed are the merciful, for they will receive mercy.'

The parable of the Sheep and the Goats

- The parable of the Sheep and the Goats is a story in the Bible in which Jesus tells his followers that in serving and caring for other people, they are serving God. It shows Christians how they should respond to those in need.
- Jesus teaches that caring for people in need is extremely important. By showing love and kindness to others, Christians will be judged favourably by God and rewarded with eternal life in heaven.

> **"**I was hungry and you gave me food, I was thirsty and you gave me something to drink, I was a stranger and you welcomed me, I was naked and you gave me clothing, I was sick and you took care of me, I was in prison and you visited me.**"**
> *Matthew 25:35–36 (NRSV)*

TIP
You can use this quote in your exam to give some examples of how Jesus expects Christians to care for others.

A Explain the meaning of 'the law'.

B 'Jesus taught that having a loving attitude is more important than anything else.'

Give arguments to support this statement. Refer to the Beatitudes and the parable of the Sheep and the Goats in your answer.

2.9 Tradition and St Irenaeus' writings about Jesus

Essential information:

☐ The theologian St Irenaeus showed how the incarnation was important for bringing God and humans closer to each other.

☐ St Irenaeus said that Jesus, as a human being who is fully alive, is 'the glory of God'.

☐ By following Jesus' example, Christians can also show that 'Life in man is the glory of God'.

St Irenaeus' teachings about Jesus

In his writings called *Adversus haereses* (Against heresies), St Irenaeus showed how Jesus – as someone who is fully God and fully human – is the **meeting point between God and humanity**. St Irenaeus wrote that Jesus 'revealed God to men':

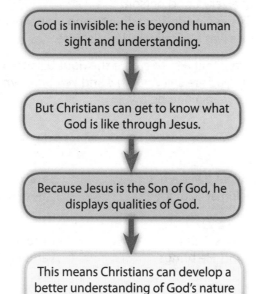

God is invisible: he is beyond human sight and understanding.

⬇

But Christians can get to know what God is like through Jesus.

⬇

Because Jesus is the Son of God, he displays qualities of God.

⬇

This means Christians can develop a better understanding of God's nature through examining the life and actions of Jesus.

The glory of God is a human being, fully alive

St Irenaeus wrote that 'Life in man is the glory of God'. This phrase is also often translated as 'the glory of God is a human being, fully alive'.

- This phrase is primarily talking about Jesus.
- For Christians, Jesus was the perfect human being. He always followed God's wishes and perfectly displayed all the qualities that God wants people to have.
- Because of this, Jesus is 'fully alive' and the 'glory of God'.
- Jesus sets the example for all other Christians to follow.
- By following Jesus' teachings and becoming more open to God, all people can become more 'fully alive', to share in God's glory.

In summary, one of the reasons the incarnation is important is because **Jesus helped humans to come to know God**. This has allowed humans to **become more 'fully alive'** and **reveal God's glory**.

A St Irenaeus wrote that 'the glory of God is a human being, fully alive'. What does this mean?

B 'Without the incarnation, God and Christians would not be able to understand each other.'

Give arguments for and against this statement. Refer to the writings of St Irenaeus in your answer.

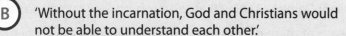

TIP

In your exam, some questions will require you to combine your knowledge from different parts of the course. Here, pages 17 and 20 will help you to think of ways that God and Christians could understand each other without the incarnation.

2.10 Different understandings of the incarnation

RECAP

Essential information:

☐ Beliefs that suggest Jesus is not both fully human and fully God are **heresies**: beliefs that go against the teachings of the Church.

☐ The documents *Dei Verbum 4* and *Verbum Domini 12* try to create a balance between presenting Jesus as fully human and fully God.

Jesus as fully human and fully God

The Catholic Church teaches that Jesus is both fully human and fully God (see page 32). But sometimes it can be difficult to present the right balance between the two.

- When the focus is too much on Jesus as human, it is possible to end up believing that Jesus wasn't really God: he was just a very good person.
- When the focus is too much on Jesus as God, it is possible to end up believing that Jesus only *appeared* to be human: he was basically God in disguise.

Two documents from the Catholic Church that aim to create the right balance of understanding between Jesus as fully human and fully God are *Dei Verbum 4* and *Verbum Domini 12*. Some quotes from these documents are explained below.

Dei Verbum 4

> ❝ For He sent His Son … so that He might dwell among men and tell them of the innermost being of God. ❞

God is revealed and speaks through Jesus. This is possible because Jesus is the Son of God. He brings salvation to all people.

> ❝ Jesus Christ, therefore, the Word made flesh, was sent as 'a man to men'. ❞

The Son of God became a human to live among other humans.

Verbum Domini 12

The Word (or Son) of God limited himself to a human form, so humans could come to understand God.

> ❝ … the eternal word became small – small enough to fit into a manger. He became a child, so that the word could be grasped by us. ❞

Jesus always knew the will of God because he *is* God. And he always carried out the will of God because he is also the perfect human being.

> ❝ In his perfect humanity [Jesus] does the will of the Father at all times … Jesus thus shows that he is the divine *Logos* [Word] … but at the same time the new Adam, the true man ❞

Through the very human act of dying, Jesus gave himself into God's hands. This led to his resurrection and to his glorification as the Word of God.

> ❝ Christ, the incarnate, crucified and risen Word of God, is Lord of all things ❞

TIP

Try to learn one or two quotes from *Dei Verbum 4* and *Verbum Domini 12*, and be able to explain how they show Jesus is both fully human and fully God.

APPLY

A Explain what is meant by 'heresies'.

B '*Dei Verbum 4* and *Verbum Domini 12* show that Jesus is both fully human and fully God.'

Give one quote from each of these documents, and explain how it shows that Jesus is both fully human and fully God.

RECAP

Essential information:

☐ Grace is the free gift of God's love to all people.

☐ As God is present in the whole of his creation, Catholics view the whole of reality as a **sacrament** – a sign of God's grace.

☐ The incarnation helped people to understand God's love and see him as a living presence in the world, leading to its sacramental nature.

What is grace?

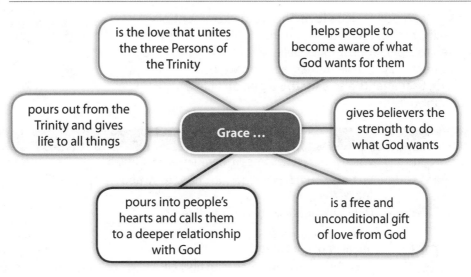

is the love that unites the three Persons of the Trinity

helps people to become aware of what God wants for them

pours out from the Trinity and gives life to all things

Grace ...

gives believers the strength to do what God wants

pours into people's hearts and calls them to a deeper relationship with God

is a free and unconditional gift of love from God

Grace and the sacramental nature of reality

The Catholic Church defines a sacrament as 'an outward sign of inward grace'. This means a sacrament is a **sign of God's love**. Catholics believe in the 'sacramental' nature of reality. This means the whole of reality can be seen as a sacrament. In other words:

- The world and everything in it is a sign of God's love.
- God's presence and love can be seen throughout the world.

The incarnation played an important role in helping Catholics to view reality as sacramental.

 Before the incarnation, God was seen as a distant (though caring) being.

 Even though Jesus is no longer present on earth, his spirit is still active, sharing God's love with all people.

 Jesus was the ultimate gift from God to show his love for humanity.

 Jesus helped to bring God's love and presence into the world. This makes the world sacramental in nature.

 Since Jesus has lived on earth, people can see God as a living and active presence.

APPLY

(A) Give two meanings of the word 'grace'.

(B) 'The whole of reality can be seen as a sacrament – a sign of God's love.'

Explain what this statement means.

TIP
When you read a statement like this in your exam, make sure you focus on the key words. Here the key words are 'reality' and 'sacrament'. You should explain in your answer how reality is sacramental, and how the incarnation affected this.

2.12 The seven sacraments

Essential information:

☐ The seven sacraments are seven rites in the Catholic Church that give grace to a person. They help to make a person's life more holy.

☐ The seven sacraments are: baptism, confirmation, the Eucharist, marriage, ordination, reconciliation and the sacrament of the sick.

What are the seven sacraments?

A sacrament is a sign of grace or God's love. The word 'sacrament' also refers to seven specific rites in the Catholic Church. These are rites through which grace is given to a person. Catholics believe that every time they take part in a sacrament they receive more grace and welcome Christ into their lives. Sacraments also **sanctify** a person's life: they make it more holy.

> **TIP**
> Try to remember how each sacrament helps a person to become closer to God, or to make their life more holy.

Sacrament		Action	Effect
Baptism		• When a person becomes a member of the Church. • Water is poured on the person's head to symbolise the washing away of sin. • Only happens once in a person's life.	• The person becomes a child of God (see page 55).
Confirmation		• When a person chooses to confirm they are a member of the Church. • Their forehead is anointed with holy oil. • Only happens once in a person's life.	• The person's faith is strengthened and deepened. • The power of the Holy Spirit is renewed in their life.
Eucharist		• When a person receives the consecrated Bread and Wine, the Body and Blood of Christ. • Can happen on a regular basis, during the Mass (see page 71).	• The person receives the life of Christ. • This helps them to keep growing in God's love.
Marriage		• When a man and woman give their consent to be married. • Usually only happens once in a person's life (see page 173).	• The couple accept that, through their love for each other, the love of God is active in their lives.
Ordination		• When a person becomes a priest, bishop or deacon. • Happens through the laying on of hands and the anointing of the hands with chrism: a symbolic gesture that passes on the power of the Holy Spirit. • For each position, this can only happen once in a person's life.	• The person commits himself to God and the Church. • He is given certain powers, such as being able to consecrate at Mass, preach and pass on from God the forgiveness of sins.
Reconciliation		• When a person confesses their sins to a priest and these are forgiven. • Can happen on a regular basis.	• The person's relationship with God is restored.
Sacrament of the sick		• When a person who is very ill is anointed with oil (see page 103). • Can happen more than once in a person's life.	• Gives strength to the person and also forgives their sins.

A Give the names of the following three sacraments:
- when a person confesses their sins
- when a person becomes a member of the Church
- when a person becomes a priest.

> **TIP**
> Pages 56 and 78 will help you to think of other ways that Catholics can become closer to God.

B 'Taking part in the sacraments is the best way for a Catholic to become closer to God.'

List arguments for and against this statement. Refer to specific sacraments in your answer.

2.13 *Imago dei* and abortion

Essential information:

☐ Catholics believe that, because humans are made in the image of God (*imago dei*), all life is holy and should be protected.

☐ Catholics believe that human life begins at the moment of **conception** (when the male sperm fertilises the female egg). Luke 1:39–45 supports this belief.

☐ These two beliefs lead Catholics to disagree with **abortion**, and to support the protection of the unborn.

When does life begin?

Luke 1:39–45 supports the Catholic belief that human life begins at the moment of conception. The events in this passage happen shortly after the annunciation (see page 30).

Mary, now pregnant, visits her cousin Elizabeth, who is pregnant with John the Baptist. When Mary greets Elizabeth, Elizabeth is 'filled with the Holy Spirit'. Her unborn baby also reacts to the presence of Jesus.

> **"** For as soon as I heard the sound of your greeting, the child in my womb leaped for joy. **"**
>
> *Luke 1:44 (NRSV)*

TIP
This verse shows that Jesus was truly present in his mother's womb from the moment of conception. It also shows that John the Baptist, while still a foetus in the womb, was able to react to the presence of Jesus.

The Catholic Church teaches that the whole person is present from the moment of conception. After this the foetus grows and develops, but it is always the same person who is growing and developing – just like a young child grows and develops into a teenager.

Imago dei and the protection of the unborn

- *Imago dei* is Latin for 'image of God'.
- The Catholic Church teaches that humans are made in the image of God.
- This means that all human life is holy and should be protected.
- Because human life begins at the moment of conception, this protection should extend to unborn foetuses.
- This is why the Catholic Church is against abortion.

To help protect unborn children, Catholics might:

- support a pro-life organisation that campaigns to reduce the abortion limit or ban abortion completely
- support an organisation that cares for women who have decided not to abort their child, but who are facing emotional or financial problems as a result.

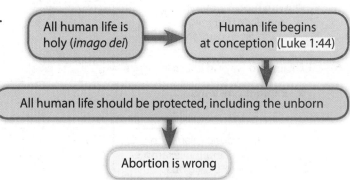

All human life is holy (*imago dei*) → Human life begins at conception (Luke 1:44)

All human life should be protected, including the unborn

Abortion is wrong

A Give two ways in which a Catholic might help to support the protection of the unborn.

B 'Abortion is murder.'

Evaluate this statement. Remember to refer to Christian teaching in your answer.

TIP
Even if you have strong views on a topic, try to answer the question objectively.

2 Exam practice

Test the 1 mark question

1 Which **one** of the following is the name given to the sacrament where a person receives the consecrated Bread and Wine.

A Baptism   B Eucharist   C Ordination   D Reconciliation   **[1 mark]**

2 Catholics believe in the sacramental nature of reality. Which **one** of the following explains what this means?

A God's love can only be experienced through the sacraments

B The seven sacraments change the nature of reality

C The world and everything in it is a sign of God's love

D Only Catholics can truly understand the nature of reality

Test the 2 mark question

3 Give **two** ways the sacraments sanctify a person's life.   **[2 marks]**

1) _____

2) _____

4 Give **two** similarities between Luke and Matthew's accounts of the annunciation.   **[2 marks]**

1) _____

2) _____

> **TIP**
>
> Questions that start with the word 'give' do not require you to write any detailed explanation in your answers.

Test the 4 mark question

5 Explain **two** ways in which the belief that humans are *imago dei* influences Catholic understandings about abortion.   **[4 marks]**

● **Explain one way.**	*For Catholics, a belief in imago dei means that all human life is valuable.*
● Develop your explanation with more detail/an example/ reference to a religious teaching or quotation.	*Because human life is valuable, it should be protected from the moment it begins (for Catholics, this is at conception).*
● **Explain a second way.**	*For Catholics, a belief in imago dei also means that all human life is holy and sacred.*
● Develop your explanation with more detail/an example/ reference to a religious teaching or quotation.	*This means that human life should not be ended early, which is what abortion does.*

6 Explain **two** ways in which Christian symbols are used.   **[4 marks]**

● **Explain one way.**	
● Develop your explanation with more detail/an example/ reference to a religious teaching or quotation.	
● **Explain a second way.**	
● Develop your explanation with more detail/an example/ reference to a religious teaching or quotation.	

7 Explain **two** Christian beliefs about the incarnation.   **[4 marks]**

Test the 5 mark question

8 Explain **two** ways in which Jesus is the fulfilment of the law.

Refer to scripture or another source of Christian belief and teaching in your answer. **[5 marks]**

● **Explain one way.**	*One way in which Jesus is the fulfilment of the law is that he always obeyed God's commands.*
● Develop your explanation with more detail/an example.	*For example, he always showed love and forgiveness to other people.*
● **Explain a second way.**	*A second way in which Jesus is the fulfilment of the law is that he developed the law to make it more perfect.*
● Develop your explanation with more detail/an example.	*Jesus taught it was more important to focus on having the right attitude than to just follow the commandments in the Old Testament.*
● Add a reference to scripture or another source of Christian belief. If you prefer, you can add this reference to your first belief instead.	*For example, he listed good attitudes to have in the Beatitudes, such as 'Blessed are the merciful, for they will receive mercy'.*

9 Explain **two** beliefs about the Word of God.

Refer to scripture or another source of Christian belief and teaching in your answer. **[5 marks]**

● **Explain one belief.**	
● Develop your explanation with more detail/an example.	
● **Explain a second belief.**	
● Develop your explanation with more detail/an example.	
● Add a reference to scripture or another source of Christian belief. If you prefer, you can add this reference to your first belief instead.	

10 Explain **two** reasons why Christians believe Jesus was the Son of God.

Refer to scripture or another source of Christian belief and teaching in your answer. **[5 marks]**

Test the 12 mark question

11 'It is impossible for Christians to follow Jesus' example and moral teachings.'

Evaluate this statement. In your answer you should:

- give reasoned arguments to support this statement
- give reasoned arguments to support a different point of view
- refer to Christian teaching
- reach a justified conclusion.

TIP

Remember, you can give your own opinion on the statement but you need to explain why this is your opinion, by supporting it with facts.

[12 marks]
Plus SPaG 3 marks

REASONED ARGUMENTS IN SUPPORT OF THE STATEMENT ● **Explain why some people would agree with the statement.** ● Develop your explanation with more detail and examples. ● Refer to religious teaching. Use a quote or paraphrase or refer to a religious authority. ● **Evaluate the arguments.** Is this a good argument or not? Explain why you think this.	Some Christians might agree with this statement because Jesus was God and we are only people, so it is impossible to be as good as him. Jesus set a very high standard for others to follow, for example he said that people should always show kindness and put the needs of other people first. Jesus went so far as to put the needs of humanity first by accepting his own crucifixion and death. But it is impossible to expect Christians today to make this sort of sacrifice for others. The Catholic Church teaches that people also have a natural tendency to sin. This makes it very hard to be good all the time and 'pure of heart', as Jesus said we should be in the Beatitudes. Everyone thinks bad things about other people sometimes and it's unreasonable to expect them not to.
REASONED ARGUMENTS SUPPORTING A DIFFERENT VIEW ● **Explain why some people would support a different view.** ● Develop your explanation with more detail and examples. ● Refer to religious teaching. Use a quote or paraphrase or refer to a religious authority. ● **Evaluate the arguments.** Is this a good argument or not? Explain why you think this.	Some Christians would disagree with this statement because Jesus knew that people make mistakes and they aren't perfect. But as long as people try to do the right things then they are following Jesus' example. This is what Jesus meant when he developed the law to put the focus more on having the right attitude. Jesus taught general principles that everyone can follow – such as being nice to others – and also showed small ways that Christians can help others, such as giving food to someone who is hungry (as explained in the parable of the Sheep and the Goats).
CONCLUSION ● **Give a justified conclusion.** ● Include your own opinion together with your own reasoning. ● **Include evaluation.** Explain why you think one viewpoint is stronger than the other or why you think they are equally strong. ● Do not just repeat arguments you have already used without explaining how they apply to your reasoned opinion/conclusion.	I think it is probably impossible for someone to be as good as Jesus, because Jesus was God and never sinned. But this doesn't mean that people can't follow Jesus' example and moral teachings. So I disagree with the statement because even if people can't be as good as Jesus, they can still try to be, by following his example and teachings.

12 'It is more helpful for Christians to focus on Jesus' humanity than to focus on his divinity.'

Evaluate this statement. In your answer you should:

- give reasoned arguments to support this statement
- give reasoned arguments to support a different point of view
- refer to Christian teaching
- reach a justified conclusion.

[12 marks]
Plus SPaG 3 marks

REASONED ARGUMENTS IN SUPPORT OF THE STATEMENT ● **Explain why some people would agree with the statement.** ● Develop your explanation with more detail and examples. ● Refer to religious teaching. Use a quote or paraphrase or refer to a religious authority. ● **Evaluate the arguments.** Is this a good argument or not? Explain why you think this.	
REASONED ARGUMENTS SUPPORTING A DIFFERENT VIEW ● **Explain why some people would support a different view.** ● Develop your explanation with more detail and examples. ● Refer to religious teaching. Use a quote or paraphrase or refer to a religious authority. ● **Evaluate the arguments.** Is this a good argument or not? Explain why you think this.	
CONCLUSION ● **Give a justified conclusion.** ● Include your own opinion together with your own reasoning. ● **Include evaluation.** Explain why you think one viewpoint is stronger than the other or why you think they are equally strong. ● Do not just repeat arguments you have already used without explaining how they apply to your reasoned opinion/conclusion.	

13 'The Catholic Church should not approve of art that depicts God or Jesus.'

Evaluate this statement. In your answer you should:

- give reasoned arguments to support this statement
- give reasoned arguments to support a different point of view
- refer to Christian teaching
- reach a justified conclusion.

[12 marks]
Plus SPaG 3 marks

Check your answers using the mark scheme on pages 230–231. How did you do? To feel more secure in the content you need to remember, re-read pages 30–41. To remind yourself of what the examiner is looking for in your answers, go to pages 8–13.

3.1 The use of music in worship

RECAP

Essential information:

☐ The Catholic Church teaches that it is good to use music to praise God.

☐ Reasons for this include the fact that music unites people and helps them to feel more involved in worship. Music also increases the beauty of worship, heightening how solemn or joyous it feels.

The value of music in worship

The Catholic Church has always approved of the use of music to praise God. Many Christians feel inspired by music and singing in the Mass, and it can make them feel closer to God.

The bishops at the Second Vatican Council stressed the benefits of using music in worship:

> **"** Sacred music is to be considered the more holy in proportion as it is more closely connected with the liturgical action, whether it adds delight to prayer, fosters unity of minds, or confers greater solemnity upon the sacred rites. **"**
>
> *Sacrosanctum Concilium 112*

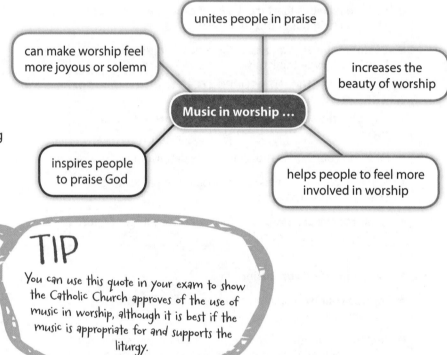

unites people in praise

can make worship feel more joyous or solemn

increases the beauty of worship

Music in worship ...

inspires people to praise God

helps people to feel more involved in worship

TIP

You can use this quote in your exam to show the Catholic Church approves of the use of music in worship, although it is best if the music is appropriate for and supports the liturgy.

APPLY

A Give two reasons why the Catholic Church approves of the use of music in worship.

B 'There is no need for church services to include music.'

Read the opinions below about the use of music in church services. Use some of them to write a paragraph in support of the statement, and others to write a paragraph which is against the statement.

Then write a concluding paragraph in which you state whether you think the statement is true or not. You can include your own opinion in this concluding paragraph.

TIP

The 12 mark question in the exam allows you to give your opinion as part of your answer. If you do choose to give your opinion, make sure you explain your reasons for it.

The words still have the same meaning even if they are not set to music

Hymns help me to join in with the worship

Music helps to make worship feel more solemn

My church is in a small village and struggles to get enough people to join the choir

Music makes going to church more interesting

I can't sing very well so don't like it when hymns are used in my church

Singing with the rest of the congregation helps me to feel part of the Christian community

The Catholic Church says it's good to use music in worship

3.2 Music in the liturgy

Essential information:

- [ ] Music is used in Catholic worship to sing parts of the **liturgy** (the practices and rituals that happen during the communal worship of God).

- [ ] Music helps to enliven the liturgy and make people feel more involved in it.

- [ ] Types of music used in the Catholic liturgy include psalms, plainchant, traditional hymns, contemporary worship songs, and mass settings.

Types of music used in the Catholic liturgy

Music	What are they?	Why are they used in worship?
Psalms	• pieces of poetry from the book of Psalms in the Old Testament. Often set to music and sung as part of worship • an important part of the **Divine Office**: a collection of psalms and readings that every priest, monk and nun has to recite (or sing) at least four times a day • also used during Mass • form the basis of many hymns used in church e.g. 'The Lord's my Shepherd'	• centre around the praise of God • talk about the joy of praising God through song • cover a wide range of human experiences and emotions • recognise that everything comes from God and without him, people are nothing
Plainchant	• ancient form of music, usually sung unaccompanied, to a limited range of notes • used in monasteries to sing the Divine Office in Latin • also used in church services, especially when the Latin parts of the Mass are sung	• the Catholic Church considers it to be ideal to use in the Mass, as it is 'specially suited to the Roman liturgy' (*Sacrosanctum Concilium 116*)
Traditional hymns	• religious songs that praise God • have been used by generations of believers • most written to be accompanied by an organ • usually sung in church by the whole congregation, such as during the Mass	• help people to feel involved in worship • have stood the test of time: their ability to help people praise God has been proven over many years
Contemporary worship songs	• religious songs that have been written recently to use in worship • usually accompanied by modern instruments, such as guitars and drums • often sound more upbeat than traditional hymns, though some are more reflective • usually sung in church by the whole congregation, such as during the Mass	• help people to feel involved in worship • some people think this type of music is disrespectful, because its upbeat nature can distract people rather than helping them to focus on God • but others think it is more accessible and appealing than traditional hymns
Mass settings	• the parts of the Mass that are sung rather than said, e.g. the Alleluia, the Sanctus, and the Gloria • before the 1960s, the music was often quite complex and sung by a choir • since the 1960s, the music has become simpler, allowing the whole congregation to join in more often	• simpler Mass settings help people to feel involved in worship • help to make the Mass appeal to the whole congregation

A What is the name for the type of religious music that is usually sung unaccompanied, to a limited range of notes?

B 'Catholic churches should modernise their music and use only contemporary worship songs or very simple Mass settings that everyone can join in with.'

List arguments to support this statement, and arguments to support a different point of view.

TIP

Try listening to some different types of religious music. This will help you to get a feel for the similarities and differences between them.

RECAP

Essential information:

☐ Certain parts of the Mass, which highlight the praise and celebration of God, are called **acclamations**.

☐ The Gloria, Alleluia, Sanctus, and Mystery of Faith in the Mass help to praise God in different ways. They are often set to music.

The Gloria, Alleluia, Sanctus, and Mystery of Faith

	What is it?	When is it used?
Gloria	• a hymn to praise God's glory and goodness • begins with the words 'Glory to God in the highest heaven' (Luke 2:14 (NRSV))	• used near the beginning of the Mass • not used during the more sorrowful seasons of Advent and Lent
Alleluia	• a Hebrew word meaning 'praise God' • a hymn of joy and triumph that praises God • announces the presence of Christ	• used to introduce the reading of the Gospel at Mass, to greet the presence of Christ • also sung three times during the Easter Vigil to announce the resurrection (see page 94) • not used during Lent
Sanctus	• a Latin word meaning 'holy' • a hymn to praise God's holiness • based on Isaiah's vision in the Temple, when the angels cried out, 'Holy, holy, holy is the Lord of hosts' (Isaiah 6:1–3 (NRSV))	• used before the Eucharistic Prayer in Mass • not used during the more sorrowful seasons of Advent and Lent
Mystery of Faith	• an acknowledgement that the whole saving event of Christ's life, death and resurrection has been made present through the consecration	• used after the consecration, when the Bread and Wine have become the Body and Blood of Christ

Music used for the acclamations

During the history of the Catholic Church, many different musical settings of the acclamations have been composed.

- Some settings are **more complex**, designed to reflect God's glory and greatness. This often includes settings of the Gloria.
- Some are much **simpler**, allowing the whole congregation to join in. For example, a simple plainchant version of the Alleluia is often sung in church.
- Some are **more modern**, appealing to a younger generation. 'The Mass of Saint Ann' by Ed Bolduc is one example.
- Some are **upbeat and joyful** in their praise of God. The Sanctus from the *Missa Luba* is one example.
- Some are **more reflective** to give a sense of peace and harmony. The Sanctus can be sung in this way to show the peace and harmony of heaven.

TIP

The Mass is discussed in more detail on page 71. Understanding the contents and structure of the Mass will help you to understand the acclamations.

APPLY

(A) Explain how the Gloria and Sanctus praise different aspects of God.

(B) 'Catholics do not need the acclamations to be set to music.'

Do you agree with this statement? Explain your reasons.

Why might someone else have a different point of view?

TIP

Always try to keep your answers focused on Christian beliefs. Here you should remember that the purpose of using music in church services is to help the congregation to praise God.

3.4 The Triune God explained in the Bible

RECAP

Essential information:

☐ Christians believe there is one God who is also three Persons. God is sometimes called the **Triune God** to emphasise this fact.

☐ The three Persons of God – the Father, Son and Holy Spirit – are known as the **Trinity**.

☐ Beliefs about the Trinity are based on Deuteronomy 6:4, Matthew 3:16–17, and Galatians 4:6 in the Bible.

Deuteronomy 6:4

- In this verse from the Old Testament, the words 'the Lord alone' stress **there is only one God**.
- Through the teachings of Jesus in the New Testament, Christians have come to believe that God is three Persons.
- But even though there are three separate Persons, there is still only one God. This verse is an important reminder of that belief, which forms the foundation for belief in the Trinity.

> ❝ Hear, O Israel: The Lord is our God, the Lord alone. ❞
>
> *Deuteronomy 6:4–5 (NRSV)*

Matthew 3:16–17

Matthew describes the baptism of Jesus:

> ❝ And when Jesus had been baptised, just as he came up from the water, suddenly the heavens were opened to him and he saw the Spirit of God descending like a dove and alighting on him. And a voice from heaven said, 'This is my Son, the Beloved, with whom I am well pleased.' ❞
>
> *Matthew 3:16–17 (NRSV)*

The **Holy Spirit** is the love that unites the Father and the Son. Here the Holy Spirit is represented by a dove, which comes down from God the Father to stay with Jesus.

The **Father** is the 'voice from heaven'.

The Father calls Jesus his **Son**. (Christians believe God the Son took on human form to become Jesus – see page 30.)

- Jesus' baptism is when **God reveals himself as the Trinity**.
- For Christians, it shows **there really are three Persons** who all coexist at the same time – not just one Person who sometimes appears as the Father and at other times as the Son or Holy Spirit.

Galatians 4:6

- This verse helps to **explain the relationship between the Trinity and a Christian**.
- Christians are God's children and brothers or sisters to Jesus.
- God the Father pours out the Holy Spirit into a Christian's heart. This is the love that unites the Father and the Son, and it fills the person with grace (see page 51).

> ❝ And because you are children, God has sent the Spirit of his Son into our hearts, crying, 'Abba! Father!' ❞
>
> *Galatians 4:6 (NRSV)*

APPLY

A Give two beliefs about the Trinity that are supported by passages from the Bible.

B 'Jesus' baptism is the most important passage in the Bible for understanding the Trinity.'

Give arguments for and against this statement. Refer to Matthew 3:16–17, Deuteronomy 6:4, and Galatians 4:6 in your answer.

TIP
Galatians 4:6 is also discussed on page 52.

RECAP

Essential information:

☐ The **Nicene Creed** is a statement of faith about what Catholics believe, which explains the nature of the Trinity and how the three Persons relate to each other.

☐ Genesis 1:1–3 shows how all three Persons shared in the act of creation.

What does the Nicene Creed teach about the Trinity?

	Teaching	Phrase that shows this
God the Father	God the Father is the creator of all things	'I believe in one God, the Father almighty, maker of heaven and earth'
God the Son	Like God the Father, God the Son is eternal	'… the Only Begotten Son of God, born of the Father before all ages.'
	There is no distinction in nature between the Father and the Son	'… consubstantial with the Father'
	The Son took on the limitations of human nature to become Jesus Jesus had a human mother but was conceived by the Holy Spirit	'… by the Holy Spirit was incarnate of the Virgin Mary, and became man.'
	The Son became human out of love for all people, to save them from being separated from God by sin He suffered and died as a human being	'For our sake he was crucified under Pontius Pilate, he suffered death and was buried, and rose again on the third day'
	After he died, Jesus rose into heaven to take his place as the Son of God Jesus did not become God at the resurrection; he had always been God, but had just limited himself to a human nature while on earth	'He ascended into heaven and is seated at the right hand of the Father.'
God the Holy Spirit	The Holy Spirit gives life to all things	'I believe in the Holy Spirit, the Lord, the giver of life'
	The Holy Spirit comes from both the Father and the Son, uniting them in love	'… who proceeds from the Father and the Son'
	The Holy Spirit is equal in majesty and power to the Father and the Son	'… who with the Father and the Son is adored and glorified'
	The Holy Spirit inspires people to let them know the will of God	'… who has spoken through the prophets.'

What does Genesis 1:1–3 teach about the Trinity?

Genesis 1:1–3 tells how God created the universe. All three Persons shared in the act of creation:

> The word 'God' here is referring to the Father; the Father created the universe.

> The phrase 'wind from God' can also be translated as 'breath' or 'spirit'. This shows that the Holy Spirit was involved in the creation of the universe.

> God created the universe with the power of his Word. Christians interpret this as a reference to the Son (or Word) of God (see page 31).

So God the Father, through God the Son (the Word of God), created the universe with the power of the Holy Spirit.

> ❝In the beginning when God created the heavens and the earth, the earth was a formless void and darkness covered the face of the deep, while a wind from God swept over the face of the waters. Then God said, 'Let there be light'; and there was light. ❞
>
> *Genesis 1:1–3* (NRSV)

APPLY

A Explain how Genesis 1:1–3 shows that all three Persons of the Trinity were involved in the creation of the universe.

B 'The Nicene Creed, not the Bible, helps people to understand the Trinity.'

Evaluate this statement. Refer to specific quotes from the Nicene Creed in your answer.

TIP

Short quotes from scripture can help you to back up your arguments in the 12 mark question. But make sure the quotes are relevant to the points you are trying to make.

RECAP

Essential information:

☐ The love of the Trinity strengthens the work of the Catholic Church, and inspires Christians to share God's love with others.

☐ The Catholic Church aims to share God's love through mission and evangelism.

How belief in the Trinity influences Christians

- The life of the Trinity flows from the love of the Father and the Son for each other, which is the Holy Spirit.
- Christians believe this love flows outwards into the lives and hearts of all believers as grace (see page 39).
- Just as the love of the Trinity is shared with Christians, so Christians believe they must pass on this love to others.

> **"** The entire activity of the Church is an expression of a love that seeks the integral good of man **"**
>
> *Deus Caritas Est 19*

The Holy Spirit is the love of the Father and the Son

It enters people's lives as grace …

… and inspires them to show love to others

TIP

You can use this quote in your exam to show that the love of the Trinity supports the Church's work in the world, and inspires Christians to help others.

Mission and evangelism

	What does it involve?	How does it share God's love?
Mission	'Mission' means sending out people to help others For example, missionaries might be sent out by the Church to work with people in poverty, by providing education or medical care	Missionaries want to share the love of God through their actions They believe they should love others as God loves them They follow the commandment that 'those who love God must love their brothers and sisters also' (1 John 4:21 (NRSV))
Evangelism	'Evangelism' means preaching the good news about Jesus to other people Evangelists share their knowledge and experience of Christianity to influence the lives and attitudes of others	Evangelists are inspired by the Holy Spirit to share their knowledge of God's love with others They want to help others experience the joy, peace and love that they experience as a Christian Jesus' last instructions to his followers included, 'Go therefore and make disciples of all nations, baptising them in the name of the Father and of the Son and of the Holy Spirit, and teaching them to obey everything that I have commanded you.' (Matthew 28:18–20 (NRSV))

APPLY

A Give two ways in which belief in the Trinity influences Christians today.

B 'Mission is a better way of sharing God's love than evangelism.'

List arguments to support this statement, and arguments to support a different point of view.

Give your opinion about which view you would support and explain why.

TIP

Think about what else you have learned about the Trinity. For example, how does a belief in the Son of God influence a Christian's approach to Jesus and his teachings?

3.7 The Trinity in the Bible

Essential information:

- ☐ Mark 1:9–11 describes Jesus' baptism. It confirms that early Christians understood the role of the Father, Son and Holy Spirit as separate yet united.

- ☐ Galatians 4:6–7 describes how the Trinity interacts with Christians.

Mark 1:9–11

> In those days Jesus came from Nazareth of Galilee and was baptised by John in the Jordan. And just as he was coming up out of the water, he saw the heavens torn apart and the Spirit descending like a dove on him. And a voice came from heaven, 'You are my Son, the Beloved; with you I am well pleased.'
>
> *Mark 1:9–11 (NRSV)*

- Matthew's account of Jesus' baptism (see page 49) is very similar to Mark's account.
- It confirms that **God is a Trinity of three Persons**, shown in this passage by the dove (the Holy Spirit), the voice from heaven (the Father), and Jesus himself (the Son).
- The presence of the Trinity at Jesus' baptism shows the importance of the Trinity in Jesus' work and teachings. It means that **the Trinity was involved in the salvation brought about by Jesus' life, death and resurrection** (see page 67).

Galatians 4:6–7

> And because you are children, God has sent the Spirit of his Son into our hearts, crying, 'Abba! Father!' So you are no longer a slave but a child, and if a child then also an heir, through God.
>
> *Galatians 4:6–7 (NRSV)*

- Galatians 4:6–7 shows that, like Jesus, Christians are **children of God**. This means they have an intimate relationship with God. They are able to call God 'Abba' (a word that means 'Father'), which is the title that Jesus used for God.
- This passage also shows that **the Holy Spirit is shared with all believers**. The Holy Spirit gives believers the strength and conviction to accept their relationship with God the Father.
- The Holy Spirit is the same Spirit that filled Jesus at his baptism. This shows that **the relationship between the Father, Son and Holy Spirit is also shared with the believer**.

A Explain how Mark 1:9–11 shows that God is a Trinity of three Persons.

B 'Christians need to follow Jesus' example and call God, "Father".'

Evaluate this statement. Refer to Christian teaching in your answer.

3.8 The Trinity and God's love

Essential information:

- [ ] St Augustine and Catherine LaCugna were two Christian theologians who wrote about the Trinity.

- [ ] St Augustine focused on the relationship within the Trinity, and how it can be understood through the concept of love.

- [ ] LaCugna focused on how the Trinity is revealed to humans as God's attempt to redeem them (to bring them back to a relationship with God).

St Augustine

St Augustine, a theologian born in the fourth century, wrote a text called *On the Trinity* in which he explained the relationship between the three Persons of the Trinity. He said that:

- the Bible states that '**God is love**' (1 John 4:16 (NRSV))
- love can't exist on its own – there must be someone to give it and someone to receive it
- therefore to have love **there must be three things**: the person who loves, the person who is loved, and the love that unites them
- the Trinity can be thought of as **three Persons united in love**
- the Father loves the Son and the Son loves the Father; the love that unites them is the Holy Spirit
- the Holy Spirit pours out into the hearts and lives of believers, **sharing God's love with all people**.

Augustine mainly focused on **the relationship *within* the Trinity**. He said that understanding this is essential for understanding God.

> "True love is: a trinity of lover, beloved and the love that binds them together into one."
> *St Augustine*

TIP
You could use this quote in your exam to show how St Augustine used the idea of love to explain the Trinity, by saying that love needs three things to exist.

Catherine LaCugna

Catherine LaCugna was an American theologian who lived in the second half of the twentieth century. She taught the following about the Trinity.

> The Father begets the Son. This means that the Son comes from the Father.
> But the Son did not just suddenly come into being – he has always been a part of God.
> So **the Son is continually, eternally coming from the Father**.

→

> The Holy Spirit **is the love that eternally unites the Father and the Son**.

→

> This continual creative act – of the Father begetting the Son, and the eternal love between them – **constantly flows outwards into the whole of creation**.

↓

> The Son came to earth as Jesus **to bring redemption**: to save people by bringing them back to a relationship with the Father.
> This means that **the Son comes from the Father to save humanity**.

←

> The Holy Spirit – God's love – is **continually guiding believers towards the Father**, to complete the work of Jesus' redemption.

←

> Once redemption is complete, through the help of the Father, Son and Holy Spirit, **all things will be brought back to God**.

In contrast to St Augustine, LaCugna placed more importance on **the *outward* effects of the Trinity**. She thought the best way to know God is through understanding God's actions in people's lives.

A Give two ways in which the Trinity contributes to people's redemption.

B 'Christians can understand the Trinity through the idea of love.'

Explain how St Augustine and LaCugna's teachings can be used to support this statement.

3.9 The authority of the Magisterium and its views on the Trinity

Essential information:

☐ The **Magisterium** refers to the authority the Pope and bishops have to shape the Catholic Church's teachings, which comes from the authority of the twelve apostles.

☐ At the councils of Nicaea and Constantinople, the Magisterium confirmed the Catholic Church's beliefs about the Trinity – in particular that each Person is fully God.

The authority of the Magisterium

- Jesus' closest followers became known as the **twelve apostles**.
- Whenever the apostles went to a new area to preach, they chose someone to lead the Church in that area.
- This person would become a **bishop**, in a ceremony that involved the **laying on of hands** – a symbolic gesture that passes on the power of the Holy Spirit and the **apostolic authority** (the authority of the apostles).
- The leader of the apostles, Peter, died in Rome. Since his death, there has been an unbroken succession of Bishops of Rome.
- The Bishop of Rome – also known as **the Pope** – is the Head of the Catholic Church.
- The Pope and the bishops form the **Magisterium**: the teaching authority of the Catholic Church.

The Councils of Nicaea and Constantinople

Sometimes the Pope and the bishops gather together to discuss and make decisions about important issues for the Church. This is known as a **Council**. Official declarations of faith that come from Councils are believed to be infallible (without error) as Catholics believe the Church is being guided by the Holy Spirit.

Two important Councils were held in the fourth century to help confirm the Church's teachings about the nature of the Trinity.

	Why was the Council called?	What was the outcome of the Council?
Council of Nicaea (325 CE)	At the start of the fourth century, a priest called Arius was teaching that only God the Father was eternal, not God the Son The bishops called a Council to discuss this idea	The Council confirmed that: • the Son is eternally begotten from the Father • the Father and Son have always co-existed together • they are both equal and of the same nature
Council of Constantinople (381 CE)	Further disputes about the nature of the Trinity, including the nature of Jesus, led the bishops to call a second Council to reaffirm Catholic beliefs	The Council confirmed that: • the Holy Spirit is the Third Person of the Trinity and fully God • Jesus is both fully God and fully human

As a result of these Councils, the Nicene-Constantinopolitan Creed was produced (usually just called the **Nicene Creed**). This is a statement of faith that all Catholics accept, which sets out the Church's beliefs about the Trinity and Jesus (see page 50).

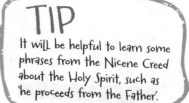

TIP

It will be helpful to learn some phrases from the Nicene Creed about the Holy Spirit, such as 'he proceeds from the Father'.

(see page 50)

APPLY

A Give two teachings about the Trinity that were confirmed by the Council of Nicaea.

B 'Without the Magisterium, Catholics wouldn't know what to believe.'

Do you agree with this statement? Give reasons to support your opinion.

Why might someone else have a different point of view?

TIP

Remember, when a question asks you to 'give' information, you don't have to explain it.

3.10 Baptism

Essential information:

☐ For all Christians except the Quakers and the Salvation Army, **baptism** is a **sign of initiation** through which a person becomes a member of the Church and a child of God.

☐ Jesus ordered his apostles to baptise all of his followers (Matthew 28:19). Jesus himself was baptised by John the Baptist.

☐ Through baptism, a person enters the life of the Trinity. They become a child of the Father, join in with Jesus' death and resurrection, and are filled with the Holy Spirit.

The symbolism of baptism

Baptism symbolises the start of **a new stage of life** as a Christian and a child of God. It also symbolises **joining in with Jesus' death and resurrection**.

- In the early Church, adults would be baptised by being totally submerged under water. This symbolised joining Jesus in the tomb after he died.
- Just as Jesus gave up his life to the will of God, so the person being baptised **commits their life to God** in the same way.
- Rising up out of the water symbolises joining in with Jesus' resurrection, to **begin a new life as a Christian**.
- Today in the Catholic Church people are no longer baptised by being fully submerged under water. Instead water is poured over their heads. But the idea of joining in with Jesus' death and resurrection is still just as important.

The use of water in baptism also **symbolises the Holy Spirit**. During baptism a person is filled with the Holy Spirit, who sustains the believer's faith and commitment to God. This is the same Spirit that filled Jesus during his baptism (see page 49).

The importance of baptism

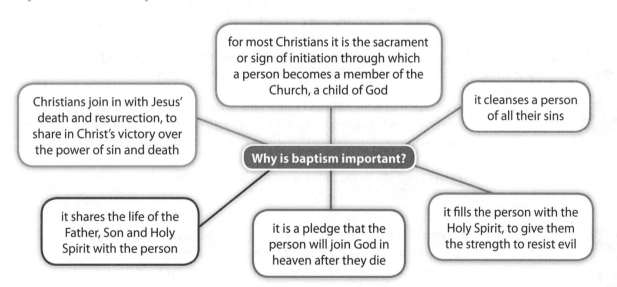

for most Christians it is the sacrament or sign of initiation through which a person becomes a member of the Church, a child of God

Christians join in with Jesus' death and resurrection, to share in Christ's victory over the power of sin and death

it cleanses a person of all their sins

Why is baptism important?

it shares the life of the Father, Son and Holy Spirit with the person

it is a pledge that the person will join God in heaven after they die

it fills the person with the Holy Spirit, to give them the strength to resist evil

In baptism, a person is baptised 'in the name of the Father and of the Son and of the Holy Spirit', thus sharing in the life of the Trinity.

A Explain two ways in which a person shares in the life of the Trinity through their baptism.

B 'The most important reason for a person to be baptised is so they can be filled with the strength of the Holy Spirit.'

List arguments to support this statement, and arguments to support a different point of view. Refer to Christian teaching in your answer.

TIP
If a question asks you to 'explain', it means you need to give some detail in your answer.

RECAP

Essential information:

☐ The Catholic Church describes **prayer** as 'raising the heart and mind to God'.

☐ **Traditional prayers** have set words that have been used by generations of believers. Some people prefer them because the familiar words help them to open up to the presence of God.

☐ **Spontaneous prayers** are made up in the moment. Some people prefer them because they feel like a more personal and sincere way of communicating with God.

What is prayer?

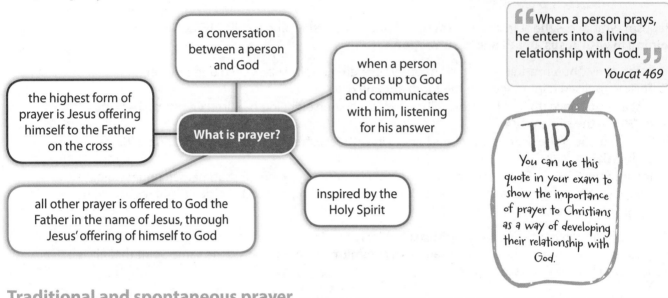

a conversation between a person and God

when a person opens up to God and communicates with him, listening for his answer

the highest form of prayer is Jesus offering himself to the Father on the cross

What is prayer?

all other prayer is offered to God the Father in the name of Jesus, through Jesus' offering of himself to God

inspired by the Holy Spirit

> "When a person prays, he enters into a living relationship with God."
> *Youcat 469*

TIP
You can use this quote in your exam to show the importance of prayer to Christians as a way of developing their relationship with God.

Traditional and spontaneous prayer

- Many Catholics like to use **traditional prayers**, which are prayers with set words that have been passed down over generations. Examples include the Our Father, Hail Mary, and the set prayers of the rosary.
- Some Christians like to use **spontaneous prayers**, which have no set format or words. Christians who use spontaneous prayers believe the Holy Spirit guides them in what to say.

I prefer traditional prayer because:

- I don't have to worry about coming up with the right words to use
- not having to focus too much on the words allows me to open up more to the presence of God; it allows my mind to go deeper than the words
- when I'm upset, using familiar words comforts me.

I prefer spontaneous prayer because:

- it feels more sincere than traditional prayer because I'm opening up to God about my own personal concerns and worries
- it helps me to develop an individual relationship with God
- it comes from the heart and reflects how I feel at the moment.

APPLY

(A) Give two reasons why prayer is important to Christians.

(B) 'Using spontaneous prayer is the best way to communicate with God.'

What is your opinion of this statement? Explain your reasoning.

Why might someone else have a different opinion? Explain why you would disagree with them.

3.12 Prauer and posture

RECAP

Essential information:

☐ Physical **postures** (particular positions of the body) can assist prayer and help to show the intention behind the prayer.

☐ Some postures emphasise respect and humility (such as kneeling), some the praise of God (such as bowing), and some asking for God's help (such as joined hands).

Postures used in prayer

What does it look like?		What does it mean?
Kneeling (bending both legs so your knees rest on the ground)		• a sign of humility • shows the person acknowledges God's authority and submits to his will • a position asking for forgiveness
Genuflecting (bending down on one knee only)		• A sign of respect • Catholics may genuflect when they enter church or pass the tabernacle, to acknowledge Christ's presence
Prostrating (lying flat with your face on the ground)		• a sign of total humility and submission to God • a position pleading for help and mercy • shows the person has given themselves up to God
Standing		• a sign of respect • for example, Catholics stand for the Gospel reading at Mass out of respect for God's word • shows readiness to act on behalf of God
Bowing (bending the upper half of the body)		• a sign of respect • a sign of praise to God • acknowledges that God is great

What does it look like?		What does it mean?
Sitting		• a more comfortable position, allowing the person to focus on their communication with God
Standing with arms stretched out in front		• a position of pleading, asking for God's help • shows the person is willing to accept whatever God sends them
Standing with arms raised up		• a sign of praise for God's greatness and glory • focuses on God 'above' in heaven • the person is totally open to God
Walking		• for Christians who don't want to confine prayer to specific moments or places, but who want God to always be with them
Joined hands		• a sign of asking • a request for help from God
Open hands		• a sign of praise • shows acceptance of whatever God sends

APPLY

A Give two postures that might be used if someone wants to ask for God's help.

B 'Using different postures for prayer is unnecessary and makes no difference.'

Evaluate this statement. Use examples of specific postures in your answer.

3 Exam practice

REVIEW

Test the 1 mark question

1   Which **one** of the following is a hymn which speaks of God as 'holy'?

   A Alleluia   B Gloria   C Plainchant   D Sanctus   **[1 mark]**

2   Which **one** of the following describes the teaching authority of the Catholic Church?

   A Magisterium   B Holy Spirit   C Mission   D Sacrament   **[1 mark]**

Test the 2 mark question

3   Give **two** ways in which music is used in the Mass.   **[2 marks]**

   1) _____

   2) _____

4   Give **two** ways in which the Trinity was involved in the creation of the universe.   **[2 marks]**

   1) _____

   2) _____

> **TIP**
> Even if you're not sure of the answer for the 1 mark question, it's worth making a guess. You might be right and gain a mark.

Test the 4 mark question

5   Explain **two** ways in which music influences Catholic worship.   **[4 marks]**

● **Explain one way.**	*One way in which music influences Catholic worship is that it helps to make it a more communal activity.*
● Develop your explanation with more detail/an example/ reference to a religious teaching or quotation.	*The use of hymns and other types of music in Catholic worship helps everyone to feel more involved in the worship.*
● **Explain a second way.**	*A second way in which music influences Catholic worship is that it can make worship feel more joyous or solemn.*
● Develop your explanation with more detail/an example/ reference to a religious teaching or quotation.	*For example, an upbeat contemporary worship song can help to make a church service feel more lively.*

6   Explain **two** reasons why Catholics can be confident in the authority of the Magisterium.   **[4 marks]**

● **Explain one reason.**	
● Develop your explanation with more detail/an example/ reference to a religious teaching or quotation.	
● **Explain a second reason.**	
● Develop your explanation with more detail/an example/ reference to a religious teaching or quotation.	

7   Explain **two** beliefs about the Trinity that can be found in the Nicene Creed.   **[4 marks]**

Test the 5 mark question

8 Explain **two** ways in which belief in the Trinity is important for the Catholic understanding of mission.

Refer to scripture or another source of Christian belief and teaching in your answer. **[5 marks]**

● **Explain one way.**	*One way in which belief in the Trinity is important is that mission involves sharing the love of the Trinity with others.*
● Develop your explanation with more detail/an example.	*Catholic missionaries believe they should share God's love with others just as God's love is shared with them. This love comes from the Trinity.*
● **Explain a second way.**	*A second way in which belief in the Trinity is important is that it sustains and inspires the work of missionaries.*
● Develop your explanation with more detail/an example.	*The love of the Trinity enters people's lives through the Holy Spirit as grace and inspires them (and the whole Church) to get involved in mission.*
● Add a reference to scripture or another source of Christian belief. If you prefer, you can add this reference to your first belief instead.	*As the Church says, 'The entire activity of the Church is an expression of a love that seeks the integral good of man' (Deus Caritas Est 19). This activity includes missionary work.*

> **TIP**
> You do not need to give the exact reference of the quotation.

9 Explain **two** reasons why prayer is important to Christians.

Refer to scripture or another source of Christian belief and teaching in your answer. **[5 marks]**

● **Explain one reason.**	
● Develop your explanation with more detail/an example.	
● **Explain a second reason.**	
● Develop your explanation with more detail/an example.	
● Add a reference to scripture or another source of Christian belief. If you prefer, you can add this reference to your first belief instead.	

10 Explain **two** beliefs about the relationship between the Trinity and a Christian.

Refer to scripture or another source of Christian belief and teaching in your answer. **[5 marks]**

Test the 12 mark question

11 'The idea of the Trinity is so clearly expressed in the Bible that it does not need to be expressed in any other way, for example by the Nicene Creed.'

Evaluate this statement. In your answer you should:

- give reasoned arguments to support this statement
- give reasoned arguments to support a different point of view
- refer to Christian teaching
- reach a justified conclusion.

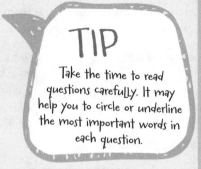

TIP

Take the time to read questions carefully. It may help you to circle or underline the most important words in each question.

[12 marks]
Plus SPaG 3 mar

REASONED ARGUMENTS IN SUPPORT OF THE STATEMENT	Some Christians would agree with this statement because the Bible gives the most important information that Christians need to know about the Trinity. For example, Deuteronomy, which says that 'The Lord is our God, the Lord alone', clearly shows there is only one God. But the baptism of Jesus shows God is also three Persons who coexist together. It mentions the Spirit of God, the Son, and the 'voice from heaven' who is the Father. The fact that all three make an appearance at Jesus' baptism at the same time shows they are three separate Persons, and not just one person who is pretending to be three.
● **Explain why some people would agree with the statement.** ● Develop your explanation with more detail and examples. ● Refer to religious teaching. Use a quote or paraphrase or refer to a religious authority. ● **Evaluate the arguments.** Is this a good argument or not? Explain why you think this.	
REASONED ARGUMENTS SUPPORTING A DIFFERENT VIEW	Some Christians would argue that the Bible doesn't actually give much detail about the Trinity, and in fact this is why the Nicene Creed had to be written. Confusion and disagreements about the nature of the Trinity meant the bishops had to call the Councils of Nicaea and Constantinople, which led to the writing of the Nicene Creed. The Nicene Creed teaches that the three Persons of the Trinity are equal. For example, it says the Son is 'consubstantial with the Father'. This is an important idea that is not clearly expressed in the Bible.
● **Explain why some people would support a different view.** ● Develop your explanation with more detail and examples. ● Refer to religious teaching. Use a quote or paraphrase or refer to a religious authority. ● **Evaluate the arguments.** Is this a good argument or not? Explain why you think this.	
CONCLUSION	If the idea of the Trinity was clearly expressed in the Bible, there wouldn't be any need for the Nicene Creed. But the bishops obviously wrote the Nicene Creed for a reason, which was to stop people saying wrong things about the Trinity. The Bible teaches that God is one and also three Persons, but the Nicene Creed teaches that the three Persons are equal, which seems just as important. So I disagree with the statement for these reasons.
● **Give a justified conclusion.** ● Include your own opinion together with your own reasoning. ● **Include evaluation.** Explain why you think one viewpoint is stronger than the other or why you think they are equally strong. ● Do not just repeat arguments you have already used without explaining how they apply to your reasoned opinion/conclusion.	

12 'Anyone who wants to be able to call themselves a Christian should first be baptised.'

Evaluate this statement. In your answer you should:

- give reasoned arguments to support this statement
- give reasoned arguments to support a different point of view
- refer to Christian teaching
- reach a justified conclusion.

[12 marks]
Plus SPaG 3 marks

REASONED ARGUMENTS IN SUPPORT OF THE STATEMENT	
● **Explain why some people would agree with the statement.**	
● Develop your explanation with more detail and examples.	
● Refer to religious teaching. Use a quote or paraphrase or refer to a religious authority.	
● **Evaluate the arguments.** Is this a good argument or not? Explain why you think this.	
REASONED ARGUMENTS SUPPORTING A DIFFERENT VIEW	
● **Explain why some people would support a different view.**	
● Develop your explanation with more detail and examples.	
● Refer to religious teaching. Use a quote or paraphrase or refer to a religious authority.	
● **Evaluate the arguments.** Is this a good argument or not? Explain why you think this.	
CONCLUSION	
● **Give a justified conclusion.**	
● Include your own opinion together with your own reasoning.	
● **Include evaluation.** Explain why you think one viewpoint is stronger than the other or why you think they are equally strong.	
● Do not just repeat arguments you have already used without explaining how they apply to your reasoned opinion/conclusion.	

13 'The best way to understand God is to understand the relationship within the Trinity.'

Evaluate this statement. In your answer you should:

- give reasoned arguments to support this statement
- give reasoned arguments to support a different point of view
- refer to Christian teaching
- reach a justified conclusion.

[12 marks]
Plus SPaG 3 marks

 Check your answers using the mark scheme on pages 231–232. How did you do? To feel more secure in the content you need to remember, re-read pages 46–57. To remind yourself of what the examiner is looking for in your answers, go to pages 8–13.

4 Redemption

4.1 How church architecture reflects Catholic beliefs

RECAP

Essential information:

☐ Catholic churches provide a space where Catholics can worship together – particularly at Mass – or pray alone.

☐ The design and decoration of a church helps to aid and inspire worship, by encouraging Christians to reflect on God and on their faith.

☐ Churches built since 1965 place more emphasis on the position of the altar, as this is the focal point of the Mass.

How do churches help Catholics to worship?

For Catholics, a church has two main purposes:

1 To provide a space where they can **meet to worship together**. The most important service in Catholic worship is the Mass (see page 71), which centres around the altar. This means that the altar should be the central focus of the church.

2 To provide a space for **individual prayer**. This means that the church should provide a quiet, peaceful space that inspires people to pray to God.

How do churches help and inspire worship?

the care that has been put into the design and decoration of the church shows devotion to God, and helps people feel that God is respected

images like the Stations of the Cross (see page 78) inspire Christians to reflect on Jesus' sufferings

statues of saints encourage and inspire Christians to follow their examples

side chapels are smaller areas where believers can pray in a quiet space

Catholic churches built before and after 1965

As a result of the Second Vatican Council (see page 81), there is a difference between Catholic churches built before and after 1965.

Before 1965, Catholic churches were usually built:

- **facing east towards Jerusalem**, as this is the city where Jesus died and rose again
- **in the shape of a cross**, as a reminder of the cross on which Jesus died
- **with the altar against the east wall**; before 1965 the Mass was said by the priest in Latin, who would usually speak very quietly with his back towards the congregation. This meant that people attending Mass did not feel very involved in the service.

After 1965, Catholic churches have been built:

- to ensure that as many people as possible can **see and join in with the Mass.**
- with **the altar more towards the centre of the church**, and seats for the congregation some or all the way around the altar.

APPLY

A Give two common features of Catholic churches built before 1965.

B 'The most important purpose of a church is to provide a space for celebration of the Mass.'

Give arguments for and against this statement.

RECAP

Essential information:

☐ The main features of a Catholic church include the lectern, altar, crucifix and tabernacle.

☐ These help to emphasise the presence of Christ in the church. They also remind Catholics of the redemption that Christ brought them through his suffering, death and resurrection.

What are the main features?

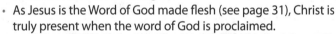

Lectern

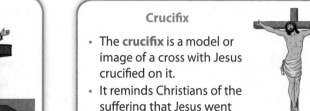

- The **lectern** is the reading stand, from where Bible readings are given.
- At least two readings are given from the lectern at every Mass.
- Readings from the Old Testament remind Christians how God has guided his people from the beginning, while readings from the New Testament tell Christians about Jesus' actions and teachings.
- As Jesus is the Word of God made flesh (see page 31), Christ is truly present when the word of God is proclaimed.
- The lectern should be in a prominent place in the church, so people can see and clearly hear the word of God.

Crucifix

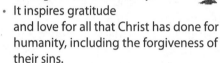

- The **crucifix** is a model or image of a cross with Jesus crucified on it.
- It reminds Christians of the suffering that Jesus went through to save humanity.
- It inspires gratitude and love for all that Christ has done for humanity, including the forgiveness of their sins.
- This gratitude which is inspired by the crucifix is clearly expressed in the Eucharist.

The main features of a Catholic church

Altar

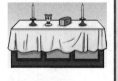

- The **altar** is the place of sacrifice, from where the bread and wine are offered to God at Mass.
- During the consecration this offering joins with Christ's offering of himself to the Father through his death on the cross, and the Bread and Wine become the Body and Blood of Christ (see page 71).
- Christ is truly present on the altar, offering himself to the Father on behalf of humanity.
- In return, the Father strengthens the lives and faith of believers when they receive the Body and Blood of Christ in Communion.

Tabernacle

- The **tabernacle** is a box where the consecrated Bread is kept after the Mass.
- It houses the Real Presence of Christ, so many Catholics like to pray in front it.
- It can inspire a deep sense of peace, as it reminds Catholics that Christ is still caring for them.
- The consecrated Bread that is saved in the tabernacle can be taken to people who can't get to Mass, such as those who are too ill to leave their homes, so they can still receive Holy Communion.

APPLY

A Explain how the tabernacle is used to help people who can't get to Mass.

B 'The main features of a church remind Christians of the importance of Jesus.'

Give arguments to support this statement. Refer to the lectern, altar, crucifix and tabernacle in your answer.

> **TIP**
> Remember, Jesus is so important to Christians because he redeemed humanity and made salvation possible. These concepts are central to Christianity so it is worth taking the time to understand them properly. See page 67 for more on this.

RECAP

Essential information:

☐ Some churches use an altar for the Mass, as a reminder of Christ's sacrifice on the cross, while other churches use a table, as a reminder of the **Last Supper** (the final meal Jesus ate with his disciples before he died).

☐ Some Catholics prefer the crucifix as a reminder of Christ's death, while others prefer a cross or Risen Christ as a reminder of Christ's resurrection.

Altar or table

During Mass, the Last Supper and Jesus' crucifixion are both remembered. Churches might choose to use an altar or a table to emphasise one of these events over the other.

Altar	Table
• An altar is a place of sacrifice and thanksgiving. • For Catholics, the most important altar is the cross on which Jesus sacrificed his life. • At Mass, the congregation joins in with giving thanks for Christ's sacrifice. • The use of an altar at Mass is a reminder that Christ's sacrifice is being made again through the offering of bread and wine.	• A table is where people eat from. • Using a table at Mass reminds the congregation that the Mass is a re-enactment of the Last Supper. • During the Last Supper, Jesus told his disciples to eat his Body and drink his Blood, 'which will be given up for you'. • By giving himself to his disciples in the form of bread and wine, Jesus was giving his disciples a share in the effects of his sacrifice. • Using a table at Mass is a reminder of this belief.

Crucifix, cross or Risen Christ

Christians view Jesus' death and resurrection as one event (though spread over a few days), where both elements are important. If Jesus hadn't offered himself to the Father on the cross through his death, the resurrection couldn't have happened. At the same time, Jesus' resurrection gave meaning to his death.

However, some Christians prefer to focus on one part of Jesus' death and resurrection over the other, and for this reason they might prefer to use a crucifix, cross or Risen Christ.

Crucifix	Cross	Risen Christ
• Shows Christ crucified on the cross. • A reminder of the suffering that Jesus endured out of his love for humanity. • Helps Christians to feel grateful for Jesus' sacrifice and love. • Many Christians like the crucifix to be present at Mass, as this service re-enacts the sacrifice of Jesus' death.	• A cross without the figure of Christ on it. • A symbol of Christ's victory over sin and death: Christ is not on the cross because he has risen. • Christians who are wary about portraying Jesus through art may prefer to use a cross (see page 35). • Emphasises Jesus' resurrection and the fact that Christians should be people of new life.	• Focuses on Christ as the risen, glorified Saviour. • Reminds Catholics that in Holy Communion, they receive the Body, Blood, Soul and Divinity of the Risen Christ. • Like the cross, the Risen Christ emphasises Jesus' resurrection and how important this was.

APPLY

A Explain how the altar and table remind Christians of two different events.

B 'A crucifix is a better source of comfort and inspiration than a cross or Risen Christ.'

What is your opinion? Explain your reasoning.

Explain why someone else might disagree with you.

> ## TIP
> When giving your opinion in an answer, remember to support it with facts. It should be clear how your opinion has been shaped by your knowledge and understanding of Christian beliefs.

RECAP

Essential information:

☐ People are able to sin because God gave humans free will.

☐ Sin broke the relationship between God and humanity, and destroyed the harmony of God's creation.

☐ Jesus helped to restore this damage by living his life in total obedience to God's will.

The relationship between free will and sin

Christians believe that for humans to have free will, sin has to exist. But the existence of sin damages the relationship between God, humanity and the whole of creation.

- God made all of creation perfect.
- But God also **gave humans free will**.
- This is because God wants humans to actively choose him, rather than follow him because they can't do anything else.

- Sin has **broken the relationship between God, humanity and the whole of creation**.
- God the Son became Jesus to help the perfect relationship with God to be restored.

- Humans can **use their free will to sin**.
- A sin is any action or thought that rejects the will of God.

- The Catholic Church teaches that **all people are born with the tendency to commit sin**.
- This inbuilt tendency is called **original sin**.

The death, resurrection and ascension of Jesus

Christians believe that Jesus' death, resurrection and ascension helped to restore the relationship between God and humanity, as well as restoring the harmony of creation.

Jesus' death	Christians believe that **Jesus lived his life in total obedience to the will of God the Father**. He always followed God's wishes and did the right thing. Jesus showed total obedience to God the Father, both in life and through the sacrifice of his death. This **helped to restore the relationship between God and humans that had been broken by sin**.
Jesus' resurrection	Because Jesus showed total obedience to the Father, fulfilled God's will and never sinned, he was not held away from God by death and sin. Three days after his death, Jesus was raised back to life by God the Father. This **destroyed the ultimate power of sin and death**. This means that, as a result of Jesus' resurrection, people are now able to be with God after they die. Sin and death still exist, but people are now able to overcome them. Jesus' resurrection also **helped to restore the harmony of creation** (see page 101).
Jesus' ascension	40 days after Jesus was resurrected, he rose up to heaven to take his place beside the Father as the Son of God. Jesus' resurrection and ascension have **helped to restore the cosmic order**, by making the whole of creation as perfect as God intended it to be.

APPLY

(A) Explain the meaning of 'the restoration of the cosmic order'.

(B) 'The existence of free will led to Jesus' death.'

Give arguments to support this statement.

4.5 The significance of Jesus' death, burial, resurrection and ascension

Essential information:

- [ ] Jesus' death, burial, resurrection and ascension were four steps in the action to redeem humanity and restore the relationship between God, humanity and the whole of creation.

- [ ] For Christians, this means that life no longer ends at the moment of death. It gives them hope that, like Jesus, they be will be resurrected after death and raised up to eternal life with God.

The significance of Jesus' death and burial

- Jesus' death **redeemed humanity** through his total obedience to God. This means he made up for the sins of humanity so people could be brought back to a relationship with God. He did this through the sacrifice of his death.
- For Christians, an important element of Jesus' death is that he **continued to show love**, even when he was suffering. For example, he forgave his executioners (Luke 23:34).
- Christians believe that when Jesus died and was buried he joined everyone else who had died before him. Christians believe this shows that **God is with them even in death**.

The significance of Jesus' resurrection

> **❝** If Christ has not been raised, your faith is futile and you are still in your sins. **❞**
>
> *1 Corinthians 15:17 (NRSV)*

TIP

You can use this quote in your exam to show that Jesus' resurrection is of central importance to the Christian faith.

- For Christians, Jesus' resurrection **made life after death possible** by destroying the ultimate power of sin and death.
- When Jesus was resurrected, all those who had died before him **rose up to heaven** with him.
- Jesus appeared to his followers in a locked room, proving he had risen from the dead. For Catholics, the accounts of the resurrection appearances in the Bible show the resurrection actually happened (rather than being myths like the Genesis creation stories).

The significance of Jesus' ascension

- For Christians, the ascension shows that **Jesus is with the Father**, sharing his glory for all eternity.
- Just before Jesus ascended to heaven, he **promised to send his Spirit to all people**. This allows Jesus to continue to work in and through his believers.
- Jesus ascension' gives believers faith that **they will also be raised up to heaven**, as Jesus promised that all his people will follow where he has gone, as the relationship between God, humanity and the whole of creation has been restored.

APPLY

A Write your own definitions for the terms 'resurrection' and 'ascension'.

B 'The resurrection of Jesus is more important than his ascension.'

Give arguments for and against this statement.

Then write a short paragraph giving your own opinion on this statement. Explain your reasoning by referring to some of the arguments you have already listed.

TIP

Remember that Jesus' resurrection and ascension are also important because they restored the relationship between God, humanity and creation. See pages 65 and 101 for more on this.

4.6 Salvation (past, present and future)

Essential information:

☐ Because Jesus redeemed humanity through his death, **salvation** is now possible. This means people can be saved from sin and eternal separation from God.

☐ Catholics believe **redemption** and salvation are ongoing processes.

☐ Redemption and salvation are the focus of the liturgy in the Mass.

Salvation in the past, present and future

Many Christians believe salvation is an ongoing process, which began with Jesus' death and resurrection and will be completed at the end of time.

In the past	In the present	In the future
• **Jesus' death and resurrection were essential to humanity's salvation**. • These events defeated the ultimate power of sin and death, and made it possible for people to enter heaven after they die. • Some Christians believe that nothing else is needed for salvation: Jesus' death and resurrection made salvation complete.	• **Salvation is an ongoing process**. • While Jesus defeated the ultimate power of sin, this does not mean that sin no longer exists. • Catholics believe that while Jesus' death and resurrection offered salvation to everyone, people still have to choose to accept it, by resisting the temptation to sin and accepting forgiveness when they do sin. • The Holy Spirit guides people to work towards salvation.	• **Salvation will be completed at the end of time**. • When the Kingdom of God is fully established (see page 81), the power of sin and death will be completely destroyed. • All believers will be able to share in the glory of Christ and experience the joy of heaven. • This will be the final victory of God's grace.

Redemption and salvation in the liturgy

Catholics believe redemption is ongoing, because Christ is offered again to the Father during every Mass.

- In the Mass, Christ's offering of himself to the Father on the cross is re-enacted (see page 63). Catholics also offer themselves up with Christ.
- Through receiving Holy Communion, Catholics receive the Body and Blood of Christ.
- Christ enters their lives to give them grace and the strength to resist sin. This helps them to get closer to salvation.
- The Mass is a chance to experience what the **heavenly banquet** will be like. This is the victory celebration that will happen when salvation is complete. It is represented by the idea of everyone in heaven joining together for a meal. So the Mass inspires Christians to work towards salvation in their everyday lives.

(A) Explain how redemption is a part of the Mass.

(B) 'Salvation was completed with the death of Jesus.'

Explain why many Christians might disagree with this statement.

> TIP
>
> Try to remember the difference between redemption and salvation. Redemption refers to the process of making up for wrongs done by others, to bring humans back into a relationship with God, and salvation is the freedom from sin which allows humans to be with God eternally.

4.7 Redemption in the Bible

Essential information:

☐ Jesus is sometimes described as the example, the restorer and the victor. This is because he set a good example for others to follow; he restored the relationship between God and humanity; and he was victorious over the power of sin and death.

☐ Redemption is an ongoing process that people have to be willing to accept. This idea is expressed in the passages in the Bible that describe the resurrection, ascension and coming of the Holy Spirit.

Jesus as the example, restorer and victor

Mark 15:21–29 tells the story of Jesus' crucifixion and death. This passage helps to show how Jesus is the example, the restorer and the victor.

Jesus as the example	Mark 14–15 tells how Jesus knew how much suffering his crucifixion would cause him, but he still went through with it. Through showing total obedience to God, Jesus set an example for all people to follow.
Jesus as the restorer	Jesus' death restored the relationship between God and humanity. Mark 15 tells how, after Jesus died, in the Holy Temple in Jerusalem the veil that separated the holiest part of the Temple from the rest tore in two. This shows that Jesus' death broke down the barrier between God and humanity.
Jesus as the victor	Mark 15 shows how Jesus experienced pain, suffering and death as a human. By bringing the presence of God into these experiences, Jesus was victorious over them. He made it possible for all people to share in the final defeat of suffering and death.

The resurrection, ascension and coming of the Holy Spirit

The resurrection, ascension and coming of the Holy Spirit are described in the Bible in John 20:1–18, Acts 1:6–11 and Acts 2:1–4. These passages help to contribute to an understanding of redemption in the following ways.

Passage	Event	Explanation
John 20:1–18	When Jesus first appeared to Mary after his resurrection, she didn't recognise him immediately.	• This suggests Jesus, while physically present, was also different. He had entered a new creation. • This reflects the idea that redemption changed creation, making it more perfect.
Acts 1:6–11	Before he ascended to heaven, Jesus told his disciples they would be his witnesses 'to the ends of the earth'.	• The disciples were witnesses to Jesus' redeeming work on earth. • Jesus expected his disciples to continue to spread his teachings after he was gone, so everyone could accept and share in his redemption.
	After Jesus ascended to heaven, two angels told the disciples he would return in the future.	• Jesus will complete the redemption of the world at the end of time, when sin and death will be completely defeated.
Acts 2:1–4	On the day of Pentecost (fifty days after the resurrection), the apostles were filled with the power of the Holy Spirit.	• The Holy Spirit gave the apostles the courage and ability to go out into the world and teach people about Jesus, so they could accept his redemption.

APPLY

A In three sentences, explain how Jesus is the example, the restorer and the victor.

B 'The Bible shows how redemption is an ongoing process.'

Give arguments to support this statement. Refer to specific passages from the Bible in your answer.

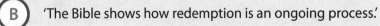

RECAP

Essential information:

- [ ] A **metaphor** is a word or phrase that is applied to something else, to suggest the two things are similar.

- [ ] St Irenaeus uses the metaphor of a tree to compare the event that created the need for salvation (the fall of Adam and Eve) with the event that brought about this salvation (Jesus' death).

- [ ] St Anselm uses the metaphor of the slave trade to show how humans were slaves to sin, and Jesus' death paid for them to be freed from this sin.

St Irenaeus

- The event that created the need for salvation is when Adam and Eve disobeyed God by eating from the tree of the knowledge of good and evil (Genesis 3).
- The event that helped to bring salvation is Jesus' death on the cross. St Irenaeus represents this event with the 'tree' of the cross.
- St Irenaeus' salvation metaphor highlights the parallels between these two events.

The tree of the knowledge of good and evil	The tree of the cross
Adam and Eve disobeyed God by eating from the tree	Jesus obeyed God by dying on the tree
Adam and Eve's rejection of God broke humanity's relationship with God	Jesus' acceptance of God restored humanity's relationship with God
The tree of the knowledge of good and evil brought death, by separating humans from God	The tree of the cross brought life, by offering the possibility of eternal life in heaven to all people

St Anselm

St Anselm compared Jesus' death with the idea of paying a ransom in the slave trade.

- In the slave trade, a slave could be freed if someone paid a ransom (a sum of money) to their owner.
- St Anselm said that after the fall of Adam and Eve, humanity became slaves to sin.
- The only way to **atone** (make up) for this is by showing total obedience to God.
- Through his total obedience to God, Jesus 'paid a ransom' for the sins of all humans, allowing them to be freed from the effects of sin.

These two metaphors have the following strengths and weaknesses.

	St Irenaeus	St Anselm
Strengths	Helps to show the parallels between the fall of Adam and Eve and Jesus' death	Reflects the idea that many Christians see themselves as slaves or servants to Christ (now they are no longer slaves to sin)
Weaknesses	Not all Christians agree with St Irenaeus' interpretation of the story of Adam and Eve	It is not clear who the 'ransom' is paid to, and some Christians think this implies there is someone greater than God

APPLY

A Explain two contrasting views about St Anselm's salvation metaphor.

B 'Metaphors are helpful for understanding Jesus' role in salvation.'

Evaluate this statement. Consider different viewpoints in your answer.

TIP

Use St Irenaeus' and St Anselm's metaphors to help you answer this question. Consider whether these metaphors are helpful or not. Do they make the ideas easier to understand?

4.9 The importance of conscience for Christians

RECAP

Essential information:

☐ Christians believe that **conscience** is the voice of God in their heart and soul, guiding them to make the right choices.

☐ Many Christians believe that their conscience is based on a natural understanding of what is right and wrong and the law of God. In addition, Catholic Christians believe that conscience needs to be guided by the teachings of the Church.

The meaning of conscience

Christians believe that a person's conscience is the **voice of God in their heart and soul**, guiding them to do what is right.

> ❝Conscience is the most secret core and sanctuary of a man. There he is alone with God, Whose voice echoes in his depths. In a wonderful manner conscience reveals that law which is fulfilled by love of God and neighbour.❞
>
> *Gaudium et Spes 16*

TIP

You can use this quote in the exam to help explain the meaning of conscience. It shows that the Church believes conscience is the voice of God, which prompts people to show love towards others and obey God's law.

Conscience can be thought of as having two different sides:

Conscience is made up of natural instincts	**Conscience has to be educated**
• The Church teaches that people are born with an understanding of right and wrong ('natural law' – see page 22) • This understanding helps to guide Catholics to instinctively do good and avoid evil	• Conscience needs to be shaped, developed and educated • This means listening to other people and paying attention to Church teachings • Catholics can only do the right thing when they have enough knowledge to make the right decision

The Catholic Church teaches that:

* people shouldn't ignore what they believe God is telling them in their hearts
* natural law means that all people instinctively know what the right thing to do is
* listening to others can help a person to understand the effects of their actions, as well as to be confident they are interpreting their conscience correctly
* the Church's teachings have been guided by the presence of the Holy Spirit over hundreds of years. These shouldn't be ignored, even if a Catholic's conscience tells them otherwise.

> ❝Personal conscience and reason should not be set in opposition to the moral law or the Magisterium of the Church.❞
>
> *Catechism of the Catholic Church 2039*

APPLY

(A) Explain how natural law affects conscience.

(B) 'In order to be faithful to God, a Catholic should always follow their conscience.'

Evaluate this statement.

TIP

To 'evaluate' this statement, explain to what extent you think it is true or not, and why. Remember to provide arguments to support two different points of view. Consider how a person could be faithful to God by following their conscience. Think carefully about the use of the word 'always' in the statement.

4.10 Redemption and the Mass

Essential information:

☐ The Mass is a re-enactment and celebration of Jesus' death, through which humans are redeemed.

☐ Through the Mass, Catholics believe that they are brought closer to Christ, accept redemption, and are given the power and grace to resist the temptation to sin.

☐ The most central points of the Mass are the Gospel reading and the Eucharistic Prayer.

Key events in the Mass

The Mass centres around the fact that people have been redeemed through Jesus' death.

	What happens?	What does it mean?
The start of the Mass	• Catholics come together to celebrate the Mass	• The congregation represents the Body of Christ on earth • Catholics believe that Christ is present among them when they gather together
	• Catholics apologise to God and each other for their sins	• This strengthens their relationship with God and each other, as they accept that God has forgiven and redeemed them
The readings	• At least two readings are given from the Bible, with one always taken from the Gospels	• The readings remind Catholics that God has guided his people • Through the Gospel, Jesus shows in his words and actions how God loves, heals, restores and forgives all people
The offertory	• The bread (the hosts) and the wine are brought to the altar, usually by members of the congregation	• These are brought to God on behalf of the congregation, as a sign of thanksgiving
The Eucharistic Prayer and consecration	• During the Eucharistic Prayer, the priest repeats the words that Jesus said at the Last Supper • At the end of the prayer, Jesus is truly present in the Bread and Wine • These are offered up to God the Father	• The command to eat and drink enables Christians to share in Jesus' offering made to God on the cross • The command, 'Do this in memory of me' reminds Christians that each time they celebrate the Eucharist, they make the event a reality, not just a past event • The Mass renews the **new covenant**. This refers to the new relationship between God and humanity that was established when Jesus died on the cross
Communion	• The priest offers the Bread and Wine to everyone in the congregation	• Catholics receive the Body and Blood of Christ • This binds them to Christ and the new covenant • They receive God's grace, which gives them the strength and guidance to resist sin and to follow Jesus' teachings
The end of the Mass	• The priest blesses and dismisses the congregation	• Catholics leave the church to share the presence of Christ with everyone they meet, so helping to spread the Kingdom of God on earth (see page 81)

(see page 81)

APPLY

A Explain two different ways in which the Mass reminds Catholics that they have been redeemed by Jesus' death.

B 'The Eucharistic Prayer is the most important part of the Mass.'

Give arguments for and against this statement.

4.11 Different Christian understandings of the Eucharist

RECAP

Essential information:

☐ Catholics believe the Mass is the 'source and summit' of Christian life, because it is the highest form of prayer they can make, and it gives them spiritual strength.

☐ The importance and meaning of the Eucharist varies between different Christian denominations.

The Mass as the source and summit of Christian life

Catholics believe the Mass is the 'summit' of Christian life because:

- the offering of Christ on the cross is the highest form of prayer to God; as the Mass re-enacts Christ's sacrifice, it is the highest form of prayer for a Christian
- the Mass celebrates and re-enacts the most important event in Christianity.

The Mass is also the 'source' of Christian life because:

- Christ's Body and Blood give life to the soul, just as normal food gives life to the human body
- offering the Mass on Sunday is a perfect way to 'keep holy the Sabbath day', as it celebrates the day of resurrection every Sunday.

> **TIP**
>
> 'Mass' and 'Eucharist' are both used to refer to the same service. 'Mass' is the term that Catholics generally use and 'Eucharist' is often used to describe the sacrament of bread and wine that takes place during the Mass.

Different Christian understandings of the Eucharist

Orthodox Christians	Many have a **very similar understanding of the Eucharist to Catholics** Like Catholics, they believe Christ is fully present in the consecrated Bread and Wine Differences to Catholicism include the following: • The Eucharist is always celebrated with the community; a Catholic priest can say Mass on his own • More emphasis is placed on symbolism and ritual • The consecration takes place behind the iconostasis – a screen that divides the holy part of the church from the congregation; this is because the consecration is too holy to be seen directly by the congregation
Anglican Christians	Some share the Catholic understanding that the Bread and Wine become the Body and Blood of Christ Many believe **the Spirit of Christ is received when Communion is given** Christ is spiritually present but the Bread and Wine do not literally become the Body and Blood of Christ Christ is present in the community that shares the Eucharist
Quakers and the Salvation Army	These groups **do not celebrate any form of Eucharist** Instead they believe that Christ is present through the Spirit, who inspires their prayers and actions They do not practise the sacraments as they believe the whole of life is a sacrament
Nonconformist Christians	Many believe the Eucharist is a **memorial of the Last Supper**; this means its purpose is to remember the Last Supper and its importance Christ is present in particular in the Bible readings Christ enters peoples' lives when they receive Communion

APPLY

A Explain two contrasting understandings of the Eucharist.

B 'The Eucharist is important to all Christians because it is the source and summit of Christian life.'

Evaluate this statement.

> **TIP**
>
> To 'evaluate' this statement, you could consider the importance of the Eucharist and your understanding of what it means to be 'the source and summit of Christian life'. Also think carefully about the use of the word 'all' in the statement.

RECAP

Essential information:

☐ Catholics believe that in the Mass the bread and wine become the Body and Blood of Christ. This means that Christ is truly present in the consecrated Bread and Wine (also called the **Blessed Sacrament**).

☐ This belief is shown in the prayers and rituals used in the Mass, and in the way the Blessed Sacrament is respected and honoured by Catholics (known as **Eucharistic adoration**).

The words of institution and the Agnus Dei

The **words of institution** are the words that Jesus said at the Last Supper. The priest repeats these in the consecration of the bread and wine.

- When these words are said, the bread and wine become the Body and Blood of Christ.
- The bread and wine look the same but the reality of what they are changes.
- This is shown in the words 'this *is* my body' (rather than 'this *symbolises* my body').
- By taking Christ's Body and Blood, his followers are able to share in the redeeming effects of his death and resurrection.

The **Agnus Dei** is the prayer that is said shortly before Communion. It refers to the 'Lamb of God' and recalls the Jews' escape from Egypt.

- The Last Supper was a Passover meal that celebrated the Jews' escape from Egypt.
- This remembered the events in Exodus 12, when God ordered each Jewish household to kill and eat a lamb, marking their front door with some of its blood. This meant nobody in the house would be killed by the Angel of Death. The sacrifice of a lamb saved the Jews.
- Jesus is the new Lamb of God, because the sacrifice of his death saved humanity from the ultimate power of sin and death. The Agnus Dei reminds Catholics of this.

> "Take this, all of you, and eat of it, for this is my body, which will be given up for you. Take this, all of you, and drink from it, for this is the chalice of my blood, the blood of the new and eternal covenant, which will be poured out for you and for many for the forgiveness of sins. Do this in memory of me."
>
> *Eucharistic Prayer II*

> "Lamb of God, you take away the sins of the world, have mercy on us… Lamb of God, you take away the sins of the world, grant us peace."
>
> *Agnus Dei*

Eucharistic adoration and the Benediction

- Eucharistic adoration refers to adoring or honouring the real presence of Christ in the consecrated Bread and Wine.
- Because Catholics believe the bread and wine become the Body and Blood of Christ, they treat it with great reverence and respect.
- Some Catholics receive Communion on their tongue rather than in their hand, as this reminds them that they are actually receiving Jesus himself.
- Eucharistic adoration is also shown in the service of **Benediction**. This is a service where the consecrated Bread is put on display in a monstrance (a large holder). The **Real Presence** of Christ is praised and the congregation are blessed with the Real Presence.

APPLY

A Explain two ways in which Catholic beliefs influence the celebration of the Mass.

B 'It is difficult to believe that Christ is truly present in the Eucharist.'

Evaluate this statement, including two different points of view and supporting these with reasoned argument. Remember to include Christian beliefs.

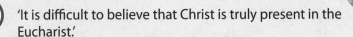

TIP

It is worth memorising the words of institution and Agnus Dei, as you may be asked about them in the exam.

REVIEW

Test the 1 mark question

1 Which **one** of the following people compared Jesus' death with the idea of paying a ransom in the slave trade?

A ☐ Catherine LaCugna   B ☐ Pope Francis   C ☐ St Anselm   D ☐ St Irenaeus   **[1 mark]**

2 Which **one** of the following Christian groups does not celebrate the Eucharist?

A ☐ Anglicans   B ☐ Nonconformist Christians

C ☐ Orthodox Christians   D ☐ Quakers   **[1 mark]**

Test the 2 mark question

3 Give **two** ways in which the main features in a church help to emphasise the presence of Christ in the church.   **[2 marks]**

1) _____

2) _____

4 Give **two** Christian beliefs about free will.   **[2 marks]**

1) _____

2) _____

Test the 4 mark question

5 Explain **two** ways in which an altar or a table helps Catholics to worship in the Mass.   **[4 marks]**

● **Explain one way.**	*One way an altar helps Catholics to worship is that it reminds them Christ's sacrifice is being made again in the Mass.*
● Develop your explanation with more detail/an example/ reference to a religious teaching or quotation.	*The altar is a place of sacrifice, so it reminds Catholics that Christ's sacrifice on the cross is being made again through the offering of Bread and Wine.*
● **Explain a second way.**	*The altar also helps Catholics to worship because it reminds them of the table round which Jesus and his disciples sat for the Last Supper.*
● Develop your explanation with more detail/an example/ reference to a religious teaching or quotation.	*Catholics may reflect on the last week in Jesus' life and of the words Jesus spoke to his disciples on that occasion, 'Do this in memory of me'.*

6 Explain **two** ways in which belief that the process of salvation is ongoing influences the way that Catholics live.   **[4 marks]**

● **Explain one way.**	
● Develop your explanation with more detail/an example/ reference to a religious teaching or quotation.	
● **Explain a second way.**	
● Develop your explanation with more detail/an example/ reference to a religious teaching or quotation.	

7 Explain **two** reasons why the Mass is seen as the source and summit of Christian life.   **[4 marks]**

4 Exam practice

Test the 5 mark question

TIP

To refer to scripture or another source of Christian belief and teaching in your answer, you could mention a passage from the Bible or a Church document, or give a quote from a religious leader.

8 Explain **two** Christian beliefs about the importance of the resurrection of Jesus in redemption.

Refer to scripture or another source of Christian belief and teaching in your answer.

[5 marks]

● **Explain one belief.**	One belief is that Jesus' resurrection made it possible for people to enter heaven after they die.
● Develop your explanation with more detail/an example.	By rising from the dead, Jesus showed that death could be defeated and eternal life with God was possible.
● **Explain a second belief.**	The resurrection is important to Christians because without it there would be no Christian faith, and no belief in Jesus' victory over sin and death.
● Develop your explanation with more detail/an example.	Jesus enabled people to have their sins forgiven and so to get close to God.
● Add a reference to scripture or another source of Christian belief. If you prefer, you can add this reference to your first belief instead.	St Paul says that if Jesus did not rise from the dead, the Christian faith is futile and 'you are still in your sins'.

9 Explain **two** reasons why Christians have different preferences for whether to use a crucifix, cross or Risen Christ.

Refer to scripture or another source of Christian belief and teaching in your answer.

[5 marks]

● **Explain one reason.**	
● Develop your explanation with more detail/an example.	
● **Explain a second reason.**	
● Develop your explanation with more detail/an example.	
● Add a reference to scripture or another source of Christian belief. If you prefer, you can add this reference to your first belief instead.	

10 Explain **two** ways in which Jesus is the example, the restorer and the victor.

Refer to scripture or another source of Christian belief and teaching in your answer.

[5 marks]

Test the 12 mark question

11 'The architecture and design of a Catholic church has no importance for Catholic worship.'

Evaluate this statement. In your answer you should:

- give reasoned arguments to support this statement
- give reasoned arguments to support a different point of view
- refer to Christian teaching
- reach a justified conclusion.

> **TIP**
>
> Remember, you need to give reasoned arguments in your answer. This means you should try to explain the arguments or points that you make by giving extra detail and examples.

[12 marks]
Plus SPaG 3 mar[ks]

REASONED ARGUMENTS IN SUPPORT OF THE STATEMENT ● **Explain why some people would agree with the statement.** ● Develop your explanation with more detail and examples. ● Refer to religious teaching. Use a quote or paraphrase or refer to a religious authority. ● **Evaluate the arguments.** Is this a good argument or not? Explain why you think this.	Some Catholics would agree with this statement because they would argue that a person should be able to worship God anywhere. They would say that the space a person worships in isn't that important and doesn't really influence the worship itself. For example, some Catholic churches are very ornate inside and some are very plain, but this doesn't change the worship that happens in the church. Likewise, some Catholic churches have the altar against the east wall and some have the altar more in the middle, but this doesn't change the content or meaning of the Mass.
REASONED ARGUMENTS SUPPORTING A DIFFERENT VIEW ● **Explain why some people would support a different view.** ● Develop your explanation with more detail and examples. ● Refer to religious teaching. Use a quote or paraphrase or refer to a religious authority. ● **Evaluate the arguments.** Is this a good argument or not? Explain why you think this.	However, other Catholics would argue that the design of a church can influence how easy it is to feel involved in worship in church services. For example, if the altar is in the centre of the church (as it tends to be in churches built after 1965) then it is easier for people to see and feel involved in the Mass. The design and decoration in a church can also help to make individual prayer easier. For example, churches which have small side chapels give people a quiet space to pray in. The decoration in a church can help people to feel that God is respected, and the art in a church can remind believers about important people or events in Christianity. For example, the Stations of the Cross remind believers about the suffering that Jesus endured before his crucifixion. Art like this can inspire people and give them something to focus on when they pray.
CONCLUSION ● **Give a justified conclusion.** ● Include your own opinion together with your own reasoning. ● **Include evaluation.** Explain why you think one viewpoint is stronger than the other or why you think they are equally strong. ● Do not just repeat arguments you have already used without explaining how they apply to your reasoned opinion/conclusion.	In conclusion, I think that although the design and decoration of a church doesn't actually change what happens in Catholic worship, it still influences it, so it does have some importance. This is because the design and decoration of a church can help make it easier to worship by providing inspiration, quiet spaces, and helping people to feel more involved.

12 'Christians should always follow their conscience if they want to become closer to God.'

Evaluate this statement. In your answer you should:

- give reasoned arguments to support this statement
- give reasoned arguments to support a different point of view
- refer to Christian teaching
- reach a justified conclusion.

[12 marks]
Plus SPaG 3 marks

REASONED ARGUMENTS IN SUPPORT OF THE STATEMENT ● **Explain why some people would agree with the statement.** ● Develop your explanation with more detail and examples. ● Refer to religious teaching. Use a quote or paraphrase or refer to a religious authority. ● **Evaluate the arguments.** Is this a good argument or not? Explain why you think this.	
REASONED ARGUMENTS SUPPORTING A DIFFERENT VIEW ● **Explain why some people would support a different view.** ● Develop your explanation with more detail and examples. ● Refer to religious teaching. Use a quote or paraphrase or refer to a religious authority. ● **Evaluate the arguments.** Is this a good argument or not? Explain why you think this.	
CONCLUSION ● **Give a justified conclusion.** ● Include your own opinion together with your own reasoning. ● **Include evaluation.** Explain why you think one viewpoint is stronger than the other or why you think they are equally strong. ● Do not just repeat arguments you have already used without explaining how they apply to your reasoned opinion/conclusion.	

13 'Jesus' resurrection is the most important event in Christianity.'

Evaluate this statement. In your answer you should:

- give reasoned arguments to support this statement
- give reasoned arguments to support a different point of view
- refer to Christian teaching
- reach a justified conclusion.

[12 marks]
Plus SPaG 3 marks

 Check your answers using the mark scheme on page 232. How did you do?
To feel more secure in the content you need to remember, re-read pages 62–73.
To remind yourself of what the examiner is looking for in your answers, go to pages 8–13.

5.1 Pilgrimage and the Stations of the Cross

Essential information:

☐ A **pilgrimage** is a journey that has a spiritual purpose, where the destination may be a sacred religious place.

☐ Catholics believe that life is a pilgrimage – a journey to meet God at death.

☐ When Catholics pray before the Stations of the Cross, they accompany Jesus on his final journey with a type of **dramatised prayer** (prayer that involves physical actions).

☐ Some Catholics make a pilgrimage to Jerusalem where they may do the Stations of the Cross on the Via Dolorosa, the street through which Jesus carried his cross (see also page 79).

What does pilgrimage mean to Catholics?

Catholics believe that **life is a pilgrimage towards heaven**. This means that:

- life is a journey towards God; Catholics will complete this journey and meet God when they die
- during their lifetime, a Catholic's actions should reflect the idea of making progress on the journey towards God
- everything they do should contribute to this purpose of getting closer to God.

This is why Catholics think of the Church as **the pilgrim people of God**.

> ❝Christians, on pilgrimage toward the heavenly city, should seek and think of these things which are above.❞
> *Gaudium et Spes 57*

> **TIP**
> You can use this quote in your exam to show that Christians view their lives as a pilgrimage towards heaven, and believe they should strive for this destination in their daily actions.

The Stations of the Cross

On the day of his crucifixion, Jesus had to carry his cross from Pilate's house to the hill of Calvary. The **Stations of the Cross** are a series of 14 images that remind Catholics of the events that happened during this journey.

The Stations of the Cross can be found in every Catholic church. During Lent, many Catholics like to **make the Stations of the Cross**. This means they walk between the Stations, reflect on a short reading about the event shown, and say a prayer at each one. This is a form of dramatised prayer, which can help a person to feel more involved in the meaning of the prayer. Moving between the Stations:

- is a way to accompany Jesus on his last journey
- is a way to share in Jesus' sufferings as a sign of gratitude and thanks
- helps the person to stay focused on their prayers.

> **TIP**
> Making the Stations of the Cross can be thought of as a type of 'pilgrimage in prayer', where the person accompanies Jesus on his final journey towards God through the action of prayer.

Ⓐ Explain what 'making the Stations of the Cross' involves and what this symbolises to Catholics.

Ⓑ 'Going on a pilgrimage involves making a physical journey to a sacred place.'

Do you think this statement is correct? Explain your reasons.

> **TIP**
> Remember to read questions carefully before you answer them. In this question the word to think about carefully is 'physical'.

RECAP

Essential information:

☐ Popular pilgrimage sites for Catholics include Jerusalem (where Jesus died), Rome (where the Pope lives), Lourdes (a place with healing waters), and Walsingham (England's Catholic national shrine).

☐ Catholics might go on pilgrimage to these places to renew their commitment to the Church and God, meet other Catholics, heal themselves, or feel spiritually inspired.

Important Catholic pilgrimage sites

Where?		Why is it important?	Why do Catholics visit?
Jerusalem		• The city in Israel where Jesus died • Catholics might visit Jesus' tomb, the Via Dolorosa (the street through which Jesus carried his cross), and other nearby places connected with Jesus' life	• To share in Jesus' life and suffering • To renew their faith and commitment to Jesus
Rome		• The centre of Catholic faith • Where St Peter died, and where the current Pope lives • Catholics might visit the Vatican (home of the Pope), the tomb of St Peter in St Peter's Basilica, and the cathedral of St John Lateran (the most important Catholic church)	• To show their commitment to the Catholic Church, and their unity with the Pope and all Catholics
Lourdes		• A town in France where a young girl called Bernadette saw visions of Mary • Mary told Bernadette to dig in the ground, and when she did a spring appeared • The waters of this spring are believed to have healing powers, and Catholics visit Lourdes to bathe in its waters	• To be healed physically or spiritually by the waters • To feel stronger and more at peace in body and mind
Walsingham		• A village in Norfolk which contains the Catholic national shrine for England • In 1061, a noblewoman had visions of the house where Mary lived in Nazareth. She built a copy of this house in Walsingham, which is now called the Holy House • Catholics often walk in procession between the Slipper Chapel and the Holy House. They might also attend Mass	• To go on pilgrimage without having to travel abroad • To spend time in prayer with other Catholics • To make themselves more aware of their place in the Church, the community of believers

APPLY

A Give the names of two Catholic pilgrimage sites, and explain why they are popular with Catholics.

B 'Catholics can't gain anything more from a pilgrimage than they could gain from visiting their local church.'

Explain why many Catholics would disagree with this statement. Use examples from the table above in your answer.

RECAP

Essential information:

☐ Catholic attitudes towards **mission** and **evangelism** – including what these should involve – are demonstrated in the films *Les Miserables* and *The Mission*.

☐ Films such as these can inspire and encourage Christians to become more involved in missionary work and evangelism.

How are mission and evangelism shown in drama?

Catholic attitude towards mission or evangelism	An example of this in a film
• For Catholics, the main idea of mission is to **show God's love through doing good actions** • Missionaries hope that actions which express God's love and forgiveness will have a real effect on other people, influencing them to do good things in turn	• In *Les Miserables*, a thief called Valjean steals silver from the Bishop of Digne • The bishop stops the police from throwing Valjean in jail for theft by saying it was a gift, and urges Valjean to use the opportunity he has been given to do good • The bishop's act of love and forgiveness persuades Valjean to become a better person • He sets up a factory to help create jobs and benefit from the wealth the bishop gave him
• Missionaries and evangelists are guided by the teachings of Jesus, who taught that **having the right attitude is more important than blindly following God's law** (see page 36) • Showing love, kindness and forgiveness are sometimes more important in missionary work than simply following the rules	• In *Les Miserables*, Valjean is constantly pursued by his former jailer, Javert. Javert refuses to forgive Valjean for his crimes and wants to send him back to prison, as the law demands • But at one point in the film, Valjean saves Javert's life and after this, Javert finds he cannot arrest Valjean • Valjean's kind act towards Javert ultimately saves Valjean from imprisonment. Goodness wins out over the law • One of the final songs has the words: 'To love another person is to see the face of God'
• Mission and evangelism require **total commitment to God** • Missionaries and evangelists may face hardships or ridicule as part of their work, but this should not lessen their commitment to their faith and work • Sometimes goodness may involve ignoring the demands of Church law	• In *The Mission*, some European priests are doing missionary work with a group of native people in South America • When the native people are attacked by their slave traders, the priests stay to defend the native people – despite the danger to their own lives and the order of their bishops to abandon the people

The influence of mission and evangelism in drama

The Catholic Church has said that 'The production and showing of films that have value … ought to be encouraged and assured by every effective means.' (*Inter Mirifica* 14). This is because films that highlight Christian values can:

• illustrate the power such values can have to change and improve people's lives
• inspire and encourage Christians to show these values in their own lives
• help to inspire Christians to preach the Gospel message to others and to show it in their lives by their actions.

APPLY

A Explain how *Les Miserables* illustrates that forgiveness is an important part of mission.

B 'The Church is right to encourage the production and showing of films that "have value".'

Do you agree with this statement? Explain why or why not. Use examples if possible. Then explain why someone else might have a different point or view.

TIP

If you are asked a question about dramas that feature mission and evangelism, you can use any relevant films or plays that you know about – not just the examples given on this page.

5.4 The Kingdom of God and the Lord's Prayer

RECAP

Essential information:

☐ The **Kingdom of God** refers not to a place but to the idea of God's authority and rule, and is seen among those who follow Jesus.

☐ The Kingdom of God was established through Jesus. It continues to grow in the present day, and will be completed at the end of time.

☐ **The Lord's Prayer** is the prayer that Jesus taught to his disciples. It gives an idea of what is required for God's Kingdom to grow on earth.

What is the Kingdom of God?

The Kingdom of God is also known as the Reign of God, when all people live as God intends. The creation of the Kingdom of God is a gradual process.

The Kingdom began when Jesus was born. This is when God's power came to earth.

It was established through Jesus' resurrection and the coming of the Holy Spirit.

It is extended by Christians, who form and help to spread the Kingdom of God on earth.

It will be completed at the end of time, when all people will enjoy the eternal happiness of heaven.

The Lord's Prayer

Phrase	What does it mean?
'Our Father, who art in heaven'	• Jesus wants all people to be able to call God their 'Father', and to have a trusting relationship with him
'hallowed be thy name'	• This is a prayer for God to be accepted as holy • When people respect the majesty and holiness of God, they recognise the importance of God in their lives, so they accept the call to become members of God's Kingdom
'thy kingdom come'	• This is a prayer for God's Kingdom to come, and for people to accept the rule of God in their hearts
'thy will be done on earth as it is in heaven'	• Accepting and following God's will is important for establishing the Kingdom • When everyone does the will of God, the Kingdom will be fully established
'Give us this day our daily bread'	• This is a prayer asking God to help provide the basics needed to survive, so people can focus more on God, thus helping the Kingdom to grow
'forgive us our trespasses'	• Forgiveness is an important part of helping people to become closer to God • To help spread the Kingdom, people need to show forgiveness to others as well as accepting God's forgiveness for their own sins
'deliver us from evil'	• This is a prayer to resist the temptation to sin, which will be assisted by God's grace • The Kingdom will grow as more people choose to accept God instead of rejecting him

APPLY

Ⓐ Explain two ways in which belief in the Kingdom of God influences Catholics today.

Ⓑ 'The Lord's Prayer teaches Christians everything important they need to know about how to help the Kingdom of God grow on earth.'

Give arguments to support this statement. Refer to phrases from the Lord's Prayer in your answer.

RECAP

Essential information:

☐ **Justice**, **peace** and **reconciliation** are signs of the Kingdom of God. The Kingdom of God is the perfect Kingdom and requires these three things.

☐ Christians can help the Kingdom of God to grow on earth by contributing to justice, peace and reconciliation, both in their own lives and in the lives of others.

Justice

To help create justice, Christians should live in a way that respects the rights of others. They should also take action to help change the systems in the world that allow injustice to continue. Helping to uphold justice will help to spread the Kingdom of God on earth.

Justice ...

- ensures all people have access to basic human rights
- '... goods created by God for everyone should in fact reach everyone' (Catechism of the Catholic Church 2459)
- recognises that all people are created and loved equally by God
- respects the dignity of every person
- treats all people fairly and equally, regardless of e.g. sex, race, religion

Peace ...

- is a state of total trust and unity between all people
- '... founded on truth, built up on justice, nurtured and animated by charity' (*Pacem in Terris* 167)
- flows from justice– there can be no peace where there is injustice
- is believed by Catholics to come from a person's heart
- is the removal of tensions caused by suspicion, resentment and mistreatment
- requires people to accept the rights of every individual

Peace

Christians should support all efforts to establish peace and harmony in the world. This includes supporting organisations that work for justice and unity. Christians believe this will lead to the peace of God's Kingdom being experienced on earth.

Reconciliation

Reconciliation breaks down the barriers that exist between people. This helps peace and justice to spread, which helps the Kingdom of God to grow.

Reconciliation ...

- brings back together people who have broken apart
- restores damaged relationships between people
- requires people to learn from the past and work together
- relies on acceptance and empathy

APPLY

A Write your own definitions for the terms 'peace', 'justice' and 'reconciliation'.

B 'For the Kingdom of God to spread on earth, Christians need to focus on fighting against injustice.'

Evaluate this statement.

TIP

To 'evaluate' this statement, decide whether you believe the statement to be true. Support two different points of view with reasoned arguments and refer to Christian beliefs and teachings in your answer. Arguments against the statement might consider whether there are better ways Christians can help the Kingdom of God to spread.

RECAP

Essential information:

☐ There is a **hierarchy** (ranking system) in the Catholic Church that recognises people's authority and responsibility, and brings about unity.

☐ The **Second Vatican Council** was a series of meetings held by the Pope and bishops between 1962 and 1965. It produced a series of documents that reflected a more modern approach to the Church and the world.

The hierarchy of the Catholic Church

Below are the main positions in the Catholic Church's hierarchy (starting with the most important on the left):

The Pope	**Cardinals**	**Bishops**	**Priests**	**Deacons**	**Lay people**
Head of the Church	Appointed by the Pope; they elect his successor	Successors to the apostles (see page 85); responsible for a diocese (a large area of churches)	Responsible for a small area of the Church called a parish; administer the sacraments and preach the word of God	Preach the word of God and assist the priests	Non-ordained members of the Church; they share in the priestly office of Christ through their baptism

- The Pope leads the Church and all authority in the Church ultimately lies with him.
- But the Pope sometimes needs to consult with other people in the hierarchy, to make sure he is making the best decisions for the whole Church.
- For this he might call a **Council**: a meeting with the bishops to discuss issues that affect the whole Church.

The Second Vatican Council

The main aim of the Second Vatican Council was to work out how to make the Church more open and accessible, and relevant to the modern world. The Council produced four major documents.

Dei Verbum **(The Word of God)**
- deals with the importance and the interpretation of the Bible
- stresses that the Bible should be taken seriously as the word of God, but should not be read in a literal way

Sacrosanctum Concilium **(On the Sacred Liturgy)**
- deals with the liturgy and church services
- emphasises that people should be able to take a full part in the worship of God
- allows Catholics to hear the Mass in their own language

Lumen Gentium **(On the Church)**
- deals with the nature and structure of the Church
- stresses that all members of the Church have important roles to play, not just the Pope
- emphasises the idea of a pilgrim Church moving forwards within modern society

Gaudium et Spes **(The Church in the Modern World)**
- deals with issues related to modern society
- stresses that the Church should not be separate from modern society, but should guide people on how to live in the modern world

---

APPLY

A Explain what a Council is, and why the Pope might call one.

B Write down three teachings that were stressed by the Catholic Church as a result of the Second Vatican Council. Then explain whether or not you agree with these teachings, and why. Do you think they are beneficial to Catholics today?

RECAP

Essential information:

☐ The **Magnificat** is a prayer that Mary said after she became pregnant with Jesus and visited her cousin Elizabeth.

☐ Catholics believe that Mary is the perfect disciple (follower of Jesus), and some of her qualities which contribute to this are shown in the Magnificat.

☐ The Magnificat is seen as a controversial Kingdom prayer, as some people think it could inspire the poor and weak to rise up against their governments as a means of spreading the Kingdom of God on earth.

The importance of Mary and the Magnificat

Catholics believe that Mary, as the mother of Jesus, is a very important figure in Christianity and the perfect disciple. Some of the qualities that make her so are shown in the Magnificat prayer.

Quality	Explanation
Mary shows humility	• Mary recognises that she is only special because of what God has done for her • For example 'for he has looked with favour on the lowliness of his servant.'
Mary praises God's greatness	• Mary is aware that God has shown his love for all people by doing great things for her and for all humanity • Her whole prayer praises God for this • For example 'My soul magnifies the Lord … for the Mighty One has done great things for me'
Mary shows her acceptance of God's will	• Mary willingly accepted the role of mother of Jesus (see page 30) • Her praise of God in this prayer confirms her readiness to follow God's will
Mary shows her trust in God	• When Mary said this prayer, she was a pregnant, unmarried teenager who could have been killed for alleged adultery • But she trusted God to protect her as she was doing his will • The prayer shows Mary's belief that God will help people who are weak and poor, like her

A controversial Kingdom prayer

The Magnificat is controversial because there is a **sense of revolution** within the prayer:

> ❝He has brought down the powerful from their thrones, and lifted up the lowly❞
> *Luke 1:52 (NRSV)*

> ❝he has filled the hungry with good things, and sent the rich away empty❞
> *Luke 1:53 (NRSV)*

- Some people think the Magnificat supports those who are **rebelling against their governments**. They believe it encourages the weak and poor to rise up against those in power to help spread the Kingdom of God on earth – by creating greater equality, promoting justice, and recognising the value of all people.
- Other people think the prayer just shows that **God supports the weak and helpless**, and that those who trust in God will be saved.

APPLY

(A) Explain why the Magnificat is controversial. Refer to scripture or another source of Christian belief and teaching in your answer.

(B) 'The Magnificat shows how Mary was the perfect disciple.'

Give three arguments to support this statement. Refer to phrases from the Magnificat in your answer.

TIP
Try to memorise a few phrases from the Magnificat so you can use them to support your answers to questions about this prayer in the exam.

RECAP

Essential information:

☐ The four marks of the Church are one, holy, catholic and apostolic. These are important characteristics that define the nature of the Catholic Church.

☐ **Apostolic succession** is the idea that the Pope and bishops are successors to the twelve apostles. This gives the Pope and bishops the authority to shape and confirm the Church's teachings (the Magisterium).

The four marks of the Church

The four marks of the Church are four qualities that are necessary for the Catholic Church to exist. They distinguish the Catholic Church from any other institution.

One

- **The Church is one united body**
- While it is made up of many individual churches, these are all part of the one Church, just as limbs form part of one human body
- At the Last Supper, Jesus prayed to God that his followers 'may all be one' (John 17:21 (NRSV)); the Church aims to achieve this today

Catholic

- The word 'catholic' means 'related to the whole' or 'worldwide'
- **The beliefs of the Church are universal**, held by Catholics everywhere in the world

The four marks of the Church

Holy

- **The presence of God makes the Church holy**
- All Christians and the Church as a whole are guided by the Holy Spirit
- Every member of the Church is also made holy through baptism

Apostolic

- **The Church's teachings are built on the teachings of the 12 apostles**
- The successors to the apostles (the Pope and the bishops) guide the Church today

Apostolic succession and the Magisterium

- Catholics believe the bishops and the Pope are **successors to the apostles**.
- This means the **authority of the apostles** has been passed down from one generation of bishops to the next. It also means the **authority of Peter** – who led the apostles and the early Church – has been passed down to the current Pope, who leads the Church today.
- The combined authority of the bishops and the Pope is known as the **Magisterium**.
- Catholics believe the Church is guided by the Holy Spirit. When the Pope makes a formal declaration of an official doctrine of the Church, he is speaking as the Head of the Church and on those occasions, he speaks infallibly – he cannot be wrong.

> **TIP**
> Apostolic succession is discussed in more detail on page 54.

APPLY

A Which two marks of the Church teach that the Church is a united, worldwide body?

B 'For Catholics today, "apostolic" is the most important mark of the Church.'

What is your opinion? Explain your reasoning.

Why might someone else disagree with you?

> **TIP**
> When you explain your opinion in an answer, refer to specific Christian beliefs. Explain how these beliefs have shaped your opinion.

RECAP

Essential information:

- [ ] The Church is **conciliar** because it makes important decisions through Councils.
- [ ] The Church is also **pontifical** because the Pope has the highest authority.
- [ ] The Church teaches that the weakest and poorest members of society should be supported and that economic exploitation should end, to help create a more equal society.

How is the Church conciliar and pontifical?

The Church is **conciliar** because:

- Councils (meetings of the Pope and bishops) are sometimes held to make important decisions and update Church teachings
- these help the Pope to discuss difficult issues with other members of the Church, and to understand the feelings of the whole Catholic community
- Councils influence the teachings and direction of the Church
- Councils express the voice of the whole Church.

The Church is **pontifical** because:

- the Pope is the leader of the Church and has the highest authority
- this authority has been passed down over generations from Peter, who was chosen by Jesus to lead the apostles
- this makes the Pope the representative of Christ on earth
- the Pope's teachings must be taken very seriously, and can be declared infallible (without error)
- the decisions of a Council have no authority until they are approved by the Pope.

Catholic social teachings

- The Church believes that God loves all people.
- The Church also acknowledges that people are vitally important to its existence: without human beings, there would be no Church.
- These beliefs have led the Church to recognise the importance of **helping to support the weakest and poorest members of society**, so all people can **live in an equal way**.

> ❝the Church sincerely professes that all men … ought to work for the rightful betterment of this world in which all alike live❞
> *Gaudium et Spes 21*

- The Church is **against economic exploitation and a culture of greed**, as this leads to inequality and suffering.

> ❝today we … have to say 'thou shalt not' to an economy of exclusion and inequality.❞
> *Evangelii Gaudium 53*

- The Church teaches that Catholics should do what they can to help support the poorest and weakest members of society, and to help relieve their suffering.

APPLY

A Explain two contrasting views about whether the Catholic Church is conciliar or pontifical.

B 'A good Catholic needs to take practical action to help others in society, rather than just focusing on their spiritual health.'

Explain why the Catholic Church would agree with this statement. Refer to *Gaudium et Spes* or *Evangelii Gaudium* in your answer.

5.10 The Church as the Body of Christ: the importance of charity for Catholics

Essential information:

☐ As members of the Body of Christ, Christians follow Jesus' command to 'love your neighbour as yourself' (Mark 12:31 (NRSV)), by showing love to those in need. Christians work through local, national and global charities to follow this teaching.

☐ SVP is an example of a Catholic charity working locally, by providing friendship and practical help to people in the local area.

☐ CAFOD is an example of a Catholic charity working nationally and globally, by trying to make a difference at a national or international level for people who live in poverty.

SVP (St Vincent de Paul Society)

SVP is an international Catholic charity that works locally. This means that SVP has members all around the world, who work in small groups to provide help to individual people in a local area. Their main aim is to offer friendship and practical help to people in need in the local area.

- SVP members visit people in need in their homes, or in hospitals, care homes and prisons
- They offer support, friendship and advice to people who are vulnerable

- SVP also help individuals with practical needs
- For example, they might help with the shopping and other household chores

- SVP run slightly bigger projects to help the local community
- For example, they might run summer camps for children or provide food for the homeless

CAFOD (Catholic Agency for Overseas Development)

CAFOD is the official charity for the Catholic Church in England and Wales. Its main aim is to help people living in poverty to become more self-reliant, by working nationally and globally. This means it offers help to people in other countries, and challenges national and international policies or companies.

- CAFOD provides emergency aid in places overseas where natural disasters or war have ruined lives
- They also help the victims of these disasters to rebuild their lives by providing long-term aid
- For example, they might provide communities with farming equipment so they can grow their own food

- CAFOD challenges national and international laws and policies that hurt those living in poverty
- For example, they campaign against policies that contribute to inequality or climate change

- CAFOD provides legal assistance to people who are being threatened by the actions of national or international companies
- For example, they provide help to farmers who are in danger of losing their land to large companies

(A) Explain two ways in which Jesus' command to 'love your neighbour as yourself' influences Catholics today.

(B) 'Catholic charities are more able to follow Jesus' teaching to show love by providing practical help on a local level instead of challenging international policies and laws.'

Do you agree with this statement? Explain your reasons. Refer to the work of two different Catholic charities in your answer.

TIP

You don't have to write about SVP and CAFOD – you could use any Catholic charities in your answer.

5.11 Kingdom values in Christian vocations

Essential information:

☐ **Kingdom values** are the values (or standards for living) that God wants people to have as members of his Kingdom.

☐ A **vocation** is a call from God to take on a certain role in life.

☐ Through the Christian vocations of priesthood, family life and religious life, people embrace Kingdom values such as serving others and showing love.

What are Kingdom values?

Kingdom values are values that God wants people in his Kingdom to show in their lives. For Christians, Jesus gave the best example of how to live according to Kingdom values. Some of these are expressed in the Beatitudes (see page 36), while others are given elsewhere in Jesus' teaching.

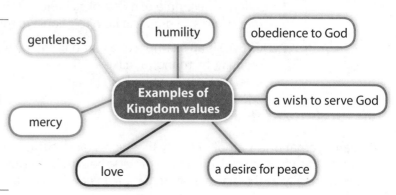

Christian vocations

Christians believe everyone has their own vocation: a calling from God to use their talents for a particular purpose. Living by Kingdom values is an important part of any vocation.

Kingdom values are expressed in the vocations of priesthood, family life and religious life in the following ways:

Priesthood	A **priest** is an ordained minister of the Catholic Church; one who is chosen to celebrate Mass, preach and forgive sins • Priests take a **promise of celibacy** (a promise not to marry or have sex). They commit themselves, body and soul, to God • Like Jesus, a priest **serves others** and, because priests don't have a family, they are always free to help others • Priests take a **promise of obedience to their bishop**, knowing they are obeying the voice of God
Family life	• **Love** is an important Kingdom value that unites a family together • Catholic parents try to show Kingdom values in their relationship with each other • They also aim to teach their children Kingdom values and by doing so they help to **spread the Kingdom of God on earth**
Religious life	**Monks** and **nuns** are people who commit themselves to God by living in a small religious community where life centres around prayer. **Religious brothers and sisters** also commit themselves to God in a similar way, but are more focused on going out into the world to help other people • Catholics who commit to a religious life as a monk or nun take **vows of poverty, chastity and obedience** to show they have committed to God's values • They live **simple lives**, dedicated to **prayer and serving others** • Monasteries have a sense of **peace** that other people can come and share in • Religious brothers and sisters centre their lives around prayer and active service • They start and end each day with prayer • They may take on roles such as teachers, nurses or care workers, to **show love through helping others** • By their care and commitment, they show people the love of God and express Kingdom values

A Explain the meaning of the word 'vocation'.

B 'Religious life is the only vocation that really allows someone to live by Kingdom values.'

List arguments to support this statement and arguments to support a different point of view.

RECAP

Essential information:

☐ Pope Francis is an example of a well known Catholic who lives by the Kingdom values of justice, peace and reconciliation.

☐ He shows his belief in justice by trying to end inequality and poverty.

☐ He shows his belief in peace and reconciliation by helping to restore relationships between nations or people that are in conflict with one another.

Justice

Pope Francis is particularly concerned with creating justice for the poor by trying to end poverty and inequality. Examples of how he has done this include the following:

- When Pope Francis became Archbishop of Buenos Aires, **he increased the number of priests working among the poor**

- By setting a good example, **he aims to inspire others to live more simply** to help reduce inequality
- For example, he lives in a small, modest flat rather than the large official apartments in the Vatican

- **He criticises economic policies that lead to inequality and exploitation**
- He also speaks out against all forms of abuse, as this damages lives and contributes to injustice

Peace

Pope Francis has helped to create or has called for peace in many different ways, including the following:

- During 2014–15, **he played a major role in restoring relations between Cuba and the USA**
- There had previously been tension between these countries since the 1950s

- **He brings together leaders of countries that have been at war with each other**
- For example, in 2014 he met and prayed with the Palestinian and Israeli presidents

- **He uses his public addresses to pray for peace**
- He often prays for areas in the world that are facing great conflict and tension

Reconciliation

Here are some examples of how Pope Francis has tried to restore relationships between people:

- Every Maundy Thursday **he goes to a local prison and washes the feet of 12 prisoners, including Muslims**
- This shows his belief that people who have committed crimes should still be accepted by society

- **He has visited areas of tension in the world**, trying to help restore harmony

- **He has helped to reconcile some of the tensions between Muslims, Jews and Christians**
- For example, as archbishop he arranged services in his cathedral where Muslim and Jewish leaders could pray together with him

APPLY

A Give two ways in which Pope Francis has showed the Kingdom value of reconciliation.

B 'If Christians want to live by the Kingdom values of peace and justice in their own lives, they should follow the example of Pope Francis.'

Give arguments to support this statement. In your answer, refer to some of the things that Pope Francis has done.

TIP
The meanings of justice, peace and reconciliation are explored on page 82.

5 Exam practice

REVIEW

Test the 1 mark question

1 Which **one** of the following pilgrimage sites is where Bernadette saw a vision of Mary?

   A Jerusalem   B Lourdes   C Rome   D Walsingham   **[1 mark]**

2 Which **one** of the following is the best definition for the term 'reconciliation'?

   A Bringing back together people who have fallen apart

   B Creating equality for everyone

   C Separating people so they cannot hurt each other

   D Preaching the good news about Jesus   **[1 mark]**

Test the 2 mark question

3 Give **two** benefits of using dramatised prayer such as the
   Stations of the Cross.   **[2 marks]**

   1) _____

   2) _____

4 Give **two** ways in which the Church is pontifical.   **[2 marks]**

   1) _____

   2) _____

> **TIP**
> Try to learn the meanings of as many key terms as you can, because they will help you to understand questions like these.

Test the 4 mark question

5 Explain **two** ways in which the belief that the Catholic Church is apostolic influences believers'
   reactions to the Magisterium (the teaching authority of the Church).   **[4 marks]**

● **Explain one way.**	*Catholics believe that the Pope – the Bishop of Rome – is the successor to St Peter and so accept his authority as handed down.*
● Develop your explanation with more detail/an example/ reference to a religious teaching or quotation.	*Because of their belief in his authority, Catholics accept that when the Pope makes an official declaration of doctrine, he is infallible and they accept what he teaches.*
● **Explain a second way.**	*The bishops are successors to the apostles and so Catholics accept their authority as they contribute to the Magisterium through the Councils.*
● Develop your explanation with more detail/an example/ reference to a religious teaching or quotation.	*For example, the Magisterium produced 'Gaudium et Spes' which influenced beliefs about family life.*

6 Explain **two** of the main teachings from the four major documents produced by the
   Second Vatican Council.   **[4 marks]**

● **Explain one teaching.**	
● Develop your explanation with more detail/an example/ reference to a religious teaching or quotation.	
● **Explain a second teaching.**	
● Develop your explanation with more detail/an example/ reference to a religious teaching or quotation.	

5 Exam practice

7 Explain **two** ways in which belief in the importance of showing Kingdom values influences Christians today. **[4 marks]**

Test the 5 mark question

8 Explain **two** ways in which justice and peace are expressions of the Kingdom of God.

Refer to scripture or another source of Christian belief and teaching in your answer. **[5 marks]**

● **Explain one way.**	*One way that peace is an expression of the Kingdom of God is that it calls for a state of trust and harmony between all people.*
● Develop your explanation with more detail/an example.	*So Christians will support work that removes tensions caused by resentment or mistreatment, because peace in peoples' hearts works to help bring about the Kingdom of God.*
● **Explain a second way.**	*One way that justice is an expression of the Kingdom of God is that it aims to create equality for everyone.*
● Develop your explanation with more detail/an example.	*In the Kingdom of God, everyone will be treated equally. Justice helps to create equality by making sure everyone has the same basic rights.*
● Add a reference to scripture or another source of Christian belief. If you prefer, you can add this reference to your first belief instead.	*The idea that equality is important for justice is expressed in the phrase, 'goods created by God for everyone should in fact reach everyone' (from the Catechism of the Catholic Church).*

> **TIP**
> This answer uses another source of Christian belief and teaching, the Catechism. Using sources other than scripture for these questions shows good breadth of knowledge.

9 Explain **two** ways the Magnificat shows that Mary was the perfect disciple.

Refer to scripture or another source of Christian belief and teaching in your answer. **[5 marks]**

● **Explain one way.**	
● Develop your explanation with more detail/an example.	
● **Explain a second way.**	
● Develop your explanation with more detail/an example.	
● Add a reference to scripture or another source of Christian belief. If you prefer, you can add this reference to your first belief instead.	

10 Explain **two** of the Catholic Church's teachings about how people could achieve a more equal society.

Refer to scripture or another source of Christian belief and teaching in your answer. **[5 marks]**

5 Exam practice

Test the 12 mark question

11   'The four marks of the Catholic Church guarantee that what the Church teaches is true.'

Evaluate this statement. In your answer you should:

- give reasoned arguments to support this statement
- give reasoned arguments to support a different point of view
- refer to Christian teaching
- reach a justified conclusion.

TIP

A 'justified conclusion' means you should write a paragraph that sums up your thoughts about the statement and explains how you have made that judgement, i.e. what the strengths or weaknesses of the arguments are.

[12 marks]
Plus SPaG 3 mark

REASONED ARGUMENTS IN SUPPORT OF THE STATEMENT ● **Explain why some people would agree with the statement.** ● Develop your explanation with more detail and examples. ● Refer to religious teaching. Use a quote or paraphrase or refer to a religious authority. ● **Evaluate the arguments.** Is this a good argument or not? Explain why you think this.	*Some Catholics would agree with this statement because the four marks show that the Church is a united body whose teachings are guided by the Holy Spirit and the authority of the apostles.* *The mark 'apostolic' means the Church's teachings are built on the teachings of the 12 apostles, and the authority of the apostles has been handed down to the current bishops and Pope. The 12 apostles were Jesus' closest followers and they led the early Church after Jesus died, so the fact that the Church's authority today stems from the apostles gives its teachings credibility.* *The mark 'holy' means the Church is holy. The whole Church is guided by the Holy Spirit. For Catholics this guarantees the Church's teachings are true, because the Holy Spirit is God and God wouldn't guide them into not telling the truth.* *The marks 'one' and 'catholic' mean the Church is united worldwide. This suggests that alternative views or disagreements are kept to a minimum – so all the Church's teachings are unified and agree with the truth.*
REASONED ARGUMENTS SUPPORTING A DIFFERENT VIEW ● **Explain why some people would support a different view.** ● Develop your explanation with more detail and examples. ● Refer to religious teaching. Use a quote or paraphrase or refer to a religious authority. ● **Evaluate the arguments.** Is this a good argument or not? Explain why you think this.	*Some Catholics might disagree with this statement because not all of the four marks necessarily mean the Church's teachings are true. For example, the marks 'one' and 'catholic' mean the Church is united, but they don't necessarily mean the Church's teachings are true. The Church could be united behind teachings that are 'lies' – or teachings that have to later be updated (as happened in the Second Vatican Council).* *Some Catholics might also say that because people make mistakes even when they are guided by the Holy Spirit, the fact that the Church is holy doesn't necessarily mean all the Church's teachings are true.*
CONCLUSION ● **Give a justified conclusion.** ● Include your own opinion together with your own reasoning. ● **Include evaluation.** Explain why you think one viewpoint is stronger than the other or why you think they are equally strong. ● Do not just repeat arguments you have already used without explaining how they apply to your reasoned opinion/conclusion.	*In conclusion, I think most Catholics would agree with the statement because they believe the fact the Church is guided by the Holy Spirit and the authority of the apostles means its teachings must be true. These teachings also come from a united body which should work together to agree what is true. If these facts mean Catholics can't be sure that what the Church teaches is true, then you might as well start to question whether their whole religion is true.*

12 'All Christians should aim to go on pilgrimage at least once in their lives.'

Evaluate this statement. In your answer you should:

- give reasoned arguments to support this statement
- give reasoned arguments to support a different point of view
- refer to Christian teaching
- reach a justified conclusion.

[12 marks]
Plus SPaG 3 marks

REASONED ARGUMENTS IN SUPPORT OF THE STATEMENT • **Explain why some people would agree with the statement.** • Develop your explanation with more detail and examples. • Refer to religious teaching. Use a quote or paraphrase or refer to a religious authority. • **Evaluate the arguments.** Is this a good argument or not? Explain why you think this.	
REASONED ARGUMENTS SUPPORTING A DIFFERENT VIEW • **Explain why some people would support a different view.** • Develop your explanation with more detail and examples. • Refer to religious teaching. Use a quote or paraphrase or refer to a religious authority. • **Evaluate the arguments.** Is this a good argument or not? Explain why you think this.	
CONCLUSION • **Give a justified conclusion.** • Include your own opinion together with your own reasoning. • **Include evaluation.** Explain why you think one viewpoint is stronger than the other or why you think they are equally strong. • Do not just repeat arguments you have already used without explaining how they apply to your reasoned opinion/conclusion.	

13 'The best way that Christians can help to spread the Kingdom of God on earth is to do charity work.'

Evaluate this statement. In your answer you should:

- give reasoned arguments to support this statement
- give reasoned arguments to support a different point of view
- refer to Christian teaching
- reach a justified conclusion.

[12 marks]
Plus SPaG 3 marks

Check your answers using the mark scheme on pages 232–233. How did you do?
To feel more secure in the content you need to remember, re-read pages 78–89.
To remind yourself of what the examiner is looking for in your answers, go to pages 8–13.

6.1 The Paschal Candle

Essential information:

☐ The **Paschal candle** is a large candle that has an important role in a number of church services, particularly the **Easter Vigil**.

☐ The candle represents the Risen Christ.

☐ It is used to help celebrate and share in Jesus' resurrection.

The Paschal candle in the Easter Vigil

The Paschal candle is an important feature of the Easter Vigil ceremony. This is a service that takes place the night before Easter Sunday, during which the resurrection of Jesus is celebrated.

What happens?	What does it represent?
After the sun has set, the priest lights a fire	The light of Christ rising from the tomb, destroying the power of sin and death through his resurrection (see page 66)
The priest traces the design of the Alpha and Omega symbols with his hand, while saying a prayer to worship Christ	The Alpha and Omega symbols always appear on the Paschal candle. They show that Christ is eternal (see page 33)
The priest inserts five little holders, each containing a grain of incense, into the candle	The five wounds that Christ received during his crucifixion
The priest lights the Paschal candle from the fire, saying, 'May the light of Christ rising in glory/ dispel the darkness of our hearts and minds'	The light of Christ coming into the world, to overcome the darkness of sin and death
The priest processes with the candle up to the altar. Light from the Paschal candle is used to light the candles held by everyone else in the church	Shows that all believers are able to share in the risen glory of Christ

Other uses for the Paschal candle

The Paschal candle is also lit at **baptisms** and **funerals**.

- When a person is baptised, they are given a candle that is lit from the Paschal candle. This shows the person has been filled with the light of Christ (see page 54). The priest tells the person's parents and godparents:

> ❝This child of yours has been enlightened by Christ. He (she) is to walk always as a child of the light. May he (she) keep the flame of faith alive in his (her) heart. ❞

- At a funeral, the Paschal candle is lit to show the deceased person has joined Christ in the resurrected life.

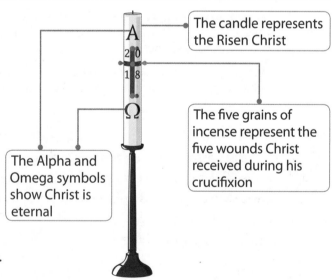

The candle represents the Risen Christ

The Alpha and Omega symbols show Christ is eternal

The five grains of incense represent the five wounds Christ received during his crucifixion

A Explain two ways the Paschal candle is used in church, other than at the Easter Vigil ceremony.

B 'The decoration on a Paschal candle reminds Catholics of important Christian beliefs.'

Give arguments to support this statement.

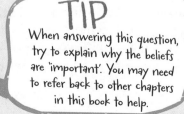

TIP

When answering this question, try to explain why the beliefs are 'important'. You may need to refer back to other chapters in this book to help.

RECAP

Essential information:

☐ Catholics believe that at the end of time, everyone will be resurrected and judged by Christ. This judgement will confirm whether a person spends the rest of eternity in heaven or hell.

☐ *The Last Judgement* is a painting by Michelangelo that depicts this event, which is itself known as the Last (or Final) Judgement.

How does *The Last Judgement* reflect Catholic beliefs?

- Christ is the central figure in the painting, emphasising his importance as the judge of all
- The wounds from his crucifixion are still visible, showing that Jesus came to glory through obedience and suffering
- Christ's right hand is raised, reflecting the parable of the Sheep and the Goats, in which Jesus promises the good will be on his right and the wicked on his left
- Here Christ is raising those on his right up to heaven

- Near to Jesus are some saints who are holding the tools that were used to torture and kill them
- Despite their torture, the saints are shown as having perfect bodies. This reflects the Catholic belief that people's bodies will be resurrected (as well as their souls), and made perfect
- This also reflects the belief that people who stick to their faith, no matter what happens to them, will be raised up to heaven

- In the original painting, everyone except for Jesus and Mary was naked
- This shows that in the Last Judgement, all people are equal before God

- Here people are rising from their graves, showing that all people will be raised up for judgement on the last day

- In the Book of Revelation, seven angels blow trumpets to bring about the end of the world and Christ's judgement
- One of the angels is holding a small book filled with the names of those who will be raised to heaven, while another angel is holding a much larger book filled with the names of those who are destined for hell
- This reflects Jesus' teaching that no one should be complacent and assume they will be raised to heaven

- Here people are shown moving towards hell, with a sense of despair
- Hell is shown as a place of darkness, which reflects the idea that the light of Christ can't reach people who have rejected God

---

APPLY

Ⓐ Explain what happens at the Last Judgement.

Ⓑ 'Michelangelo's *The Last Judgement* teaches Catholics that if they spend their lives trying to become closer to God, they will be rewarded in the afterlife.'

List arguments to support this statement. Refer to specific parts of the painting in your answer.

TIP
If you are asked a question about Michelangelo's *The Last Judgement* in your exam, you won't be given a copy of the painting to look at. So make sure you can accurately describe the most important parts of the painting in words.

RECAP

Essential information:

☐ Catholics believe in the resurrection of the body (the whole person, body and soul, will be judged in God's presence). Since the body is the temple of the Holy Spirit, the body should be treated with respect even after death.

☐ **Memorials** are structures or areas that are built to honour and show respect to the dead.

☐ Christian memorials express various beliefs about life after death, such as a belief in heaven, judgement, resurrection, and eternal life after death.

Tombstones

A **tombstone** is a large carved stone that is placed over a person's grave. It indicates the location of the person's grave, so it can be treated with respect.

Feature	What does it mean?
Often inscribed with the letters 'R.I.P.'	• Stands for 'Requiescat in pace' or 'May (s)he rest in peace': a prayer expressing hope that the person is in heaven, enjoying the peace and happiness of eternal life
Catholic tombstones are often shaped like a cross	• Indicates the person believed in Jesus • Expresses the hope they will be resurrected with Jesus to eternal life
Some Catholic tombstones have an angel carved on them	• Reflects the belief that all people have their own guardian angel, who takes care of them during their life • This angel will present them to God to be judged, and ask for a merciful judgement

Monuments

A **monument** is a structure that is built to remember an important person or event. Some monuments have been built for Catholic saints to indicate how important they were, such as for St Edward the Confessor (in Westminster Abbey) and St Thomas Becket (in Canterbury Cathedral).

Feature	What does it mean?
In the past, some wealthy Christians were buried in sarcophagi (highly decorated coffins) with the Chi-Rho symbol on them	• Shows the person believed in Jesus (see page 33) • A reminder of the belief that Jesus died so everyone would be able to experience eternal life in heaven
In the Middle Ages, monuments were often decorated with skeletons and other symbols of decay	• Reflects the belief that no matter how important or wealthy a person is, they face death and God's judgement just like everyone else

Remembrance gardens

A **remembrance garden** is an outside area where the ashes of people who have been cremated (burnt) can be kept. Many Catholics today choose to be cremated because there is not enough space to be buried. Their ashes are kept in a container or urn, which may be placed in a remembrance garden or a cemetery.

Feature	What does it mean?
Remembrance gardens are designed to be areas of peace and beauty	• Helps mourners to reflect on the peace and beauty of heaven, where the person who died is now hopefully present
Remembrance gardens are quiet, reflective spaces	• Helps people to mourn for their loved ones in peace in a place where they feel close to them, as this is where their bodily remains are at rest

APPLY

Ⓐ Write definitions for the following terms: tombstone; monument; remembrance garden.

Ⓑ 'A tombstone is the memorial that best reflects Catholic beliefs about the afterlife.'

What is your opinion? Explain your reasoning.

Explain why someone else might disagree with you.

TIP

You will not be asked to write definitions like this in your exam. But remembering the meanings of key terms, and being able to use key terms in your answers, will help you to gain more marks.

6.4 Eschatology and life after death

Essential information:

☐ **Eschatology** is the study of what will happen at the end of time.

☐ Jesus' resurrection is important for eschatology, as Jesus is the only person who has been able to give some idea of what happens after death.

☐ In 1 Corinthians 15:42–44, Paul explains how a person's resurrected body will be different from the body they had while they were alive.

Eschatology and the resurrection

The Bible suggests the end of time will be signalled by cosmic disasters – frightening, large-scale events such as the sun darkening or the stars falling from heaven (Mark 13:24–25). After this:

- the Son of Man (Jesus) will come to judge the whole of creation (see page 99)
- the end of the current world order will lead to the creation of a new one
- the Reign of God will be established.

Much of what Christians believe about the afterlife and the end of time **is based on Jesus' resurrection**. Most importantly, Jesus' resurrection taught Christians that **life continues after death in the presence of God**.

Beliefs about resurrection and the end of time have changed over the years:

- The early Christians believed Jesus' resurrection meant the end of the world would happen shortly
- All people would then be resurrected and taken up into the presence of God

- As time passed and the world didn't end, this view changed
- Christians realised they have to live in the life of the resurrection while they are still alive on earth
- This means following Jesus' teachings and resisting the temptation to sin
- This prepares them for judgement after death

St Paul's letter on resurrection

In one of his letters, Paul wrote the following about resurrection:

> ❝ So it is with the resurrection of the dead. What is sown is perishable, what is raised is imperishable. It is sown in dishonour, it is raised in glory. It is sown in weakness, it is raised in power. It is sown a physical body, it is raised a spiritual body. If there is a physical body, there is also a spiritual body. ❞
>
> *1 Corinthians 15:42–44 (NRSV)*

> **TIP**
>
> You can use this quote, or part of it, in your exam to show that Paul thought a resurrected body will live forever (it is 'imperishable'), will be sinless and perfect (it is 'raised in glory'), and will be powerful and strong (it is 'raised in power').

Here Paul compares the relationship between the earthly body and the resurrected body to the relationship between a seed and the plant that grows from it. In some ways they are the same thing, but they are also different from each other.

John 20:19–29 also helps to give an idea of what a resurrected body is like. This passage tells how Jesus was resurrected in a physical body – he was not limited by any physical barrier, but he was fully present and touchable.

A Give two ways in which, according to Paul, a resurrected body is different from an earthly body.

B 'Catholics can learn everything they need to know about the afterlife from Jesus' resurrection.'

List arguments for and against this statement.

> **TIP**
>
> Try to memorise some of Paul's descriptions of what a resurrected body is like, and be able to explain what these descriptions mean.

6.5 The four last things

Essential information:

☐ Christians believe the **four last things** – death, judgement, heaven and hell – are what all people face at the end of their life.

☐ Many Christians believe that when they die, they are judged by God and sent to either heaven or hell.

☐ Belief in the four last things encourages Christians to live good lives that are committed to God.

What are the four last things?

Death

- For Christians, death is a transition to a new phase of life
- Death is not something to fear, because it is the start of eternal life without the limitations of the earthly body
- While the body dies, the soul continues to live on
- The soul is judged by God and sent to heaven or hell (Catholics believe souls might also be sent to purgatory – see page 99)
- At the end of time, at the final judgement, the body and soul will be reunited in a perfect form

Judgement

- Catholics believe that after they die they will be judged by God
- God will consider everything a person has done during their lifetime
- This is the moment of truth when people have to accept responsibility for all of their actions
- Some Catholics believe that while God judges them, they also judge themselves in the light of his love
- Because Jesus died so all people could be saved, Christians believe God's judgement will be merciful

The four last things

Heaven

- If people are judged favourably, they will enter heaven
- Heaven is the state of eternal happiness in the presence of God
- In heaven, God's love removes all cares and worries
- God wants all people to join him in heaven, but he also respects people's free will. This means people have to choose to accept God in order to enter heaven

Hell

- If people are judged unfavourably, they will enter hell
- Hell is the state of eternal separation from God
- Christians believe God doesn't send people to hell; people send themselves by not accepting God
- People in hell are aware of what they have thrown away, and exist in a state of frustration and anger at themselves

A Explain two contrasting Christian beliefs about what might happen to people when they die.

B 'Christians have nothing to fear from death.'

Give arguments to support this statement. Refer to the four last things in your answer.

Why might some Christians disagree with this statement?

TIP
Aim to explain both sides of an argument in a neutral and objective way, even when you have strong personal beliefs about it.

6.6 Purgatory and judgement

Essential information:

☐ Catholics believe that after judgement, some people go through **purgatory**: a process of cleansing, which removes the effects of sin, to help a person accept the full presence of God.

☐ Catholics believe judgement happens twice: once immediately after death (particular judgement) and once at the end of time (final judgement).

☐ Christian beliefs about the afterlife vary. For example, some Christians don't believe in purgatory or judgement immediately after death.

Purgatory

- Catholics believe that when people are judged before God, many want to accept the offer of heaven.
- But the presence and overwhelming love of God makes some people ashamed of the bad things they have done in their life.
- Even though God has forgiven their sins, they still want to make up for the things they have done wrong.
- In this case they might enter purgatory. This is a **cleansing process**, where the effects of sin are removed so the person can feel happy in the presence of God.
- Catholics believe the process of purgatory can be quickened with the **help of prayers** from those who are still alive.

Particular and final judgement

Catholics believe there are two types of judgement after death:

Particular judgement

- Happens immediately after a person dies
- When God judges someone on a personal, individual basis. This means they are judged on all the actions they took during their life
- Results in the person going to heaven, hell or purgatory

Final judgement

- Happens at the end of time
- Christ will come in glory at the end of time and judge the whole of creation
- After this happens, the Reign of God will be established and everything made perfect. Those who have been judged favourably by God will stay with him forever in this perfect creation

Other Christian beliefs about the afterlife

- All Christian denominations believe in the resurrection and in heaven.
- **Many Christians do not believe in purgatory.** They believe that, after judgement, people will either totally accept God and go to heaven or totally reject God and go to hell.
- **Some Christians believe judgement doesn't happen immediately after death.** Instead all people wait in their graves for the second coming of Christ, when they will be judged and sent to heaven or hell.

A Explain two ways in which a belief in judgement might influence Catholics today.

B 'All Christians should enter purgatory before they enter heaven.'

Develop one religious argument against this statement, and one religious argument in support of this statement.

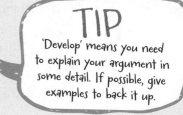

TIP

'Develop' means you need to explain your argument in some detail. If possible, give examples to back it up.

Essential information:

☐ The parable of the Rich Man and Lazarus is a story in the Bible (Luke 16:19–31) that tells of what happens to a rich man and a poor man in the afterlife.

☐ It teaches Christians about the nature of heaven and hell, and what type of actions and behaviour might result in a person being sent to heaven or hell.

What does the parable of the Rich Man and Lazarus teach?

The parable tells the story of a rich man who had everything he wanted in life. But he never gave any food or help to the poor, homeless man called Lazarus who lay at the gates to his house. When both men died, the rich man went to hell and Lazarus went to heaven. In hell, the rich man calls out to Abraham (the father of the Jews), who is in heaven. The parable teaches the following about the afterlife:

Teaching	How this is shown in the parable
Showing love and kindness to others will lead people to heaven	• By not showing love and kindness to Lazarus, the rich man went to hell
Wealth can make it easier to forget the needs of others	• The rich man 'feasted sumptuously every day' but didn't share any of his food with Lazarus • He didn't use his wealth to help others, so went to hell
Hell is a place of torment where people are cut off from any relationship with God	• The torment and suffering of hell are shown by the rich man pleading for some water; he says that he is 'in agony in these flames'
People in hell are conscious and aware of those in heaven	• In hell, the rich man is aware that Abraham and Lazarus are in heaven • This shows that people in hell are aware of the happiness of those in heaven • This increases their suffering
It is not possible to move between heaven and hell	• Abraham tells the rich man that there is a 'great chasm' between heaven and hell, and it is not possible to cross from one to the other • This shows a person can't escape hell by repenting or apologising for the things they did wrong in their life • A person's actions and choices during their lifetime determine the state in which they will spend the afterlife
Having faith in God, and following Jesus' teachings, will lead people to heaven	• The rich man asks Abraham to send someone from the dead to warn his brothers that heaven and hell are real, and they need to change their ways in order to enter heaven • Abraham replies that, 'If they do not listen to Moses and the prophets, neither will they be convinced even if someone rises from the dead.' • This means that everything people need to know to get into heaven is in the scriptures. If people do not believe in the scriptures – if they don't already have faith in God – then seeing someone rise from dead will not change their minds

A Explain two Christian beliefs about heaven and hell which are shown in the parable of the Rich Man and Lazarus.

Refer to scripture or another source of Christian belief and teaching in your answer.

B 'An important point the parable of the Rich Man and Lazarus teaches Christians is that they shouldn't have too much money.'

Do you agree with this statement? Explain your reasons.

TIP
Remember to read the question carefully. Here you should think about the difference between having money and using money.

6.8 Cosmic reconciliation

Essential information:

- [ ] **Cosmic reconciliation** refers to the idea that, at the end of time, the whole of creation will be reconciled (brought together in harmony) with God.

- [ ] Jesus' death and resurrection played an important role in starting the process of cosmic reconciliation.

- [ ] Julian of Norwich was a medieval writer who had a vision of Jesus telling her that 'all shall be well', suggesting that all of creation will be made perfect at the end of time.

What is cosmic reconciliation?

Sin broke the relationship between humans and God (see page 65), and Jesus' death and resurrection helped to restore this relationship. A similar process has happened with the whole of creation:

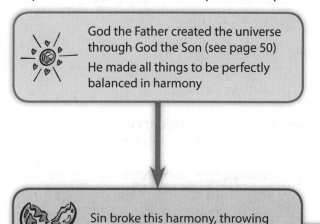

God the Father created the universe through God the Son (see page 50)

He made all things to be perfectly balanced in harmony

The whole of creation will be fully restored and made perfect at the end of time

At this point the cosmos (or universe) will be fully reconciled with God

This is known as cosmic reconciliation

Sin broke this harmony, throwing the whole of creation out of balance

As the Son of God, Jesus was able to destroy the power of sin and death, which had disrupted God's perfect creation

Jesus' death and resurrection helped to restore harmony to the world

> ❝ … through him [Jesus] God was pleased to reconcile to himself all things, whether on earth or in heaven, by making peace through the blood of his cross. ❞
>
> *Colossians 1:20* (NRSV)

Julian of Norwich

Julian of Norwich was a medieval writer who received a series of visions (or revelations) from Jesus. In one of these visions she asked Jesus why there is sin and hell, and he replied by saying:

> ❝ It was necessary that there should be sin; but all shall be well, and all shall be well, and all manner of thing shall be well. ❞
>
> *Revelations of Divine Love 32* (NRSV)

TIP
You can use this quote in your exam to show that Jesus' death helped to start the process of cosmic reconciliation.

The first phrase reflects the Christian teaching that sin is necessary because God has given humans free will. If people are able to make free choices for or against God then sin has to exist.

But 'all shall be well' because sin will be defeated and all things made perfect at the end of time. The whole of creation will be brought together in harmony and reconciled with God.

(A) Explain the meaning of the term 'cosmic reconciliation'.

(B) 'It is unlikely that all things will be perfect at the end of time.'

Evaluate this statement. Make sure you include Christian belief and teaching in your answer.

RECAP

Essential information:

☐ The Catholic Church teaches that no one is predestined to go to heaven or hell. Instead, the actions a person takes during their lifetime determine what happens to them after death.

☐ The Church teaches that no one knows when the end of time will happen. Catholics must therefore live their lives in the expectation that this could happen at any time, by constantly striving to do good deeds and committing themselves to God.

Preparing for the end of time

The Second Vatican Council (see page 83) helped to shape the Catholic Church's teachings about the end of time. It confirmed the following beliefs:

- At the end of time, **Christ will come in glory as the judge and saviour**. Catholics must live on earth in this hope.
- **No one is predestined to go to heaven or hell**. People have the free will to choose whether to accept God or not.
- This means that **God doesn't send people to hell**; people send themselves to hell by choosing to reject God.
- All Catholics can therefore determine what happens to them after they die through the choices they make during their lives.
- The Church teaches that **people should be constantly preparing for the end of time**, as no one knows when this will happen. They should **always strive to follow Jesus' teachings** while they are alive.

> " Since however we know not the day nor the hour, on Our Lord's advice we must be constantly vigilant "
> *Lumen Gentium 48*

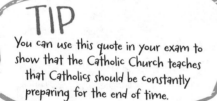

TIP
You can use this quote in your exam to show that the Catholic Church teaches that Catholics should be constantly preparing for the end of time.

To prepare for the end of time with the hope of getting into heaven, the Church teaches that Catholics should obey the following advice:

Teaching	Quote that shows this
Keep faith in God, as it is only through choosing to reject God that someone ends up in hell	'The promised restoration … is carried forward in the mission of the Holy Spirit and through Him continues in the Church in which we learn the meaning of our terrestrial life **through our faith**, while we perform with hope in the future **the work committed to us in this world by the Father, and thus work out our salvation**.' (*Lumen Gentium* 48)
Perform good deeds and actions that share God's love with others	
Do not commit mortal sins. These are the most serious sins (such as murder or adultery), which totally destroy a person's relationship with God	'God predestines no one to go to hell; for this, **a wilful turning away from God (a mortal sin) is necessary**, and **persistence in it until the end**.' (Catechism of the Catholic Church 1037)
If someone does commit a mortal sin, they should **confess** and be truly sorry for it	

APPLY

(A) Explain what is meant by the teaching 'God predestines no one to go to hell'.

(B) 'It is easy to get into heaven. So long as they believe in God, Catholics can do what they like.'

Do you agree with this statement? Give reasons for your answer.

Explain why someone else might disagree with you, putting forward their arguments.

TIP
Predestination is the idea that a person's actions are already fixed or determined before they happen. It suggests that people have no control over what happens to them, because this has already been determined by fate or God.

RECAP

Essential information:

☐ The **anointing of the sick** is one of the seven sacraments. It is given to a person who is seriously ill and may be facing death.

☐ The **commendation of the dying** is a short service that is held for a person who is dying.

☐ These last rites help to give a person who is sick or dying hope, strength, courage and forgiveness.

The anointing of the sick

The anointing of the sick is a sacrament centred around the action of anointing a sick person with holy oil. During the sacrament, there is a reading from the Bible, and prayers for the sick and the 'Our Father' are said. The following actions also take place:

Action	Meaning
The sacrament begins with the priest sprinkling the room and patient with holy water	• This is a reminder of baptism
The priest lays their hands on the head of the sick person, calling down the power and strength of the Holy Spirit	• The Holy Spirit fills the person to give them a sense of peace, and the strength to resist the temptation of sin • It also gives them the courage to overcome the doubt and despair their illness may have caused
The priest blesses a small amount of oil (the oil of the sick), then he anoints the forehead and hands of the sick person with this oil	• Through this anointing, the priest asks God to help the person, saying, 'Through this holy anointing may the Lord in his love and mercy help you with the grace of the Holy Spirit.' • The anointing gives hope of a new life, whether this is a restoration to full health in this life or the promise of eternal happiness with God
The sick person confesses their sins to the priest, who forgives them	• The person can face the future with a clear conscience, which helps them to feel more positive
Holy Communion is given to the sick person	• This shows that Christ is present with the person, supporting them through their illness

Commendation of the dying

The commendation of the dying is a short service centred around the dying person receiving their last Holy Communion, which is called **Viaticum**. During the service the following things may happen:

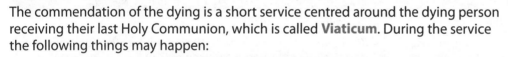

Action	Meaning
The dying person may hold a crucifix	• A reminder they are sharing in Christ's death
The dying person may repeat the promises that were made at their baptism	• The dying person is reminded of their faith in God • This gives them confidence in the hope they will experience God's love in heaven after they die
A Bible reading and prayers are given, including a Litany of the Saints	• The reading assures the person that God is with them • The Litany of the Saints asks the saints for their prayers as the dying person faces God's judgement
The dying person receives their last Holy Communion	• Shows that Christ is with the person on their journey from death to new life
At the moment of death a prayer might be said which includes the words, 'go forth, Christian soul, from this world … May you live in peace this day, may your home be with God in Zion'	• Expresses the hope that the person will be able to experience eternal peace and happiness with God in heaven after they die

APPLY

 A Write your own definitions for the terms 'anointing of the sick' and 'commendation of the dying'.

B 'It is not important whether a Catholic receives the last rites or not.'

Evaluate this statement and refer to Catholic beliefs and teachings in your answer.

TIP
Understanding and being able to explain key terms will be very useful in your exam.

6.11 The funeral rite

RECAP

Essential information:

- [ ] A **funeral** is a ceremony to mourn a person who has died.
- [ ] Catholic funerals reflect the hope that the deceased person has been judged favourably by God and is now experiencing the eternal happiness of heaven.

Reception of the body

What happens?	What does it mean?
• The body is taken to church in its coffin	• This represents the deceased person being taken back to God
• At the church doors, the coffin is sprinkled with holy water (the water that is blessed and used in baptism)	• This is a reminder of baptism • The person was baptised into Christ's death and now joins in Christ's resurrection (see page 55)
• The coffin is placed beside the lit Paschal candle	• This shows the light of the Risen Christ is shining on the person (see page 94)

The funeral Mass

What happens?	What does it mean?
• The priest holds a Mass • This funeral Mass is often called a **requiem**, which is a Latin word meaning 'rest'	• The whole Mass is centred around praying that the deceased person is now resting in the presence of God in heaven, with all their sins forgiven
• The readings of the Mass focus on the effects of Christ's resurrection • John 11:25–26 is often used as a reading, which includes the line 'I am the resurrection and the life … everyone who lives and believes in me will never die'	• This reflects the belief that Christ's death and resurrection made life after death possible, by opening up heaven to those who accept God

The committal and burial or cremation

What happens?	What does it mean?
• Holy water is sprinkled over the coffin	• A reminder of baptism
• The priest waves smoke from burning incense over the coffin	• God gave the dead person to the community for a time and now the family is returning the person to God • The rising smoke of the incense represents people's prayers being offered up to God on behalf of the deceased
• As the coffin is blessed, the congregation says or sings, 'May the angels lead you to paradise and with poor man Lazarus of old may you enjoy eternal life'	• This expresses the hope the deceased will spend eternity in heaven • The mention of Lazarus is a reference to the parable of the Rich Man and Lazarus (see page 100)
• A prayer is said for the mourners	• This reflects the hope they will meet the deceased person again in heaven
• At the burial or cremation, the Lord's Prayer is said • The coffin is sprinkled with holy water • There are prayers for the person's eternal happiness with God	• This reflects the belief the deceased person was a child of God, who has now hopefully been returned to his loving care

APPLY

A Explain two ways in which Catholic funerals and baptisms are linked.

B 'Funerals should be very solemn occasions.'

Write a paragraph giving your opinion on this statement. Refer to Christian beliefs in your answer.

TIP

Pages 55 and 94 will help you to answer this question.

RECAP

Essential information:

☐ Catholics believe in the **sanctity of life**: all life is holy and sacred, because it has been created by God. This means that all life should be respected, valued and cared for up until the moment of death.

☐ For this reason the Catholic Church is against **euthanasia** (killing someone painlessly and with compassion in order to end their suffering).

Care of the dying

Because of a belief in the sanctity of life, the Catholic Church teaches that:

- **All human life is holy and sacred**, because it has been created by God.
- **All life should therefore be respected and valued**. Life does not become any less valuable when a person becomes ill or elderly.
- **All life belongs to God**. If anyone intentionally damages or destroys a human life then they are rejecting a gift from God.
- **People have a duty to give the ill and elderly all the care and support they need**, so they can maintain their dignity until they die. Showing care for the dying should be central to any decisions that are made about their treatment.

Euthanasia

Euthanasia describes a situation where someone intentionally helps another person to die in order to end their suffering. The Catholic Church is against euthanasia for the following reasons:

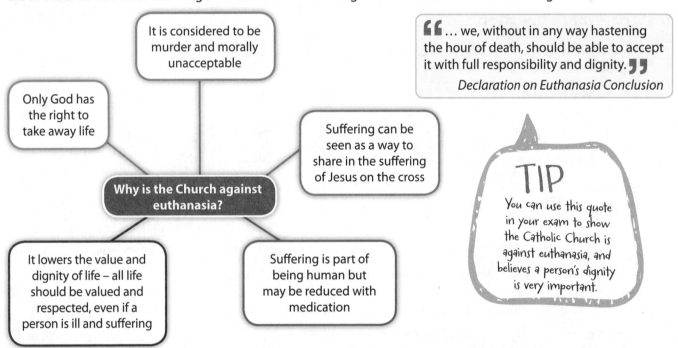

It is considered to be murder and morally unacceptable

Only God has the right to take away life

Why is the Church against euthanasia?

Suffering can be seen as a way to share in the suffering of Jesus on the cross

It lowers the value and dignity of life – all life should be valued and respected, even if a person is ill and suffering

Suffering is part of being human but may be reduced with medication

❝ … we, without in any way hastening the hour of death, should be able to accept it with full responsibility and dignity. **❞**
Declaration on Euthanasia Conclusion

TIP
You can use this quote in your exam to show the Catholic Church is against euthanasia, and believes a person's dignity is very important.

While the Catholic Church is against euthanasia, it does not believe a person's life should be deliberately prolonged by treatments that have no real benefit for the dying person. This means **a person who is close to death shouldn't receive treatment that will only prolong their suffering** but has no other real benefits.

APPLY

 A Explain two ways in which a belief in the sanctity of life influences Christians today.

B 'It is important that the Catholic Church never accepts euthanasia.'

Evaluate this statement.

TIP
To 'evaluate' this statement, give arguments for and against it to help decide whether you agree with it or not.

6 Exam practice

Test the 1 mark question

1   Which **one** of the following do the grains of incense in the Paschal candle represent?

- A The Body and Blood of Christ
- B The four last things
- C The three Persons of the Trinity
- D The wounds Jesus received during his crucifixion   [1 mark]

2   Which **one** of the following describes the time when God judges an individual person after their death?

- A Direct judgement
- B Final judgement
- C Particular judgement
- D Terminal judgement   [1 mark]

Test the 2 mark question

3   Give **two** ways in which the Paschal candle is used in church services.   [2 marks]

1) _____

2) _____

4   Give **two** teachings from the Catholic Church about preparing for the end of time.   [2 marks]

1) _____

2) _____

Test the 4 mark question

5   Explain **two** ways in which Catholic beliefs about life after death influence the types of memorials that are chosen to remember people.   [4 marks]

● **Explain one way.**	One way is that a belief that each person has their own guardian angel might influence someone to choose a tombstone with an angel carved on it.
● Develop your explanation with more detail/an example/ reference to a religious teaching or quotation.	Catholics believe this angel presents the dead person to God to be judged, and asks for a merciful judgement.
● **Explain a second way.**	A second way is that a belief in Jesus and resurrection might influence someone to choose a tombstone shaped like a cross.
● Develop your explanation with more detail/an example/ reference to a religious teaching or quotation.	This expresses the hope that the dead person will be resurrected with Jesus to eternal life in heaven.

> **TIP**
> A question that asks you to 'explain' means you need to make a point and then develop it with some more detail. You will get one mark for the point and one mark for the extra detail.

6   Explain **two** contrasting Christian beliefs about heaven and hell.   [4 marks]

● **Explain one belief.**	
● Develop your explanation with more detail/an example/ reference to a religious teaching or quotation.	
● **Explain a second belief.**	
● Develop your explanation with more detail/an example/ reference to a religious teaching or quotation.	

7   Explain **two** beliefs about final judgement which are expressed in Michelangelo's *The Last Judgement*.   [4 marks]

Test the 5 mark question

8 Explain **two** ways in which the prayers and actions in a Catholic funeral express beliefs about an afterlife.

Refer to scripture or another source of Christian belief and teaching in your answer. **[5 marks]**

● **Explain one way.**	*One way is that the prayers and actions express the belief that life after death is a reality because of Jesus' death and resurrection.*
● Develop your explanation with more detail/an example.	*For example, the coffin is sprinkled with holy water as a reminder that, like in baptism, the dead person is joining in with Jesus' death and resurrection.*
● **Explain a second way.**	*A second way is that the prayers express the hope that the dead person will spend their afterlife in heaven.*
● Develop your explanation with more detail/an example.	*For example, as the coffin is blessed the following prayer is said:*
● Add a reference to scripture or another source of Christian belief. If you prefer, you can add this reference to your first belief instead.	*'May the angels lead you to paradise and with poor man Lazarus of old may you enjoy eternal life.' This expresses the hope the dead person will enter heaven (paradise) and spend eternity there.* *This is a reference to the parable of the Rich Man and Lazarus in the Bible, in which the beggar Lazarus ends up in heaven after he dies.*

9 Explain **two** beliefs about the afterlife that are expressed in the parable of the Rich Man and Lazarus.

Refer to scripture or another source of Christian belief and teaching in your answer. **[5 marks]**

● **Explain one belief.**	
● Develop your explanation with more detail/an example.	
● **Explain a second belief.**	
● Develop your explanation with more detail/an example.	
● Add a reference to scripture or another source of Christian belief. If you prefer, you can add this reference to your first belief instead.	

10 Explain **two** Christian beliefs about cosmic reconciliation.

Refer to scripture or another source of Christian belief and teaching in your answer. **[5 marks]**

Test the 12 mark question

11 'Catholic funerals should be happy occasions.'

Evaluate this statement. In your answer you should:

- give reasoned arguments to support this statement
- give reasoned arguments to support a different point of view
- refer to Christian teaching
- reach a justified conclusion.

[12 marks]
Plus SPaG 3 mar

REASONED ARGUMENTS IN SUPPORT OF THE STATEMENT ● **Explain why some people would agree with the statement.** ● Develop your explanation with more detail and examples. ● Refer to religious teaching. Use a quote or paraphrase or refer to a religious authority. ● **Evaluate the arguments.** Is this a good argument or not? Explain why you think this.	*Some Catholics believe that death is just a transition to a new stage of life. So funerals should celebrate the fact that, if the dead person lived a good Catholic life, they are now experiencing eternal peace and happiness in heaven in the presence of God.* *For example, at the start of the funeral the coffin is taken to the church, which represents the dead person being taken back to God. Catholics would say this should be something to celebrate because the dead person is now in the presence of God.* *Also, Catholics believe they will be reunited with the dead person when they die and enter heaven themselves. So Catholics don't need to be sad at a funeral because they know they will see the dead person again.*
REASONED ARGUMENTS SUPPORTING A DIFFERENT VIEW ● **Explain why some people would support a different view.** ● Develop your explanation with more detail and examples. ● Refer to religious teaching. Use a quote or paraphrase or refer to a religious authority. ● **Evaluate the arguments.** Is this a good argument or not? Explain why you think this.	*Other Catholics would disagree with this statement because it is obviously sad when someone you love dies and to pretend otherwise could be seen as disrespectful, like you're happy that they are dead. Some Catholics might say that funerals should be serious, solemn occasions because the person's death isn't a trivial or funny matter.* *Also, even though the dead person might now be in heaven, there's no guarantee this is the case – they could also be in purgatory or hell. Michelangelo's 'The Last Judgement' even suggests that it's harder to get into heaven than into hell. This uncertainty means that you can't happily assume the dead person is now in heaven.*
CONCLUSION ● **Give a justified conclusion.** ● Include your own opinion together with your own reasoning. ● **Include evaluation.** Explain why you think one viewpoint is stronger than the other or why you think they are equally strong. ● Do not just repeat arguments you have already used without explaining how they apply to your reasoned opinion/conclusion.	*In conclusion, I think that Catholic funerals should maybe be happy occasions when it seems likely that the dead person is now in heaven. This is something good to celebrate. But I also think that Catholic funerals should treat the person's death seriously and respectfully. Catholic funerals shouldn't be too happy, especially when there is uncertainty over whether the dead person is now in heaven or not.*

12 'The main reason for Christians to show kindness to others during their lifetime is so they can enter heaven after they die.'

Evaluate this statement. In your answer you should:

- give reasoned arguments to support this statement
- give reasoned arguments to support a different point of view
- refer to Christian teaching
- reach a justified conclusion.

[12 marks]
Plus SPaG 3 marks

REASONED ARGUMENTS IN SUPPORT OF THE STATEMENT ● **Explain why some people would agree with the statement.** ● Develop your explanation with more detail and examples. ● Refer to religious teaching. Use a quote or paraphrase or refer to a religious authority. ● **Evaluate the arguments.** Is this a good argument or not? Explain why you think this.	
REASONED ARGUMENTS SUPPORTING A DIFFERENT VIEW ● **Explain why some people would support a different view.** ● Develop your explanation with more detail and examples. ● Refer to religious teaching. Use a quote or paraphrase or refer to a religious authority. ● **Evaluate the arguments.** Is this a good argument or not? Explain why you think this.	
CONCLUSION ● **Give a justified conclusion.** ● Include your own opinion together with your own reasoning. ● **Include evaluation.** Explain why you think one viewpoint is stronger than the other or why you think they are equally strong. ● Do not just repeat arguments you have already used without explaining how they apply to your reasoned opinion/conclusion.	

13 'Belief in the sanctity of life means that very ill patients should be kept alive as long as possible.'

Evaluate this statement. In your answer you should:

- give reasoned arguments to support this statement
- give reasoned arguments to support a different point of view
- refer to Christian teaching
- reach a justified conclusion.

> **TIP**
> Even when you have very strong views about a topic, try to write a balanced answer that takes into account different viewpoints.

[12 marks]
Plus SPaG 3 marks

Check your answers using the mark scheme on page 233. How did you do?
To feel more secure in the content you need to remember, re-read pages 94–105.
To remind yourself of what the examiner is looking for in your answers, go to pages 8–13.

7.1 The Oneness of God and the supremacy of God's will

RECAP

Essential information:

☐ Islam is a **monotheistic** religion. This means that Muslims believe there is only one God (**Allah**).

☐ The belief in one, indivisible God is known as **Tawhid**.

☐ Muslims believe in the **supremacy** of God's will: the idea that God's will is above all things. This means that things only happen if God wants them to.

The Oneness of God

Tawhid is a fundamental belief in Islam. Surah 112 from the **Qur'an** (the main holy book in Islam) helps to explain this belief:

Verse in Surah 112	Meaning
'He is God the One'	• There is only one God • God is a unified, undivided being; God cannot be divided into different persons
'God the eternal'	• God has always existed
'He begot no one nor was He begotten'	• God was not born or came into being out of something else • God does not have any children
'No one is comparable to Him'	• God is unique • No other person or thing has God's qualities and attributes • No one can accurately picture or describe God because there is nothing to compare him to

The word 'Allah' in Arabic

Belief in Tawhid means that Muslims should:

- worship only one God
- never make anything in their lives more important than God, as God has no equal
- not use images or pictures of God, as it is impossible to portray God accurately.

The supremacy of God's will

- Muslims believe **God's will is supreme** (most powerful). This means God can make anything happen that he wants to happen (see page 114).
- It also means that **nothing happens unless God allows it to happen**.
- This helps to give Muslims confidence when something goes wrong, because they know it is part of God's plan for them.
- Muslims try to live according to God's will in their everyday lives, accepting that God knows best.

> **TIP**
>
> Remember that Christianity and Islam are both monotheistic religions. This means they both believe in only one God. The difference is that Christians believe God is also three Persons.

APPLY

A Give two beliefs about God found in Surah 112 and explain what each teaches Muslims about God.

B 'Tawhid is the most important belief in Islam because it influences everything that Muslims do.'

Evaluate this statement.

> **TIP**
>
> To 'evaluate' this statement, explain the extent to which you think it is true or not and why. Consider how a belief in Tawhid affects the way a Muslim lives their life.

7.2 Key beliefs of Sunni Islam and Shi'a Islam

Essential information:

- [ ] **Muhammad** was the last and most important of the prophets in Islam. After Muhammad died, there were disagreements about who should succeed him as the leader of Islam. The religion split into two branches: **Sunni** and **Shi'a**.

- [ ] The central beliefs of Sunni Muslims are given in the **six articles of faith**, while the central beliefs of Shi'a Muslims are shown in the **five roots of 'Usul ad-Din**.

Sunni and Shi'a Islam

Sunni Islam	Shi'a Islam
The Sunni leader (called the Caliph) should be elected	The Shi'a leader (called the Imam) should be a descendant of Muhammad and chosen by God
Only the Qur'an and the **Sunnah** (Muhammad's teachings and actions) have the authority to provide religious guidance	The Qur'an, Sunnah *and* the Shi'a leader have the authority to provide religious guidance
Abu Bakr, Muhammad's advisor, was the rightful leader after Muhammad died	Ali, Muhammad's cousin and son-in-law, was the rightful leader after Muhammad died
The six articles of faith give the main beliefs for Sunni Muslims	The five roots of 'Usul ad-Din give the main beliefs for Shi'a Muslims
There are many shared beliefs in Sunni and Shi'a Islam. For example, both Sunni and Shi'a Muslims: • believe in the same God • follow the teachings in the Qur'an • follow the teachings in the Sunnah • acknowledge the importance of the prophets.	

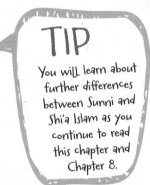

TIP

You will learn about further differences between Sunni and Shi'a Islam as you continue to read this chapter and Chapter 8.

The six articles of faith in Sunni Islam

1. **Tawhid** – belief that there is only one God.
2. **Angels** – belief in angels, who passed on God's message to the prophets.
3. **The holy books** – respect for the holy books and particularly the Qur'an, which is the highest authority in Islam.
4. **The prophets** – respect for the prophets and particularly Muhammad, who received the final revelation of Islam from God.
5. **The Day of Judgement** – belief that at the end of the world, every person will be judged by God and sent to paradise or hell.
6. **The supremacy of God's will** – belief that nothing happens unless God wants it to happen.

The five roots of 'Usul ad-Din in Shi'a Islam

1. **Tawhid** – belief that there is only one God.
2. **Prophethood** – respect for the prophets and particularly Muhammad, who received the final revelation of Islam from God.
3. **The justice of God (Adalat)** – belief that God will judge everyone on the Day of Judgement in a fair and just way, and hold them to account for their actions.
4. **The Imamate** – respect for the twelve Imams, who were chosen by God to lead Islam after Muhammad died.
5. **Resurrection** – belief that after death, Muslims will be resurrected and judged by God.

APPLY

(A) Explain two contrasting Muslim beliefs about God's nature

(B) 'The similarities between Sunni and Shi'a Islam are more important than the differences.'

Do you agree with this statement? Explain your reasoning. Make sure you refer to some of the key similarities and differences in your answer.

TIP

Being able to understand and use key terms such as 'Tawhid', 'Sunnah' and others will gain you marks in the exam.

7.3 The nature of God

Essential information:

☐ There are 99 different names for God in the Qur'an and Hadith (Muhammad's sayings). These names describe God's characteristics, and help to give Muslims some idea of what God is like.

☐ Some of God's most important qualities are: **immanent**, **transcendent**, **omnipotent**, **beneficent**, **merciful**, **fair** and **just**.

The main qualities of God

Muslims believe God is so great he is beyond human understanding and imagination. But the 99 names for God can help them to understand what God is like. These names are given in the Qur'an and Hadith, and help to describe God's different qualities.

Transcendent
- God created the universe, so is beyond and outside it. He is not limited by the physical world
- Muslims believe that God can be both transcendent and immanent because although he created the universe (so is outside it), he is also within all things and able to act within it

Immanent
- God is present everywhere in the world and the universe
- God is within all things and is involved with life on earth

Beneficent
- God is benevolent: all-loving and all-good
- God's generosity is seen in his gift to humans of everything they need to live on earth

The qualities of God

Omnipotent
- God is all-powerful
- God has the power to create and sustain everything in the universe
- God is aware of everything, including human actions and thoughts

Merciful
- God shows compassion and mercy
- God cares for people and understands their suffering
- God forgives people who are truly sorry for the things they have done wrong

Fair and just
- God treats everyone fairly and justly
- God will judge all people equally on the Day of Judgement
- Shi'a Muslims in particular believe that people have full responsibility for their actions, and God will reward or punish people depending on the choices they make (see page 114)

> **TIP**
> Remember that Christians and Muslims share similar beliefs about how God is the all-powerful creator of everything.

A Explain how God can be both transcendent and immanent.

B 'Of all God's qualities, his omnipotence is the most important one for Muslims to know about.'

Read the following response:

"I think it is more important for Muslims to know about God's mercy, because it's important to know that God will forgive them if they are sorry for what they have done wrong. People aren't perfect and always make mistakes, so knowing that God will forgive them helps people to keep trying to be better. Otherwise they might just give up, because it's impossible to be good all the time."

Write your own short paragraphs explaining why the most important quality of God for Muslims to understand is:

- fairness and justice
- immanence
- omnipotence.

Now write a short conclusion, in which you weigh up the arguments you have just written, to decide whether you consider the statement is true or not.

> **TIP**
> Remember, when you give your opinion in an answer, make sure you back it up by referring to religious beliefs and teachings.
>

7.4 Angels

RECAP

Essential information:

☐ **Angels** are spiritual beings who serve God and pass on his word to people through the prophets.

☐ **Jibril** is the angel of revelation, who revealed the Qur'an to Muhammad.

☐ **Mika'il** is the angel of mercy, who rewards good deeds and provides nourishment for the earth and human life.

The nature and role of angels

are spiritual beings, created by God from light

are pure and sinless

Angels ...

constantly serve and praise God

have no free will, so can only do what God wants them to do

are able to take on a human form to give messages to people

Muslims believe that angels have a number of different roles.

- Some act as **messengers of God**. They receive God's words directly from him and pass them on perfectly to the prophets.
- Some **take care of people** throughout their lives.
- Some **record everything a person does** in their own 'book of deeds'. This book is presented to God on the Day of Judgement, who will use it to judge the person and decide whether to send them to paradise or hell.
- Some **take people's souls to God** after they die, and escort them into paradise or hell.

Jibril and Mika'il

Jibril (Gabriel) and Mika'il (Michael) are two of the most important angels in Islam.

Jibril	Mika'il
The angel of revelation	The angel of mercy
Purified Muhammad's heart when he was a child, so he would later be able to receive God's revelation	Responsible for sending rain, thunder and lightning to earth
Recited the Qur'an to Muhammad and continued to pass on God's messages to Muhammad to guide him through the rest of his life	Brings nourishment to earth, and helps to provide food for humans, by sending rain to the ground
Therefore played an important role in communicating the final version of Islam to humanity	Believed to reward people who do good deeds

APPLY

A Give two different roles that angels have in Islam.

B 'Without angels, Islam would not exist.'

Do you think this statement is true or not? Explain your reasoning.

7.5 Predestination

Essential information:

- [ ] **Predestination** is the idea that God knows or determines everything that will happen in the universe.
- [ ] Most Muslims believe that predestination means God knows everything that will happen, but people still have free will and can make their own choices.
- [ ] Most Muslims believe that they are responsible for their own actions, and will be rewarded or punished for them by God on the Day of Judgement.

What is predestination?

In Islam, ideas about predestination vary. Some Sunni Muslims believe that **God has already determined everything that will happen in the universe**. They believe that:

- God has written down everything that will happen in a 'book of decrees'
- because God created people, they must act according to his will
- God's will is so powerful that he is able to make anything happen that he wants to happen (see page 110)
- humans do not have the freedom to change their destiny, or the overall plan that God has set for them; but they do have some choice over how they behave.

Surah 9:51 from the Qur'an is sometimes used to support the view that God has already determined everything that will happen:

> ❝ Only what God has decreed will happen to us. ❞
>
> *Qur'an 9:51*

In contrast, many Shi'a Muslims believe that **God *knows* everything that is going to happen**, but this does not mean he *decides* what is going to happen. They believe that:

- as God is the creator of time, he is outside time and so not bound by it. This means that God can see everything that happens in the past, present and future
- God knows what choices people will make, but they still have the free will to make these choices for themselves.

Surah 13:11 from the Qur'an is sometimes used to support the view that people have the free will to change their own future:

> ❝ God does not change the condition of a people [for the worse] unless they change what is in themselves ❞
>
> *Qur'an 13:11*

The Day of Judgement

- Muslims who believe they have the free will to make their own choices also believe they will be judged by God for these choices.
- They believe that on the Day of Judgement, God will judge them for everything they have done during their lives, and reward or punish them as a result.
- Even though God knows everything that will happen, people are still responsible for their actions, and will be rewarded or punished for them on the Day of Judgement.

(A) Explain why Muslims believe it is important to take responsibility for their actions.

(B) 'Predestination means that Muslims have no free will to make their own choices.'

Evaluate this statement.

TIP

Sunni and Shi'a Muslims have slightly different ideas about whether or not predestination limits human freedom. Try to use their different understandings to support your evaluation of this issue.

7.6 Life after death

Essential information:

☐ Muslims believe in **Akhirah** – everlasting life after death.

☐ They believe that after death, they enter a state of waiting until the Day of Judgement, when God judges them and sends them to **heaven** (**jannah**) or **hell** (**jahannam**).

☐ Belief in life after death encourages Muslims to take responsibility for their actions and to live in a way that pleases God.

Life after death

Muslims believe that after death the following three stages happen:

Barzakh

- After death, the state of waiting until the Day of Judgement is called **barzakh**, which means a 'barrier'. People are unable to come back across the barrier to right wrongs or to warn people
- While they are waiting, God sends two angels to question them about their faith
- Depending on how they answer, they will either see the rewards that will come or the punishments they will have to endure after the Day of Judgement

The Day of Judgement

- When God's purpose for the universe has been fulfilled, the world will be destroyed
- Everyone who has ever lived will be raised from the dead (**resurrected**)
- Everyone will be given their own 'book of deeds', which is a record of everything they did during their lives
- If they are given the book in their right hand, they will go to heaven; if they are given it in their left hand, they will go to hell

Heaven and hell

- People who have kept their faith in God and done good deeds will be rewarded with heaven (paradise)
- Heaven is described as a beautiful garden – it is a state of eternal happiness in the presence of God
- People who have rejected God and done bad things will be punished with hell
- Hell is described as a place of fire and torment, where people are separated from God

The importance of belief in Akhirah

- Belief in Akhirah encourages Muslims to **take responsibility for their actions**, because they know God will hold them accountable for their actions and reward or punish them accordingly.
- This motivates Muslims to follow the teachings in the Qur'an and to dedicate their lives to God.
- Belief in Akhirah helps to **give hope to Muslims who suffer**, as they know there is something better to look forward to. It also helps Muslims to **accept unjust situations**, because they know God will provide justice in the afterlife, and everyone will be fairly rewarded or punished for their actions on the Day of Judgement.

APPLY

Ⓐ Which one of the following is the name given to the state of waiting that a Muslim enters after they die?

Akhirah/ Purgatory/ Paradise/ Barzakh

Ⓑ 'A Muslim's approach to life should be based on their beliefs about the afterlife.'

Explain why some Muslims would agree with this statement.

Why might some people disagree with this statement?

7.7 Prophethood and Adam

Essential information:

- [ ] **Prophethood** refers to when someone is made a **prophet**: a messenger of God's word.
- [ ] **Risalah** is belief in the prophets and their importance as messengers of God.
- [ ] Muslims believe that Adam (the first human) was the first prophet.

What is prophethood?

Muslims believe that:

- prophethood is a gift from God to help humans to understand his message
- when people have forgotten, misunderstood or changed God's message, God has sent prophets to call people back to the right path
- there have been around 124,000 prophets, who have been sent to every nation on earth
- Muhammad was the last and most important of the prophets (see page 118).

Prophets are important in Islam because they are good role models and help Muslims to understand how to follow God. They do this both by conveying God's words and by setting a good example for how to live a life in obedience to God.

> ## TIP
>
> Jesus (Isa) is an important prophet in Islam. Muslims believe he was sent by God to help guide them in their faith. Muslims and Christians believe Jesus was fully human but only Christians believe that he was also fully God. Christians believe that Jesus had a unique relationship with God and they refer to him as the Son of God.

Adam

Adam is considered to be the father of the human race and the first prophet. The Qur'an teaches the following about Adam's beginnings:

```
God created Adam from     →   God gave Adam knowledge and   →   God told the angels to bow
the dust of the ground, and   understanding and he taught        down to Adam out of respect
breathed his Spirit into him   Adam the names of all things      for his knowledge
                                                                        ↓
God told Adam and Hawwa   ←   God created Hawwa (Eve) to    ←   Iblis (Satan) refused to bow
they could eat anything in the   keep Adam company, and they      down to Adam, so God
garden, except for the fruit     lived together in the Garden of   threw him out of paradise.
from the forbidden tree          Bliss                             Iblis vowed to always tempt
                                                                   humans to sin against God
      ↓
Iblis deceived Adam and   →   God expelled Adam and        →   God forgave Adam after he
Hawwa into eating fruit from   Hawwa from the garden and        accepted his mistake, and he
the tree                       their actions brought sin into     became the first prophet
                               the world
```

Adam is important to Muslims because God gave him knowledge and understanding. God taught Adam how to live a good life in obedience to God, and Adam passed on this knowledge to the rest of the human race through his descendants.

A Give two reasons why prophets are important in Islam.

B 'Adam is just as important a prophet as Muhammad.'

Explain why many Muslims would disagree with this statement.

What arguments could be given in support of this statement?

> ## TIP
>
> Some questions in the exam will require you to combine your knowledge from different parts of the course. Here, page 118 will help you to explain why Muslims disagree with this statement.

7.8 Ibrahim

Essential information:

- [ ] Ibrahim (Abraham) is an important prophet in Islam.

- [ ] Ibrahim is a good role model for Muslims because he always had faith in God and showed obedience to God, at a time when many people worshipped a variety of gods and idols (statues).

Why is Ibrahim important?

he fulfilled all the tests and commands given to him by God

he proclaimed belief in only one God at a time when people worshipped many different gods and idols

Ibrahim is important because …

he showed great faith in God

Muhammad was one of his descendants through his son, Ishmael

he is a good role model for Muslims

The Ka'aba in Makkah

How was Ibrahim a good role model?

How was Ibrahim a good role model?	Further explanation
He refused to worship idols and instead preached that there is only one God	• When Ibrahim was a young man, many people worshipped a number of different gods and idols • Ibrahim questioned their beliefs and decided there was only one God who had created everything in the universe • Ibrahim became determined to stop idol worship. One day, he took an axe and destroyed all the idols in the temple of his town • People were furious and demanded that Ibrahim be burned alive. He was thrown into a huge fire, but the fire only burned his chains and he walked out of it alive • This miracle prompted many people to start following Allah
He rebuilt the Ka'aba	• The **Ka'aba** is a small, cube-shaped building in the centre of the Grand Mosque in Makkah (Mecca). It is considered to be the house of God and the holiest place in Islam • The original Ka'aba was built by Adam but destroyed in the great flood • Following God's command, Ibrahim rebuilt the Ka'aba on the same site (see page 129) • When Muslims take part in Hajj (see pages 129–130), which starts at the Ka'aba, they remember Ibrahim and the steadfastness of his faith
He was willing to sacrifice his son to God	• Ibrahim had a dream in which God asked him to sacrifice his son to him • Ibrahim was willing to do this, but just before he carried out the sacrifice God stopped him, and told him he had passed the test • During the festival of Id-ul-Adha each year, Muslims kill an animal to remember Ibrahim's willingness to sacrifice his own son out of obedience to God

A What is the Ka'aba, and why is it important to Muslims?

B 'Ibrahim is the perfect role model for Muslims.'

Evaluate this statement.

> **TIP**
>
> To 'evaluate' this statement, consider whether you think it is true or not and explain why. Are there any reasons why Ibrahim might not be a perfect role model (for example, regarding how he tried to stop idol worship)?

Essential information:

☐ Muhammad is the last and most important prophet in Islam. He received the final revelation of Islam from God, which is recorded in the Qur'an.

☐ Shi'a Muslims believe in the importance of the **Imamate**: the leadership of the **Imams**. Shi'as believe that as the Imams have been appointed by God, they are able to maintain and interpret Islamic teachings without fault.

Why is Muhammad important?

Muhammad is the most important prophet in Islam because he is 'God's messenger' (Qur'an 33:40). He received the Qur'an from God, which all Muslims use as the basis of their faith. He is also remembered for helping to fully establish the religion by conquering Makkah, and for having travelled to heaven where he was in the presence of God.

Revelation of the Qur'an

- Muhammad grew up in Makkah (Mecca) and he would sometimes visit a cave in the mountains nearby to meditate and pray
- In 610 CE, Muhammad visited the cave and experienced a revelation from the angel Jibril
- Over the next 22 or so years, Muhammad continued to receive revelations from Jibril
- These were combined together to form the Qur'an

Conquering Makkah

- After the first revelation from Jibril, Muhammad started challenging people in Makkah to follow God's teachings
- Muhammad was persecuted for his preaching and fled with his followers to Madinah
- In Madinah he united the warring tribes, and with their help he conquered Makkah, converting the city to Islam
- This helped to bring harmony to the region, and firmly established Islam as a religion

The Night Journey

- Before Muhammad fled to Madinah, the angel Jibril took him on a miraculous journey to Jerusalem and then into heaven, where he spoke to prophets and saw great signs of God
- In heaven, Muhammad agreed with God that Muslims should pray five times a day
- Sunni Muslims still follow this practice (see page 125)

The Imamate

- The leader of Shi'a Muslims is called the Imam. The leadership of the Imams is known as the Imamate.
- Shi'as believe the Imam should be a **descendent of Muhammad and chosen by God**.
- The Twelver branch of Shi'a Islam teaches there have been **twelve Imams in total**. Each has been related to Muhammad in some way. The twelfth Imam has been kept alive by God and hidden somewhere on earth. He will return in the future to bring justice and equality to all.
- Because the Imams have been appointed by God, they are able to **interpret the Qur'an and Islamic law without fault**.
- Shi'as believe the Imams are necessary because people **need divine guidance on how to live correctly**. Although the final version of God's law was received by Muhammad, the Imams are important for helping to preserve and explain this law.

 A Give two reasons why the Imamate is important to Shi'a Muslims.

B 'Muhammad has had more impact on Muslims' lives than any other prophet.'

List arguments to support this statement, and arguments to support a different point of view.

RECAP

Essential information:

☐ The Qur'an is the most important holy book in Islam, and the highest source of authority for all matters relating to Islamic teaching, practice and law.

☐ The Qur'an was revealed to the prophet Muhammad by the angel Jibril.

☐ Other holy books in Islam are the Torah, Psalms, Gospel and Scrolls of Abraham.

The Qur'an

What is the Qur'an?

- includes a mixture of historical accounts and advice on how to follow God
- contains 114 surahs (chapters), roughly arranged in order of length
- nearly every chapter starts with the words 'In the name of God, the Lord of Mercy, the Giver of Mercy'
- written in Arabic
- the foundation of every believer's faith

• The Qur'an was revealed to Muhammad by the angel Jibril • Jibril was directly passing on God's words, so the Qur'an is considered to be the word of God • Jibril's revelations occurred over a period of about 22 years	• Muhammad learned by heart each revelation he received • He recited these revelations to his followers • Scribes later wrote them down	• As Islam spread, there was a danger that the original words would be distorted • The third Caliph asked a team of Muslim scholars to compile an official version of the Qur'an that everyone could use • This was completed around 650 CE

Other holy books

- Muslims believe there are other holy books that have been revealed by God.
- These holy books are mentioned in the Qur'an.
- Some Muslims think these books have been completely lost and no longer exist today.
- Others think they can still be found to some extent in the Bible. However, the original text has been corrupted or distorted, so it does not have the same authority as the Qur'an.

Name of the book	Who it was revealed to	Its authority in Islam
The Torah	Moses (Musa)	Some Muslims think the Torah is the first five books of the Bible, but altered from the original text
The Psalms	David	Many Muslims accept the Psalms mentioned in the Qur'an are similar to the ones in the Bible
The Gospel	Jesus (Isa)	Muslims believe the Gospel has been lost but some of its message is still found in the Bible
The Scrolls of Abraham	Ibrahim	These are considered to be one of the earliest scriptures in Islam, and no longer exist

APPLY

A What is the name of the holy book that was revealed to David?

B 'The Qur'an is the highest authority in Islam.'

Why would many Muslims agree with this statement? List arguments to support it.

7 Exam practice

Test the 1 mark question

1 Which **one** of the following is the name of the holy book that was revealed to Moses?

A ☐ The Gospel   B ☐ The Psalms

C ☐ The Scrolls of Abraham   D ☐ The Torah   **[1 mark]**

2 Which **one** of the following revealed the Qur'an to Muhammad?

A ☐ Iblis   B ☐ Israfil   C ☐ Jibril   D ☐ Mika'il   **[1 mark]**

Test the 2 mark question

3 Give **two** differences between Sunni and Shi'a Islam.   **[2 marks]**

1) _____

2) _____

4 Give **two** of the six articles of faith in Sunni Islam.   **[2 marks]**

1) _____

2) _____

Test the 4 mark question

5 Explain **two** ways in which a belief in prophethood influences Muslims today.   **[4 marks]**

● **Explain one way.**	*A belief in prophethood influences Muslims to respect and follow the teachings in the Qur'an.*
● Develop your explanation with more detail/an example/reference to a religious teaching or quotation.	*This is because the Qur'an was revealed to the prophet Muhammad. Believing in prophethood means believing that Muhammad passed on God's words in the Qur'an.*
● **Explain a second way.**	*A belief in prophethood also influences Muslims by encouraging them to show complete obedience to God.*
● Develop your explanation with more detail/an example/reference to a religious teaching or quotation.	*This is because the prophets were always obedient to God. For example, Ibrahim was willing to sacrifice his son to God after God told him to.*

TIP

If you see a question asking you to explain how a belief in something influences people today, make sure your answer focuses on how people in the world today are affected by the belief. How does the belief change the way they practise their faith?

6 Explain **two** of God's qualities.   **[4 marks]**

● **Explain one quality.**	
● Develop your explanation with more detail/an example/reference to a religious teaching or quotation.	
● **Explain a second quality.**	
● Develop your explanation with more detail/an example/reference to a religious teaching or quotation.	

7 Explain **two** ways in which a belief in the afterlife influences Muslims today.   **[4 marks]**

Test the 5 mark question

8 Explain **two** Muslim teachings about predestination.

Refer to scripture or another source of Muslim belief and teaching in your answer. **[5 marks]**

● **Explain one teaching.**	One teaching about predestination is that God has already determined everything that will happen in the universe.
● Develop your explanation with more detail/an example.	God has already written down everything that will happen in a 'book of decrees', and people have limited freedom to change their future.
● **Explain a second teaching.**	Another teaching about predestination is that God knows everything that will happen, but hasn't already decided what will happen.
● Develop your explanation with more detail/an example.	Because God is outside time, he already knows everything that will happen, but people can still make their own choices.
● Add a reference to scripture or another source of Muslim belief. If you prefer, you can add this reference to your first belief instead.	This teaching is supported by Surah 13:11 in the Qur'an: 'God does not change the condition of a people... unless they change what is in themselves.'

TIP

To refer to Muslim belief and teaching in your answer, you could write out a short quote from the Qur'an or mention a specific passage from this text.

TIP

This answer is good because it explains a teaching about predestination and then supports it by referring to a specific passage from the Qur'an. If you cannot remember an exact quotation you can always paraphrase it.

9 Explain **two** reasons why Muhammad is considered to be the most important prophet in Islam.

Refer to scripture or another source of Muslim belief and teaching in your answer. **[5 marks]**

● **Explain one reason.**	
● Develop your explanation with more detail/an example.	
● **Explain a second reason.**	
● Develop your explanation with more detail/an example.	
● Add a reference to scripture or another source of Muslim belief. If you prefer, you can add this reference to your first belief instead.	

10 Explain **two** meanings of the concept of Tawhid.

Refer to scripture or another source of Muslim belief and teaching in your answer. **[5 marks]**

Test the 12 mark question

11 'The best way of understanding God is to describe God as transcendent.'

Evaluate this statement. In your answer you should:

- give reasoned arguments to support this statement
- give reasoned arguments to support a different point of view
- refer to Muslim teaching
- reach a justified conclusion.

TIP

'Some [Muslims/Christians/Jews, etc.] might [agree/disagree] with this answer because...' can be a good way to introduce your arguments in the 12 mark answer.

[12 marks]
Plus SPaG 3 mar

REASONED ARGUMENTS IN SUPPORT OF THE STATEMENT ● **Explain why some people would agree with the statement.** ● Develop your explanation with more detail and examples. ● Refer to religious teaching. Use a quote or paraphrase or refer to a religious authority. ● **Evaluate the arguments.** Is this a good argument or not? Explain why you think this.	Some Muslims might agree that the best way of understanding God's nature is to think of God as transcendent because this makes sense of God's ability to do things that humans can't. 'Transcendence' means that God is beyond and outside the universe. Because he is outside the universe, God is not limited by its rules. This is a good description of God because Muslims believe that God is above them and much greater than them. God created the universe, something humans cannot do. It also suggests that God can be omniscient and know everything that happens in the past, present and future because he is outside time. The Qur'an says, 'He is in charge of everything.'
REASONED ARGUMENTS SUPPORTING A DIFFERENT VIEW ● **Explain why some people would support a different view.** ● Develop your explanation with more detail and examples. ● Refer to religious teaching. Use a quote or paraphrase or refer to a religious authority. ● **Evaluate the arguments.** Is this a good argument or not? Explain why you think this.	Some Muslims might disagree with this statement because they think there are other qualities that describe God better. For example, God is also immanent. This means he is present in the world and involved with life on earth. Some Muslims might think this is the best way to understand God because it shows how people are able to have a relationship with God and be guided by him in their everyday lives. Another example of a way that God can be described is omnipotent. This means he is all-powerful. Some Muslims might think this is a good word for understanding God because it explains how he is able to create the whole universe, and make anything happen that he wants to happen.
CONCLUSION ● **Give a justified conclusion.** ● Include your own opinion together with your own reasoning. ● **Include evaluation.** Explain why you think one viewpoint is stronger than the other or why you think they are equally strong. ● Do not just repeat arguments you have already used without explaining how they apply to your reasoned opinion/conclusion.	In conclusion, I think all of the different qualities of God probably help Muslims to understand him in different ways. Knowing that God is transcendent helps to understand his greatness and special abilities, but knowing that God is immanent helps to understand how he can be close to humanity, and other qualities, for example that he is One, help to understand God in other ways too. All of these qualities teach Muslims something important about God.

TIP

It is helpful to explain what transcendence means before evaluating whether it is a good description of God. Also, accurate use of key religious terms gains more marks for SPaG.

12 'The Qur'an contains all the guidance that Muslims need to live a perfect Muslim life.'

Evaluate this statement. In your answer you should:

- give reasoned arguments to support this statement
- give reasoned arguments to support a different point of view
- refer to Muslim teaching
- reach a justified conclusion.

[12 marks]
Plus SPaG 3 marks

REASONED ARGUMENTS IN SUPPORT OF THE STATEMENT ● **Explain why some people would agree with the statement.** ● Develop your explanation with more detail and examples. ● Refer to religious teaching. Use a quote or paraphrase or refer to a religious authority. ● **Evaluate the arguments.** Is this a good argument or not? Explain why you think this.	
REASONED ARGUMENTS SUPPORTING A DIFFERENT VIEW ● **Explain why some people would support a different view.** ● Develop your explanation with more detail and examples. ● Refer to religious teaching. Use a quote or paraphrase or refer to a religious authority. ● **Evaluate the arguments.** Is this a good argument or not? Explain why you think this.	
CONCLUSION ● **Give a justified conclusion.** ● Include your own opinion together with your own reasoning. ● **Include evaluation.** Explain why you think one viewpoint is stronger than the other or why you think they are equally strong. ● Do not just repeat arguments you have already used without explaining how they apply to your reasoned opinion/conclusion.	

13 'For Muslims, the prophets make better role models than the angels.'

Evaluate this statement. In your answer you should:

- give reasoned arguments to support this statement
- give reasoned arguments to support a different point of view
- refer to Muslim teaching
- reach a justified conclusion.

[12 marks]
Plus SPaG 3 marks

 Check your answers using the mark scheme on page 234. How did you do?
To feel more secure in the content you need to remember, re-read pages 110–119.
To remind yourself of what the examiner is looking for in your answers, go to pages 8–13.

8.1 The Five Pillars, the Ten Obligatory Acts and the Shahadah

RECAP

Essential information:

☐ The **Five Pillars** are the five most important duties for all Muslims. They are the fundamental practices of Islam on which everything else is built, and are seen as the key to living a perfect Muslim life.

☐ The **Ten Obligatory Acts** combine the Five Pillars with some additional duties. These are followed by Twelver Shi'a Muslims.

☐ The **Shahadah** is the Muslim declaration of faith. It expresses the basic beliefs of Islam.

The Five Pillars

1. **Shahadah** – the declaration of faith
2. **Salah** – prayer
3. **Zakah** – charitable giving
4. **Sawm** – fasting
5. **Hajj** – pilgrimage

The Ten Obligatory Acts

Salah – prayer
Sawm – fasting
Zakah – charitable giving
Khums – 20% tax (half goes to charity and half to religious leaders)
Hajj – pilgrimage
Jihad – the struggle to maintain the faith and defend Islam
Amr-bil-Maruf – encouraging people to do what is good
Nahi Anil Munkar – discouraging people from doing what is wrong
Tawallah – showing love for God and people who follow him
Tabarra – not associating with the enemies of God

Shahadah

> There is no God but Allah and Muhammad is the Prophet of Allah.

- This phrase is called the Shahadah. It is important to Muslims because it **expresses the core beliefs of Islam**.
- The Shahadah is considered to provide the foundation for the other four pillars, which tell a Muslim how to live according to the beliefs expressed in the Shahadah.
- Shi'a Muslims add an extra phrase to the Shahadah: **'and Ali is the friend of God'**. This shows their belief that Ali, Muhammad's cousin and son-in-law, was the true successor to Muhammad (see page 111).
- To become a Muslim, a person only has to **sincerely recite the Shahadah in front of Muslim witnesses**.
- The Shahadah is recited many times during a Muslim's life. If they are born into a Muslim family, it is the first thing they hear. If possible, it is also the last thing they say before they die.

APPLY

A Name two of the Ten Obligatory Acts, and describe what they are.

B 'The Shahadah summarises the most important beliefs in Islam.'

Give arguments to support this statement. As part of your answer, explain how these beliefs influence Muslims in their practice of Islam.

TIP
To answer this question, think about why these beliefs are important and how they affect a Muslim's everyday life. For example, why is the belief that there is only one God central to Islam? And how does this belief affect the way a Muslim practises Islam?

RECAP

Essential information:

☐ To observe the duty of **salah** (prayer), Sunni Muslims pray five times a day and Shi'a Muslims three times a day.

☐ Muslims perform ritual washing (**wudu**) before they pray to make themselves spiritually clean. They always face the city of Makkah when they pray.

☐ When Muslims pray in a mosque, men and women are divided into separate groups. The prayers are led by an imam (religious leader).

The times of prayer

The times for each prayer are worked out from the times of sunrise and sunset, so they change slightly each day. Prayer timetables help Muslims to know when to pray. For Sunni Muslims, the five times for prayer are:

Fajr: just before sunrise   **Zuhr:** just after midday   **Asr:** afternoon   **Maghrib:** just after sunset   **Isha:** night

Differences between Shi'a and Sunni Muslims in prayer

Shi'a Muslims combine the midday and afternoon prayers, and sunset and night prayers, so they pray the same prayers but only pray three times a day. There are also a few differences in the movements Shi'a and Sunni Muslims make during salah. Another difference is that Shi'a Muslims believe in using only natural elements when prostrating themselves in prayer, so they place a clay tablet at the spot where their forehead will rest.

Preparing for prayer and the direction of prayer

	Preparing for prayer	**The direction of prayer**
What should Muslims do?	• Perform ritual washing (wudu) before they pray, to make themselves spiritually clean	• Face the city of Makkah
How is this achieved?	• Muslims wash their faces, hands and feet under running water • Mosques have two special rooms set aside for this, one for women and one for men • If water isn't available, Muslims can 'wash' themselves using sand or dust instead. This illustrates the fact that wudu is about becoming spiritually clean, not physically clean	• In a mosque, the **mihrab** indicates the direction of Makkah • This is a small niche in the **qiblah wall**, which is the wall that faces Makkah. Muslims use this to face the right direction when they pray • Muslims can also use a special compass to indicate the right direction
Why is it important?	• The purification of wudu helps Muslims to fully focus on God in their prayers	• Praying in the same direction means that all Muslims are focusing on one place associated with God

Prayer inside a mosque

- Many mosques have carpets that look like rows of prayer mats, giving each person their own space to pray.
- Prayers in the mosque are led by an imam, who is positioned at the front of the congregation, facing the mihrab.
- Men and women pray at the same time but in separate spaces.
- The imam will lead the prayers from the men's prayer room, but his voice is usually also broadcast in the women's prayer room, so he can lead everyone's prayers together.

APPLY

A Explain how Muslims prepare for prayer, and why this is important.

B 'Prayer is the most difficult of the Five Pillars for Muslims to follow.'

Give arguments for and against this statement.

Then write a short conclusion where you weigh up the arguments and decide whether you agree with the statement or not.

TIP
Some questions in the exam will require you to combine your knowledge from different sections of the course. This is one example.

Essential information:

- ☐ Prayers are made up of a number of **rak'ah**: set sequences of actions and recitations.
- ☐ The **Jummah prayer** is a special prayer that is held at midday on Friday. Men are expected to attend a mosque for this prayer, but Muslims are otherwise allowed to pray at home if they want to.
- ☐ God commanded Muslims to pray, so it is important for Muslims to observe this pillar of Islam. Prayer is also important because it unites Muslims and brings them closer to God.

The rak'ah

Each prayer consists of a certain number of rak'ah. The rak'ah changes slightly depending on which prayer it is used in, and where it comes in the overall sequence, but it usually includes the following basic actions:

Stand and recite the first chapter from the Qur'an	Bow (showing respect to God) and recite in Arabic 'Glory be to my Lord who is the very greatest' three times	Stand and make a recitation praising God	Kneel with the forehead, nose, hands, knees and toes touching the floor (**prostration**) – this shows complete obedience to God. Recite 'How perfect is my Lord the most high'	Recite 'God is the greatest', first while sitting and then while prostrating

Jummah prayer and prayer at home

- The Jummah prayer is a special communal prayer held every Friday at midday.
- All men are expected to attend a mosque for this prayer, and women may do so if they wish.
- After the prayer, the imam will give a sermon that reminds Muslims about their duties to God.
- Muslims are otherwise allowed to pray at home, and women often do so if they have children to look after or find it hard to attend a mosque.
- Muslims must still perform wudu at home, although they do not need a special room to pray in.
- Many Muslims use a prayer mat at home, which is positioned facing Makkah.

The significance of prayer

Some Muslims may emphasise the ritualistic aspects of prayer, while others focus more on the spiritual quality of prayer. Either way, all Muslims agree that prayer is a very important part of worship in Islam.

the actions of bowing and prostrating remind Muslims that God is greater than them

it unites Muslims around the world, as they all pray in the same way

Prayer is important because ...

Muslims have been commanded by God to pray (see page 118)

it helps Muslims to become closer to God

it motivates Muslims to do God's will

A Explain two contrasting ways in which prayer is practised in Islam.

B 'It is best that prayers are structured, with set actions and recitations.'

Give your opinion on this statement. Explain your reasoning, referring to Muslim practices in your answer.

TIP
Page 57 in this Revision Guide might help you to develop your opinion on this statement. But make sure your answer focuses on the religion in question, which in this case is Islam.

RECAP

Essential information:

- [ ] **Ramadan** is the most important month in the Islamic calendar, as it is when the angel Jibril started to reveal the Qur'an to Muhammad (see page 118).

- [ ] Muslims focus on their faith during this month by **fasting** (not eating or drinking during daylight hours), studying the Qur'an, giving to charity, and trying to please God.

- [ ] The **Night of Power** is the night when Jibril first started to recite the Qur'an to Muhammad. Muslims celebrate this night during Ramadan.

Fasting during Ramadan

Origins of fasting	• The command to fast was revealed to Muhammad and can be found in the Qur'an: 'It was in the month of Ramadan that the Qur'an was revealed as guidance for mankind … So any one of you who sees in that month should fast' (Qur'an 2:185) • It has been obligatory for Muslims to fast during Ramadan since the seventh century
What it involves	• Muslims get up every day before sunrise to eat and drink enough to keep them going until sunset • Food, drink, smoking and sex are forbidden during daylight hours • The fast is broken at sunset. The evening meal is often shared with family and friends, and followed by extra prayers and readings from the Qur'an
The exceptions	• Children and people who are ill, pregnant or breastfeeding can be excused from fasting • People who can't fast are expected to make up for it later if they can
Its importance	• The self-discipline that is required to fast shows obedience and dedication to God • Fasting inspires Muslims to help those in poverty who can't afford enough to eat or drink

The Night of Power

- The Night of Power is when Jibril first appeared to Muhammad and started revealing the Qur'an.
- The words that Jibril spoke to Muhammad on this night can be found in Qur'an 96:1–5. They describe how Jibril instructed Muhammad to start reciting his words:

> ❝Read! In the name of your Lord who created: He created man from a clinging form [a blood clot]. Read! Your Lord is the Most Bountiful One who taught by [means of] the pen, who taught man what he did not know.❞
>
> *Qur'an 96:1–5*

- The exact date of the Night of Power is unclear, but it is believed to be one of the odd-numbered dates in the second half of Ramadan.
- Muslims try to stay awake throughout the night on each of these dates, praying and studying the Qur'an.
- Observing the Night of Power is thought to give Muslims the benefits of worshipping for a thousand months.

> ❝What will explain to you what that Night of Glory is? The Night of Glory is better than a thousand months❞
>
> *Qur'an 97:2–3*

APPLY

A Explain two Muslim beliefs about the Night of Power.

Refer to scripture or another source of Muslim belief and teaching in your answer.

B 'It is more important to study the Qur'an during Ramadan than it is to fast.'

Evaluate this statement.

TIP
To 'evaluate' this statement, explain whether you think it is true or not and why. Consider arguments for and against the statement, then weigh them up to decide whether you agree or disagree with it.

8.5 Zakah: almsgiving

Essential information:

☐ **Zakah** requires Muslims to give 2.5% of their savings to charity every year. Muslims believe that giving Zakah helps them to purify their souls, by removing selfishness and greed.

☐ In addition to giving Zakah, Shi'a Muslims also give **Khums**. This is 20% of their savings, half of which goes to Shi'a religious leaders and half to charity.

Zakah

Origins of Zakah	• Giving to charity is mentioned a number of times in the Qur'an; for example 'Whatever ... you give should be for parents, close relatives, orphans, the needy, and travellers. God is well aware of whatever good you do.' (Qur'an 2:215) • The exact amount that should be given was worked out at a later date by Muslim scholars
How much is given	• Only Muslims with savings greater than a certain amount (known as the nisab) are required to give Zakah • Muslims with savings greater than the nisab are expected to give 2.5% of their savings once a year
Who it is given to	• Zakah can be donated directly to a charity such as Islamic Relief or Muslim Aid • It can also be collected by a mosque, which will distribute the money among those in need
The importance of Zakah	• By giving Zakah, Muslims are fulfilling a duty to God • It helps to strengthen the Muslim community by supporting the poorest and weakest • It encourages Muslims to have a good attitude towards money, and to use their wealth in a way that would please God • It is a type of purification that helps Muslims to become closer to God

Khums

- Khums means 'fifth'. The giving of Khums started as a requirement for Muslim armies to donate one fifth (20%) of the spoils of war to their religious leader.
- Today, Shi'a Muslims give 20% of their savings.
- Half goes to Shi'a religious leaders, to be used for religious education or other religious matters, and the other half is given to charity or the poor.

In addition to giving Zakah, Muslims are encouraged to voluntarily give their money and time to charity at any point of the year. This is called Sadaqah.

> **ff** Alms are meant only for the poor, the needy, those who administer them, those whose hearts need winning over, to free slaves and help those in debt, for God's cause, and for travellers in need. **JJ**
>
> *Qur'an 9:60*

A Give two differences between Zakah and Khums.

B 'The most important reason to give Zakah or Khums is because it teaches Muslims to have a good attitude towards money.'

Do you agree with this statement? Explain your reasons.

Then explain why someone else might have a different point of view.

 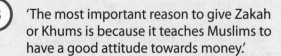

TIP

When you evaluate this question think about what 'a good attitude to money' would mean for a Muslim compared to a non-religious person.

8.6 Hajj: pilgrimage – origins and significance

Essential information:

☐ **Hajj** is an annual pilgrimage that starts and ends in the city of Makkah (Mecca) in Saudi Arabia. Every Muslim is expected to take part in Hajj at least once during their life.

☐ Hajj remembers the actions of the prophet Ibrahim and his family, who rebuilt the **Ka'aba** (the cube-shaped building in the centre of the Grand Mosque, and the holiest place in Islam).

☐ Hajj strengthens a Muslim's faith and shows their commitment to God.

The origins of Hajj

Around 4000 years ago, God told the prophet Ibrahim to take his wife Hajira and son Ishmael to Arabia	God then told Ibrahim to leave Hajira and Ishmael on their own with some supplies of food and water	After a few days the supplies ran out, and Hajira and Ishmael were suffering from hunger and dehydration
Hajira and Ishmael survived by trading some of the water for food and supplies. This source of water became known as the well of Zamzam	Hajira prayed to God for help. Ishmael then struck his foot on the ground, and water began to gush up from the earth	Hajira ran up and down two hills called Safa and Marwah, looking for help or a source of water. After running between the hills seven times, she collapsed beside her son
When Ibrahim returned, God told him to build a shrine dedicated to him – the Ka'aba. Ibrahim was told to make the Ka'aba a pure place of worship and to call people to perform Hajj there	Over the years, as the city of Makkah grew, God's instructions to Ibrahim were forgotten. People worshipped idols and stored them in the Ka'aba	In 628 CE, Muhammad journeyed from Madinah to Makkah with a large group of Muslims to convert the city to Islam (see page 118). This is thought to have been the first pilgrimage in Islam

The significance of Hajj

- produces inner peace
- brings a person closer to God
- reminds Muslims of the good examples set by the prophets

Hajj is important because it ...

- leads to a person's sins being forgiven
- shows self-discipline and dedication to God
- emphasises equality and unity
- fulfils a religious obligation

> "Pilgrimage to the House is a duty owed to God by people who are able to undertake it."
>
> *Qur'an 3:97*

A Explain why the Ka'aba is important to Muslims.

B 'Going on Hajj is the best way for a Muslim to show their commitment to Islam.'

Give arguments for and against this statement.

Then write a short conclusion where you weigh up these arguments and decide whether you agree or disagree with the statement.

TIP

To answer this question, you need to explain why particular actions (such as going on Hajj, praying or fasting) show commitment to Islam. Then think about which of these actions is the 'best' way to show commitment to Islam, and why.

RECAP

Essential information:

☐ Hajj takes place over five days, during which time pilgrims travel from Makkah to Mina, Arafat, Muzdalifah and back to Makkah.

☐ The actions that are performed on Hajj remember events in the lives of the prophet Ibrahim and his family, such as Hajira's search for water and Ibrahim's willingness to sacrifice his own son.

What happens on Hajj?

	What is involved	Its significance
Entering a state of Ihram	• Before Hajj begins, pilgrims must enter a state of purity called **Ihram** • This involves performing ritual washing, praying, and putting on Ihram clothing • Men dress in two sheets of white cloth, and women wear a single colour (usually white) as well	• The colour white symbolises purity • The fact that everyone wears similar clothes emphasises unity and equality • It shows everyone is equal before God
Circling the Ka'aba	• Hajj starts in Makkah at the Grand Mosque. Pilgrims walk in a circle seven times around the Ka'aba • As they circle the Ka'aba, they touch the black stone set into a corner of the building, or raise a hand towards it as they pass	• This stone is an ancient Islamic relic • It is believed to be the only surviving stone from the original Ka'aba • Some Muslims believe it comes from paradise, and was given by God to Adam
Walking between the two hills	• After circling the Ka'aba, pilgrims walk seven times between the two hills of Safa and Marwah • They then collect water from the well of Zamzam	• This remembers Hajira's search for water (see page 129), and the miraculous appearance of the well of Zamzam
Standing at Arafat	• Pilgrims travel to Arafat, where Muhammad preached his last sermon • They spend a whole afternoon praying under the hot summer sun (a reminder of what the Day of Judgement will be like) • Some Muslims stand while they pray to show the depth of their faith	• This afternoon is physically draining but allows Muslims to show their devotion to God • God is believed to forgive the sins of everyone at Arafat, providing they are sincerely sorry for what they have done wrong
Throwing pebbles at Mina	• Pilgrims walk to Muzdalifah, where they spend the night. On their way they collect a handful of pebbles • The next day, at Mina, they throw these pebbles at three stone walls called the Jamarat	• The walls represent the devil and temptation • Pilgrims throw pebbles at the walls to show they reject evil and the temptation to sin
Sacrificing an animal	• If they can, pilgrims then sacrifice an animal, as part of the celebration of Id-ul-Adha (see page 132) • The leftover meat is given to the poor	• This sacrifice remembers Ibrahim's willingness to sacrifice his own son out of obedience to God (see page 117)

APPLY

 A Describe what must happen before Hajj starts, and what this signifies.

B 'The most important reason for performing Hajj is to remember the actions of the prophets.'

What is your opinion on this statement? Explain your reasoning.

8.8 Jihad

Essential information:

☐ **Jihad** refers to the struggle against evil. It requires Muslims to strive to improve themselves and the societies they live in, in a way that would please God.

☐ **Greater jihad** is the inward, personal struggle to live according to the teachings of Islam.

☐ **Lesser jihad** is the outward, collective struggle to defend Islam from threat.

Greater jihad

Greater jihad refers to the constant struggle that Muslims undertake to improve themselves spiritually and to deepen their relationship with God, by living according to the teachings of Islam. It is considered to be more important than lesser jihad, and might involve some of the following actions.

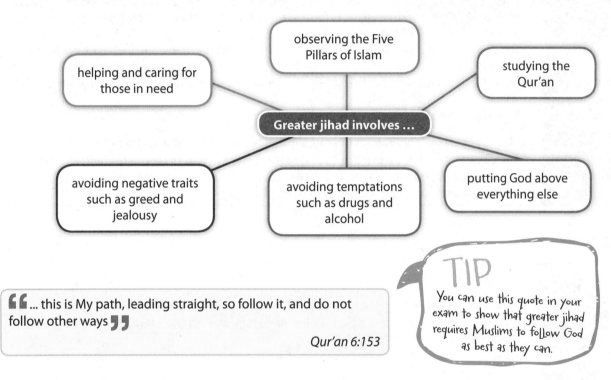

observing the Five Pillars of Islam

helping and caring for those in need

studying the Qur'an

Greater jihad involves …

avoiding negative traits such as greed and jealousy

avoiding temptations such as drugs and alcohol

putting God above everything else

> 〝 … this is My path, leading straight, so follow it, and do not follow other ways 〞
>
> *Qur'an 6:153*

TIP
You can use this quote in your exam to show that greater jihad requires Muslims to follow God as best as they can.

Lesser jihad

Lesser jihad refers to the outward struggle to defend Islam from threat. In the early days of Islam, this was important when Muslims were being persecuted and they needed to fight for their freedom to practise the faith.

Fighting for a religious cause is also sometimes called **holy war**. This refers to a war that must be:

- approved by a fair religious leader
- fought in self-defence in response to a threat
- not used to gain territory or wealth
- not used to convert people to Islam
- fought only after all peaceful methods to resolve the situation have been tried first.

This list shows that lesser jihad or holy war can only be used as a last resort, to defend the faith when it is under severe attack. Islam teaches that lesser jihad or holy war can never be used to justify terrorist attacks.

APPLY

Ⓐ Explain two ways in which a belief in greater jihad influences Muslims today.

Ⓑ 'Greater jihad is harder to follow than lesser jihad in today's world.'
Give arguments for and against this statement.

8.9 The festivals of Id-ul-Fitr and Id-ul-Adha

Essential information:

☐ **Id-ul-Fitr** is a Muslim festival that celebrates the end of Ramadan.

☐ **Id-ul-Adha** is a Muslim festival that celebrates Ibrahim's willingness to sacrifice his son to God, and marks the end of Hajj.

Id-ul-Fitr

Origins	• The festival was started by Muhammad after he arrived in Madinah, having fled from persecution in Makkah (see page 118) • Muhammad told the people in Madinah that God had set aside two days for festivities: Id-ul-Fitr and Id-ul-Adha
Celebrations	• Muslims gather together in mosques or large outdoor areas to say special prayers. The imam's sermon usually reminds Muslims to forgive any disputes that have happened during the year, and focus instead on helping the poor • Muslims decorate their homes, wear new clothes, eat special foods, and exchange cards and presents • Many Muslims visit their local cemetery to remember and pray for family members who have died • In the UK, Islamic businesses may give Muslims time off to celebrate
Importance	• The festival allows Muslims to celebrate the end of a month of fasting (see page 127) • It is a way for Muslims to give thanks to God for giving them the strength to complete the fast • It is also a way for Muslims to thank God for giving his wisdom and guidance in the Qur'an, which was first revealed to Muhammad during Ramadan

Id-ul-Adha

Origins	• Like Id-ul-Fitr, this festival was started by Muhammad (see above)
Celebrations	• Special prayers are held in the mosque, and the sermon will usually be on the theme of sacrifice • Muslims visit family and friends, and enjoy meals together. An effort is made to make sure everyone is included in the celebrations • Muslims who are able to, including those who are taking part in Hajj, will slaughter an animal (see page 130) • In Britain, some Muslims buy an animal from their local slaughterhouse, and share the meat with their family and friends. Traditionally some of the meat is given to the poor, but today Muslims usually donate money to the poor instead
Importance	• The festival remembers and celebrates Ibrahim's willingness to sacrifice his son to God, as described in Surah 37 in the Qur'an. This reminds Muslims about the importance of showing complete obedience to God • The festival also celebrates the completion of Hajj, which is a demanding pilgrimage that helps strengthen a Muslim's faith • The festival allows Muslims around the world to connect with those on Hajj, even if they can't be there themselves

A Describe the origins of Id-ul-Fitr and Id-ul-Adha.

B 'Muslim festivals are mainly about having fun.'

Read the following response:

"During Id-ul-Fitr and Id-ul-Adha, Muslims give each other presents, eat lots of nice food and have fun together. If they were really thinking about the religious meaning of the festival then they would be more solemn. Also, Id-ul-Adha remembers an event that happened years and years ago which isn't relevant to Muslims today, so I think the festival is mainly an opportunity to get together and share a meal with family and friends."

Write a paragraph in reply to this response, which argues against the statement above. Keep your answer focused on the festivals of Id-ul-Fitr and Id-ul-Adha.

8.10 The festival of Ashura

RECAP

Essential information:

☐ The **Day of Ashura** (Day of Remembrance) is an important Shi'a festival that remembers the death of Husayn at the battle of Karbala.

☐ Many Shi'a Muslims observe Ashura by taking part in mourning rituals or processions.

☐ Ashura is also observed by Sunni Muslims, for whom the festival is known as the Day of Atonement. However, for Sunni Muslims it is not as important or solemn an occasion as for Shi'a Muslims.

The origins and meaning of Ashura

- The Day of Ashura is important for Shi'a Muslims in particular, who view it as a day of great sorrow. This is because it remembers the death of Husayn, who was the son of Imam Ali and grandson of Muhammad.
- Husayn died in the battle of Karbala. This battle was held on 10 October 680 CE in Karbala, Iraq. It was fought between Husayn and his supporters (around 70 men, women and children) against the much larger army of Caliph Yazid I. Husayn and most of his supporters were killed in the battle.
- Husayn's death is seen by Shi'a Muslims as a symbol of the struggle against injustice, tyranny and oppression.

Sunni Muslims also observe Ashura, which they call the Day of Atonement. For some Sunni Muslims the festival celebrates the day the Israelites were freed from slavery in Egypt, while for others it celebrates the day Noah left the ark after the flood.

How Ashura is commemorated

Shi'a Muslims commemorate Ashura in the following ways:

Action	Further explanation
Shi'a Muslims perform plays and re-enactments to tell the story of Husayn's death	• These help Muslims to remember the events at Karbala
Many Shi'a Muslims take part in public expressions of grief and mourning	• In London, thousands of Shi'a Muslims gather at Marble Arch to listen to speeches and take part in a procession of mourning • In some cities in Britain, some Shi'a men gather in the streets and beat themselves on their chests as part of a mourning ritual • Some Muslims believe they should cut themselves and shed blood to connect with Husayn's suffering and death • Some Shi'a religious leaders condemn this practice and encourage Muslims to donate blood to the blood transfusion service instead
In Iraq, many Shi'a Muslims visit Husayn's tomb	• Husayn's tomb is believed to be located in the Mashhad al-Husayn, which is a shrine in Karbala • Many Shi'a Muslims go on pilgrimage to the Mashhad al-Husayn each year for Ashura

Many Sunni Muslims observe Ashura by fasting for the day. They may also give to charity, show extra kindness to their family and the poor, recite prayers, and learn from Islamic scholars.

APPLY

A Give two ways in which Shi'a Muslims observe Ashura.

B On page 132, question B asked you to write a paragraph arguing against the statement 'Muslim festivals are mainly about having fun', focusing on the festivals of Id-ul-Fitr and Id-ul-Adha.

Now add another paragraph to your answer, arguing that the festival of Ashura is not 'mainly about having fun.'

> **TIP**
> When writing about Ashura, try to be specific about whether you are referring to Shi'a or Sunni Muslims. Remember that each group observes the festival in different ways, for different reasons.

8 Exam practice

Test the 1 mark question

1 Which **one** of the following is *not* one of the Ten Obligatory Acts?

   A ☐ Hajj   B ☐ Jihad   C ☐ Shahadah   D ☐ Zakah   **[1 mark]**

2 Which **one** of the following people do Shi'a Muslims remember on the Day of Ashura?

   A ☐ Hajira   B ☐ Husayn   C ☐ Muhammad   D ☐ Ali   **[1 mark]**

Test the 2 mark question

3 Give **two** objects or features that Muslims can use to know they are facing the right direction when they pray.   **[2 marks]**

   1) _____

   2) _____

4 Give **two** ways in which Muslims can give Zakah.   **[2 marks]**

   1) _____

   2) _____

Test the 4 mark question

5 Explain **two** ways in which a belief in the importance of prayer influences Muslims today.   **[4 marks]**

● **Explain one way.**	*A belief in the importance of prayer means that Muslims pray at least three times a day.*
● Develop your explanation with more detail/an example/ reference to a religious teaching or quotation.	*Muslims believe prayer is an important duty in their daily lives because it is one of the Five Pillars of Islam. One way that Muslims show it is important is by praying five times a day (Sunni Muslims) or three times a day (Shi'a Muslims). This helps Muslims remember God is with them throughout each day of their lives.*
● **Explain a second way.**	*A belief in the importance of prayer also means that Muslim men are expected to attend a mosque every Friday lunchtime.*
● Develop your explanation with more detail/an example/ reference to a religious teaching or quotation.	*Another way in which a belief in the importance of prayer is shown is by attending Friday prayers in the mosque to take part in the Jummah prayer, a special communal prayer that is said once a week. This is important to Muslims because it unites them with other members of the Muslim community and helps to strengthen their faith in God.*

> **TIP**
> Remember to be careful not to make generalisations in your answers. For example, here the student has correctly pointed out that Shi'a and Sunni Muslims pray a different number of times each day.

6 Explain **two** ways in which the actions of the prophet Ibrahim and his family are remembered on Hajj.   **[4 marks]**

● **Explain one way.**	
● Develop your explanation with more detail/an example/ reference to a religious teaching or quotation.	
● **Explain a second way.**	
● Develop your explanation with more detail/an example/ reference to a religious teaching or quotation.	

7 Explain **two** contrasting Muslim beliefs about why it is important to fast during Ramadan.   **[4 marks]**

Test the 5 mark question

8   Explain **two** Muslim beliefs about the importance of festivals.

Refer to scripture or another source of Muslim belief and teaching in your answer.   **[5 marks]**

● **Explain one belief.**	*Muslims believe festivals are important because they allow them to give thanks to God.*
● Develop your explanation with more detail/an example.	*For example, during the festival of Id–ul–Fitr Muslims give thanks to God for giving them the strength to complete a month of fasting.*
● **Explain a second belief.**	*Muslims also believe festivals are important because they help them to remember important events in the history of Islam.*
● Develop your explanation with more detail/an example.	*For example, Id–ul–Adha remembers Ibrahim's willingness to sacrifice his son to God.*
● Add a reference to scripture or another source of Muslim belief. If you prefer, you can add this reference to your first belief instead.	*In Surah 37, the Qur'an describes the dream Ibrahim had where God asked him to sacrifice his son, and tells how Ibrahim was willing to obey God's command.*

9   Explain **two** reasons why Muslims go on Hajj.

Refer to scripture or another source of Muslim belief and teaching in your answer.   **[5 marks]**

● **Explain one reason.**	
● Develop your explanation with more detail/an example.	
● **Explain a second reason.**	
● Develop your explanation with more detail/an example.	
● Add a reference to scripture or another source of Muslim belief. If you prefer, you can add this reference to your first belief instead.	

10   Explain **two** Muslim beliefs about jihad.

Refer to scripture or another source of Muslim belief and teaching in your answer.   **[5 marks]**

Test the 12 mark question

11 'The Shahadah is the most important pillar of Islam.'

Evaluate this statement. In your answer you should:

- give reasoned arguments to support this statement
- give reasoned arguments to support a different point of view
- refer to Muslim teaching
- reach a justified conclusion.

[12 marks]
Plus SPaG 3 mar

> **TIP**
> Try to use religious terms in your answer, if it is appropriate, as this helps you to demonstrate your knowledge of the subject. For example, in this answer some of the names of the different pillars are given.

REASONED ARGUMENTS IN SUPPORT OF THE STATEMENT ● **Explain why some people would agree with the statement.** ● Develop your explanation with more detail and examples. ● Refer to religious teaching. Use a quote or paraphrase or refer to a religious authority. ● **Evaluate the arguments.** Is this a good argument or not? Explain why you think this.	Many Muslims would agree with this statement because the Shahadah expresses the core belief of Islam. It provides the foundation for the other four pillars, which tell Muslims how to put into practice the belief expressed in the Shahadah. It is also the only pillar which people have to observe in order to become a Muslim, by reciting it sincerely in front of other Muslims. The Shahadah states that 'There is no God but Allah and Muhammad is the Prophet of Allah'. Muslims should carry out the other four pillars with this statement in mind. This means when they pray, they should pray only to God. When they go on Hajj, they should focus on God throughout the pilgrimage. If Muslims don't believe in the Shahadah, the other pillars become meaningless.
REASONED ARGUMENTS SUPPORTING A DIFFERENT VIEW ● **Explain why some people would support a different view.** ● Develop your explanation with more detail and examples. ● Refer to religious teaching. Use a quote or paraphrase or refer to a religious authority. ● **Evaluate the arguments.** Is this a good argument or not? Explain why you think this.	Some Muslims might disagree with this statement because the Shahadah doesn't tell Muslims how to live in a way that pleases God. It just tells Muslims what they should believe. But the other four pillars tell Muslims how to live a good life that gets them closer to God and helps them to get into heaven when they die. For example, the pillar of salah teaches Muslims they should pray three or five times a day. The pillar of sawm teaches Muslims they should fast during Ramadan. Observing these pillars helps Muslims to develop their relationship with God, so it could be argued they are more important than the Shahadah.
CONCLUSION ● **Give a justified conclusion.** ● Include your own opinion together with your own reasoning. ● **Include evaluation.** Explain why you think one viewpoint is stronger than the other or why you think they are equally strong. ● Do not just repeat arguments you have already used without explaining how they apply to your reasoned opinion/conclusion.	I think all of the pillars are important in Islam, because they all teach Muslims how to live in a way that would please God. This is important for becoming closer to God and getting into heaven in the afterlife. However, I also agree with the statement because Muslims have to believe in the Shahadah before they can observe the other four pillars. Also the Shahadah is a clear summary of the faith which Muslims share.

> **TIP**
> This is a good answer that compares the Shahadah with the other pillars and comes to a justified conclusion about which is the most important.

12 'Giving to charity is the most important practice in Islam.'

Evaluate this statement. In your answer you should:

- give reasoned arguments to support this statement
- give reasoned arguments to support a different point of view
- refer to Muslim teaching
- reach a justified conclusion.

[12 marks]
Plus SPaG 3 marks

REASONED ARGUMENTS IN SUPPORT OF THE STATEMENT ● **Explain why some people would agree with the statement.** ● Develop your explanation with more detail and examples. ● Refer to religious teaching. Use a quote or paraphrase or refer to a religious authority. ● **Evaluate the arguments.** Is this a good argument or not? Explain why you think this.	
REASONED ARGUMENTS SUPPORTING A DIFFERENT VIEW ● **Explain why some people would support a different view.** ● Develop your explanation with more detail and examples. ● Refer to religious teaching. Use a quote or paraphrase or refer to a religious authority. ● **Evaluate the arguments.** Is this a good argument or not? Explain why you think this.	
CONCLUSION ● **Give a justified conclusion.** ● Include your own opinion together with your own reasoning. ● **Include evaluation.** Explain why you think one viewpoint is stronger than the other or why you think they are equally strong. ● Do not just repeat arguments you have already used without explaining how they apply to your reasoned opinion/conclusion.	

13 'Id-ul-Fitr should be made an official public holiday in Britain.'

Evaluate this statement. In your answer you should:

- give reasoned arguments to support this statement
- give reasoned arguments to support a different point of view
- refer to Muslim teaching
- reach a justified conclusion.

[12 marks]
Plus SPaG 3 marks

Check your answers using the mark scheme on page 234–235. How did you do?
To feel more secure in the content you need to remember, re-read pages 124–133.
To remind yourself of what the examiner is looking for in your answers, go to pages 8–13.

9.1 The nature of God: God as One

Essential information:

☐ Judaism is a **monotheistic** religion. This means that Jews believe there is only one God.

☐ The belief in God as One is expressed in the **Shema** – an important Jewish prayer.

God as One

The belief in one God forms the foundation of Judaism.

* This belief influences the way that Jews view the world.
* Jews believe that God is always present in people's lives. In addition, everything they see and experience is considered to be a meeting with God.

> **TIP**
>
> Remember that Christianity and Judaism are both monotheistic religions. This means they both believe in only one God. The difference is that Christians believe God is also three Persons.

God as One means ...

* God is a single, whole, indivisible being
* God is the only being who should be praised and worshipped
* everything in the universe has been created and is sustained by this one God
* God is the source of all Jewish morality, beliefs and values

The belief in one God is expressed in the Shema. This is an important Jewish prayer that is formed from passages in Deuteronomy and Numbers. It starts with the following words:

This phrase confirms the belief there is only one God.

> **"** Hear, O Israel! The LORD is our God, the LORD alone. You shall love the LORD your God with all your heart and with all your soul and with all your might. **"**
>
> *Deuteronomy 6:4–5*

This sentence shows how Jews should respond to this belief – by showing total loyalty, love and dedication towards God.

> **TIP**
>
> Some Jews write 'G-d' instead of 'God' as a sign of respect. Either spelling is acceptable in your exam.

Many Jews cover their eyes while reciting the first line of the Shema, to avoid distractions

 A Write out Deuteronomy 6:4–5 (the start of the Shema), and explain what it means to Jews.

B 'For Jews, the belief in God as One simply means they should not worship any other gods.' Give arguments against this statement.

RECAP

Essential information:

☐ Jews believe God is the **creator** and sustainer. God created the universe out of nothing, exactly as he wanted it to be, and sustains the world so all species are able to live on it.

☐ Jews believe God gave humans free will, and because of this, evil has to exist (see page 147).

God as creator and sustainer

The Jewish Bible is called the Tenakh, and the first section of the Tenakh (the five books of Moses) is called the **Torah**. Genesis, which is the first book in the Torah, tells how God took six days to create the universe and everything in it:

| God took four days to make the universe fit to support life | → | God took two days to create all living creatures | → | God then rested and made the seventh day holy. When Jews celebrate Shabbat on this day (see page 156), they are reminded of God's importance and role as the creator |

- Many Orthodox and ultra-Orthodox Jews believe the events in Genesis literally happened about 6000 years ago. They reject scientific theories of evolution.
- Other Jews interpret the Genesis creation story less literally. They still believe God is the creator of everything, but accept the universe is much older and life has evolved over many years.

Jews believe that in addition to creating the universe, God also sustains it. He provides all the resources needed for life on earth to survive.

> **TIP**
> Orthodox Jews (and particularly ultra-Orthodox Jews) believe it is important to follow the laws and guidance in the Torah as strictly as possible. They are more traditional than Reform Jews, who form the other main group in Judaism (see page 154).

Evil and free will

In order for God to have the power and ability to create everything in the universe, Jews believe that God must be:

- **omnipotent** – all-powerful
- **omniscient** – all knowing
- **omnipresent** – everywhere at all times.

The belief that God created everything also means that God must have created evil. The existence of evil is considered to be a necessary consequence of free will:

| God gave people free will because he wants people to be able to choose to do good. This makes the act of doing good more significant | → | But in order to exercise free will, there must be a choice between good and bad | → | This means that evil has to exist |

The existence of free will explains why the world's resources are distributed unevenly. Jews who exercise free will to help to improve the balance of resources, by giving to those less fortunate, are helping to fulfil God's plan for his creation.

> **TIP**
> You can use this quote in your exam to show that Jews believe there is one God who created everything, including evil.

> ❝I am the LORD and there is none else, I form light and create darkness, I make weal and create woe – I the LORD do all these things.❞
>
> *Isaiah 45:6–7*

Ⓐ Explain two contrasting ways in which Jews interpret the Genesis creation story.

Ⓑ 'Jews would have a better relationship with God if free will didn't exist.'

Evaluate this statement.

> **TIP**
> To 'evaluate' this statement, explain whether you think it is true or not and why. Consider how the existence of free will affects a Jew's relationship with God.

9.3 The nature of God: God as lawgiver and judge; the divine presence

Essential information:

☐ To help Jews use their free will correctly, God has given them many laws which he expects them to obey. This is why Jews view God as the lawgiver.

☐ God is also viewed as a judge, as he judges how well people follow his laws and rewards or punishes them as a result.

☐ Jews believe there are occasions in their history when God's presence has been experienced on earth. The divine presence of God on earth is called the **Shekhinah**.

God as lawgiver and judge

Jews believe God has given them many laws to follow. These laws help them to use their free will in a way that would be approved by God.

- There are **613 laws in the Torah** which teach people how they should behave. These are called **mitzvot**. They form the basis of the Halakah, which is the accepted code of conduct for Jewish life.
- The first ten mitzvot are the **Ten Commandments**. These are the ten laws that God gave to Moses after he rescued the Jewish slaves from Egypt. They are particularly important and form the foundation for all the other mitzvot.

Jewish children studying the mitzvot

Jews believe God judges them for how well they follow these laws, based on their actions, behaviour and beliefs. God's judgements are considered to be fair and tempered by his loving, merciful nature. For Jews there are two main times when God judges people:

1 **During the festival of Rosh Hashanah** (the Jewish new year). This is when God judges people for their actions over the past year and decides what the coming year will bring them (see page 164).
2 Many Jews also believe they will be **judged after death**, when God determines how they will spend the afterlife (see page 141).

The divine presence (Shekhinah)

The Shekhinah is the presence of God on earth. Jewish writings tell how the divine presence of God was experienced by the early Jews:

- In early Judaism, the **Tabernacle** was considered to house the divine presence of God. This was a portable temple, similar in structure to a tent, that the Jews carried with them on their journey through the wilderness to Canaan (see page 144).
- After Canaan was conquered, the Tabernacle was replaced with **Solomon's Temple** in Jerusalem. This Temple was the centre of Jewish worship at the time, and several of the prophets experienced the presence of God in the Temple. For example, Isaiah 6:1–2 makes reference to the presence of God in the Temple:

> **"** In the year that King Uzziah died, I beheld my Lord seated on a high and lofty throne; and the skirts of His robe filled the Temple. Seraphs stood in attendance on Him. **"**
>
> *Isaiah 6:1–2*

- The Tenakh describes how the Jews were led at times by **a pillar of fire or a cloud** on their journey to Canaan. These were considered to be appearances from God that demonstrated his power and glory.

APPLY

A Give two examples of when Jews have experienced the divine presence of God on earth.

B 'It is more important for Jews to know about God's role as lawgiver and judge than it is to know about his role as creator and sustainer, as it has a greater impact on their lives today.'

Give arguments for and against this statement.

TIP
When giving arguments for or against a statement, it may first help to explain what parts of the statement mean. Here you could explain what it means to say that God is 'lawgiver and judge', or 'creator and sustainer'. Then explain how these beliefs impact upon the lives of Jews today.

9.4 Life after death, judgement and resurrection

Essential information:

- ☐ There is little agreement among Jews about the afterlife, and many do not think it is important to know what happens after death. They are more concerned with focusing on the present and living in a way that pleases God.

- ☐ Some Jews believe God will judge them after they die: some will go to heaven and others to Sheol (a place of waiting where souls are cleansed).

- ☐ Some Jews believe in **resurrection** (rising from the dead to live again). However, many Jews reject the idea of resurrection.

Life after death

The Jewish holy books do not contain much information about the afterlife, so beliefs about it have developed gradually over the centuries. This has led to differences among Jews about what happens after death.

One reason for the lack of agreement is that, in general, **Jews are not too concerned with the afterlife**. They think it is more important to focus on the present and to live in a way that is pleasing to God.

Heaven and Sheol

- Many Jews believe that if they follow their faith correctly, they will go to **heaven or paradise** (Gan Eden) when they die.
- There is no clear teaching about what heaven is like. It is considered to be where people are with God, but it is not known if this is a state of consciousness, or a physical or spiritual place.
- Some Jews believe that people who do not enter heaven go to **Sheol**, a place of waiting where souls are cleansed. Jews do not believe in a place of eternal punishment.

Judgement and resurrection

- Some Jews believe they will be judged by God **as soon as they die**. This belief is supported by Ecclesiastes 12:7.
- Others believe God will judge everyone **on the Day of Judgement**, after the coming of the Messiah (see page 142). This belief is supported by Daniel 12:2.
- Some Jews believe in the idea of physical or spiritual resurrection, but many do not.

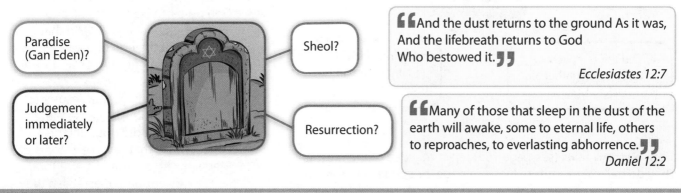

Paradise (Gan Eden)?

Sheol?

Judgement immediately or later?

Resurrection?

> **"** And the dust returns to the ground As it was, And the lifebreath returns to God Who bestowed it. **"**
>
> *Ecclesiastes 12:7*

> **"** Many of those that sleep in the dust of the earth will awake, some to eternal life, others to reproaches, to everlasting abhorrence. **"**
>
> *Daniel 12:2*

A Explain two contrasting Jewish beliefs about judgement.

Refer to scripture or another source of Jewish belief and teaching in your answer.

B 'It does not matter if there are different beliefs about life after death within a religion.'

The start of two paragraphs have been written below, one against the statement and one in support of it. Finish the paragraphs by developing the arguments further and referring to Jewish beliefs.

"It matters if there are different beliefs about life after death within a religion because then believers don't know how to live their lives in a way that would guarantee them a good afterlife ..."

"It doesn't matter if there are different beliefs about life after death within a religion because it is more important to focus on the present ..."

TIP
When writing about a topic where there are different views on something (such as beliefs about the afterlife), start your sentences by saying 'Some/most/many people believe ...' to reflect this difference.

RECAP

Essential information:

☐ In Judaism, the **Messiah** ('the anointed one') is a future leader of the Jews who will rule over humanity with kindness and justice.

☐ The Messiah will rule during the **Messianic age**, which will be a time when the world is united in peace.

Origins of the Messiah

- The word 'Messiah' was originally used in the Tenakh to refer to the **kings of Israel**.
- The first king of Israel was **Saul**, who lived around the eleventh century BCE.
- Before Saul was made king, the prophet Samuel **anointed him with oil** to show he was chosen by God to rule over the Jews. (The word 'Messiah' means 'the anointed one'.)
- Today, the word 'Messiah' is used to refer to a **future leader of the Jews**.
- This leader is expected to be a future king of Israel – a descendent of Saul's successor, King David.

The nature of the Messiah

The Messiah is expected to lead the Jews during the Messianic age. This will be a time in the future of global peace and harmony, when everyone will want to become closer to God.

Orthodox Jews believe there is a descendent of King David in every generation who has the potential to become the Messiah. If the Jews are worthy of redemption, this person will be directed by God to become the Messiah.

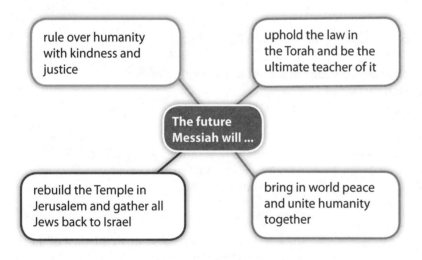

rule over humanity with kindness and justice

uphold the law in the Torah and be the ultimate teacher of it

The future Messiah will …

rebuild the Temple in Jerusalem and gather all Jews back to Israel

bring in world peace and unite humanity together

Many **Reform Jews** (see page 155) reject the idea of the Messiah. They do believe in a future Messianic age, but believe this will be achieved by everyone working together to create world peace, rather than as the result of the leadership of one person.

Was Jesus the Messiah?

- **Christians** believe that Jesus was the Messiah. They believe this is because, through his death and resurrection, he saved humanity and established the Kingdom of God on earth (see pages 66 and 81). Some Christians believe that he will come at the end of the world to complete the Kingdom of God – a Messianic age.

- **Jews** do not believe that Jesus was the Messiah. This is because they believe that he did not fulfil the expectations that Jews have for the Messiah – he did not observe Torah law strictly enough or establish the Messianic age.

APPLY

(A) Explain two contrasting Jewish beliefs about the Messianic age.

(B) The idea of a Messianic age is not relevant in today's world.

Give arguments for and against this statement.

TIP

This question asks you to consider carefully the differences between Christian and Jewish beliefs about the Messiah.

RECAP

Essential information:

☐ The **Promised Land** is the land of Canaan, which God promised to Abraham and the Jews.

☐ After Abraham had travelled to Canaan, he made a **covenant** (agreement) with God. God promised Abraham he would be the father of many nations. In return, Abraham was required to live a life dedicated to God.

Abraham and the Promised Land

Abraham travelled to Canaan after he was promised this land by God, as a place where Abraham and his descendants could make 'a great nation'.

> Abraham was born in the city of Ur, probably in the twentieth or nineteenth century BCE

> At that time people worshipped idols (statues) of many different gods

> From an early age, Abraham became convinced there was only one God who had created everything, and that worshipping idols was wrong

> Before they reached Canaan, they settled on the way at Haran in Northern Mesopotamia

> Abraham and some of his family (including his wife Sarah) decided to leave Ur to travel to Canaan

> Abraham tried to convince the people in Ur to stop worshipping idols, but had little success

> Many years later, God told Abraham to continue the journey to Canaan, promising to make a great nation through him

> " The LORD said to Abram [Abraham], 'Go forth from your native land and from your father's house to the land that I will show you. **I will make of you a great nation, And I will bless you** …' "
> *Genesis 12:1–2*

> Once Abraham and Sarah reached Canaan, God told Abraham, 'I give all the land that you see to you and your offspring forever' (Genesis 13:15). This became known as the Promised Land

The covenant with Abraham

- In Judaism, a covenant is an agreement between God and an individual person (made on behalf of the rest of the Jews).
- Various covenants have been made during the history of Judaism, and Jews believe these covenants are still binding today.
- After Abraham travelled to Canaan, God made a covenant with him.

What did God promise?	• To make Abraham the father of many nations
What was required of Abraham?	• To agree to 'Walk in My [God's] ways and be blameless.' (Genesis 17:1)
How was the covenant sealed?	• Through the action of **circumcision** (the removal of the foreskin from the penis) • Abraham proved his acceptance of the covenant by being circumcised himself and by circumcising all the males in his household
How did God keep his side of the covenant?	• To make Abraham the father of many nations, God made it possible for Abraham's wife Sarah to conceive, despite the fact she was very old • Sarah gave birth to a son called Isaac. His birth is seen by some as a gift from God to mark the start of the covenant between Abraham and God

APPLY

A Write out a quote from the Torah which tells how God promised Abraham a land where he would make a 'great nation'.

B 'Abraham is a perfect role model for Jews because he showed complete dedication and obedience to God.'

Give arguments to support this statement.

> **TIP**
> Memorising short extracts from scripture will help you to gain marks in the 5 and 12 mark questions in your exam.

RECAP

Essential information:

☐ The **covenant at Sinai** is the covenant between God and Moses, who represented the Jewish people. This requires Jews to follow God's laws (including the Ten Commandments) in return for his protection and blessing.

☐ The Ten Commandments are ten laws which were given to Moses by God after the Jews escaped from Egypt.

The escape from Egypt

The Ten Commandments were given to the Jews after they escaped from slavery in Egypt.

About 400 years after God made the covenant with Abraham, the Jews were being forced to work as slaves in Egypt → God chose Moses to lead their escape. He told Moses to ask the Egyptian Pharaoh to release the Jews from slavery, so they could return to Canaan → After God had sent a number of plagues to Egypt, the Pharaoh finally agreed to release the Jews

This is where God gave Moses the Ten Commandments – these were carved on two tablets of stone that Moses carried down the mountain ← When they arrived at Mount Sinai, Moses climbed the mountain, leaving the rest of the Jews at the base ← The Jews left Egypt and wandered for many years in the desert in the Sinai region between Egypt and Canaan

The Ten Commandments

The Ten Commandments form the foundation of Jewish law. They give Jews important guidance on how to have a good relationship with God (the first four commandments), and how to have good relationships with each other to create a peaceful society (the last six commandments). They are recorded in Exodus 20:2–14.

1. You shall have no other gods besides Me
2. You shall not make for yourself a sculptured image, or any likeness
3. You shall not swear falsely by the name of the LORD your God
4. Remember the sabbath day and keep it holy

5. Honour your father and your mother
6. You shall not murder
7. You shall not commit adultery
8. You shall not steal
9. You shall not bear false witness against your neighbour
10. You shall not covet

The Ten Commandments form the basis of the **covenant at Sinai**. This is a covenant between God and the Jews, which was agreed at Mount Sinai under the following terms:

- God would protect the Jews from harm and be their God.
- In return, Jews would have to obey his laws (including the Ten Commandments and the other laws in the Torah).

This covenant is one of the main reasons why the Jews believe they are the chosen people of God.

APPLY

A Give two of the Ten Commandments.

B 'The covenant at Sinai requires too much from the Jews for what they get in return.'

Write two paragraphs in response to this statement, one arguing for it and one arguing against it.

TIP
When writing arguments for or against a statement, make sure your arguments are backed up by facts. Here you should refer to the terms of the covenant at Sinai.

RECAP

Essential information:

☐ The concepts of justice, healing the world, and kindness to others are important moral principles in Judaism.

☐ These principles help Jews to live in a way that is pleasing to God. They involve helping to create a just world through showing love to others.

Justice

- **Justice** refers to bringing about what is right and fair, according to the law, or making up for a wrong that has been committed.
- Pursuing justice is a sacred duty for Jews. For example, in the Torah, the prophet Micah states that God requires people 'to do justice and to love goodness' (Micah 6:8).
- The laws in the Torah give guidance to Jews on how to treat the poor and vulnerable, to help achieve justice.
- Jews believe the Torah and the prophets were sent by God to help people understand how to bring about justice in a way that demonstrates mercy.

Healing the world

- **Healing the world** is an important concept in Judaism, which involves taking actions to help God's work in sustaining the world.
- Many Jews help to heal the world by contributing to social justice or helping to protect the environment. For example, they might volunteer for a charity such as World Jewish Relief, which helps those living in poverty.
- Some Jews believe healing the world involves more than just doing charity work or similar actions. They believe it should also include obeying the mitzvot and trying to become closer to God.

> TIP
> The concept of healing the world links to Jewish beliefs about God as the creator and sustainer. By helping to heal the world, Jews are helping to sustain the world that God created (see page 139).

Kindness to others

- Jews aim to show **kindness to others** by showing positive, caring actions towards all living things.
- Many of the laws in the Torah give guidance to Jews on how to be kind to others.
- The Torah teaches that Jews should love others as they love themselves. This instruction is given twice in Leviticus 19:

> ❝You shall not take vengeance or bear a grudge against your countrymen. Love your fellow as yourself❞
>
> *Leviticus 19:18*

> ❝The stranger who resides with you shall be to you as one of your citizens; you shall love him as yourself, for you were strangers in the land of Egypt❞
>
> *Leviticus 19:34*

APPLY

(A) Give two ways in which a belief in healing the world influences Jews today.

(B) 'The moral principles of justice, healing the world, and kindness to others are all interlinked and equally important.'

Give arguments to support this statement.

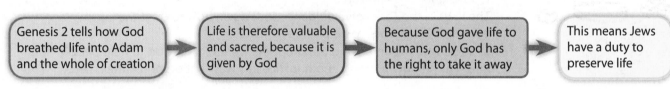

9.9 Sanctity of life

RECAP

Essential information:

☐ **Sanctity of life** refers to the idea that life is sacred and holy because it has been created by God.

☐ For Jews, belief in the sanctity of life means only God has the right to take life away. Jews are against practices such as murder and active euthanasia, as these quicken a person's natural death.

☐ Belief in the sanctity of life also means Jews have a duty to save a person's life if they can, even if this breaks Jewish law. This duty is called **pikuach nefesh**.

Sanctity of life

For Jews, belief in the sanctity of life stems from the creation story in Genesis.

Genesis 2 tells how God breathed life into Adam and the whole of creation → Life is therefore valuable and sacred, because it is given by God → Because God gave life to humans, only God has the right to take it away → This means Jews have a duty to preserve life

For Jews, belief in the sanctity of life means they should **not do anything to quicken a person's natural death**. For example, this means active euthanasia and murder are wrong.

However, while Jewish law states that Jews have a duty to preserve life, there are different opinions about what this means in practice. For example, some Jews think a sick patient should be kept alive at all costs. Others think a patient's death shouldn't be prolonged if they are in great pain.

The importance of preserving life is expressed in Sanhedrin 4:5 in the Talmud:

> ❝He who destroys one soul of a human being, the Scripture considers him as if he should destroy a whole world ❞
>
> *Sanhedrin 4:5*

Saving a life (pikuach nefesh)

- A belief in the sanctity of life is behind the concept of pikuach nefesh. This is the obligation that Jews have to save a person's life if they can, even if doing so breaks Jewish laws.
- Pikuach nefesh emphasises how valuable human life is to Jews, as it puts human life above Jewish law.

Examples of laws that might be broken to save a life
- Jews are required to observe Shabbat, which means they are not allowed to do certain types of work from sunset on Friday to sunset on Saturday (see pages 156–157). But Jews are allowed to break Shabbat law in order to save a life.
- Examples in the Talmud of where it is possible to break Shabbat law include rescuing a child from the sea or putting out a fire. Examples today might include driving a sick person to hospital or performing a life-saving operation.

APPLY

A Give an example of a Jewish law that could be broken to save a person's life.

B 'People shouldn't interfere with God's plan for each person, including his decision to take away their life.'

Write two paragraphs in response to this statement, one arguing against it and one arguing for it. Refer to Jewish beliefs in each paragraph.

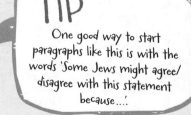

TIP

One good way to start paragraphs like this is with the words 'Some Jews might agree/ disagree with this statement because ....'

9.10 Free will and mitzvot

Essential information:

☐ Jews believe God has given people **free will**: the ability to make their own decisions. Jews also believe their decisions have consequences, and will either bring them closer to God or lead them away from God.

☐ Mitzvot are the Jewish rules or commandments. Some of these teach Jews how to form a good relationship with God, while others teach Jews how to form good relationships with each other.

Free will

Jews believe God has given them the free will to make their own choices.
But this does not mean people can do what they like without any consequences:

- Good actions lead to a life of fulfilment. They bring Jews closer to God and ensure they are judged favourably by him.
- Bad actions will not bring people closer to God, in life or after death.

In Genesis 3, Adam and Eve use their free will to disobey God and eat from the tree. They were banished from the garden of Eden as a result. This story shows God has given humans the choice of how to live their lives, but using free will to go against God has serious consequences.

Mitzvot

A mitzvah is a Jewish rule or commandment. There are 613 mitzvot in the Torah and others in the Talmud.

The mitzvot **give guidance to Jews on how to use their free will correctly**, to live in a way that pleases God. Jews believe that, as the mitzvot in the Torah came from God while the Jews were under the leadership of Moses, following them carefully makes it impossible to disobey God.

Mitzvot can be divided into two categories:

Mitzvot between man and God	Mitzvot between man and man
• These are mitzvot that tell Jews how they can improve their relationship with God • They cover areas such as worship, sacrifice, and the observance of festivals • The most important are the first four of the Ten Commandments • For example, the first commandment tells Jews to worship no other gods, and the fourth commandment tells Jews to remember God every Shabbat	• These are mitzvot that tell Jews how to improve their relationship with other people • This is important because the Torah teaches that Jews should show love towards other people and by doing this, Jews are showing their love for God • They cover areas such as the treatment of workers and how to settle disputes • They help Jews to live as members of their faith and community in a way that pleases God

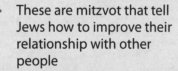

A Explain two teachings that Genesis 3 gives Jews about free will.

Refer to scripture or another source of Jewish belief and teaching in your answer.

B 'Obeying the mitzvot between man and man should be more important to Jews than obeying the mitzvot between man and God.'

What is your opinion on this statement? Explain your reasoning.

Why might someone else have a different opinion?

9 Exam practice

Test the 1 mark question

1　Which **one** of the following is *not* one of the Ten Commandments?

　A ☐ Do not cause harm to anyone　　B ☐ Do not steal

　C ☐ Do not worship any other God　　D ☐ Honour your father and mother　　**[1 mark]**

2　Which **one** of the following people sealed the covenant with God through the action of circumcision?

　A ☐ Abraham　　B ☐ Moses　　C ☐ King David　　D ☐ The Messiah　　**[1 mark]**

Test the 2 mark question

3　Give **two** different Jewish beliefs about the creation of the universe.　　**[2 marks]**

　1) _____

　2) _____

4　Give **two** different occasions when Jews believe they will be judged by God.　　**[2 marks]**

　1) _____

　2) _____

Test the 4 mark question

5　Explain **two** ways in which a belief in the sanctity of human life influences Jews today.　　**[4 marks]**

● **Explain one way.**	One way a belief in the sanctity of life influences Jews today is that it means they shouldn't take any action that would quicken a person's natural death.
● Develop your explanation with more detail/an example/ reference to a religious teaching or quotation.	For example, they shouldn't perform euthanasia because this makes a person die quicker than they would naturally.
● **Explain a second way.**	A second way a belief in the sanctity of life influences Jews today is that it means they should save someone's life even if this breaks Jewish law.
● Develop your explanation with more detail/an example/ reference to a religious teaching or quotation.	For example, they're allowed to drive someone to the hospital during Shabbat, even though they're not supposed to do work on this day.

6　Explain **two** ways in which the covenant at Sinai influences Jews today.　　**[4 marks]**

● **Explain one way.**	
● Develop your explanation with more detail/an example/ reference to a religious teaching or quotation.	
● **Explain a second way.**	
● Develop your explanation with more detail/an example/ reference to a religious teaching or quotation.	

7　Explain **two** Jewish beliefs about life after death.　　**[4 marks]**

Test the 5 mark question

8 | Explain **two** Jewish beliefs about the divine presence (Shekhinah).

Refer to scripture or another source of Jewish belief and teaching in your answer.

TIP
To refer to scripture or Jewish belief and teaching in your answer, you could write out a short quote from the Torah or mention a specific passage from this text.

[5 marks]

● **Explain one belief.**	*One belief about the divine presence is that God's divine presence was once housed in the Tabernacle.*
● Develop your explanation with more detail/an example.	*God manifested his glory to the Jews while they were travelling through the wilderness after escaping from Egypt. They carried a portable tent called the Tabernacle to represent God's constant presence with them throughout this journey.*
● **Explain a second belief.**	*Another belief about the divine presence is that God has sometimes made appearances on earth.*
● Develop your explanation with more detail/an example.	*God's presence on earth is sometimes very dramatic and changes lives.*
● Add a reference to scripture or another source of Jewish belief. If you prefer, you can add this reference to your first belief instead.	*For example, he once appeared to the prophet Isaiah in Solomon's Temple and called him to be a prophet. This story is given in Isaiah 6:1–2 in the Torah.*

9 | Explain **two** moral principles that Jews can follow to live in a way that pleases God.

Refer to scripture or another source of Jewish belief and teaching in your answer.

[5 marks]

● **Explain one moral principle.**	
● Develop your explanation with more detail/an example.	
● **Explain a second moral principle.**	
● Develop your explanation with more detail/an example.	
● Add a reference to scripture or another source of Jewish belief. If you prefer, you can add this reference to your first belief instead.	

10 | Explain **two** meanings of the Jewish belief that God is One.

Refer to scripture or another source of Jewish belief and teaching in your answer.

[5 marks]

Test the 12 mark question

11   'The mitzvot help Jews to use free will properly.'

Evaluate this statement. In your answer you should:

- give reasoned arguments to support this statement
- give reasoned arguments to support a different point of view
- refer to Jewish teaching
- reach a justified conclusion.

[12 marks]
Plus SPaG 3 ma

REASONED ARGUMENTS IN SUPPORT OF THE STATEMENT	
● **Explain why some people would agree with the statement.**	Most Jews would agree with this statement because the mitzvot tell Jews how to behave in a way that is pleasing to God. There are 613 mitzvot in the Torah which give Jews rules for how to behave in all areas of life, from worship and the observance of festivals to settling disputes and treating workers fairly. They teach Jews how to have a good relationship with God and with each other.
● Develop your explanation with more detail and examples.	
● Refer to religious teaching. Use a quote or paraphrase or refer to a religious authority.	Jews believe these rules are necessary because God has also given them free will. This means they have the ability to make bad choices and decisions that would turn them away from God. But the mitzvot help Jews to make good choices and use their free will in a way that would be approved by God.
● **Evaluate the arguments.** Is this a good argument or not? Explain why you think this.	

TIP

The answer begins well by explaining what the mitzvot are before saying how they help Jews. The student also addresses how free will might make it difficult to follow God if there were no mitzvot to help keep people on the right track. Always try to address all parts of the statement you are asked to evaluate.

REASONED ARGUMENTS SUPPORTING A DIFFERENT VIEW	
● **Explain why some people would support a different view.**	Some Jews might argue that there are too many mitzvot to be helpful, and that trying to follow 613 separate rules is confusing and overwhelming. They might argue that general principles – such as showing kindness to others, and healing the world – are more useful in guiding Jews to use their free will properly.
● Develop your explanation with more detail and examples.	
● Refer to religious teaching. Use a quote or paraphrase or refer to a religious authority.	For example, the principle of showing kindness to others means that Jews should help and care for other people. This teaches Jews that a loving attitude is important. Some Jews might say that having a loving attitude towards everything will help them to use their free will better than trying to follow lots of specific mitzvot.
● **Evaluate the arguments.** Is this a good argument or not? Explain why you think this.	

TIP

Rather than arguing that the mitzvot are unhelpful, the student argues that other moral principles might be more helpful in making wise choices. But it would also be acceptable to argue that keeping rigidly to rules may stop people growing up and being able to make mature choices of their own. A variety of different views will be credited as long as you provide reasons for them.

CONCLUSION	
● **Give a justified conclusion.**	I believe that God gave the mitzvot to the Jews to help them live in a way he approves. Jews believe if they follow the mitzvot carefully, it is impossible to disobey God, so this means they must be using their free will properly. I think the detail in the 613 mitzvot gives helpful guidance to keep people close to God.
● Include your own opinion together with your own reasoning.	
● **Include evaluation.** Explain why you think one viewpoint is stronger than the other or why you think they are equally strong.	
● Do not just repeat arguments you have already used without explaining how they apply to your reasoned opinion/conclusion.	

12 'Jews do not need to worry about trying to create a more peaceful society, because this will be achieved by the Messiah.'

Evaluate this statement. In your answer you should:

- give reasoned arguments to support this statement
- give reasoned arguments to support a different point of view
- refer to Jewish teaching
- reach a justified conclusion.

[12 marks]
Plus SPaG 3 marks

REASONED ARGUMENTS IN SUPPORT OF THE STATEMENT ● **Explain why some people would agree with the statement.** ● Develop your explanation with more detail and examples. ● Refer to religious teaching. Use a quote or paraphrase or refer to a religious authority. ● **Evaluate the arguments.** Is this a good argument or not? Explain why you think this.	
REASONED ARGUMENTS SUPPORTING A DIFFERENT VIEW ● **Explain why some people would support a different view.** ● Develop your explanation with more detail and examples. ● Refer to religious teaching. Use a quote or paraphrase or refer to a religious authority. ● **Evaluate the arguments.** Is this a good argument or not? Explain why you think this.	
CONCLUSION ● **Give a justified conclusion.** ● Include your own opinion together with your own reasoning. ● **Include evaluation.** Explain why you think one viewpoint is stronger than the other or why you think they are equally strong. ● Do not just repeat arguments you have already used without explaining how they apply to your reasoned opinion/conclusion.	

13 'For Jews, it is more important to understand God as a judge than as anything else.'

Evaluate this statement. In your answer you should:

- give reasoned arguments to support this statement
- give reasoned arguments to support a different point of view
- refer to Jewish teaching
- reach a justified conclusion.

[12 marks]
Plus SPaG 3 marks

Check your answers using the mark scheme on page 235. How did you do?
To feel more secure in the content you need to remember, re-read pages 139–147.
To remind yourself of what the examiner is looking for in your answers, go to pages 8–13.

10.1 The importance of the synagogue

Essential information:

☐ The **synagogue** is a building where Jews meet for worship, study, social activities and charitable events. It is also where Jews celebrate festivals and rites of passage.

☐ The synagogue forms the centre of the Jewish religious community.

What is a synagogue?

- A synagogue provides a space for Jews to **meet and take part in a wide range of activities**, from worship and prayer to community meetings and social clubs.
- Synagogues are usually identified from their **use of Jewish symbols** on the outside of the building. For example, synagogues may display an image of a **menorah** (a many-branched candlestick) or the **Star of David** (a six-pointed star that represents King David, who ruled Israel in the tenth century BCE).
- Jews have a **number of different names** for the synagogue. It is sometimes called the 'house of prayer' or 'house of study'. Orthodox Jews often call it the 'shul', which means 'school'. Reform Jews sometimes call it the 'temple', in reference to the Temple in Jerusalem (an important centre of worship for early Jews).

The importance of the synagogue

The synagogue is important to Jews because it strengthens their community by providing a space for a variety of activities, including the following:

Worship and prayer

- The synagogue **provides a space for worship and communal prayer**
- Although Jews can pray anywhere, they believe it is good to pray together in a group: certain prayers can only be said in the presence of a **minyan** – a group of at least 10 adults
- Services are regularly held in the synagogue for Jews to pray and worship together

Education

- The synagogue helps to **educate Jews of all ages in their faith**
- Synagogues may provide classes in Hebrew for young Jews, to help them learn the language used in Jewish prayer
- Most synagogues have a library that helps older Jews to continue improving their understanding of the faith and its scriptures

Social activities

- Most synagogues **host a variety of activities for children, teenagers and adults in their social hall**
- Examples include youth clubs, music or drama groups, and groups for senior citizens
- The synagogue provides a place to discuss matters that are important to the community

Charitable events

- The synagogue **helps Jews to donate their time and money to charity**
- Synagogues often hold events to raise money for charity
- They also collect money or other items to be given to charity or distributed among the poor and needy

A Give two ways in which someone might recognise a synagogue from the outside.

B 'The most important role of the synagogue is to provide a space for communal prayer.'

Evaluate this statement.

TIP

To 'evaluate' this statement, explain whether you think it is true or not and why. Consider why the activities held in a synagogue are important to Jews. For example, is it more important for Jews to be able to pray together, or to be educated in their faith?

RECAP

Essential information:

☐ The Ark (**Aron Hakodesh**) is the cabinet where the Torah scrolls are kept. It is the holiest place in the synagogue.

☐ The ever-burning light (**ner tamid**) is a light that is kept on at all times, and sits above the Ark. It symbolises God's presence.

☐ The reading platform (**bimah**) is the raised platform from where the Torah is read.

The prayer hall

- The prayer hall is the room in the synagogue where Jews come together for communal worship and prayer.
- It is usually rectangular in shape, with seats on three sides of the hall facing inwards towards the bimah, which is situated in the centre. The fourth side is where the Ark is kept, which is the focal point of the synagogue.
- The prayer hall might be decorated with patterns, Jewish symbols or extracts from scripture. Images of God, the prophets or other religious figures are not allowed, as this goes against the second commandment.

Important features of the prayer hall include the following:

Feature	Description	Significance
The Ark (Aron Hakodesh) *(illustration of ornamental cabinet)*	• An ornamental cabinet or container where the Torah scrolls are kept • Situated at the front of the synagogue, usually set into the wall facing Jerusalem • Usually reached by climbing up some steps • There are usually two stone tablets placed above the Ark, on which the start of each of the Ten Commandments is written	• The holiest place in the synagogue • Represents the original Ark of the Covenant. This first Ark was built to hold the stone tablets that contained the Ten Commandments, which God gave to Moses • The first Ark was taken to Jerusalem and placed in the Temple built by King Solomon. The Temple was the focal point of Jewish worship in early Judaism • Today, when Jews face the Ark in the synagogue, they face the city where the Temple once stood • By climbing up steps to reach the Ark, Jews are reminded that God is above his people and the sacred Torah is above humanity
The ever-burning light (ner tamid) *(illustration of oil lamp)*	• A light that is placed in front of and slightly above the Ark • Traditionally an oil lamp, but most synagogues now use electric lights (with an emergency power source in case of a power cut)	• Symbolises God's presence, so it is never put out • A reminder of the menorah that was lit every night in the Temple in Jerusalem
The reading platform (bimah) *(illustration of raised platform)*	• A raised platform situated in most synagogues in the centre of the prayer hall • Where the Torah is read from during services	• Provides a focal point when the Torah is being read, making it easier for the congregation to see the reader and hear what is being said • To some Jews it is a reminder that the altar was the central feature of the courtyard in the Temple in Jerusalem

APPLY

(A) Write three sentences to describe what the Ark, the ner tamid and the bimah are.

(B) 'The prayer hall in a synagogue shows how important the Temple in Jerusalem was to Jews.'

List arguments in support of this statement.

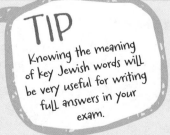

TIP

Knowing the meaning of key Jewish words will be very useful for writing full answers in your exam.

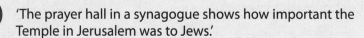

RECAP

Essential information:

☐ In the UK today, there are two main groups within Judaism: **Orthodox** Judaism (which is more traditional) and **Reform** Judaism (which is more progressive).

☐ Jews are expected to pray three times a day. Orthodox synagogues hold daily services so Jews can pray together.

☐ Orthodox and Reform services differ in a number of ways.

Orthodox and Reform Judaism

Orthodox Judaism	Reform Judaism
• The traditional branch of Judaism	• A type of progressive Judaism
• Orthodox Jews emphasise the importance of **strictly following the laws in the Torah** • They believe the Torah was given directly to Moses by God, so should be followed as closely as possible	• Reform Jews emphasise the importance of **individual choice in deciding how to worship and practise the faith** • They believe the Torah was inspired by God but written by humans, so it can be adapted for modern times
• Orthodox Jews believe **men and women should have different roles** • Currently all Orthodox rabbis are male, although there are women within the tradition who are working towards greater equality	• Reform Jews believe **men and women should be able to undertake the same roles** • This means women in Reform Judaism can take on roles traditionally reserved for men, such as becoming a rabbi or being part of the minyan

Public worship

Services in the synagogue are led by either a rabbi (a Jewish religious leader and teacher), a cantor (a person who leads or chants prayers in the synagogue), or a member of the congregation. Orthodox and Reform services differ in the following ways:

Orthodox services	Reform services
Synagogues usually hold daily services	Synagogues often do not hold daily services; the focus instead is on celebrating Shabbat and festivals
The service is in Hebrew	The service is in Hebrew and the country's own language (English in the UK)
The person leading the service has his back to the congregation, so he is facing the Ark	The person leading the service faces the congregation most of the time
Men and women sit separately	Men and women sit together
Some of the congregation may arrive late and catch up at their own pace	Services are shorter than Orthodox ones but tend to be more rigidly structured; there is a set time and worshippers are usually present at the start
Men always cover their heads by wearing a skull cap and married women cover their heads by wearing a hat or scarf. This shows respect for God, and a recognition that God is above humanity	Most men wear a skull cap and some women do as well (or they might wear a hat instead)
The singing in the service is unaccompanied	The singing may be accompanied by musical instruments

APPLY

A Explain how Orthodox and Reform Judaism differ in their beliefs about the Torah. How does this influence their approach to worship?

B 'Reform services make it easier for people to understand what is happening than Orthodox services'.

What is your opinion about this statement? Explain your reasoning.

10.4 Daily services and prayer

Essential information:

☐ Orthodox Jewish men (and some Reform Jews) often wear a **tallit** (a prayer shawl) and **tefillin** (small leather boxes containing extracts from the Torah) when they pray.

☐ Weekday services in the synagogue consist of a number of prayers, including the **Amidah** (the 'standing prayer'), which is the central prayer in Jewish worship.

Tallit and tefillin

During morning prayers, Orthodox Jewish men wear a tallit, and on weekdays they wear tefillin as well. Some Reform Jewish men and women wear them too.

	Description	**Significance**
Tallit	A prayer shawl made from wool or silk A long tassel is attached to each corner	The shawl reminds Jews they are obeying God's word whenever they wear it The tassels represent the mitzvot (see page 147)
Tefillin	A pair of small leather boxes containing extracts from the Torah, including some of the words of the Shema One is fastened with leather straps to the centre of the forehead, and the other is wound around the upper arm in line with the heart	Reminds Jews that their mind should be concentrating fully on God when they pray, and their prayers should come from the heart

The format of Jewish services

On weekdays, prayer services are held in Orthodox synagogues in the morning, afternoon and evening. The service often consists of the following parts:

- **Opening prayers** are said. These might consist of prayers and psalms that praise and thank God.
- The **Shema** is recited, and accompanied by blessings.
- The **Amidah** ('standing prayer') is said. This is the central prayer of Jewish worship, and on a weekday it forms the core of all Jewish prayer services. It is prayed in silence while standing and facing Jerusalem.
  It consists of a series of blessings:
  - the first three blessings praise God and ask for his mercy
  - the middle thirteen blessings ask for God's help
  - the final three blessings thank God for the opportunity to serve him and pray for peace, goodness, kindness and compassion.
- The Amidah is sometimes followed by a **reading** from the Torah.
- **Final prayers** are said. These include the closing Aleinu prayer, which gives praise and thanks to God.

it is a way to communicate with God

communal prayer strengthens the Jewish community

Prayer is important to Jews because …

it brings Jews closer to God

it helps Jews to remember what their faith is all about

A Describe two parts of a prayer service in an Orthodox synagogue.

B 'Prayer is more important to Jews than helping to heal the world.'
Give arguments for and against this statement.

TIP
The concept of 'healing the world' is discussed on page 145.

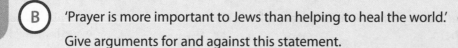

RECAP

Essential information:

☐ **Shabbat** is the Jewish holy day of the week. It is a day of rest and renewal, starting just before sunset on Friday and continuing to sunset on Saturday.

☐ Services that are held in the synagogue for Shabbat include a brief service on Friday evening, the main service on Saturday morning, and sometimes an extra service especially for families with children.

What is Shabbat?

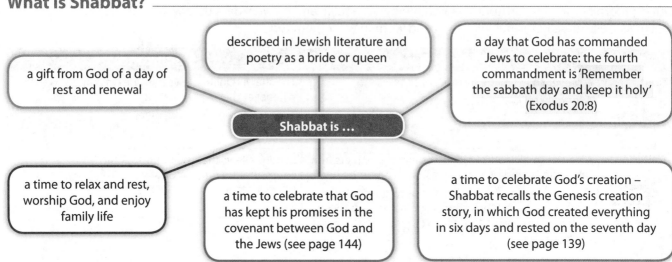

described in Jewish literature and poetry as a bride or queen

a day that God has commanded Jews to celebrate: the fourth commandment is 'Remember the sabbath day and keep it holy' (Exodus 20:8)

a gift from God of a day of rest and renewal

Shabbat is ...

a time to relax and rest, worship God, and enjoy family life

a time to celebrate that God has kept his promises in the covenant between God and the Jews (see page 144)

a time to celebrate God's creation – Shabbat recalls the Genesis creation story, in which God created everything in six days and rested on the seventh day (see page 139)

Shabbat services

- On **Friday evening**, there is a brief service in the synagogue, during which Shabbat is welcomed like a bride coming to meet her husband (the Jewish people).
- Some synagogues hold a service during Shabbat for **families with children**, which includes storytelling, games and music.
- The main service is on **Saturday morning**. This service is longer than the weekday prayer services, as it includes a reading from the Torah and often a sermon, as well as prayers and blessings.

Before the reading is given, the following often happens:

Action	Significance
The congregation stands when the Ark is opened to reveal the Torah scrolls	This is a reminder of how the Jews stood at the bottom of Mount Sinai when Moses returned with the Ten Commandments
The Torah is taken from the Ark and dressed with a cover and various ornaments, such as a crown or belt	This is a reminder of the vestments worn by priests in early Judaism
The Torah is held in front of the congregation while verses from scripture are chanted; it is then paraded round the synagogue	This represents the march through the wilderness, when Jews carried the original Ark (containing the Ten Commandments) from Mount Sinai to Jerusalem
When the Torah passes through the synagogue, many Jews touch it with their prayer book or the tassels on their prayer shawl, and then touch their lips	This recalls Ezekiel 3:3, which tells Jews that God's words should be on their lips, and sweet like honey

- After the reading is finished, the Torah scrolls are dressed and paraded around the synagogue again, before being placed back in the Ark.
- The rabbi or visiting speaker then gives a sermon, which may be based on the reading or something important in the news.

APPLY

(A) Explain two actions that happen before the reading from the Torah is given in the main Shabbat service.

(B) 'Shabbat is a day for Jews to celebrate all that God has given them.'

Write a paragraph to explain why Jews would agree with this statement.

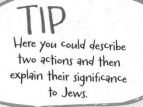

TIP

Here you could describe two actions and then explain their significance to Jews.

RECAP

Essential information:

☐ To help make Shabbat a special occasion when no work is done, various preparations need to be made beforehand, such as cleaning the house and preparing the food.

☐ In the home, the start of Shabbat is marked through the lighting of the candles, and the end of Shabbat is marked through the havdalah service.

☐ The main celebration in the home is the Friday evening meal, which allows the family to relax and enjoy each other's company.

Shabbat preparations

Preparation	Significance
• All the work is done and the home is prepared before Shabbat begins on Friday evening • This involves cleaning the house, preparing the food, washing, and changing into smart clothes	• Most types of work are not allowed during Shabbat, as stated in the fourth commandment • Jews try to make their homes neat and presentable to welcome in Shabbat, which is seen as being like welcoming a special bride or queen into the home
• At least two candles are placed on the table	• The two candles represent the two commandments to 'remember' and 'observe' Shabbat
• Two loaves of challah bread are placed on the table	• These represent the food that God provided for the Jews on Shabbat while they were wandering in the wilderness
• Wine or grape juice is placed on the table (the wine is drunk from a special goblet called the Kiddush cup)	• Drinking Shabbat wine symbolises joy and celebration

Shabbat celebrations

Shabbat is welcomed through the **lighting of the candles**:

- A female member of the family (usually the wife) lights the two candles, shortly before sunset on Friday.
- She waves or beckons with her arms around the candles, then covers her eyes to say a blessing.
- She also says a prayer asking God to bless the family.

After the Friday evening service in the synagogue, the family **shares a special meal**:

- Before the meal, the parents bless their children, and the head of the household recites the Kiddush blessings while holding up the Kiddush cup.
- To begin the meal, the bread is blessed and passed round so everyone has a piece.
- The meal might last for a few hours, giving the family time to relax and enjoy each other's company. After each course, religious stories might be told to the children or songs might be sung.
- The meal ends with a prayer of thanksgiving for the food.

After the Saturday morning service in the synagogue, the family **shares another special meal**. During the afternoon, parents may **spend time with their children** and **study the Torah**. The end of Shabbat is marked by the **havdalah service**:

- This is performed at home after the sun has set.
- Blessings are performed over a cup of wine, sweet smelling spices and a candle with several wicks.
- The spices and candle are believed to soothe and bring light to the house after Shabbat has ended.

APPLY

 A Give two preparations that are made in the home before Shabbat begins, and explain their significance.

 B 'Shabbat is most important for Jews as a time to relax and enjoy being together as a family.'

Give arguments for and against this statement.

RECAP

Essential information:

☐ Jews may pray in the home instead of attending a synagogue. They are also reminded to focus on God in other ways in the home, such as through touching the mezuzah (a small box containing verses from the Torah).

☐ The **Tenakh** is the main Jewish sacred text and contains the written law. The **Talmud** is a commentary which helps Jews to put the laws in the Tenakh into practice.

☐ Studying the Tenakh and Talmud is very important to Orthodox Jews in particular.

Worship in the home and private prayer

- Jews are expected to **pray three times a day**, which they can do in the home or in the synagogue. They traditionally stand to pray, and if they are alone they pray silently.
- Jews are also reminded of God in the home in other ways. For example, many Jewish homes have one or more **mezuzot**. A mezuzah is a small box that contains a handwritten scroll of verses from the Torah, which is attached to a doorpost. Jews touch the mezuzah as a sign of respect to God and a reminder to obey his laws.
- In Jewish Orthodox homes, the layout of the kitchen will also remind Jews of God and the need to obey the dietary laws (see page 163).

Study of sacred writings

The Tenakh and the Talmud teach Jews how to obey God's laws in their everyday lives:

Writing	Overview	Contents
Tenakh (the written law)	• The Jewish sacred scriptures • A collection of 24 books (which can all be found in the Old Testament in the Christian Bible)	The Tenakh is in three main parts: 1 the **Torah**: the five books of Moses, which form the basis of Jewish law 2 the **Nevi'im** (the Prophets): eight books that continue to trace Jewish history and expand on the laws in the Torah 3 the **Ketuvim** (the Writings): eleven books that contain a collection of poetry, stories, advice, historical accounts and more

Talmud (the oral law)	• A commentary by the early rabbis on the Torah
	• Contains a collection of discussions and teachings about how to interpret the Torah and apply its laws to everyday life
		The Talmud is in two main parts:
		1 the **Mishnah**: a commentary on the Torah compiled by Rabbi Judah Ha'Nasi in 200 CE
		  • Ha'Nasi wrote down the oral law: the early teachings about how to interpret the Torah, which had been passed down from generation to generation by word of mouth
		  • there was a danger these teachings would be altered or misinterpreted without a written record of them, so Ha'Nasi compiled the Mishnah to stop this from happening
		2 the **Gemara**: a collection of discussions on the Mishnah, written down in 500 CE

- For Orthodox Jews, the Torah and Talmud are considered to be the source of all Jewish laws, legal teachings and decisions that affect their daily lives.
- For this reason they are studied extensively by Orthodox Jews, who may attend classes and lectures to develop their understanding.
- Reform Jews do not regard the Torah and Talmud with the same absolute authority and may not study them as much.

APPLY

(A) Give two ways in which Jews are reminded of God in the home.

(B) 'All Jews should carefully study the Talmud if they want to live in a way that pleases God.'

Evaluate this statement.

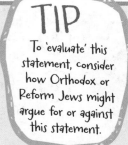

TIP

To 'evaluate' this statement, consider how Orthodox or Reform Jews might argue for or against this statement.

RECAP

Essential information:

☐ Family life is central to Jews, as it is where the Jewish faith is preserved and passed on to the next generation. Birth is an important rite of passage which the wider Jewish community helps to celebrate.

☐ Three Jewish ceremonies associated with birth are the **naming ceremony** (when the baby is formally named), **Brit Milah** (when a boy is circumcised), and the **redemption of the firstborn son** (when the firstborn son is 'redeemed' from Temple service).

Ceremonies for newborn Jews

In Judaism, there are three ceremonies which help a family to celebrate the birth of their child and welcome them into the Jewish community:

Ceremony	What it involves	Significance
Naming ceremony	• Boys and girls born into Orthodox families are **blessed in the synagogue on the first Shabbat after their birth** • The father recites the Torah blessing, and asks God for the good health of his wife and baby • **A baby girl's name will be announced at this point** • A boy will be named later at his circumcision • In Reform synagogues, both parents will take part in the naming ceremony, which may not necessarily be held on the first Shabbat after the child's birth	• The naming ceremony formally introduces the baby to the community and God
Brit Milah	• **This ceremony happens when a baby boy is eight days old** • A close friend or relative places the baby on an empty chair that symbolises the presence of the prophet Elijah • A trained circumciser picks up the baby and places him on the knee of the person who has been given the honoured role of being 'the companion of the child' • The baby's father blesses his son • A blessing is said over wine and the baby is formally named • **The baby is circumcised in a simple operation that quickly heals** • Family and guests then enjoy a festive meal to celebrate	• Brit Milah recalls the covenant God made with Abraham (see page 143), where God told Abraham that circumcision would 'be the sign of the covenant between Me and you' (Genesis 17:11) • It provides a lifelong reminder to a male Jew that they are one of God's chosen people
Redemption of the firstborn son	• Some Orthodox Jews give a small amount of money 31 days after the birth of their firstborn son, to 'redeem' him from Temple service (the Temple in Jerusalem no longer exists, but some Orthodox Jews maintain this tradition anyway) • **Five silver coins are given to a kohen**: a descendent of the priests who used to work in the Temple • Prayers are also said, asking that the child may 'enter into Torah, into marriage, and into good deeds.'	• This tradition comes from the following command in Numbers 18 'but you shall have the first-born of man redeemed … Take as their redemption price … the money equivalent of five shekels' (Numbers 18:15–16).

APPLY

A Give two ways in which Orthodox and Reform Jews differ in their celebrations of a birth.

B 'Jewish ceremonies associated with birth remind Jews of the importance of following God's laws.'

Give arguments to support this statement.

TIP

Even if you can't remember all the details of these ceremonies, try to remember why they are important to Jews.

Essential information:

☐ When Jewish boys turn 13 and girls turn 12, they are considered to be old enough to take full responsibility for practising their faith.

☐ Boys celebrate coming of age at 13 with a **Bar Mitzvah** ceremony and become a 'son of the commandment'.

☐ In Reform Judaism, girls celebrate coming of age at 12 with a **Bat Mitzvah** ceremony and become a 'daughter of the commandment'.

The significance of Bar and Bat Mitzvah

it is when a Jew is seen to become an adult

preparing carefully for it brings Jews closer to God and the Jewish community

Bar or Bat Mitzvah is significant because …

it is when a Jew is expected to start strictly following Jewish law, and takes full responsibility for doing so

it is when a Jewish boy is allowed to become part of the minyan (see page 152)

Celebrating a Bar Mitzvah

- At the first opportunity after his thirteenth birthday (usually the first Shabbat), the boy reads from the Torah at the normal service in the synagogue. Many synagogues hold classes to prepare boys for this occasion.
- The boy wears a tallit for the first time, may lead part of the service – reading from the Torah or saying prayers – and makes a short speech.
- The boy's father thanks God for bringing his son to maturity, and declares he is now responsible for his own actions.
- After the service there is often a celebratory meal or party, where the boy receives gifts.

Celebrating a Bat Mitzvah

- Reform Jewish girls often have a Bat Mitzvah ceremony and celebrations that are very similar to a Bar Mitzvah.
- The girl reads from the Torah, gives a short speech, and may lead part of the service in the synagogue.
- This is often followed by a celebratory meal or party.
- Orthodox Jews sometimes mark a girl's Bat Mitzvah with a family meal and small religious gifts.

APPLY

A Give two ways in which a Jew might participate in a service as part of their Bar or Bat Mitzvah.

B 'The Bar or Bat Mitzvah ceremony is the most significant moment in a Jewish peson's life.'

The start of two paragraphs have been written below, one arguing against the statement and one in support of it. Finish the paragraphs by developing the arguments further.

"I agree with this statement because the Bar or Bat Mitzvah ceremony marks the point when a Jewish person has to take full responsibility for following Jewish law …"

"I disagree with this statement because there are other moments in a Jewish person's life that some might think are equally significant. For example, the Brit Milah ceremony …"

10.10 Marriage

Essential information:

☐ In Judaism, **marriage** is a two-step process. A period of engagement called the **betrothal**, which typically lasts for a year, is then followed by the wedding itself.

☐ A Jewish wedding can be divided into three main parts: the betrothal ceremony, the signing and reading of the marriage contract, and the marriage of the couple.

☐ For Jews, marriage creates a spiritual bond between a couple and helps them to experience holiness in their everyday lives.

Betrothal

- Betrothal refers to the period of time before the wedding ceremony when the couple are engaged or promised to each other. This traditionally lasts for 12 months.
- Betrothal has legal status in Jewish law and can only be broken by death or divorce.
- During the year of betrothal the couple do not live together, but they do prepare for their future lives together.
- Traditionally a special betrothal ceremony was held a year before the wedding, but this ceremony is now held at the wedding itself.

The wedding

Jewish weddings take place in the synagogue or in a venue such as a hotel, on any day except Shabbat or a festival. A typical Jewish wedding includes the betrothal ceremony, the signing and reading of the marriage contract, and the marriage itself.

Before the wedding	• The couple may fast before the wedding to cleanse themselves of sin and come to the ceremony with the right attitude
The betrothal ceremony	• The bride joins the groom underneath the chuppah, which is a canopy that symbolises the couple's home • The bride and groom recite two blessings over wine, and in Orthodox weddings the groom places a plain ring on the bride's finger (Reform couples usually exchange rings)
The marriage contract	• The marriage contract is signed in the presence of witnesses, then read out and given to the bride • For Orthodox Jews this covers aspects such as the husband's duties to his wife, the conditions of inheritance upon his death, and how he will provide for his wife if they get divorced • For Reform Jews, the marriage contract usually focuses on spiritual aspirations rather than legal rights. It often describes mutual hopes for the marriage, which are the same for the husband and wife
The marriage itself	• Seven wedding blessings are recited • The rabbi makes a short speech and blesses the couple in front of the congregation • The groom breaks a glass under his heel to show regret for the destruction of the Temple in Jerusalem – this is a reminder that life involves hardship as well as joy • The congregation wishes the couple good luck
The wedding reception ♪	• After the ceremony, the couple spend a short time together in a private room to symbolise their new status as a married couple • A wedding reception follows that includes music and dancing

For Jews, marriage is a way of experiencing holiness in everyday life. It creates a spiritual bond between a couple, where two souls are fused to become one. This is described in the Torah in Genesis 2.

> ❝Hence a man leaves his father and mother and clings to his wife, so that they become one flesh.❞
>
> *Genesis 2:24*

A Explain what the term 'betrothal' means in Judaism.

B 'Jewish weddings show equality between men and women.'
Give arguments for and against this statement.

TIP
Don't forget that marks are added for spelling, so learn how to spell any key terms you may use in your answer.

10.11 Mourning for the dead

Essential information:

- [ ] In Judaism there are set periods of mourning which decrease in intensity over the period of a year. These allow a family to grieve fully but also help them to get back to normal life.

- [ ] Most Jews are buried rather than cremated. A short funeral service is held at the cemetery, ideally within 24 hours after the person's death.

The periods of mourning

When the death is announced
- When Jews first hear of the death of a close family member, they make a small tear in their clothes, to follow the example of Jacob, as described in Genesis 37:34
- Jews also say a blessing that refers to God as the true judge, which shows they accept God's decision to take the person's life

The first period of mourning
- Most Jews are buried as soon after death as possible, usually within the first 24 hours
- Until then, Jews believe the deceased's soul should be comforted and supported by family members, because it does not fully leave the person until they are buried
- Close family are left to grieve without having to follow certain Jewish laws

The second period of mourning (shiva)
- Shiva is an intense period of mourning that lasts for seven days, starting on the day of the burial
- Mourners do not work but stay at home and hold prayer services three times a day
- One of the prayers said is the kaddish, which praises God and asks for peace
- Mourners do not wear make-up, shave or cut their hair: mirrors are covered over so mourners can't focus on their appearance

After the first year
- Formal mourning ends after a year
- Children continue to mark the anniversary of a parent's death by lighting a candle each year that burns for 24 hours
- Sons also recite the kaddish and, if possible, make a Torah blessing

The final period of mourning
- This lasts for eleven months
- Mourners do not attend parties
- Children continue to say the kaddish for a parent who has died

The third period of mourning
- This begins after shiva and lasts until 30 days after the person's death
- Normal life resumes but mourners do not listen to music, go to parties, shave or cut their hair
- Male mourners say the kaddish daily in the synagogue

The funeral

- Before the funeral, the body is carefully washed and wrapped in a plain linen cloth, as well as a tallit for men. It is placed in a simple coffin to show that everyone is equal in death.
- Funerals do not usually take place in the synagogue as this is considered to be a place for the living. Instead the body is taken straight to the cemetery.
- The funeral service includes prayers, psalms, readings from scripture, and a short speech by the rabbi.
- After the funeral, everyone washes their hands to show they are leaving death behind.
- Jewish law states a tombstone must be placed on the grave so the person is remembered.

A Describe two actions a Jewish person takes when they first hear of the death of a close family member, and explain their significance.

B 'Jewish mourning customs help a family to accept and cope with a person's death.'

What is your opinion on this statement? Explain your reasoning.

> **TIP**
> Remember, even when you are writing about an emotional subject such as death, try to keep your answers as objective and balanced as possible.

RECAP

Essential information:

☐ Jews follow **dietary laws**: strict rules about what can and cannot be eaten, and how food should be prepared.

☐ Food that is acceptable to eat is called **kosher**, while food that is unacceptable to eat is called **trefah**.

☐ Milk and meat cannot be mixed, so many Jewish kitchens have two food preparation areas to keep these separate.

Jewish dietary laws

The dietary laws **originate from passages in the Torah**, particularly Leviticus 11 and Deuteronomy 14. Some Jews think the laws were originally for hygiene or health reasons.

The laws categorise food as being **acceptable (kosher)** or **unacceptable (trefah)**.

- **Orthodox Jews** follow the dietary laws strictly. They believe the laws have come from God to test their obedience and help develop their self-control. The laws remind people daily of their faith, and mark out Jewish people as different from others.
- Many **Reform Jews** think the laws are outdated in modern British society, and it is up to an individual whether to follow them or not.

Preparing food

Kosher animals must be **killed in a certain way**. For example:

- the animal must be slaughtered with a very sharp knife by a trained Jew
- the animal has to be conscious when it is killed
- blood is drained from the animal as Jews are not permitted to consume food containing blood.

> **"** But make sure that you do not partake of the blood; for the blood is the life, and you must not consume the life with the flesh. **"**
>
> *Deuteronomy 12:23*

Jews must also be careful to **keep milk and meat separate**. Dairy products and meat are not allowed to be eaten at the same time. In addition, several hours must pass between eating meat and anything containing milk. Most Jews believe the reason for this comes from an instruction in Exodus: You shall not boil a kid in its mother's milk. (Exodus 23:19)

For this reason:

- many Orthodox homes have kitchens with two sinks and two food preparation areas, to keep milk and meat separate
- Jews may also colour-code their utensils, cutlery and crockery, so one set is used for meat dishes and another for dairy products
- most synagogues have kosher kitchens, so they can prepare food for events without breaking dietary laws
- Jews who live in non-Jewish communities often find it difficult to eat out and make sure their food is prepared correctly.

APPLY

A Write out a passage from the Torah which deals with the dietary laws, and explain what it means for Jews today.

B 'The Jewish dietary laws should be relaxed because they are too difficult to follow.'

Evaluate this statement.

TIP

To 'evaluate' this statement, consider whether you think Jews would agree with it or not. Think about the different arguments that Orthodox and Reform Jews might have in response to the statement.

10.13 Rosh Hashanah and Yom Kippur

Essential information:

☐ **Rosh Hashanah** is a festival that marks the start of the Jewish new year. Many Jews believe that during Rosh Hashanah, God judges their actions over the past year and decides their fortune for the coming year.

☐ **Yom Kippur** is the holiest and most important day in the year, when God's judgement from Rosh Hashanah is finalised.

☐ During the ten days between the start of Rosh Hashanah and Yom Kippur, Jews try to make up for their wrongdoings over the past year and seek forgiveness from God.

Rosh Hashanah

Origins and meaning	• Rosh Hashanah **remembers God's creation of the world,** and is also a **day of judgement** • It is considered to be the anniversary of the day on which God created humans, as described in Genesis 1. Some Jews believe that on this day, God weighs up and judges a person's actions over the past year, deciding what their fortune will be like in the year to come
Observance	**Improving God's judgement:** • Jews believe God's judgement can be influenced by their behaviour during the festival, so they try to **take actions that will improve God's judgement** • This might include praying, doing charity work, and atoning or making up for any harm they have caused over the past year **Celebrating at home:** • The day before Rosh Hashanah, preparations are made similar to those made for Shabbat • The evening Rosh Hashanah starts, families **share a festive meal** with symbolic foods. For example, apples dipped in honey symbolise hope for a sweet new year **Attending services in the synagogue:** • At the evening service in the synagogue, prayers are said asking God to continue to be the king of the world for the coming year • Next morning at the synagogue a ram's horn is blown 100 times • This is followed by a service which is longer than usual, with special prayers

Yom Kippur

Origins and meaning	• Yom Kippur, which is known as the **Day of Atonement**, is the holiest day in the Jewish calendar • Its origins stem from Leviticus 16:30, which tells Jews that on Yom Kippur, 'atonement shall be made for you to cleanse you of all your sins' • Jews believe God's judgement is finalised on this day, so it is the last chance to repent for any sins
Observance	**Attending services in the synagogue:** • Many Jews spend much of Yom Kippur in the synagogue • They focus on **asking God to forgive their sins**, to help restore their relationship with him • Jews take part in a general confession of sins as a community • During the final service, Jews are given one last chance to confess their sins. The doors of the Ark are then closed, showing that God's judgement is now sealed **Observing other rituals:** • During Yom Kippur, Jews fast for 25 hours and do no work • They wear white as a symbol of purity • Bathing, wearing leather shoes, and having sex are also forbidden

Ⓐ Give two differences between the ways in which Rosh Hashanah and Yom Kippur are observed.

Ⓑ 'It is more important to show kindness to others during Rosh Hashanah than at any other time in the year.'

Do you think Jews would agree with this statement? Explain your reasoning.

RECAP

Essential information:

☐ **Pesach** (also called Passover) is a festival that lasts for seven or eight days. It celebrates the Jews' escape from slavery in Egypt.

☐ One of the most important parts of the festival is the Passover Seder, which is a meal with special foods that families share on the first evening of Pesach.

Origins of, importance of and preparations for Pesach

- Pesach **celebrates the Jews' escape from slavery in Egypt**, after which they spent many years wandering in the desert before reaching the land of Canaan (see page 144).
- In particular, Pesach remembers the **final plague** that God sent to Egypt to persuade the Pharaoh to release the Jews. This killed the firstborn children of the Egyptians but 'passed over' the houses of the Jewish slaves.
- Pesach is important for Jews as it celebrates their escape from slavery to create the birth of the Jewish nation, when they were given the law that made them God's chosen people. It is a time for Jews to gives thanks to God for their redemption, and to feel empathy with those who still live under oppression.
- The most important preparation is to **remove leaven (yeast) from the home**. Removing leaven ecalls how the Jews did not have time to let their bread rise when they escaped from Egypt.
- After cleaning the house, some parents or children hide bread crumbs to find and burn, to show all leaven has been removed.
- Some firstborn males fast before Pesach starts, in thanksgiving for their ancestors' escape from death.

The Passover Seder

- On the first evening of Pesach, families **celebrate with a special meal** (called the Passover Seder).
- During the meal, the youngest member of the family asks four questions about the meaning of Pesach rituals. In reply, the story of the escape from Egypt is told from a book called the Haggadah.

During the meal, the following are served:

Item	Significance
Red wine	• A reminder of the lambs' blood the Jews smeared on their doorposts to save their children from the final plague • During the meal, four glasses of wine are blessed and shared to represent the four freedoms God promised in Exodus 6:6–7
Unleavened bread	• This fulfils God's command to celebrate the escape from Egypt by eating unleavened bread for seven days each year (Exodus 12:15) • Some of the bread is hidden for children to hunt for later – the finder receives a small prize
On the Seder plate: • a green vegetable, often parsley, to dip in salt water • two bitter herbs such as horseradish and romaine lettuce • charoset (a sweet paste) • an egg and a lamb bone	• The green vegetable symbolises new life in the Promised Land • The salt water represents the tears shed in slavery • The bitter herbs represent the bitterness of slavery • The sweet charoset symbolises the mortar Jews had to use when slaves, and reminds Jews that life is now sweeter • The egg and lamb bone are reminders of sacrifices made in the Temple of Jerusalem

APPLY

A Explain two ways in which Pesach celebrations remember the Jews' escape from Egypt.

B 'Pesach rituals are important because they teach Jewish children about the history of Judaism.'

Write a paragraph that supports this statement. Then write a paragraph which supports a different point of view.

TIP
Think about why Pesach rituals might be important for other reasons.

10 Exam practice

REVIEW

Test the 1 mark question

1　Which **one** of the following is a light that is kept on at all times in the synagogue?

　　A Aron Hakodesh　　B Bimah　　C Ner tamid　　D Tefillin　　　**[1 mark]**

2　Which **one** of the following is the name of the 'standing prayer', which forms the core of all Jewish prayer services?

　　A Aleinu　　B Amidah　　C Havdalah　　D Shema　　　**[1 mark]**

Test the 2 mark question

3　Give **two** ways in which Jews celebrate when a boy becomes 13 years old.　　**[2 marks]**

　　1) _____

　　2) _____

4　Give **two** ways in which Orthodox and Reform prayer services differ from each other.　　**[2 marks]**

　　1) _____

　　2) _____

Test the 4 mark question

5　Explain **two** ways in which the synagogue is used.　　**[4 marks]**

● **Explain one way.**	One way the synagogue is used is to provide education for young Jews.
● Develop your explanation with more detail/an example/ reference to a religious teaching or quotation.	For example, young Jews might take classes in Hebrew in preparation for their Bar or Bat Mitzvah.
● **Explain a second way.**	Another way the synagogue is used is for communal prayer.
● Develop your explanation with more detail/an example/ reference to a religious teaching or quotation.	For example, Orthodox synagogues hold daily services in the prayer hall so Jews can pray together.

6　Explain **two** reasons why Jews study the Tenakh and the Talmud.　　**[4 marks]**

● **Explain one reason.**	
● Develop your explanation with more detail/an example/ reference to a religious teaching or quotation.	
● **Explain a second reason.**	
● Develop your explanation with more detail/an example/ reference to a religious teaching or quotation.	

7　Explain **two** ways in which Jews celebrate Rosh Hashanah.　　**[4 marks]**

10 Exam practice

Test the 5 mark question

8 Explain **two** ways in which Shabbat is celebrated in the home.

Refer to scripture or another source of Jewish belief and teaching in your answer. **[5 marks]**

● **Explain one way.**	*One way in which Shabbat is celebrated in the home is with a special meal on the Friday evening.*
● Develop your explanation with more detail/an example.	*The meal is relaxed and might last for a few hours, with religious stories or songs between the courses.*
● **Explain a second way.**	*Another way Shabbat is celebrated in the home is through the lighting of two candles.*
● Develop your explanation with more detail/an example.	*The candles are lit just before sunset on Friday to mark the start of Shabbat.*
● Add a reference to scripture or another source of Jewish belief. If you prefer, you can add this reference to your first belief instead.	*Judaism teaches that Shabbat is like a bride or queen, and the candles are lit to welcome her into the home.*

9 Explain **two** ceremonies that take place after a Jewish baby is born.

Refer to scripture or another source of Jewish belief and teaching in your answer. **[5 marks]**

TIP

Remember that the reference to scripture or Jewish belief and teaching needs to be relevant to the point you are making. This means it should back up the point, instead of being about something else.

● **Explain one ceremony.**	
● Develop your explanation with more detail/an example.	
● **Explain a second ceremony.**	
● Develop your explanation with more detail/an example.	
● Add a reference to scripture or another source of Jewish belief. If you prefer, you can add this reference to your first belief instead.	

10 Explain **two** dietary laws that are followed by Orthodox Jews.

Refer to scripture or another source of Jewish belief and teaching in your answer. **[5 marks]**

Test the 12 mark question

11 'The most important duty of Jews is to attend the synagogue.'

Evaluate this statement. In your answer you should:

- give reasoned arguments to support this statement
- give reasoned arguments to support a different point of view
- refer to Jewish teaching
- reach a justified conclusion.

[12 marks]
Plus SPaG 3 ma

REASONED ARGUMENTS IN SUPPORT OF THE STATEMENT ● **Explain why some people would agree with the statement.** ● Develop your explanation with more detail and examples. ● Refer to religious teaching. Use a quote or paraphrase or refer to a religious authority. ● **Evaluate the arguments.** Is this a good argument or not? Explain why you think this.	*Some Jews might agree with this statement because the synagogue is the centre of the Jewish community. It is where Jews can worship, celebrate festivals and rites of passage, and meet other Jews. Attending the synagogue helps to strengthen the Jewish community.* *Jews believe it is good to pray together, and some prayers can only be said in the presence of a minyan (10 or more adults). The synagogue provides a space for prayer, which is very important to Jews because it is how they develop their relationship with God.* *Many synagogues also provide classes for Jews and have a library so Jews can learn more about their faith. This also helps them to become closer to God.*
REASONED ARGUMENTS SUPPORTING A DIFFERENT VIEW ● **Explain why some people would support a different view.** ● Develop your explanation with more detail and examples. ● Refer to religious teaching. Use a quote or paraphrase or refer to a religious authority. ● **Evaluate the arguments.** Is this a good argument or not? Explain why you think this.	*Some Jews might argue that there are more important duties for Jews. For example, they might say the most important duty is to obey the mitzvot. God expects Jews to follow his laws in return for his blessing and protection. This was made official in the covenant at Sinai so it is a duty that Jews are expected to follow.* *Other Jews might say the most important duty is simply to worship God. But they don't have to attend a synagogue to do this. For example, Jews are allowed to pray at home, and they can study the Torah at home. They can also take part in Jewish celebrations at home like the Passover Seder and the havdalah service.*
CONCLUSION ● **Give a justified conclusion.** ● Include your own opinion together with your own reasoning. ● **Include evaluation.** Explain why you think one viewpoint is stronger than the other or why you think they are equally strong. ● Do not just repeat arguments you have already used without explaining how they apply to your reasoned opinion/conclusion.	*I think most Jews would say that their most important duty is to worship God and obey his laws. Attending a synagogue, for example to pray and study, probably makes this a lot easier. But I think most Jews would say it isn't necessary, whereas obeying the mitzvot and worshipping God is.*

TIP

This is a well balanced answer, providing good support and argument for the opinions expressed, and a justified conclusion.

12 'Men and women are treated equally in Jewish practices.'

Evaluate this statement. In your answer you should:

- give reasoned arguments to support this statement
- give reasoned arguments to support a different point of view
- refer to Jewish teaching
- reach a justified conclusion.

**[12 marks]
Plus SPaG 3 marks**

> **TIP**
>
> Remember, some questions in the exam will require you to combine your knowledge of different topics. Try to consider links and connections between different topics when you revise.

REASONED ARGUMENTS IN SUPPORT OF THE STATEMENT ● **Explain why some people would agree with the statement.** ● Develop your explanation with more detail and examples. ● Refer to religious teaching. Use a quote or paraphrase or refer to a religious authority. ● **Evaluate the arguments.** Is this a good argument or not? Explain why you think this.	
REASONED ARGUMENTS SUPPORTING A DIFFERENT VIEW ● **Explain why some people would support a different view.** ● Develop your explanation with more detail and examples. ● Refer to religious teaching. Use a quote or paraphrase or refer to a religious authority. ● **Evaluate the arguments.** Is this a good argument or not? Explain why you think this.	
CONCLUSION ● **Give a justified conclusion.** ● Include your own opinion together with your own reasoning. ● **Include evaluation.** Explain why you think one viewpoint is stronger than the other or why you think they are equally strong. ● Do not just repeat arguments you have already used without explaining how they apply to your reasoned opinion/conclusion.	

13 'Jewish mourning rituals are helpful for a person who is mourning the death of someone they love.'

Evaluate this statement. In your answer you should:

- give reasoned arguments to support this statement
- give reasoned arguments to support a different point of view
- refer to Jewish teaching
- reach a justified conclusion.

**[12 marks]
Plus SPaG 3 marks**

Check your answers using the mark scheme on pages 235–236. How did you do?
To feel more secure in the content you need to remember, re-read pages 152–165.
To remind yourself of what the examiner is looking for in your answers, go to pages 8–13.

11.1 Human beings as sexual, male and female

RECAP

Essential information:

☐ The Bible says that God created men and women.

☐ Both male and female were created in the image of God and so are of equal importance and are designed to complement each other.

☐ It was part of God's plan that Adam and Eve should 'Be fruitful and multiply.'

☐ The Catholic Church views sex as exclusively **marital** (for marriage) as it is **unitive** (something that joins people together) and **procreative** (open to creating new life).

Foundational biblical understanding

Both men and women are created in the image of God and blessed by him, therefore they are equal.	66 So God created humankind in his image, in the image of God he created them; male and female he created them. God blessed them, and God said to them, 'Be fruitful and multiply' 99 *Genesis 1:27–28* (NRSV)	God created men and women.
		Men and women are expected to procreate.

In Genesis 2 God takes 'Adam' (humanity) and splits it into two complementary parts. This shows the idea of equality between sexes, as men and women complement each other. Together each person is able to give to the other what the other lacks, producing a harmony which isn't possible in isolation.

Catholic teaching about the nature and purpose of sexual love

sexual intercourse should be within marriage	**The nature and purpose of sexual love ...**	sex should be open to creating new life (procreative)

sex should be unitive (join people together)

- The sacrament of marriage enables two people in love to commit themselves publicly and exclusively to each other
- The promises made before God in the Catholic Church include a commitment to be together for life
- After these promises have been made, the commitment is **consummated** (completed or fulfilled) by the physical union of sex. For a marriage to be valid there has to be sexual intercourse
- Sex before or outside marriage is not allowed

- Through sex God creates new life
- The Catholic marriage ceremony contains the commitment to accept children lovingly from God
- 'Each and every marriage act must remain open to the transmission of life' (Humanae Vitae 11)

- Sexual love expresses and deepens the couples' love for each other
- '... the two shall become one flesh.' (Mark 10:8 (NRSV))
- Sexual intercourse between a married person and a person who is not their spouse (**adultery**) is forbidden because it destroys the unity of the married couple

APPLY

A Give two reasons why the Catholic Church views men and women as equals.

B 'Sex is so special that it should only happen in marriage.'

Explain three arguments Catholics would give to support this statement. Which do you think is the most important argument?

What arguments might a non-religious person give against this statement?

TIP

When doing an evaluation (12 mark) question it is important to be able to give judgements concerning the strengths of the arguments that may be used in supporting different points of view.

11.2 Pope John Paul II's 'Theology of the Body'

RECAP

Essential information:

- [ ] In a series of talks Pope John Paul II gave a summary of traditional Catholic teaching about the human body and sexual relationships. He said:
  - [ ] God loves every person and created both sexes to have dignity and value.
  - [ ] The full meaning of the body is appreciated through a deep relationship with the opposite sex in marriage.
  - [ ] Sex is an essential part of marriage and should only occur within marriage.
  - [ ] True mutual love includes having only the number of children that can be lovingly cared for.

Pope John Paul II's teaching about sex and the human body

Marital sex (sex within marriage)	Extramarital sex (sex outside of marriage)
Unites a couple in self-giving and love	Is a form of exploitation for personal pleasure
Brings two people into a communion of persons (sharing together)	Can make people selfish, caring only for themselves and not their marriage partner
Shows commitment, mutual love and respect, and leads to greater intimacy	Adultery breaks the marriage vows and shows no commitment to a spouse
Gives the possibility of creating new life (contraceptives should not be used)	Is a sin and distorts God's original plan for human beings
Can make use of natural periods of infertility to reduce the chances of pregnancy. Sometimes it is more loving to express fondness through non-sexual acts	Can lead people to think of others as sex objects rather than individuals with dignity and value

Contrasting views: sexual relationships and contraception

- Other Christian denominations agree with Catholics that sex should be treated with respect and consideration, and intercourse should only take place within marriage
- Catholic teaching says that sex should be open to the creation of new life
- Other Christians may differ about this point (see page 168)

Many peoples' views are somewhere in-between these two opposites

- Some people in Britain have casual sex with many partners
- Many people in Britain, including some Christians, view using contraceptives as a responsible way of preventing sexually transmitted diseases and unplanned pregnancies (see page 172)

APPLY

A Pope John Paul II's teaching shows that Catholics should respect the body and relationships. Give two examples of his teachings and explain why you think he made these points.

B 'Pope John Paul II is right to say that sexual intercourse should only take place within marriage.'

Write a paragraph to explain whether you agree or disagree with this statement. Use the table above that shows Catholic teaching about sex within and outside marriage.

TIP
Be aware not only of Catholic teaching, but also of contrasting views about the body and relationships which are found in British society today.

11.3 Human sexuality and its expression

RECAP

Essential information:

☐ The Catholic Church teaches that sex should be between a man and a woman, exclusively within marriage. Adultery is seen as wrong and an act of betrayal.

☐ Homosexual sex is not acceptable to the Catholic Church.

Sex before marriage: the teaching of the Catholic Church

> Sex before marriage devalues or trivialises it.

> As there has been no sex before marriage there is no danger of sexually transmitted diseases.

> The gift of virginity offered in marriage makes both husband and wife feel special, privileged and loved.

> " Because love is so great, so sacred, and so unique, the Church teaches young people to wait until they are married before they start to have sexual relations. "
>
> *Youcat 407*

Contrasting views

- Other Christian denominations generally share the Catholic view that sex should be saved for marriage.
- Many Christians and non-Christians in British society do have sex before marriage.
- Some have casual sex and many use contraceptives to prevent pregnancy.

Adultery

Adultery is voluntary sexual intercourse between a married person and a person who is not their spouse.

The teaching of the Catholic Church	Other Christian denominations	Contrasting/non-religious views
It breaks the vows made in marriage: 'To have and to hold from this day forward, for better, for worse'	It's wrong as it breaks the promises made in marriage	It may break a marriage promise but there may be a reason why, such as if one partner refuses to have sex. Some may not have made a 'life-long' promise
It betrays trust in the marriage and causes harm and suffering to the innocent partner		Personal happiness is important even if it may cause harm to someone else
It brings distress and tensions into the home and causes the whole family to be unhappy		There may be other reasons why the marriage is falling apart e.g. a very unhappy marriage
It can cause the break-up of the marriage		Maybe the couple made a serious mistake in getting married and have found a more suitable partner

Homosexuality: the teaching of the Catholic Church

> Sex should be open to the possibility of creating new life

> Homosexuals should live celibate lives

> Homosexual relations are not acceptable as there is no possibility of new life

> People are loved by God regardless of their sexual orientation, so should be treated with respect

Contrasting views

- The Church of England supports the idea of same-sex civil partnerships.
- Same-sex marriage was legalised in 2014 in England and Wales, reflecting the views of many in British society.
- Some United Reformed churches perform same-sex marriages.

APPLY

A Give two reasons why the Catholic Church teaches that it is wrong to have sex before marriage.

B 'The Catholic Church is unfair to homosexuals.'

Explain an argument non-Catholics would give to support this statement.

Explain reasons why a Catholic might argue against this statement. Include a relevant religious quotation.

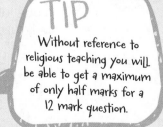

TIP

Without reference to religious teaching you will be able to get a maximum of only half marks for a 12 mark question.

11.4 A valid marriage in the Catholic Church

Essential information:

☐ For the Catholic Church to acknowledge a marriage as valid, it must meet a set of conditions.

☐ Only then can the consent (the moment when the couple commit themselves to each other for life) be made.

☐ Same-sex marriages are not recognised as valid in the eyes of the Catholic Church, as they do not allow for the acceptance of children from God.

The conditions for a valid marriage

A valid Catholic marriage …

- the marriage is not valid until it is **consummated** (the couple have given themselves to each other physically through sex)

- both promise that they will **remain together** 'for richer for poorer, in sickness and in health, to love and to cherish, till death do us part.'

- the couple must be **free to marry** (not married already to someone who is still alive, or bound by vows to the priesthood or a religious community)

- the two people must declare that they are willing to accept God's **gift of children**

- both people must be getting married of their own **free will** (pressure to get married might lead to the marriage being declared **null and void** – not valid)

- the **promises** must be made in the presence of a Catholic priest

- the actual moment of marriage is the **consent**

- the couple must not be **closely related** e.g. first cousins

> ❝The consent consists in a 'human act by which the partners mutually give themselves to each other': 'I take you to be my wife' – 'I take you to be my husband.' This consent that binds the spouses to each other finds its fulfilment in the two 'becoming one flesh.'❞
>
> *Catechism of the Catholic Church 1627*

The extension of marriage laws to same-sex couples

Catholic view	Contrasting view
• Marriage is a sacrament between a man and a woman	• In 2014, the British government legalised same–sex marriages
• Same–sex couples cannot have children naturally and lovingly from God, so cannot meet the requirements for a valid marriage	• Many people in British society (including some Christians) believe homosexuals should have the same rights as heterosexuals and so should be able to marry • They do not see being able to have children as an essential part of marriage

Pope Francis on homosexuality

When interviewed in 2013, Pope Francis set out the Catholic position. He said that the Catholic Church says that while homosexual acts are sinful, homosexuality in itself is not. Homosexuals should be integrated into society, not marginalised.

A The consent is the most important element of a Catholic marriage. Give two reasons why this is important.

B 'The Catholic Church is right not to allow same-sex marriages.'

Explain two arguments that support this statement and two that oppose it.

Consider the strength of each of the arguments. Give reasons for your judgements.

TIP
Make sure you are able to explain the conditions necessary to make a marriage valid in the Catholic Church.

RECAP

Essential information:

☐ The Church teaches that marriage is a valuable commitment that can strengthen over time.

☐ The Church disagrees with cohabitation, although many people believe it is acceptable.

The nature of marriage

Marriage is seen as …

- providing the **loving relationship** and atmosphere through which children can grow and flourish
- an **exclusive** union of a man and woman
- a **sacrament** through which God's love and blessing is given to a couple
- a **sign** of the love of Christ for the Church.

TIP

Use a mnemonic to help you remember these points: LESS – loving relationship, exclusive, sacrament, sign.

The marriage promises

These promises are made after the consent is given in the marriage ceremony.

| The **public declaration** assures each other that their love is genuine and asks for the church community's support. |

> ❝I call upon these persons here present to witness that I, (full name), take you (full name) to be my lawful wedded husband/wife, to have and to hold from this day forward, for better for worse, for richer for poorer, in sickness and in health, to love and to cherish, till death do us part.❞

| The commitment only **ends** when one partner dies. |

| The full names are used to ensure everyone knows the **identity** of those making the promises. |

| By making the **same promises** the husband and wife show that there is equal commitment in marriage. |

| The promises recognise that there may be **difficulties** as well as good times e.g. health or financial problems. |

| They promise to fulfil a loving **relationship**. |

Cohabitation

Cohabitation (a couple living together and having a sexual relationship without being married to one another) is quite common in Britain today. Some people want to see if the relationship works out, or live together for financial reasons. Some live in committed relationships throughout their lives. Others are in same-sex relationships and cohabit until they decide if they wish to have a civil partnership or get married.

| it may destroy the sense of family | it breaks the sanctity of the sexual union | it breaks the sanctity of marriage |

| if the couple split up it affects children | **The Catholic Church disagrees with cohabitation because …** | it may reduce effort to make the relationship last |

| it may create insecurity as one might leave | it may destroy a sense of need for faithfulness | it removes commitment from the sexual union |

APPLY

 A Explain two contrasting beliefs about cohabitation.

 B 'The marriage promises strengthen a marriage.'

Develop an argument to support this statement and include why most Catholics would agree with it.

TIP

Number each of the two beliefs to show you have written about two different ones as required. Don't write about just one, or three, or more.

RECAP

Essential information:

- [ ] If there is a reason why a marriage was not valid according to the Catholic Church, it will allow an **annulment** (a statement by the Catholic Church that there was no valid marriage in the first place).
- [ ] This means that the two people are free to marry again in the Catholic Church.
- [ ] The Catholic Church does not accept the possibility of remarriage in a valid sacramental marriage after a divorce.

Annulment

An annulment may be allowed if:

- one partner does not take the exclusive nature of marriage seriously, e.g. continues to have affairs
- the couple never had sexual intercourse
- they always insist on using contraception, so refusing to accept God's gift of children
- they didn't freely enter into marriage, e.g. were forced by parents to marry.

Divorce and remarriage

Catholics recognise that sometimes people make a serious mistake and cannot continue to live together. This might result in a legal divorce, e.g. to settle financial affairs. Remarriage is when a person who has been married before goes on to marry another person.

The Catholic position on divorce

- marriage promises made before God cannot be broken
- God made man and woman to be united as one
- Jesus taught that a divorcee remarrying commits adultery (Mark 10:11–12)
- marriage is 'till death do us part'

The Catholic position on remarriage

- can happen if the original partner has died
- anyone who divorces and remarries cannot receive communion
- allowed if the first 'marriage' is annulled, so is not classed as remarriage
- not allowed to remarry in church if the original spouse is still alive

Contrasting views

Topic	Catholic view	Other views
Divorce	• People should stick by their marriage promises • The couple knew what they were committing to	• It is impossible to know what the future holds • If the marriage has broken down, divorce may be the compassionate solution
Remarriage	• Should not happen if the original partner is still alive as Catholics believe in the sanctity of marriage • 'a new union cannot be recognised as valid, if the first marriage was.' (Catechism of the Catholic Church 1650) • The couple will not be able to receive communion	• Anglicans, Methodists and other free churches do not encourage remarriage but will sometimes marry divorcees • Most Protestant denominations will not stop those who remarry from receiving communion

APPLY

A Give two reasons why the Catholic Church might annul a marriage.

B 'Catholics should be allowed to get divorced.'

Develop an argument to support this statement and one which opposes it. Include Catholic teaching in your answer.

TIP
It is important to understand the difference between an annulment and a divorce.

RECAP

Essential information:

☐ The Catholic Church does not allow artificial contraception but does allow natural family planning.

☐ Many people disagree with the Church's view on artificial contraception, for both family planning and health reasons.

Catholic teaching on family planning and contraception

The Catholic Church believes:

- sex is important within marriage as it is the final expression of the total commitment of the couple to each other
- every act of sex should be both unitive and procreative – these two purposes cannot be separated
- using **artificial contraception** (unnatural methods used to prevent a pregnancy from taking place) is not allowed as it makes sex non-procreative and separates the two purposes
- **family planning** (the practice of controlling how many children couples have, and when they have them) is allowed if it is done naturally.

natural family planning reduces the chances of conception but leaves the final decision to God

The Catholic Church and family planning ...

recent Popes have stressed the need for responsible parenthood

couples should only have the number of children they can care for

the use of natural family planning (using the woman's natural monthly cycle to reduce or increase the chance of conception) is acceptable

Contrasting views

Views in British society	Catholic response
Many people (including some Christians) say contraceptives are essential to stop the spread of sexually transmitted infections (STIs)	If both partners do not have sex with others before or outside marriage there is little chance of contracting an STI
It is responsible to use contraceptives to prevent unwanted pregnancies	The final decision about pregnancies should be left up to God
Many Christian denominations say that using contraception prevents the family from having too many children to support	Natural family planning can prevent families from being too large
The world is becoming over-populated, so limiting family sizes is a responsible action	Genesis 1:22 says, 'Be fruitful and multiply': it is wrong to stop God's gift, lovingly intended for a married couple
It is acceptable to use the morning-after pill as it prevents the egg developing and an unwanted pregnancy	Life begins at conception so using the morning-after pill is wrong as fertilisation may have already taken place

APPLY

A Explain the difference between using natural family planning and using contraceptives. Why does the Catholic Church support one but not the other method of limiting the number of children in a family?

B 'The Church's teaching on the use of contraception ignores the needs of the modern world.'

Evaluate this statement. Consider arguments that would support it and those that would oppose it. Write a paragraph explaining your conclusion and the reasons for it.

TIP

You are marked for your spelling, punctuation and grammar (SPaG) in 12 mark answers. Make sure that you include specialist terminology where appropriate, and that you spell the terms correctly.

Essential information:

☐ The Church views the family as a Church in miniature, with several important roles.

☐ The family is the best place for procreation and raising children.

☐ The family provides children with stability and education for life.

Catholic views on the family

The Catholic Church values the family as a Church in miniature with four main tasks:

- to form a community (group of people)
- to help with the life and personal development of each other
- to take part in the development of the wider society
- to be part of the life and mission of the Church.

The Catholic Church sees the stability and happiness of family life as vitally important for the development of society. A family is made up of a number of related individuals, and there are different types of family:

Nuclear family	Extended family	Other families
Consists of mother, father and children living together	Has additional relatives to the nuclear family, such as grandparents, aunts, uncles	May consist of a single parent with children or a same-sex couple with or without children
The usual type of family for most Catholic families in British society	This is common in some cultures and religions. Sometimes Catholics also live with their grandparents	Becoming more common in British society but not normally among Catholics

Procreation and security

The Catholic Church teaches that:

- the family is the best environment to bring up children
- children are signs of the parents' love for each other
- the family provides a stable and safe place for children to develop
- the family provides the opportunity to be mutually supportive.

Education

The Catholic Church believes that:

- parents are the first and most important teachers of their children
- parents are the role models for their children
- parents should encourage their children to become independent, well balanced individuals who respect everyone
- parents need to provide an atmosphere where everyone is valued.

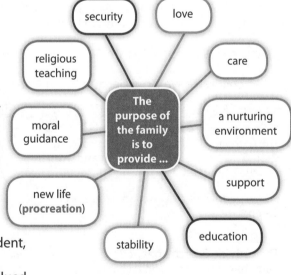

The purpose of the family is to provide ... security, love, care, a nurturing environment, support, education, stability, new life (procreation), moral guidance, religious teaching

A 'The welfare and future of a State depend on the ability of the smallest unit, the family, to live and develop.' (Youcat 370)

This quote means that the future and wellbeing of a country is determined by what happens in family life. Explain two ways in which the Catholic Church encourages family life to flourish.

B 'The main purpose of the family is to provide security.'

Develop arguments to support this statement and arguments to oppose it.

TIP
Examiners will be looking to see if you have commented on the strength of the arguments you have given.

RECAP

Essential information:

☐ The Catholic Church believes that people play different roles within a family, with the purpose of working together to produce a harmonious whole.

☐ The Church encourages families to be founded on the marriage between a man and a woman.

Roles within the family

Paul, in writing his letter to the Ephesians, said:

> People should live family lives as if they are serving Jesus.

> Wives should show their love by doing what their husbands ask.

> Children should honour their parents by obeying them as God commands it.

> Fathers should show love and kindness to children, so they should bring them up in the Christian faith.

> Husbands should love their wives so much they would be prepared to die for them.

> 66 Be subject to one another out of reverence for Christ. Wives, be subject to your husbands as you are to the Lord ... Husbands, love your wives, just as Christ loved the church and gave himself up for her ... Children, obey your parents in the Lord, for this is right. 'Honour your father and mother' ... fathers, do not provoke your children to anger, but bring them up in the discipline and instruction of the Lord. 99
>
> *Ephesians 5:21 and 6:1–4 (NRSV)*

The dignity of work in the home

- Traditionally, Catholics have believed that the important role of the mother is to look after the home and children. The father's role included protecting and providing for the needs of the family, and teaching by word and example.
- Catholics regard men and women as equally important in contributing different qualities to help in bringing up children, and providing security and stability in the home.
- Nowadays, many mothers also go out to work part- or full-time to help provide for the family financially.
- Gender equality has resulted in traditional roles sometimes being shared or even switched.

Families with single or same-sex parents

Not all children have a mother and father living at home.

Catholic teaching	Parenthood in Britain
The Catholic Church teaches that procreation should take place between a man and woman who have married	There is a growing acceptance and number of single parent families or same-sex parents in British society
Single people are not encouraged to become parents	Around a quarter of children in Britain today live with one parent
The Catholic Church does not encourage same-sex parenting as it teaches that children need a mother and a father	Same-sex parents may say that it is the love between parents and children that really matters

APPLY

A What do Catholics believe about the importance of a mother's role in the family? Explain how that role is changing in modern Britain.

B 'The Catholic Church should support families that have same-sex parents.'

Evaluate this statement. This may include considering what the word 'support' may mean, and thinking about the roles of families and the Catholic Church.

TIP

It is important to know the similarities and differences between Catholic teaching and non-religious responses to the specified issues.

11.10 Gender equality in the Bible

Essential information:

☐ The Bible was written during times when men were perceived as superior to women.

☐ However, women play a very important role in the Bible and the early Christian Church.

☐ The Genesis stories show that men and women were created as equals.

The creation of men and women as equals

Genesis 2:23–24 says that woman was created from the bone of a man but only together are they the full form of a human being – they are two equal parts that complement and complete each other.

Paul taught that men and women are equal:

> **"** There is no longer Jew or Greek, there is no longer slave or free, there is no longer male and female; for all of you are one in Christ Jesus. **"**
> *Galatians 3:28* (NRSV)

> **"** … in the image of God he created them; male and female he created them. **"**
> *Genesis 1:27* (NRSV)

The importance of women in the Bible

In the Old Testament, women have special roles on the same level as men. In the New Testament, the importance and dignity of women is symbolised in Mary, the mother of Jesus. Jesus always treated women with respect, and his teachings about divorce and adultery applied the same standard to women as to men.

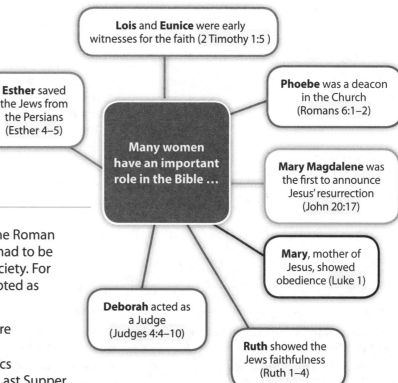

Lois and **Eunice** were early witnesses for the faith (2 Timothy 1:5)

Esther saved the Jews from the Persians (Esther 4–5)

Many women have an important role in the Bible …

Phoebe was a deacon in the Church (Romans 6:1–2)

Mary Magdalene was the first to announce Jesus' resurrection (John 20:17)

Mary, mother of Jesus, showed obedience (Luke 1)

Deborah acted as a Judge (Judges 4:4–10)

Ruth showed the Jews faithfulness (Ruth 1–4)

The importance of men in the Bible

Society was very different in Biblical times. The Roman Empire was male-dominated and Christians had to be careful about challenging the structure of society. For example, women would not have been accepted as travelling preachers.

- Most of the events recorded in the Bible are about men.
- Jesus chose 12 male apostles who Catholics believe were made the first priests at the Last Supper.
- The first missionaries and main leaders of the Church were men.

APPLY

A Explain two ways in which the Bible shows that men and women are of equal importance.

B 'Christianity has always undervalued women.'

Consider arguments that could be used in a debate on this issue. Include Christian beliefs about the role of men and women, and consider the views of the society in which they live. Write a paragraph giving your opinion and justifying your conclusion.

TIP
Consider the significance of the role of two of the women mentioned in the diagram above.

TIP
Be aware that men were regarded as superior to women in society in biblical times, and this limited what a woman was allowed to do.

RECAP

Essential information:

☐ The Catholic Church believes in the equality of men and women, as God made both in his image and likeness (Genesis 1:27).

☐ This does not mean that men and women are the same, but that they have equal dignity and equal rights.

☐ God gave men and women differences but when they unite in marriage, they create a natural bond that strengthens and completes them as individuals and as a couple.

☐ The fact that men and women are not identical helps them to value the gifts and qualities of each other.

Catholic teaching on equality

The attributes of a woman are as important as that of a man.

❝The personal resources of femininity are certainly no less than the resources of masculinity: they are merely different.❞

Mulieris Dignitatem 10

Equality is not the same as uniformity.

It was God's deliberate choice to create men and women as a pair.

❝Man and woman were made 'for each other' – not that God left them half-made and incomplete: he created them to be a communion of persons, in which each can be 'helpmate' to the other, for they are equal as persons … and complementary as masculine and feminine.❞

Catechism of the Catholic Church 372

Men and women have equal roles in supporting each other.

God designed men and women to care for each other.

Contrasting views

Catholic view	Non-religious (including humanist or atheist) view
Men and women are equally important	Most agree with the equality of sexes
Men and women have different roles, for example men may be priests	Treating women as equals means allowing them equal opportunities
Women and men have different yet complementary roles to perform	Men and women are equally capable of fulfilling the same roles, including roles in the home

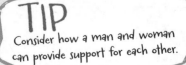

APPLY

Ⓐ Explain what Catholics mean when they say that men and women are equal but different.

Ⓑ 'The Catholic view of men and women is sexist.'

Write one paragraph giving arguments that agree or disagree with this statement, and a second paragraph supporting a different point of view.

TIP
Consider how a man and woman can provide support for each other.

TIP
Be able to compare Catholic beliefs with what other people in Britain today, religious or non-religious, believe.

RECAP

Essential information:

☐ The attitude that women are superior to men or men are superior to women is **gender prejudice**. This might result from stereotyping – expecting a man or woman to behave in a certain way because of their gender.

☐ Putting this attitude into action is **gender discrimination**. For example, a manager of a building site may refuse to employ a woman because s/he thinks a man is stronger.

☐ The Church does not accept gender discrimination, although some people say that the Church's view on the different roles of men and women can lead to gender discrimination.

Catholic teachings on gender discrimination

Catholic teaching does not generally support gender discrimination because of the negative effect it can have on individuals and society. The Catholic Church has championed the rights of women in the home and family, in the workplace, and within society.

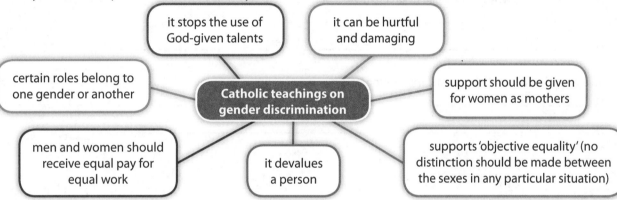

- it stops the use of God-given talents
- it can be hurtful and damaging
- certain roles belong to one gender or another
- **Catholic teachings on gender discrimination**
- support should be given for women as mothers
- men and women should receive equal pay for equal work
- it devalues a person
- supports 'objective equality' (no distinction should be made between the sexes in any particular situation)

Gender discrimination in Britain today

Catholic view	Non-religious viewpoints
• In general, gender discrimination should not happen	• The 1975 Sex Discrimination Act was designed to prevent gender discrimination
• Catholics do not support women being paid less for doing the same job as men • Pope Francis said, 'They [women] have the same rights. The disparity is a pure scandal.'	• Men and women should be given equal pay • It is wrong that, while women make up about half of the workforce, men hold most of the senior positions
• Men and women should be able to fulfil particular roles, for example, women who choose to look after the home and children should be supported. However, only men are allowed to become priests	• The Catholic view of the different roles of men and women is a form of discrimination • Increasingly, roles traditionally reserved for women and men are being shared or switched. Other Christian denominations allow women as vicars, ministers or pastors
• Positive discrimination may have a good intention but 'labour should be structured in such a way that women do not have to pay for their advancement by abandoning what is specific to them.' (Compendium of the Social Doctrine of the Church 295) • In others words, defending women's rights must not detract from a woman's role in the family and in the home	• There is a need for positive discrimination if, for example, a company has nearly all male managers and they wish to deliberately promote some women to create a more gender-balanced situation • This would be particularly the case where there had been discrimination against female employees in the past

APPLY

A Give two examples of gender discrimination in Britain today.

B 'There will always be gender prejudice.'

Evaluate this statement, considering both positive and negative discrimination, and what the law, the Catholic Church, and society says and does. Outline the arguments you would use and write a justified conclusion.

> **TIP**
> For a 'give' question examiners expect a brief answer. Explanation is not required. Number your points 1 and 2 so it is clear you have given two examples.

11 Exam practice

Test the 1 mark question

1. The Catholic Church teaches that sexual intercourse should only take place within marriage.
   Which **one** of the following is a term given to having sex outside of marriage?

   A ☐ Marital   B ☐ Unitive   C ☐ Adultery   D ☐ Consummation **[1 mark]**

2. Catholic teaching does not support sexual relationships between people of the same gender.
   Which **one** of the following is the term used for such a relationship?

   A ☐ Heterosexual   B ☐ Transsexual   C ☐ Asexual   D ☐ Homosexual **[1 mark]**

Test the 2 mark question

3. Give **two** reasons why the Catholic Church will not marry same-sex couples. **[2 marks]**

   1) _____

   2) _____

4. Give **two** Christian beliefs about cohabitation. **[2 marks]**

   1) _____

   2) _____

Test the 4 mark question

5. Explain **two** contrasting beliefs in British society about the use of contraception.
   - You must refer to a Christian belief or view.
   - Your contrasting belief or view may come from Christianity or from another religious or non-religious tradition. **[4 marks]**

   > **TIP**
   > By 'contrasting' the examiner means that they are looking for different beliefs.

● **Explain one belief.**	The Catholic Church teaches that it is wrong to use artificial contraception, as it makes sexual intercourse non-procreative.
● Develop your explanation with more detail/an example/ reference to a religious teaching or quotation.	This means that it prevents God deciding whether or not, through the couple's relationship, there should be new life.
● **Explain a second contrasting belief.**	Many Christians support the use of contraception as it helps the planning of when the family has children.
● Develop your explanation with more detail/an example/ reference to a religious teaching or quotation.	This prevents unwanted pregnancies and ensures that the family is able to care and financially provide for their children.

6. Explain **two** contrasting beliefs in contemporary British society about sex before marriage.
   - You must refer to a Christian belief or view.
   - Your contrasting belief or view may come from Christianity or from another religious or non-religious tradition. **[4 marks]**

● **Explain one belief.**	
● Develop your explanation with more detail/an example/reference to a religious teaching or quotation.	
● **Explain a second contrasting belief.**	
● Develop your explanation with more detail/an example/reference to a religious teaching or quotation.	

7 Explain **two** similar beliefs in contemporary British society about a married person having an affair.

- You must refer to a Christian belief or view.
- Your similar belief or view may come from Christianity or from another religious or non-religious tradition.

TIP
Be aware that you can be asked for similarities as well as contrasts in the 4 mark theme questions.

[4 marks]

Test the 5 mark question

8 Explain **two** Christian beliefs about divorce.

Refer to scripture or another source of Christian belief and teaching in your answer.

[5 marks]

● **Explain one belief.**	Christians believe that when a couple gets married in Church they make the promise before God to stay together until one partner dies.
● Develop your explanation with more detail/an example.	This means that divorce is not something the Christian Church wants to happen as divorce is breaking the solemn promise made as part of the marriage vows 'till death do us part'.
● **Explain a second belief.**	A second Christian belief concerns the teaching of Jesus, as he said that anyone who has divorced and then married another person commits adultery.
● Develop your explanation with more detail/an example.	Catholics believe that divorce is wrong because if the person remarries while his or her original partner is still alive they will be committing adultery. The Church regards adultery as a sin and therefore it should be avoided.
● Add a reference to scripture or another source of religious belief. If you prefer, you can add this reference to your first belief instead.	'Whoever divorces his wife and marries another commits adultery against her; and if she divorces her husband and marries another, she commits adultery.' (Mark 10:11–12)

9 Explain **two** religious beliefs about the nature of marriage.

Refer to scripture or another source of Christian belief and teaching in your answer.

[5 marks]

● **Explain one belief.**	
● Develop your explanation with more detail/an example.	
● **Explain a second belief.**	
● Develop your explanation with more detail/an example.	
● Add a reference to scripture or another source of religious belief. If you prefer, you can add this reference to your first belief instead.	

10 Explain **two** Christian beliefs about gender equality.

Refer to scripture or another source of Christian belief and teaching in your answer.

[5 marks]

Test the 12 mark question

11 'A family is still a family, no matter what gender the parents are.'

Evaluate this statement. In your answer you:

- should give reasoned arguments in support of this statement
- should give reasoned arguments to support a different point of view
- should refer to Christian arguments
- may refer to non-religious arguments
- should reach a justified conclusion.

[12 marks]
Plus SPaG 3 mar▶

REASONED ARGUMENTS IN SUPPORT OF THE STATEMENT ● **Explain why some people would agree with the statement.** ● Develop your explanation with more detail and examples. ● Refer to religious teaching. Use a quote or paraphrase or refer to a religious authority. ● **Evaluate the arguments.** Is this a good argument or not? Explain why you think this.	Many people would agree with this statement as same-sex marriages are now allowed by law in Britain today. Although same-sex couples are unable to have a family naturally they may adopt or use in vitro fertilisation or surrogates to have children. Many non-religious people believe that this is fine as long as same-sex parents are loving and caring, have good parenting skills, and are willing to put a lot of time and effort into nurturing their children. They would argue that they are just as much a family as those who have heterosexual parents. Same-sex couples will teach their children what is right and wrong just as other parents do. They will ensure their children have respect for others no matter what their sexuality. The children will learn to love and relate to people through the example of the love shown by the same-sex couple for each other. This is just the same as any family and so is a strong and convincing argument in favour of the statement.
REASONED ARGUMENTS SUPPORTING A DIFFERENT VIEW ● **Explain why some people would support a different view.** ● Develop your explanation with more detail and examples. ● Refer to religious teaching. Use a quote or paraphrase or refer to a religious authority. ● **Evaluate the arguments.** Is this a good argument or not? Explain why you think this.	The Catholic Church would disagree with this statement because it disapproves of same-sex parents. It teaches that children in a family need both a mother and father. It argues that God made people male and female so that they would 'be fruitful and multiply' (Genesis 1:28). Same-sex couples cannot do this naturally so the children will not be the fulfilment of the love of the husband and wife. Therefore to Catholics the gender of the parents does matter and is basic to their beliefs about the family. A family exists where children are able to grow up with a male and female role model as parents. Moreover, some religious people disagree with homosexual relationships and so would not accept same-sex parents as they would regard their behaviour as wrong. The Ten Commandments say that children should honour their mother and father but this couldn't be done if the parents are both of the same sex.
CONCLUSION ● **Give a justified conclusion.** ● Include your own opinion together with your own reasoning. ● **Include evaluation.** Explain why you think one viewpoint is stronger than the other or why you think they are equally strong. ● Do not just repeat arguments you have already used without explaining how they apply to your reasoned opinion/conclusion.	In conclusion, I think that whether or not you agree with the statement depends on your definition of a family. A dictionary definition says that a family is a group of people related to each other such as a mother and father and their children. A family with same-sex parents might not be related to each other by blood and there would be either two fathers or two mothers but not one of each. If you believe, like most Catholics, in that definition then it is clear that the statement is incorrect. Personally though I think that the definition is a narrow one because there are different types of family including extended families, single-parent families and same-sex parent families. A family to me is a group of people bringing up their children and so I would disagree with the statement. Same-sex parents can give the same love to their children as any other type of family and that is what I think is important.

TIP

The final sentence shows a judgement being made of the strength of the argument.

TIP

This is a detailed explanation of a viewpoint that is different from that in the statement. There is clear and accurate reference to a religious viewpoint, including specific religious teachings.

TIP

This is a justified conclusion.

12 'There is really no difference between a divorce and an annulment.'

Evaluate this statement. In your answer you:

- should give reasoned arguments in support of this statement
- should give reasoned arguments to support a different point of view
- should refer to Christian arguments
- may refer to non-religious arguments
- should reach a justified conclusion.

TIP

For 'should' read 'must', and it is also useful to refer to non-religious arguments.

[12 marks]
Plus SPaG 3 marks

REASONED ARGUMENTS IN SUPPORT OF THE STATEMENT

- **Explain why some people would agree with the statement.**

- Develop your explanation with more detail and examples.

- Refer to religious teaching. Use a quote or paraphrase or refer to a religious authority.

- **Evaluate the arguments.** Is this a good argument or not? Explain why you think this.

REASONED ARGUMENTS SUPPORTING A DIFFERENT VIEW

- **Explain why some people would support a different view.**

- Develop your explanation with more detail and examples.

- Refer to religious teaching. Use a quote or paraphrase or refer to a religious authority.

- **Evaluate the arguments.** Is this a good argument or not? Explain why you think this.

CONCLUSION

- **Give a justified conclusion.**

- Include your own opinion together with your own reasoning.

- **Include evaluation.** Explain why you think one viewpoint is stronger than the other or why you think they are equally strong.

- Do not just repeat arguments you have already used without explaining how they apply to your reasoned opinion/conclusion.

13 'People should not be allowed to remarry in a church.'

Evaluate this statement. In your answer you:

- should give reasoned arguments in support of this statement
- should give reasoned arguments to support a different point of view
- should refer to Christian arguments
- may refer to non-religious arguments
- should reach a justified conclusion.

[12 marks]
Plus SPaG 3 marks

Check your answers using the mark scheme on pages 236–237. How did you do?
To feel more secure in the content you need to remember, re-read pages 170–181.
To remind yourself of what the examiner is looking for in your answers, go to pages 8–13.

12.1 Biblical perspectives on violence and bullying

RECAP

Essential information:

☐ In the beginning God created a world that was 'very good' (Genesis 1:31 (NRSV)). It included a place of **paradise** – the garden of Eden.

☐ The Bible says that humans **rejected God's rules** and this disobedience brought sin, which **corrupted human nature**.

☐ Sin brought feelings of anger, which lead to violence and bullying.

Ideas about violence in the Bible

- Some Christians believe the early chapters of Genesis to be myths, but whether the stories are literally true or not, they make important points about human nature and the result of turning against God.
- **Violence** (using actions that can threaten or harm others) is a rejection of the ideals God wants for the world.
- Jesus taught that the seeds of bitterness, anger and jealousy need to be controlled, as they may lead to violence and murder.
- People need a deep feeling of wellbeing and an inner calm – the peace that Jesus gives (John 14:27) – to face life's challenges.

> ❝You have heard that it was said to those of ancient times, 'You shall not murder'; and 'whoever murders shall be liable to judgement.' But I say to you that if you are angry with a brother or sister, you will be liable to judgement; and if you insult a brother or sister, you will be liable to the council; and if you say, 'You fool', you will be liable to the hell of fire. ❞
>
> *Matthew 5:21–22* (NRSV)

TIP

If a quote is too long to remember, you can summarise it, e.g. 'In the Old Testament it was said that murderers would be judged, but Jesus said that those who are angry will also receive judgement.'

Wrong thoughts can turn into action, as in the story of Cain and Abel:

| Cain was jealous of his brother Abel | → | God said to Cain 'sin is lurking at the door … you must master it' (Genesis 4:7 (NRSV)) | → | Cain's angry thoughts led to violence | → | Cain plotted to kill his brother out in the field | → | 'Cain rose up against his brother Abel, and killed him' (Genesis 4:8 (NRSV)) | → | God said to Cain 'your brother's blood is crying out to me from the ground' (Genesis 4:10 (NRSV)) |

Bullying

- **Bullying** (the deliberate intimidation of a person through words or physical actions) is a destructive form of violence.
- Words can destroy a person's self-esteem, cause fear, and leave them with a sense of powerlessness. James 3:3–12 refers to the power of words to harm.
- Comments published on social media or the internet can bring more distress.

APPLY

Ⓐ James said, 'but no one can tame the tongue – a restless evil, full of deadly poison. With it we bless the Lord and Father, and with it we curse those who are made in the likeness of God.' (James 3:8–9 (NRSV))

Explain what James meant and why it is important for people to be careful about what they say.

TIP

Quotations from scripture help to get high marks in an evaluation question, but you can express them in your own words.

Ⓑ 'The key to preventing violence is to control one's thoughts.'

Develop arguments to support this idea. Refer to biblical teaching.

12.2 Forgiveness and reconciliation

RECAP

Essential information:

- [ ] A central message in Jesus' teaching is the importance of forgiveness.
- [ ] If people want God's forgiveness they must forgive others.
- [ ] Jesus taught that reconciliation is important and should take place before giving an offering to God.

Forgiveness

Forgiveness is showing grace and mercy, and pardoning someone for what they have done wrong. Jesus asked God to forgive those who crucified him.

> **❝**Father, forgive them; for they do not know what they are doing.**❞** *Luke 23:34 (NRSV)*

There are many biblical teachings on forgiveness:

- Jesus forgave Peter for denying him (John 21:15–17).
- Peter asked how many times he should forgive his brother, 'As many as seven times?' Jesus replied, 'seventy-seven times' (Matthew 18:21–22), meaning we should always forgive.
- The Lord's Prayer says, 'forgive us our debts, as we also have forgiven our debtors' (Matthew 6:12), teaching that Christians must forgive others.
- The message of the parable of the Unforgiving Servant is that God only forgives those who are willing to forgive others (Matthew 18:23–35).

Reconciliation

Reconciliation is the restoring of harmony after relationships have broken down.

- Pope Francis has called for reconciliation and respect between religions.
- In Matthew 5:24, Jesus emphasised the importance of reconciliation by saying that if you are bringing a gift to God but have a problem with someone you need to sort it out first.
- Reconciliation leads to the peace that Jesus prayed for at the Last Supper:

> **❝**Peace I leave with you; my peace I give to you. I do not give to you as the world gives. Do not let your hearts be troubled and do not let them be afraid.**❞** *John 14:27 (NRSV)*

Reconciliation brings … appreciation and acceptance of each other; a stronger relationship; a more peaceful future; an opportunity to live without fear; respect for others' religions and beliefs; opportunities to learn from the past

APPLY

A Explain two things that the Bible teaches about reconciliation.

B 'If everyone followed the biblical teachings about forgiveness it would end all hatred in the world.'

Write one paragraph supporting this statement and another paragraph giving a different point of view. Write a justified conclusion stating your opinion. Below are some ideas which may help you start your answer.

> **TIP**
> All 4 mark questions will ask for two reasons, names, examples, teachings, ways, etc.

One view	Another view
"18-year-old Anthony Walker was killed in a racial attack but his mother and sister said that they forgave his murderers because Jesus forgave those who crucified him."	"Unfortunately this is idealistic. There will never be a time when everyone follows biblical teaching about forgiveness, as many do not believe in the Bible and what it says."

12.3 Justice

Essential information:

- ☐ Christians believe that establishing justice helps God's Kingdom to spread on earth.
- ☐ **Justice** is bringing about what is right and fair, according to the law, or making up for a wrong that has been committed.
- ☐ Some Christians believe that **righteous anger** (anger against injustice) can be effectively used to help create justice.
- ☐ Christians generally support peaceful protests against injustice but most do not believe in violent protests.

The importance of justice

- The Catholic Church teaches that it is God's desire that everyone should be treated fairly.
- The Old Testament prophet Amos taught that creating justice is more important than ensuring that worship is done correctly.

Injustice can cause people to lose their sense of self-worth and self-respect. It can deny people dignity because they have been treated unfairly, e.g. black people suffered during the apartheid era in South Africa.

> ❝Take away from me the noise of your songs; I will not listen to the melody of your harps. But let justice roll down like waters, and righteousness like an ever-flowing stream.❞
>
> *Amos 5:23–24 (NRSV)*

> ❝Building a just social and civil order, wherein each person receives what is his or her due, is an essential task which every generation must take up anew.❞
>
> *Deus Caritas Est 28*

Righteous anger as a response to injustice

- Although Jesus taught that anger should be avoided whenever possible, he showed righteous anger when he drove the sellers from the Temple as they had turned it into a market place (John 2:13–17).
- Many Christians believe that righteous anger is acceptable because it can be controlled and channelled into positive action, which can improve a situation.

Violent protest as a response to injustice – contrasting views

Most Christians are against violent protest 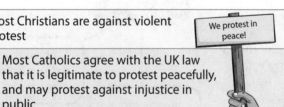	Some people will support violent protest in some circumstances providing no people are harmed 
• Most Catholics agree with the UK law that it is legitimate to protest peacefully, and may protest against injustice in public • They may take part in a peaceful march or procession to make their point	• Some people will join others in taking part in protests which they accept may lead to violence, if they believe that it is the only way to get the government to take notice and end injustice
• Many Christians believe that violent protest is an ineffective and damaging way to create change, and may result in loss of life	• Some people supported violent protests by the suffragette movement in the early twentieth century • The Church took part in protests which became violent against the government in the Democratic Republic of Congo in 2015

A Explain two reasons why some Catholics would agree with the idea of righteous anger.

B 'It is never right to use violent protest to end injustice.'

Write a paragraph giving reasons to support the statement and then one explaining why some people may consider that it may be sometimes right to use violent protest. Remember to refer to Christian beliefs or teaching. Add a conclusion which may include your own opinion.

> **TIP**
> Look for the key words in the statement to ensure that your focus is correct: 'never right', 'use violent protest', 'end injustice' – make sure you use these terms in your answer.

12.4 The just war theory

Essential information:

☐ The New Testament contains teachings that suggest a limited use of violence is acceptable.

☐ St Augustine and St Thomas Aquinas devised a set of conditions that made fighting a war justifiable.

☐ Many Catholics accept the **just war theory** (a set of criteria that a war needs to meet before it can be justified) and that war is sometimes necessary.

Background to the just war theory

- Jesus said, 'The one who has no sword must sell his cloak and buy one' (Luke 22:36 (NRSV)).
- The early Christians refused to fight in wars as they did not believe they had the right to take someone else's life.
- After 370 CE, Christianity became the official religion of the Roman Empire. Christians faced the choice of either fighting or allowing the empire to be overrun by invaders.

Conditions for a just war

The Catechism of the Catholic Church gives strict conditions for a just war:

> **"** At one and the same time:
> - the damage inflicted by the aggressor … must be lasting, grave, and certain;
> - all other means of putting an end to it must have been shown to be impractical or ineffective;
> - there must be serious prospects of success;
> - the use of arms must not produce evils and disorders graver than the evil to be eliminated. **"**

Just war criteria include …

- it must be a just **cause** e.g. self-defence
- it must be the **last resort**, having tried to solve the dispute
- there must be a reasonable **chance of winning** and bringing lasting peace
- **innocent civilians** should not be attacked
- only **proportional force** should be used – weapons must not be too destructive
- it must be declared by a legitimate authority e.g. by a **state** or sovereign (government)

Contrasting views on the just war theory

The army should only go to war when there has been a major abuse of power or there is a serious threat to the security of Britain

The just war theory is dangerous as it could be used to defend the concept of war. It is outdated and not relevant to twenty-first century warfare

Opinions in British society

It is so much better if war can be avoided by working together, including with the United Nations, to avoid conflict

We should only support a war that meets the just war criteria, as only then can it be justified

A Explain two of the conditions which may make a war 'just'.

B 'No war can ever be just.'

Evaluate this statement. Include more than one point of view, and refer to Catholic beliefs and teachings in your answer. Be sure to give reasons for your opinion. Make sure you give a strong conclusion.

TIP

Use a mnemonic to help remember some just war criteria e.g. CLIPS:

C – just cause
L – last resort
I – innocent civilians
P – proportional force
S – state or sovereign.

RECAP

Essential information:

☐ The Catholic Church opposes nuclear war and the use of other weapons of mass destruction such as chemical weapons and biological weapons.

☐ Many people, including some Catholics, have different opinions about possessing weapons of mass destruction.

Catholic attitudes to nuclear war and weapons of mass destruction

There are five main reasons why the Catholic Church opposes the use of **nuclear weapons** (which work by creating a nuclear reaction in order to devastate huge areas and kill large numbers of people) and **weapons of mass destruction** (WMDs – weapons that can kill large numbers of people and/or cause great damage), including **chemical weapons** (these use chemicals to harm humans and destroy the natural environment) and **biological weapons** (these use living organisms to cause disease or death).

1: They are completely indiscriminate and have long-term effects	**2:** They are totally disproportionate to any possible success that may follow	**3:** With WMDs the possibility of success is small; there are no 'victors, only victims' (Pope Benedict XVI)	**4:** The cost of researching, building and maintaining these weapons is great; it prevents governments from spending to improve people's lives	**5:** Possession of these weapons increases tension and fear, making the world less safe

Pope John XXIII made the following comments, which summed up Catholic beliefs about weapons of mass destruction:

> " We are deeply distressed to see the enormous stocks of armaments that have been, and continue to be, manufactured … involving a vast outlay of intellectual and material resources … while other countries lack the help they need …
>
> Consequently people are living in the grip of constant fear …
>
> Hence justice, right reason, and the recognition of man's dignity cry out insistently for a cessation to the arms race … Nuclear weapons must be banned …
>
> The warning of Pope Pius XII stills rings in our ears: 'Nothing is lost by peace; everything may be lost by war.' "
>
> *Pacem in Terris 109–116*

Contrasting views

Some people, including some Catholics, believe that it is right for Britain to have nuclear weapons		Many Christians and others call for nuclear disarmament and may support organisations such as the Campaign for Nuclear Disarmament (CND)	
Having nuclear weapons deters aggressive attacks from other countries		Some non-religious people and some Christians oppose WMDs for similar reasons to those given by the Catholic Church	
Having such weapons is important for self-defence, particularly when other countries have them		Someone needs to start the process of disarmament: Britain should do this	

APPLY

A Explain why the Catholic Church is opposed to the use of weapons of mass destruction.

B 'As long as there are nuclear weapons in the world there is always the danger they will be used, whether by accident or intention.'

Do you think that this statement by the Campaign for Nuclear Disarmament is correct? Develop arguments for and against it.

TIP

Some statements may not refer specifically to religion and it would be possible to write a purely secular (non-religious) response. However, it is important to refer to Church teaching or quote other religious sources, or only up to half marks can be given.

RECAP

Essential information:

☐ Modern warfare can be far more destructive than previous wars, and can have devastating long-term effects.

☐ War in the twenty-first century usually results in far more civilian deaths than military deaths.

☐ Modern wars can cause refugee crises as thousands flee their homes.

☐ Environmental damage through warfare can be huge, contaminating an area for generations.

Civilian casualties

- The Catholic Church teaches that it is wrong for civilians (non-combatants) to be attacked or threatened; instead, they should be protected.
- The Catechism of the Catholic Church 2313 states that 'Non-combatants, wounded soldiers, and prisoners must be respected and treated humanely.'

Refugees

- Many civilians are forced to flee the fighting either because their homes have been destroyed or because they face serious risk of death.
- Most flee with few possessions and have difficulty in finding somewhere safe to rebuild their lives.
- Many end up living in refugee camps in very poor conditions.
- The Catholic Church believes that refugees should be welcomed and protected by all countries. The Church actively campaigns for governments and individuals to help.

> ❝We cannot insist too much on the duty of giving foreigners a hospitable reception. It is a duty imposed by human solidarity and by Christian charity … This must be done … that they may be shielded from feelings of loneliness, distress and despair that would sap their strength.❞
>
> *Populorum Progressio 67*

- At the height of the Syrian refugee crisis Pope Francis preached, 'May every parish, every religious community, every monastery, every sanctuary in Europe host a family, starting with my diocese of Rome.'
- Many people are unable to take in a refugee family, and instead give money to a charity that helps refugees.

Environmental damage

The problem	The Catholic Church's response
Modern warfare can do great damage to the environment – huge areas of land can be destroyed	As stewards of the earth, people have a responsibility to limit any damage done to the environment
Using chemical weapons can affect the vegetation for decades after a war has ended	Popes have condemned the use of practices that ruin the environment such as the use of chemical weapons

Contrasting views

- Some people believe that it is acceptable to use powerful destructive weapons as, although they may cause more civilian deaths and environmental damage, they can end wars more quickly.
- Some people argue that Britain has not got enough resources to support lots of refugees or asylum seekers.
- Other people believe that providing asylum is the humane thing to do and that refugees can positively contribute to the economy of the country to which they move.

APPLY

A Give two examples of the consequences of modern warfare.

B 'Britain should be prepared to take more refugees.'

Write a paragraph explaining why the Catholic Church would support this statement. In a second paragraph explain arguments which might be used to disagree with taking in more refugees. In a final paragraph explain your opinion on the issue.

TIP
Examiners will be looking for the development of good reasons why people agree or disagree and your judgement about which are the strongest arguments.

Essential information:

☐ There have been many wars in which religion has been a difference between the two sides, but it is seldom the only or the main reason for the conflict.

☐ There are many examples of violence and war in the Old Testament, as the Israelites fought to conquer and defend the land they believed God had promised them.

☐ **Holy war** is fighting for a religious cause or God, probably controlled by a religious leader.

Religion and belief as a reason for war and violence

- There is rarely one reason for war, although some people claim that difference in religion is one of the major causes, e.g. the Crusades, the Thirty Years War, the Troubles in Northern Ireland, and conflicts in the Middle East.
- Jesus taught that the use of violence is very rarely justified.

> ❝You have heard that it was said to those of ancient times, 'You shall not murder'; and 'whoever murders shall be liable to judgement.' But I say to you that if you are angry with a brother or sister, you will be liable to judgement❞
> *Matthew 5:21–22* (NRSV)

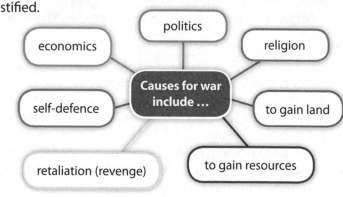

War and violence in the Old Testament

- The Israelites fought to establish themselves in the Promised Land and to defend the country.
- It could be argued that they were a persecuted people fighting for their survival.
- Exodus 21:24 says, 'eye for eye, tooth for tooth' which is often taken as meaning that it is acceptable to return violence with violence. When it was written it was an attempt to reduce punishment to only the individuals involved – not the families or tribes of the offenders, as was often the case at this time.
- Many Old Testament passages show that **God's wish is for peace** for all people, not war, for example Isaiah 2:4.

Holy War

- For Christians, a holy war must be approved by a religious leader with great authority, such as the Pope.
- The purpose of the war should be to defend the Christian faith from attack.
- It is believed that those who take part will gain spiritual rewards.
- The concept of a holy war does not feature in current Christian belief – Christians are more likely to use the power of argument rather than military strength.
- The Crusades are the best known example of a holy war.

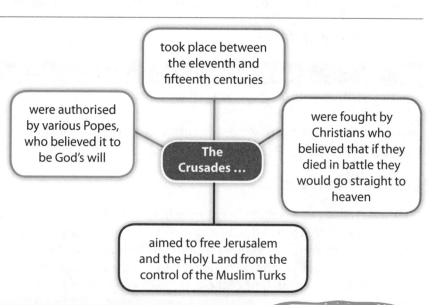

A Explain two contrasting views in the Bible about war.

B 'People should never use violence to defend religion.'

Evaluate this statement.

TIP
Don't just give simple points – you need to give some explanation of the two points you make.

12.8 Pacifism

Essential information:

☐ Some people think that Jesus held pacifist views.

☐ The early Christians were pacifists, refusing to take part in war or any form of violence.

☐ Throughout history there have been influential Christians who have refused to use violence, such as Martin Luther King.

☐ Although the Catholic Church strives for peace, it does teach that it is sometimes necessary to use force in self-defence or to defend the weak, but that the force must be limited.

Christian views on pacifism

* Jesus taught that it is much better to try to bring peace than to use violence:

  'if anyone strikes you on the right cheek, turn the other also.' (Matthew 5:39 (NRSV))
  'Blessed are the peacemakers, for they will be called children of God.' (Matthew 5:9 (NRSV))
  'all who take the sword will perish by the sword.' (Matthew 26:52 (NRSV)).

* The early Christians would not fight. For example, Martin of Tours (336–397 CE) resigned from the army when he became a Christian saying, 'It is not right for me to fight.'

* Martin Luther King, leader of the US civil rights movement during the twentieth century, refused to use violence.

* The Quakers (Religious Society of Friends) promote pacifism and acted as stretcher-bearers in the First World War. Pacifist Christians joined the Friends Ambulance Unit in the Second World War, but did not fight.

* After the Second World War, some Catholics founded Pax Christi (The Peace of Christ) to try to reconcile war-torn countries.

Teachings of the Catholic Church

* The Catholic Church believes that everyone and every nation has the right to protect itself, but emphasises the need to use non-violent approaches to resolve conflicts:

> **❝** in this age which boasts of its atomic power, it no longer makes sense to maintain that war is a fit instrument with which to repair the violation of justice. **❞**
>
> *Pacem in Terris 127*

* Pope Francis wrote, 'War never again! Never again war!' but he has acknowledged that force may be necessary in self-defence or to protect the weak:

> **❝** The Church strives for peace but does not preach radical pacifism. **❞**
>
> *Youcat 398*

Contrasting views

Pacifist beliefs	Other views
It is **always wrong to fight**, even in self defence	**Force is sometimes necessary** to solve disputes
Jesus taught that **peace is better than violence**	It is the **duty** of a country to **defend its peoples**
Some people have a religious or moral (though non-religious) belief in the **sanctity of life**	Peace can only be built on **mutual respect** which is unlikely if one party isn't prepared to defend itself
War never solves problems	A country that isn't prepared to fight is **seen as weak**
War causes such **destruction** that problems need to be solved through more peaceful, humane means	Sometimes all **negotiations fail** and war is necessary to bring about justice for the weak or to defend against attack

A Explain two reasons why some Christians are pacifists.

Refer to scripture or another source of Christian belief and teaching in your answer.

B 'Christians should never support violence.'

Evaluate this statement. Is it possible to resolve all situations peacefully?

TIP

Creating a mnemonic might help you to remember the main points, e.g. **TEMPS**:
Turn the other cheek
Early Christians were pacifists
Martin Luther King and Martin of Tours were pacifists
Peacemakers will be called children of God
Society of Friends (Quakers) are pacifists.

12.9 The role of religion in conflicts of the twenty-first century

Essential information:

☐ The Catholic Church believes that it is important to try to both **prevent war** and help **victims of war**.

☐ Each week the Pope highlights the need to **pray for peace** as he addresses the crowds in the Vatican Square.

☐ Catholic agencies such as **CAFOD**, **Aid to the Church in Need** and **Caritas International** help to support victims of war.

The efforts of the Pope

- Recent Popes such as Pope Francis have tried to bring about peaceful solutions to areas of conflict. Pope Francis said, 'War is madness … It also ruins the most beautiful work of his [God's] hands: human beings … War is irrational; its only plan is to bring destruction: it seeks to grow by destroying.'
- In 2013, Pope Francis urged people to pray for peace in eastern Ukraine, highlighting the number of civilian casualties.
- In 2014, Pope Francis organised a **meeting of prayer between the presidents of Israel and Palestine**. By using Jewish, Muslim and Christian prayers he hoped to help to bring the two leaders into a position where change could occur.
- In 2014, Pope Francis organised a **football match in Rome's Olympic stadium** to raise funds for children in need, particularly those affected by war. International players – including Buddhists, Christians, Hindus, Jews and Muslims took part, in an effort to break down barriers.

The work of Catholic agencies

Catholic agencies do not take sides in a war but try to help those who are victims.
Examples of their work include the following:

CAFOD	Aid to the Church in Need	Caritas International
• After civil war in Sierra Leone (1991–2002), CAFOD set up orphanages and rehabilitation programmes to help children who had been forced to become child soldiers get back to a normal way of life	• The civil war in Syria has caused thousands to flee; others have lost their homes and needed shelter • Aid to the Church in Need has provided shelter, blankets, medicine and food both inside and outside Syria	• After the fighting in Niger in 2015, many people fled their homes and were living under trees • Caritas International provided food, water and shelter, even where the aid workers were themselves in danger of being attacked

 A Name two examples of Catholic agencies that help victims of war.

B 'Christian leaders cannot stop wars.'

Evaluate this statement.

Write one paragraph supporting the idea that this is an accurate statement and another paragraph giving reasons why this might not be true. Write a final justified paragraph stating your opinion. Below are some ideas to start you off.

TIP

For this question you do not have to write in full sentences. Just giving the names is enough.

Agree	Disagree	Conclusion
"Wars are often started because of complex reasons. Many are the result of political differences or people wanting power or resources. It is very difficult for Christian leaders to have any influence in these situations because …"	"Pope Francis has worked hard to try to bring an end to conflicts in places like the Ukraine and in the Middle East. He has provided initiatives to bring people of different sides together to meet each other and to pray. In so doing he has encouraged leaders to respect each other …"	"In my opinion it is hard to prevent wars, but people can provide opportunities to talk and hopefully find ways of ending conflicts. I have therefore come to the conclusion that … because …"

12.10 Terrorism

Essential information:

- [ ] **Terrorism** is the unlawful use of violence, usually against innocent civilians.
- [ ] The Bible does not support terrorism as it goes against the state of peace that God wants for all people.
- [ ] The Catholic Church opposes the use of terror in any situation.

What is terrorism?

- In order to further their beliefs, some individuals or groups use a terror campaign with the **aim of frightening people** so that they are afraid to go about their normal daily lives.
- The violence is usually against **innocent civilians** and is usually designed to **undermine governments** and force authorities to give way to certain demands.

Biblical perspectives

- Paul taught that everyone should **obey the authorities** as they have been put in charge by God. 'Let every person be subject to the governing authorities; for there is no authority except from God, and those authorities that exist have been instituted by God. Therefore whoever resists authority resists what God has appointed, and those who resist will incur judgement.' (Romans 13:1–2 (NRSV))
- Paul's command **never to take vengeance** suggests that violence and terrorism is always wrong. 'Beloved, never avenge yourselves, but leave room for the wrath of God; for it is written, "Vengeance is mine, I will repay, says the Lord."' (Romans 12:19 (NRSV))
- The **Jewish Maccabees** resorted to violent terrorist attacks against the non-Jewish power that was **trying to force them to give up their religious beliefs and practices** (1 Maccabees 2:44–48). Some argue that without this action **Judaism might not have survived** and so in those circumstances these actions are justifiable.

Contemporary Catholic teachings

Pope Francis has said that it is wrong to carry out acts of terrorism in the name of God: 'Terrorism threatens, wounds, and kills indiscriminately; it is gravely against justice and charity.' (Catechism of the Catholic Church 2297.)

Terrorism in Britain

the IRA (Irish Republican Army) detonated bombs in Warrington (1993), London (1993), Manchester (1996) and Omagh (1998)	**Examples of terrorism in Britain**	Islamist extremists carried out attacks in London (2005), Glasgow (2007), and in London and Manchester in 2017

- Some people believe that terrorists are motivated by their religion.
- Others say that they have a **distorted and inaccurate view of the world** and what God would want: their actions have been completely rejected by the religion they claim to represent.
- Christian and Muslim leaders have strongly condemned the attacks and shown solidarity against terrorism.

(A) Give two examples of terrorist attacks which have been carried out in Britain.

(B) 'All terrorist attacks are sinful.'

Explain why many Christians would agree with this statement. Refer to Catholic belief and teaching in your answer.

What arguments might be used to disagree with this statement?

TIP

Usually it is good to give a balanced response to the evaluation questions, for example, two developed arguments on each side. With this statement it might be difficult to do this but make sure you do give two different points of view.

195

RECAP

Essential information:

☐ The Catholic Church is opposed to the use of torture.

☐ The Catholic Church urges people to reject radicalisation, as it can lead to terrorism and encourages tension in the world.

☐ Suicide bombers are not regarded as martyrs by the Catholic Church.

Torture

Some people argue that using **torture** – severe physical or psychological pain – to get information to prevent a greater wrong may be justified, for example, to prevent a terrorist attack.

> ❝Torture which uses physical or moral violence to extract confessions, punish the guilty, frighten opponents, or satisfy hatred is contrary to respect for the person and for human dignity.❞
> *Catechism of the Catholic Church 2297*

it is illegal

international law does not allow it even in war

The Catholic Church opposes torture because …

it denies the victim their basic human rights

Catholics see it as always wrong and inhuman

it views it as barbaric

Radicalisation and its prevention

- The Catholic Church focuses on **mutual respect**, so it is concerned about **radicalisation** (adopting extreme views) as it can make people unwilling to accept any alternative views.
- Radicalisation tends to take place among **younger people who feel rejected by their society or religion**.
- It is seen by most people as a **threat to the unity and stability of society**, and can potentially lead to terrorism.
- Schools now have a legal duty to stop people from being drawn into terrorism.
- Some people say that radicalisation is the fault of individuals or groups, who must be stopped.
- Others say that society must prevent people from feeling left out by using the education system, tackling inequality, and ensuring that nobody feels rejected: 'In the past, cultural differences have often been a source of misunderstanding between peoples and the cause of conflicts and wars.' (Pope John Paul II, Message for the World Day of Peace).

Martyrdom

- The term martyr is usually used to describe Christians who have been persecuted and put to death for refusing to give up their beliefs. Catholic martyrdom – the suffering or death of a martyr – does not include people who, for example, act as suicide bombers in the name of their religion.
- 'A Christian martyr is a person who is ready to suffer violence or even to be killed for Christ, who is the truth, or for a conscientious decision made on the basis of faith.' (Youcat)
- Christian martyrs follow the teaching and example of Jesus who said, 'If any want to become my followers, let them deny themselves and take up their cross and follow me.' (Matthew 16:24 (NRSV)).

APPLY

(A) Explain two reasons why the Catholic Church rejects the use of torture.

(B) 'Radicalisation is the greatest threat British society faces.'

Complete a paragraph supporting the statement:

"Radicalisation may result from people feeling isolated and rejected by society. They begin to think that no one listens to them and they develop their own very strong views, believing that they are right and everyone else is wrong. This may lead to …"

Complete a paragraph disagreeing with the statement:

"There are many other threats British society faces. Some of them include the divide between the rich and the poor, the proliferation of nuclear weapons, and growing individual and national debt. These may be seen as greater threats than radicalisation because …"

> **TIP**
> You can draw on knowledge gained in other chapters when answering evaluation questions, for example, nuclear war and weapons of mass destruction are discussed on page 190.

12.12 Conflict resolution and peacemaking

Essential information:

- [ ] The Bible teaches that it is the duty of Christians to be at **peace with one another** and to **help to bring about reconciliation**.

- [ ] The Catholic Church teaches that all believers should be involved in **peacemaking** and **conflict resolution** (creating peace where there have been disputes and war).

- [ ] Two organisations, **Pax Christi** and the **Justice and Peace Commission**, work with the Catholic Church to help bring mutual respect, justice, reconciliation and peace.

- [ ] Some Christians believe in **non-violent resistance** to pursue justice.

Biblical perspectives and Christian teaching

The Bible teaches that an end to war will be a sign of God's Kingdom having come on earth, so Christians should work to help solve conflicts.	Paul asks people to help bring reconciliation between Euodia and Syntyche: 'I ask you also, my loyal companion, help these women' (Philippians 4:2–3 (NRSV)).	The Catholic Church encourages everyone to work together towards lasting peace built on mutual respect and trust: 'Peace, however, is not merely a gift to be received: it is also a task to be undertaken.' (Pope Benedict XVI, Message for the World Day of Peace).	The Bible teaches that living in harmony shows that God is present: 'agree with one another, live in peace; and the God of love and peace will be with you.' (2 Corinthians 13:11 (NRSV)).

Catholic organisations working for peace

- All Catholics are encouraged to help with **peacemaking within their family and the local community**.
- The Church also believes in working for peace on a **global scale** (throughout the world).
- **Pax Christi** works in over 50 countries. It aims to get involved at an early stage of a conflict to encourage people, in order to solve disputes peacefully and fairly, rather than use violence.
- **Justice and Peace Commission** works in each Catholic diocese in England and Wales. It raises awareness of situations where people are deprived of their rights and needs, and campaigns against nuclear weapons and the arms trade.

Non-violent resistance

- Gandhi (a Hindu) successfully used non-violent resistance in his efforts to gain India's independence in 1947.
- Martin Luther King, a Baptist minister, used non-violent resistance in the USA to gain equal rights for black people.
- Many Christians believe that Jesus supported non-violent protest, as he said, 'Love your enemies, do good to those who hate you, bless those who curse you, pray for those who abuse you.' (Luke 6:27–28 (NRSV)).
- The Catholic Church supports the use of non-violent resistance in order to gain justice.

APPLY

A Give two examples of what the Bible says about peacemaking.

B 'All Christians must help to prevent individuals and countries getting into conflicts.'

Evaluate this statement. Be sure to include more than one point of view, and refer to what the Catholic Church teaches and does in your answer.

> **TIP**
> Key words in the statement include 'all' and 'must'. Make sure you refer to these important words by including judgement about whether every Christian should help and whether it should be compulsory or voluntary.

12 Exam practice

Test the 1 mark question

1   Which **one** of the following means the restoring of harmony after relationships have broken down?

    A Reconciliation   B Forgiveness   C Grace   D Mercy   **[1 mark]**

2   Which **one** of the following is a Catholic organisation set up to assist in peacemaking?

    A Christian Aid   B Save the Children   C Pax Christi   D Shelter Box   **[1 mark]**

Test the 2 mark question

3   Give **two** reasons why some Catholics would agree with the idea of righteous anger.   **[2 marks]**

1) _____

2) _____

4   Give **two** of the conditions for a just war.   **[2 marks]**

1) _____

2) _____

Test the 4 mark question

5   Explain **two** contrasting beliefs in contemporary British society about the use of nuclear weapons.

- You must refer to a Christian belief or view.
- Your contrasting belief or view may come from Christianity or from another religious or non-religious tradition.   **[4 marks]**

TIP

This is a basic point which would gain the first mark.

● **Explain one belief.**	The Catholic Church opposes the use of nuclear weapons as the effects are so devastating.
● Develop your explanation with more detail/an example/ reference to a religious teaching or quotation.	Pope Benedict XVI said in 2006 that in a nuclear war there would be 'no victors, only victims' as the survivors would end up living in a world that is in a state of total chaos because of the destruction.
● **Explain a second belief.**	Some people argue that it is necessary to have nuclear weapons for effective self-defence, although it would be wrong to use them first.
● Develop your explanation with more detail/an example/ reference to a religious teaching or quotation.	If other countries attack with nuclear weapons it is right to be able to retaliate, and the threat of this is likely to deter aggressive attacks in the first place.

TIP

This is a good development and would gain the second mark.

6   Explain **two** similar religious beliefs about the use of weapons of mass destruction.

- You must refer to a Christian belief or view.
- Your contrasting belief or view may come from Christianity or from another religious or non-religious tradition.   **[4 marks]**

● **Explain one belief.**	
● Develop your explanation with more detail/an example/ reference to a religious teaching or quotation.	
● **Explain a second belief.**	
● Develop your explanation with more detail/an example/ reference to a religious teaching or quotation.	

7 | Explain **two** contrasting beliefs in contemporary British society about helping refugees.

- You must refer to a Christian belief or view.
- Your contrasting belief or view may come from Christianity or from another religious or non-religious tradition.

[4 marks]

Test the 5 mark question

8 | Explain **two** Christian beliefs about the use of torture.

Refer to scripture or another source of Christian belief and teaching in your answer.

[5 marks]

● **Explain one belief.**	The Catholic Church believes that the use of torture is always wrong as it is inhumane and barbaric. Catholics oppose such cruelty.
● Develop your explanation with more detail/an example.	This is summed up in the Catechism of the Catholic Church 2297 which says that torture is against the beliefs in 'respect for the person and for human dignity.'
● **Explain a second belief.**	The use of torture is illegal under international law, even in a war, and so most Christians would not support its use.
● Develop your explanation with more detail/an example.	Christians, along with many others, believe that torture denies a victim their basic human rights.
● Add a reference to scripture or another source of religious belief. If you prefer, you can add this reference to your first belief instead.	Paul, in writing to the Romans, explained that Christians should obey the law: 'Let every person be subject to the governing authorities; for there is no authority except from God, and those authorities that exist have been instituted by God.' (Romans 13:1).

> **TIP**
> You do not have to include two references to scripture or another source of Christian belief and teaching, but do so if you are able to, just in case one is not accurate.

9 | Explain **two** Christian teachings about the need to forgive.

Refer to scripture or another source of Christian belief and teaching in your answer.

[5 marks]

● **Explain one teaching.**	
● Develop your explanation with more detail/an example.	
● **Explain a second teaching.**	
● Develop your explanation with more detail/an example.	
● Add a reference to scripture or another source of religious belief. If you prefer, you can add this reference to your first belief instead.	

10 | Explain **two** reasons why some Christians are pacifists.

Refer to scripture or another source of Christian belief and teaching in your answer.

[5 marks]

Test the 12 mark question

11 'It is impossible for Catholics to support the use of terrorism.'

Evaluate this statement. In your answer you:

- should give reasoned arguments in support of this statement
- should give reasoned arguments to support a different point of view
- should refer to Christian arguments
- may refer to non-religious arguments
- should reach a justified conclusion.

[12 marks]
Plus SPaG 3 ma

REASONED ARGUMENTS IN SUPPORT OF THE STATEMENT ● **Explain why some people would agree with the statement.** ● Develop your explanation with more detail and examples. ● Refer to religious teaching. Use a quote or paraphrase or refer to a religious authority. ● **Evaluate the arguments.** Is this a good argument or not? Explain why you think this.	The Catholic Church opposes the use of terrorism as many innocent people get injured or killed. The aim of terrorism is to create fear among the public so that they are frightened to go about their daily work. Most Catholics would say that morally terrorism should never be supported and it goes against the idea of the sanctity of life. The Ten Commandments include the teaching that it is wrong to kill, and suicide bombs or driving vehicles into crowds of people do just that. Furthermore, terrorist acts are usually aimed at challenging the government and the Bible teaches that it is right to obey the authorities. Paul says this in his letter to the Romans as he says that the government has been put in charge by God to look after the people in their care. These are strong arguments in support of the statement as they are important beliefs in the Bible.
REASONED ARGUMENTS SUPPORTING A DIFFERENT VIEW ● **Explain why some people would support a different view.** ● Develop your explanation with more detail and examples. ● Refer to religious teaching. Use a quote or paraphrase or refer to a religious authority. ● **Evaluate the arguments.** Is this a good argument or not? Explain why you think this.	A minority of Catholics might feel that terrorism is justified in very extreme cases. If, for example, Catholics were being persecuted by a vicious government they may feel that they have to take action to try to stop the persecution happening. They may feel that the Jewish Maccabees were right in rebelling against the authorities who were trying to force the Jews to abandon their religious beliefs and practices. The Maccabees used terrorist type tactics and some would argue that without it Judaism may not have survived. So some Catholics might argue that in a similar situation they might need to fight back using whatever methods they could. However, this is not a strong argument as most Catholics would not feel able to support such actions as a state of terror goes against their belief in the need to strive for peace and reconciliation.
CONCLUSION ● **Give a justified conclusion.** ● Include your own opinion together with your own reasoning. ● **Include evaluation.** Explain why you think one viewpoint is stronger than the other or why you think they are equally strong. ● Do not just repeat arguments you have already used without explaining how they apply to your reasoned opinion/conclusion.	I agree with the statement as to support the use of terrorism would go totally against the beliefs and teachings of the Catholic Church. It is very clear that the Church condemns putting innocent peoples' lives at risk and the creation of a climate of fear. Even where there is injustice the Bible teaches that vengeance is in the hands of God, not man. With such beliefs it would be very hard indeed for Catholics to support the use of terrorism, even in extreme circumstances. To follow such important teachings of their faith would in my opinion make it impossible to use terrorism to kill or injure innocent men, women and children. The evidence therefore overwhelmingly supports the statement.

TIP
Good use has been made of reference to the Bible which is a main source for Catholic belief.

TIP
The judgement of this argument in the last sentence is good practice.

TIP
This answer shows logical chains of reasoning and ends with a justified conclusion.

12 'It is never right to go to war.'

Evaluate this statement. In your answer you:

- should give reasoned arguments in support of this statement
- should give reasoned arguments to support a different point of view
- should refer to Christian arguments
- may refer to non-religious arguments
- should reach a justified conclusion.

[12 marks]
Plus SPaG 3 marks

REASONED ARGUMENTS IN SUPPORT OF THE STATEMENT ● **Explain why some people would agree with the statement.** ● Develop your explanation with more detail and examples. ● Refer to religious teaching. Use a quote or paraphrase or refer to a religious authority. ● **Evaluate the arguments.** Is this a good argument or not? Explain why you think this.	
REASONED ARGUMENTS SUPPORTING A DIFFERENT VIEW ● **Explain why some people would support a different view.** ● Develop your explanation with more detail and examples. ● Refer to religious teaching. Use a quote or paraphrase or refer to a religious authority. ● **Evaluate the arguments.** Is this a good argument or not? Explain why you think this.	
CONCLUSION ● **Give a justified conclusion.** ● Include your own opinion together with your own reasoning. ● **Include evaluation.** Explain why you think one viewpoint is stronger than the other or why you think they are equally strong. ● Do not just repeat arguments you have already used without explaining how they apply to your reasoned opinion/conclusion.	

13 'All nuclear weapons should be destroyed.'

Evaluate this statement. In your answer you:

- should give reasoned arguments in support of this statement
- should give reasoned arguments to support a different point of view
- should refer to Christian arguments
- may refer to non-religious arguments
- should reach a justified conclusion.

[12 marks]
Plus SPaG 3 marks

 Check your answers using the mark scheme on pages 237–238. How did you do?
To feel more secure in the content you need to remember, re-read pages 184–197.
To remind yourself of what the examiner is looking for in your answers, go to pages 8–13.

13.1 Human dignity and religious freedom

Essential information:

☐ Christians believe that humans are created in the image of God which gives them a sense of **dignity** (being worthy of honour and respect).

☐ God loves and values everyone, as shown by his willingness to become man in Jesus and to die to save all human beings.

☐ The Catholic Church believes that everyone should have the right to religious freedom to believe what they wish.

Biblical teaching about human dignity

" God created humankind in his image, in the image of God he created them; male and female he created them. **"** *Genesis 1:27* (NRSV)	Being created in God's image doesn't mean that humans look like God, but that they **share in the qualities of God** and are superior to other creatures These qualities give humans a sense of dignity
" there is no longer Greek and Jew, circumcised and uncircumcised, barbarian, Scythian, slave and free; but Christ is all and in all! **"** *Colossians 3:11* (NRSV)	Paul in his letter reminds his readers that Jesus died for all people; therefore there should be **no division of any type** between people and all are given dignity by the love God has for them all
" You shall love your neighbour as yourself. **"** *Mark 12:31* (NRSV)	Christians should put the **needs of others** on the same level as their own needs
" what does the Lord require of you but to do justice, and to love kindness, and to walk humbly with your God? **"** *Micah 6:8* (NRSV)	Christians should not be selfish but should **strive for justice and equality**

Freedom of religion or belief

- One way of accepting other human beings is to recognise every person's right to have a different set of beliefs. This has not always been the case, as shown in the religious persecution in England in the seventeenth and eighteenth centuries and the treatment of the Jews during the Second World War.
- The Second Vatican Council declared that 'no one is to be forced to act in a manner contrary to his own beliefs' (*Dignitatis Humanae* 2).
- Pope Francis has called for a world where 'believers and non-believers can work together to promote a society where injustice can be overcome'.
- The rights and differences of individuals should be recognised and respected. 'Everyone shall have the right to freedom of thought, conscience and religion.' (International Covenant on Civil and Political Rights 18).
- Freedom of religion should not give people the right to try to force others to accept a religion.

TIP
Don't just quote what the Bible says. You need to explain the meaning of the quotes.

(A) Explain two teachings from the Bible about human dignity.

(B) 'People should have the freedom to say whatever they want about Christianity or any other religion.'

Evaluate this statement. Consider positive and negative issues such as basic human rights, freedom of speech, human dignity, peoples' passion, loving your neighbour, being offensive, stirring up hatred, and persecution.

Include Catholic beliefs and teachings in your response.

TIP
It may help if you consider, for example, how you would feel if you were unable to voice an opinion in support of your favourite team or band, or respond if you heard someone saying horrible things about them.

RECAP

Essential information:

☐ The Catholic Church promotes the rights of the individual, regardless of status, race or religion.

☐ The Catholic Church's teaching on **human rights** (the basic rights and freedoms to which all human beings should be entitled) is clearly shown in *Gaudium et Spes* 26.

☐ All countries are legally required to uphold the UN Declaration of Human Rights.

Catholic teaching on human rights

Pope John XXIII began his teachings on peace by recognising how important it is for every person to have rights and dignity:

> ❝each individual man is truly a person. His is a nature, that is, endowed with intelligence and free will. As such he has rights and duties❞
>
> *Pacem in Terris 9*

Gaudium et Spes 26	Meaning
'the common good … involves rights and duties with respect to the whole human race.'	The rights and duties of people throughout the world need to be considered
'Every social group must take account of the needs and legitimate aspirations of other groups, and even of the general welfare of the entire human family.'	Careful thought must be given to the needs and ambitions of every group of people; this includes the wellbeing of everyone
'there is a growing awareness of the exalted dignity proper to the human person, since he stands above all things'	It is right to give dignity to every person because humans are superior to all other living beings
'and his rights and duties are universal and inviolable.'	Peoples' rights and duties are the same all over the world and should be respected and protected
'Therefore, there must be made available to all men everything necessary for leading a life truly human'	Every person should receive the necessities of life such as food, clothing and shelter
'the right to choose a state of life freely and to found a family … to activity in accord with … one's own conscience, to protection of privacy and rightful freedom even in matters religious.'	Other rights include the right to have children, an education, employment, respect, freedom of conscience and religion, and privacy
'This social order … must be founded on truth, built on justice and animated by love'	Society must be built on truth and justice and motivated by love

- The Catholic Church teaches that anyone who does not receive these human rights is being treated as less than human and loses their human dignity.
- The teaching of the parable of the Sheep and Goats shows that whoever helps a person, who doesn't have basic human rights, helps Jesus.

Ensuring human rights

- The UN Declaration of Human Rights (similar to the rights expressed in *Gaudium et Spes* 26) should legally be followed by all countries.
- Many people are being denied these basic rights and the Church asks Catholics to work towards greater equality.

APPLY

(A) Explain two points made in *Gaudium et Spes* 26 about human rights.

(B) 'The Catholic Church should campaign more to help everyone get basic human rights.'

Evaluate this statement. This requires saying what the Catholic Church already says and does, and judging whether or not it is enough. Is it fair just to single out one Christian denomination and say that they should do more?

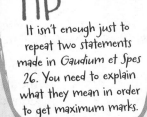
TIP

It isn't enough just to repeat two statements made in *Gaudium et Spes* 26. You need to explain what they mean in order to get maximum marks.

RECAP

Essential information:

☐ Insisting on people having basic human rights also means accepting the responsibility to respect other people's rights, and to help make those rights available.

☐ People have a duty to use their rights responsibly and not cause harm to others.

☐ Catholics believe that it is important to work together to bring about change, especially in unjust situations.

The relationship between rights and responsibilities

> ❝These rights and duties derive their origin … from the natural law … for example, the right to live involves the duty to preserve one's life … in human society one man's natural right gives rise to a corresponding duty in other men; the duty, that is, of recognising and respecting that right.❞
>
> *Pacem in Terris 28–30*

rights

- If people want rights they must realise that other people should be able to have the same rights
- There is a need to ensure people have access to human rights
- Vulnerable people are often deprived of rights

responsibilities

- This sometimes limits what a person is allowed to do; for example, the right to free speech is not being used responsibly if it is used to encourage violence
- For example, a right to education would be impossible unless people are prepared to provide that education; the student also has the responsibility to want to learn
- Christians should show solidarity with the weak and vulnerable by demanding that they receive their just rights

The pursuit of human rights in action

The Church teaches that all Catholics, as members of the Body of Christ on earth, should work together to end injustice and the denial of human rights. Some Catholic agencies work to bring human rights to those who do not have them:

The Justice and Peace Commission	Caritas International	Agencies from other religions
• Tries to ensure people's human rights are respected • Raises awareness and takes practical action such as providing food and shelter	• Raises awareness of situations like human trafficking and takes action to stop this abuse • Puts pressure on the United Nations to improve access to human rights worldwide	• In non-Christian countries Catholics work with other agencies, such as Islamic Aid, to help people get justice • This is done because some governments prevent Christian agencies working in their countries

APPLY

A Explain two examples of how rights are linked with responsibilities.

B 'There is no point in Catholics trying to influence governments where there are human rights abuses.'

Evaluate this statement. Write three paragraphs: one supporting the statement, one opposing it, and one giving your conclusion. Consider issues such as: are governments likely to take notice of Catholics protesting, writing letters, or using the media? Many of these abuses are in other countries – are they likely to listen to foreigners but is it right to stand aside and do nothing?

TIP
You are awarded marks for your spelling, punctuation and grammar (SPaG) in these answers. Make sure that your sentences are not too long, that they begin with a capital letter, and that you write in paragraphs.

RECAP

Essential information:

☐ Some Christians believe the Bible teaches them to reject money and be poor. Others believe that having wealth is acceptable as long as people use it wisely.

☐ There is a danger that wealth may distort people's values and perspectives.

☐ Christians should share their God-given wealth to help those who are poor.

☐ Helping to correct the imbalance of wealth in the world is known as **stewardship of wealth**.

Teachings in the Bible

- Jesus told his disciples 'to **take nothing** for their journey except a staff; no bread, no bag, no money in their belts; but to wear sandals and not to put on two tunics'. (Mark 6:8–9 (NRSV)). Some Christians interpret this to mean they should reject money and be poor.
- The parable of the Talents (Mathew 25:14–30) teaches that wealth is a **gift from God** which needs to be used wisely, as God will judge how the wealth is used.
- 1 John 3:17 teaches that wealth should be used to **help others**: 'How does God's love abide in anyone who has the world's goods and sees a brother or sister in need and yet refuses help?'
- Wealth can distort people's values and perspectives, for example, in the parable of the Rich Man and Lazarus (Luke 16:19–31) the rich man didn't even notice the poor man at the gate.
- It is not wealth itself that is the problem, but people's use of wealth and their attachment to it. 'For the **love of money** is a root of all kinds of evil' (1 Timothy 6:10 (NRSV)).

> **TIP**
> Note that this verse doesn't say that 'money is the root of evil' – it is the desire, 'the love of money', that causes wrongdoing.

Teachings of the Catholic Church

- The Catholic Church has strongly spoken out against unequal wealth. It says poor people are deprived of their dignity by those who are greedy for wealth.
- Paul sums up Catholic teaching by saying that Christians are not expected to make themselves poor, but should share what they are able to afford with the needy: 'For if the eagerness [the desire to be of help] is there, the gift is acceptable according to what one has – not according to what one does not have.' (2 Corinthians 8:12 (NRSV))

Stewardship of wealth

- Many Christians believe that they are **stewards** of God's wealth. As wealth is a gift from God it should be used wisely and responsibly, as God would want.
- If the rich shared their wealth everyone would have a reasonable standard of living. Paul encourages Christians to use wealth responsibly. 'They are to do good, to be rich in good works, generous, and ready to share'. (1 Timothy 6:18)
- Pope Francis taught that the life of all people is more important than the gaining of private wealth by a few people. The way Christians should think about making money is that its purpose is 'to restore to the poor what belongs to them'. (*Evangelii Gaudium* 189)

Food banks supply emergency food parcels to people in need

APPLY

A Give two examples of what the Bible teaches about wealth.

B 'There is nothing wrong with being rich.'

Do you agree with this statement? Why might someone else have a different point of view? Explain your reasoning.

> **TIP**
> Although the statement does not mention religion it is very important to refer to religious beliefs and teachings in your answer.

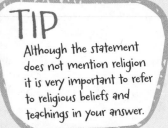

13.5 Wealth creation and exploitation

Essential information:

☐ The Catholic Church teaches that wealth creation is essential for people's survival and prosperity, but it should not be done at the expense of depriving people of their rights.

☐ The Church is against **exploitation** (when people misuse power or money to get others to do things for little or unfair reward) and **human trafficking** (a form of modern-day slavery).

☐ The Catholic Church has a lot of wealth but it is mainly tied up in its church buildings.

Catholic teachings about wealth creation

- Christians should be productive, as Paul told the early Christians: 'Anyone unwilling to work should not eat. For we hear that some of you are living in idleness, mere busybodies, not doing any work.' (2 Thessalonians 3:10–11 (NRSV))
- Genesis 41 tells the story of Joseph storing spare grain, during the years of surplus, in order to feed the nation during the famine which followed. Catholics are taught to use wealth positively to provide for needy times.

Exploitation of the poor

- Wealth creation should not be at the expense of the poor.
- The prophet Amos forcefully condemned the exploitation of the poor (Amos 8:4–7).
- The Catechism of the Catholic Church explains that the motivation for wealth should not be greed, but to provide for the family and, where possible, the wider community.

> **❝**Work is for man, not man for work. Everyone should be able to draw from work the means of providing for his life and that of his family, and of serving the human community. **❞**
> *Catechism of the Catholic Church 2428*

Human trafficking

- Some vulnerable people, who flee from war or persecution in search of a better quality of life, get exploited by groups who promise to help. Instead of helping, they sell them into prostitution or slavery.
- The Bakhita Foundation was set up by the Catholic Church in memory of an African girl, Bakhita, who escaped from traffickers and became a nun and a saint. It gives practical and emotional support to those caught up in human trafficking, and works with international agencies to enforce laws to prevent it happening.

The wealth of the Church

- Pope Francis has pointed out that practical action is required, not just talk.
- Some people criticise the Catholic Church for being wealthy, as it owns a significant amount of land. To sell it would be difficult as the buildings which stand on the land include hospitals, schools and churches. All of these provide important services for people.
- Popes since John XXIII have been gradually selling works of art which the Church owns and using the proceeds to help in situations of great need.

(A) Explain two reasons, using examples from the Bible, which show why there is a need for wealth creation.

TIP
You may be asked in the exam to give two contrasting (different) or two similar reasons given in the Bible or believed by Christians.

(B) 'The Catholic Church should sell off its huge wealth to help the poor.'

Give arguments for and against this statement. Are most Catholic leaders likely to agree or disagree with this idea? Write a final paragraph including your opinion, and explain your reasoning.

TIP

A one-sided response to a 12 mark question will only be able to get a maximum of half marks.

RECAP

Essential information:

☐ Greed is the desire to have more, regardless of need, and is against the teaching of Jesus.

☐ **Materialism** (the belief that physical objects matter far more than other things) places great value on having many possessions. The Catholic Church believes spiritual or intellectual things are more important

☐ Some people take a vow of poverty to show that they are willing to go without wealth and possessions, as a sign that they have committed themselves to the service of God and others.

Greed and materialism

Jesus warned his followers:

> ❝Take care! Be on your guard against all kinds of greed; for one's life does not consist in the abundance of possessions. ❞
> *Luke 12:15 (NRSV)*

- However, some people don't believe that greed is all bad, as they think it helps the economy if people desire possessions.
- Some people think that if they work hard to earn money they should spend it however they wish, and should put their own desires before others.

Pope Francis warned of the dangers of materialism:

```
is a desire for more
makes people ignore spiritual things
Jesus warned against it
Greed ...
destroys a person's relationship with God
is one of the seven deadly sins
makes people put their own needs first
goes against the teaching to 'love your neighbour'
```

> ❝Whenever material things, money, worldliness, become the centre of our lives, they take hold of us, they possess us; we lose our very identity as human beings ❞
> *Pope Francis*

This means that being materialistic distorts a person's sense of value, gives people a false sense of purpose, and takes control of life. The Catholic Church also teaches that a materialistic approach to life:

- encourages judging people on what they earn and makes people little more than objects, lacking value
- can make people seem falsely important because they have possessions
- leads to shallowness of life and destroys appreciation of the beauty of creation.

The vow of poverty

- Monks, nuns, some priests, and religious brothers and sisters take a vow of poverty in order to commit themselves to fully serving God and others.
- Jesus told a rich young man: 'If you wish to be perfect, go, sell your possessions, and give all the money to the poor, and you will have treasure in heaven; then come, follow me.' (Matthew 19:21 (NRSV))

Contrasting views

Those who support the idea of taking a vow of poverty ...	Those who believe that a vow of poverty is not for them ...
• Some Christians and non-believers think that living simply will help solve the imbalance of wealth in the world	• The call to live a life of poverty can only apply to those with limited family responsibilities
• They believe that simplicity in life leads to happiness as it removes stress and the mentality of having to match other people's wealth	• Having worked for their money they believe that they should enjoy their wealth and possessions

APPLY

A Explain two reasons why Catholics are against people being greedy. Refer to scripture or another source of Christian belief and teaching in your answer.

B 'There is no point in taking a vow of poverty.'

Evaluate the statement, providing well reasoned arguments.

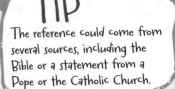

TIP

The reference could come from several sources, including the Bible or a statement from a Pope or the Catholic Church.

13.7 Catholic teachings about poverty

Essential information:

- **Poverty** is being without money, food, or other basic needs of life (being poor).
- Catholics believe that poverty degrades people and threatens their dignity.
- The Catholic Church teaches that the needs of poor people should be put first – this is called 'the preferential option for the poor'.

The preferential option for the poor

The Catholic Church teaches that the poor deserve preferential treatment because they have suffered from not having had the basic requirements for life. Paul told Christians to be concerned about the interests of others.

> ❝Let each of you look not to your own interests, but to the interests of others. Let the same mind be in you that was in Christ Jesus.❞
>
> *Philippians 2:4–5 (NRSV)*

Evangelii Gaudium 198	In this passage Pope Francis teaches:
❝God shows the poor 'his first mercy'. This divine preference has consequences for the faith life of all Christians … Inspired by this, the Church has made an option for the poor … This option – as Benedict XVI has taught – 'is implicit in our Christian faith in a God who became poor for us, so as to enrich us with his poverty.❞	• The poor are first to receive the mercy of God, so caring for the poor is a demand on Christians • Christians should put the needs of others first, especially those in the most need, as Jesus offered his life for all people
❝This is why I want a Church which is poor and for the poor. They have much to teach us … in their difficulties they know the suffering Christ. We need to let ourselves be evangelised by them … We are called to find Christ in them, to lend our voice to their causes, but also to be their friends, to listen to them, to speak for them.❞	• The Catholic Church must focus on the needs of the poor • Poor people can teach the rich because they are closer to the spirit of Jesus as they share his rejection and suffering • Christians who are rich need to see Jesus in the poor, to speak up for them, to befriend and listen to them

Catholics have a duty to protest and work against those that create poverty. Poverty degrades not only the poor, but also those who exploit people or those who do nothing to stop or prevent exploitation.

> ❝Poverty in the world is a scandal. In a world where there is so much wealth, so many resources to feed everyone, it is unfathomable that there are so many hungry children, that there are so many children without an education, so many poor persons…
>
> A way has to be found to enable everyone to benefit from the fruits of the earth … satisfy the demands of justice, fairness and respect for every human being.❞
>
> *Pope Francis, 7 and 20 June 2013*

A Explain two points made by Pope Francis about the treatment of the poor.

B 'The preferential option for the poor means that the Catholic Church should give up all its wealth to benefit the poor.'

Evaluate this statement. Give two arguments which can be used to support it and two to oppose it. Give reasons for the arguments and refer to Christian beliefs.

RECAP

Essential information:

- [ ] The Church teaches that love is not shown through words but through deeds, that is, by giving practical help to the poor.

- [ ] One way of assisting those in poverty is to give money and aid directly to the poor.

- [ ] Many people argue that the best ways to fight poverty in the long term are those that tackle the root causes of poverty.

The duty to take action on poverty

- Catholics believe that they are part of the Body of Christ: if one part is suffering they should provide support.
- Christians believe that to 'love your neighbour' means not ignoring those in need.
- John writes, 'Those who say, "I love God", and hate their brothers or sisters, are liars; for those who do not love a brother or sister whom they have seen, cannot love God whom they have not seen.' (1 John 4:20 (NRSV))
- James challenges Christians to take action by saying, 'So faith by itself, if it has no works, is dead.' (James 2:17 (NRSV))

Directly helping the poor

- Most people living in poverty are desperate to become self-sufficient but need immediate help because of their present situation.
- Some people argue that just giving money to the poor does little to help, as they may come to rely on aid. What is needed are ways of solving the causes of poverty.
- Some people say that the problem of poverty can only be solved by governments and organisations with power: 'The rich countries have the moral obligation to help the underdeveloped nations out of poverty through developmental aid and the establishment of just economic and commercial conditions.' (Youcat 448)
- Individuals could boycott multinational companies who pay unfair wages, forcing them to change their policies.
- People could buy more Fairtrade products, meaning more money would go to the people who produced them – this would help more people in the developing world become more self-sufficient.

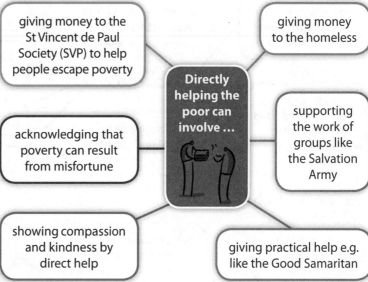

giving money to the St Vincent de Paul Society (SVP) to help people escape poverty

giving money to the homeless

Directly helping the poor can involve …

acknowledging that poverty can result from misfortune

supporting the work of groups like the Salvation Army

showing compassion and kindness by direct help

giving practical help e.g. like the Good Samaritan

The responsibility to help those in poverty

- Many people agree that most people are in poverty because of unfortunate circumstances that are the result of how society works, so it is society's responsibility to help them.
- Some people say that those in poverty should show more responsibility, either to not fall into poverty in the first place, or to make a greater effort to improve their situation.

APPLY

A Give two ways in which Christians can help those struggling with poverty.

B 'Those suffering from poverty have a responsibility to help themselves get out of it.'

Write a paragraph explaining why this could be seen as a fair comment. Should people do more to get skills and a job? Compose a second paragraph suggesting that it is not possible, in many circumstances, for people to do this – natural disasters, extreme weather, illness or exploitation may be preventing them. What religious references could you include in a question like this?

TIP

Don't just list reasons. To get high marks it is vital to explain why the reasons are relevant and important.

RECAP

Essential information:

☐ CAFOD is a Catholic charity that works with communities across the world, helping people to tackle the poverty and injustice they face.

☐ Christian Aid is a UK charity that works in over 60 countries and has a vision to stop poverty and tackle its causes.

☐ CAFOD and Christian Aid work with other agencies and charities, and have formed the Disasters Emergency Committee (DEC).

Taking action against poverty as an expression of Christian values

- Christians accept the need to be Good Samaritans (Luke 10:29–37) and help individuals and sections of society when they are in need.
- There are many Christian charities that believe they should be 'my brother's keeper' (Genesis 4:9 (NRSV)) and not ignore the causes of poverty and the poor.

> **"**In all places and circumstances, Christians, with the help of their pastors, are called to hear the cry of the poor. **"**
>
> *Evangelii Gaudium 191*

The work of CAFOD

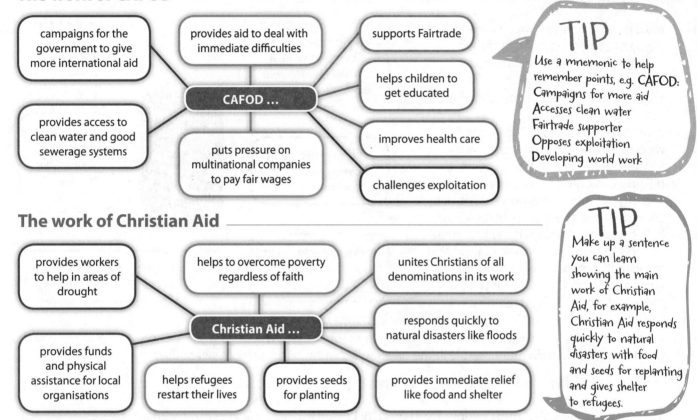

campaigns for the government to give more international aid

provides aid to deal with immediate difficulties

supports Fairtrade

helps children to get educated

CAFOD ...

provides access to clean water and good sewerage systems

puts pressure on multinational companies to pay fair wages

improves health care

challenges exploitation

TIP

Use a mnemonic to help remember points, e.g. CAFOD:
Campaigns for more aid
Accesses clean water
Fairtrade supporter
Opposes exploitation
Developing world work

The work of Christian Aid

provides workers to help in areas of drought

helps to overcome poverty regardless of faith

unites Christians of all denominations in its work

Christian Aid ...

responds quickly to natural disasters like floods

provides funds and physical assistance for local organisations

helps refugees restart their lives

provides seeds for planting

provides immediate relief like food and shelter

TIP

Make up a sentence you can learn showing the main work of Christian Aid, for example, Christian Aid responds quickly to natural disasters with food and seeds for replanting and gives shelter to refugees.

Other views (including atheist and humanist views)

- Many people support the work of other non-religious charities such as Oxfam, Save the Children and Live Aid
- They see the need and respond on a humanitarian basis

- Some people do not donate to charities because they believe that it isn't the most effective way to solve the causes of poverty
- They prefer to campaign for governments to change their policies and for financial systems to help in the developing world

APPLY

A Explain two ways in which CAFOD tries to overcome poverty.

B 'All Christians should give money to Christian Aid.'

List reasons to support this statement and then reasons to oppose it. Write a conclusion in which you express your personal point of view.

RECAP

Essential information:

☐ As all human beings are created in the image and likeness of God (Genesis 1:27), Christians believe that **prejudice** (unfairly judging someone or holding biased opinions about an individual or group) is wrong.

☐ Racial **discrimination** (actions or behaviour that result from prejudice) is unacceptable to the Catholic Church. It can cause great harm to individuals and lead to tensions within society.

Christian teachings about prejudice and discrimination

Catechism of the Catholic Church 1934	Meaning
'Created in the image of the one God and equally endowed with rational souls, all men have the same nature and the same origin.'	God created everyone in his image and is present in each person regardless of gender, nationality, colour, faith, disability and sexual orientation
'Redeemed by the sacrifice of Christ, all are called to participate in the same divine beatitude: all therefore enjoy an equal dignity.'	All people are saved by the death and resurrection of Jesus so there are no grounds for prejudice and discrimination as everyone has the same dignity

Racial prejudice and discrimination

- This means having a negative attitude towards someone who belongs to a different race or ethnic group.
- Catholics believe that everyone should be respected, as they are children of God, and are loved and valued by God as he brought them into existence.
- Catholics are warned in *Evangelium Vitae* 34 that those who practise racial prejudice and discrimination are also harmed.

> ❝ whatever insults human dignity ... poison[s] human society, but [the insults] do more harm to those who practise them than those who suffer from the injury. ❞
>
> *Evangelium Vitae 34*

- means people are not treated as full human beings
- can cause tensions and harm
- leads to negative actions
- stops people from developing their full potential
- **Racial prejudice and discrimination ...**
- affects individuals and groups
- is against Catholic teaching to treat each person fairly
- is against the teaching that all are children of God
- are linked: prejudice turns into discrimination

In Britain today

Positive beliefs about racial diversity	Negative beliefs about racial diversity
Britain has a history of different races working together and getting married regardless of race, and most people accept and celebrate this	Some people wrongly believe that historically only one racial group belongs to the British Isles
Different races and cultures have greatly contributed to the genetic make-up and culture of Britain	Misunderstandings can lead to tensions between different groups in society
Britain is a multicultural society with a wide range of racial groups making a large contribution to society	Racism, although illegal, still occurs. For example, racial abuse is sometimes a problem at football matches
Racial prejudice is often based on lack of knowledge and understanding, simply because some people have different customs, beliefs and values	Some people fear that Britain's security and prosperity is threatened by an increase in immigration, which leads to prejudice against ethnic minorities

APPLY

(A) Give two reasons why some people are racially prejudiced.

(B) 'It is impossible to stop racial discrimination.'
Evaluate this statement.

TIP
Don't limit your response to one side of the debate in an evaluation question, even if you have very strong views.

RECAP

Essential information:

☐ Christians believe that men and women are both created in the image of God and so God regards them as equals.

☐ Catholics believe that men and women may have different roles, but they complement each other and are of equal value.

☐ Catholics teach that homosexuals should live chaste lives, without having sex, as they cannot be open to the possibility of conceiving children.

Equality in the Bible

> Humans are made in the image and likeness of God:
>
> 'So God created humankind in his image, in the image of God he created them; male and female he created them.' (Genesis 1:27 (NRSV))

> Men and women complete each other – neither is subservient or inferior to the other (Genesis 2)

> Peter's vision taught him that God wanted him to preach to Jews and non-Jews alike:
>
> 'I truly understand that God shows no partiality' (Acts 10:34 (NRSV))

> Paul said that everyone is equal in Christ:
>
> 'There is no longer Jew or Greek, there is no longer slave or free, there is no longer male and female; for all of you are one in Christ Jesus.' (Galatians 3:28 (NRSV))

Equality and gender

- The Catholic Church teaches that men and women have equal dignity with equal rights, but 'equal dignity and equal rights do not mean uniformity' (Youcat 401).
- Catholics believe that the role of the woman within the home is irreplaceable but they also appreciate the value women can bring to society through going out to work.

Contrasting views about the role of women in leadership in the Church

The Catholic Church	The Church of England (Anglicans)
Both Catholic and Orthodox Christians have allowed only men to be priests, following Jesus' example	The Church of England has allowed women to be priests since 1993 and bishops since 2014
Church teaches that Jesus ordained his male followers, the apostles, as priests during the Last Supper	Anglicans have allowed women to be ordained, believing that the call of God is what is important, not the gender
Catholics do not see this as diminishing the role and status of women but an example of how men and women are equal but different	Allowing women to be ordained leaders reflects the majority view in Britain that access to equal opportunities is an important part of equality

Equality and sexuality

The Catholic Church opposes practising homosexuality because:

- sexual union should be open to God blessing the couple by creating new life
- the creation of new life is impossible with two people of the same sex
- the purpose of homosexual sex is distorted and so is seen as sinful

Although calling on homosexuals not to have same-gender sex, the Catholic Church believes that homosexuals should have their rights and dignity as human beings.

TIP
For other views on homosexuality, see page 172.

> ❝ [Homosexuals] must be accepted with respect, compassion, and sensitivity. Every sign of unjust discrimination in their regard should be avoided. ❞
> *Catechism of the Catholic Church 2358*

APPLY

Ⓐ Explain two reasons why the Catholic Church opposes homosexual sex.

Ⓑ 'The Catholic Church should allow women to be ordained as priests.'

Give developed arguments either in support of this statement, or in support of a different point of view.

TIP
In completing the evaluation bring in quotes, teachings or examples from the Bible, such as Galatians 3:28, but ensure that they are relevant to the question.

RECAP

Essential information:

☐ Seeking justice and fairness is an important duty for all Christians.

☐ Catholics support laws and actions which promote tolerance, racial equality and respect.

☐ Catholics offer support to those who have been targets of racial prejudice and abuse.

Justice

Individually, in following the teaching 'love your neighbour', Christians should treat others fairly. They may also take part in campaigns to promote equality and justice to all sections of society.

> ❝Social justice comes about where the inalienable dignity of every person is respected and the resulting rights are safeguarded and championed … A society is not perfected by laws, however, but rather by the love of neighbour❞
> *Youcat 302*

The promotion of tolerance and racial equality

Christians say **YES** to laws that respect the rights of every member of society. Christians say **NO** to laws that could be used to undervalue individuals or groups.

> ❝If a state [government] should establish laws and procedures that are racist, sexist, or destructive of human life, a Christian is obliged in conscience to refuse to obey, to refrain from participation, and to offer resistance.❞
> *Youcat 377*

Ways the Catholic Church promotes tolerance and racial equality include:

Through Catholic Schools	• Children of all races and religions are welcome to attend UK Catholic schools • Catholic and non-Catholic students (including many Muslims) mix together. This promotes understanding and acceptance of differences
Through Catholic priests, bishops and clergy working in other countries	• Recent Popes have been Italian, Polish, German and Argentinian • The College of Cardinals is made up of over 120 senior bishops representing every continent • Many Catholic priests in the UK are from other countries • 'All nations form but one community.' (Catechism of the Catholic Church 842)

Support for victims of racial prejudice

The Catechism of the Catholic Church 1930 stresses the importance of the Church supporting efforts to end injustice including racial abuse:

> ❝Respect for the human person entails respect for the rights that flow from his dignity as a creature … It is the Church's role to remind men of good will of these rights❞

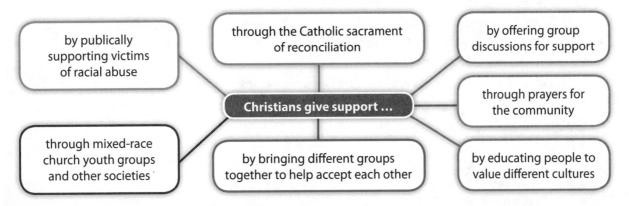

by publically supporting victims of racial abuse

through the Catholic sacrament of reconciliation

by offering group discussions for support

Christians give support …

through prayers for the community

through mixed-race church youth groups and other societies

by bringing different groups together to help accept each other

by educating people to value different cultures

APPLY

A Give two ways in which the Catholic Church tries to promote tolerance and racial equality.

B 'All Catholics must help to stop racial prejudice.'

Write an argument in support of this statement and one that opposes it.

TIP
Key words include 'all' and 'must'. Make sure you address the key words in your answer.

REVIEW

Test the 1 mark question

1. Which **one** of the following is a charity organised by the Catholic Church?

   A ☐ Oxfam   B ☐ Save the Children

   C ☐ Christian Aid   D ☐ CAFOD   **[1 mark]**

2. Which **one** of the following is *not* an action which goes against human rights?

   A ☐ People trafficking   B ☐ Promoting tolerance

   C ☐ Racial prejudice   D ☐ Exploiting the poor   **[1 mark]**

Test the 2 mark question

3. Give **two** points made in *Gaudium et Spes* 26 about human rights.   **[2 marks]**

   1) _____

   2) _____

4. Give **two** ways in which Catholics may take action to try to promote human rights.   **[2 marks]**

   1) _____

   2) _____

> **TIP**
>
> The 'give' questions do not require any explanation.

Test the 4 mark question

5. Explain **two** similar beliefs in contemporary British society on freedom of religion.

   • You must refer to a Christian belief or view.

   • Your contrasting belief or view may come from Christianity or from another religious or non-religious tradition.   **[4 marks]**

● **Explain one belief.**	The Catholic Church teaches that religious freedom is a basic right of every human being.
● Develop your explanation with more detail/an example/ reference to a religious teaching or quotation.	The Second Vatican Council (1962–65) set out this belief in the 'Dignitatis Humanae 2' saying that 'no one is to be forced to act in a manner contrary to his own beliefs'.
● **Explain a second belief.**	The right to freedom of belief applies equally to religious and non-religious beliefs.
● Develop your explanation with more detail/an example/ reference to a religious teaching or quotation.	It is part of the International Covenant on Civil and Political Rights: 'Everyone shall have the right to freedom of thought, conscience and religion.'

6. Explain **two** contrasting beliefs in contemporary British society about racial prejudice.   **[4 marks]**

   • You must refer to a Christian belief or view.

   • Your contrasting belief or view may come from Christianity or from another religious or non-religious tradition.

● **Explain one belief.**	
● Develop your explanation with more detail/an example/ reference to a religious teaching or quotation.	
● **Explain a second belief.**	
● Develop your explanation with more detail/an example/ reference to a religious teaching or quotation.	

7 Explain **two** contrasting views about homosexuality.

- You must refer to a Christian belief or view.
- Your contrasting belief or view may come from Christianity or from another religious or non-religious tradition.

[4 marks]

Test the 5 mark question

8 Explain **two** Christian beliefs about the preferential option for the poor.

Refer to scripture or another source of Christian belief and teaching in your answer.

[5 marks]

● **Explain one belief.**	*Catholics believe that the needs of the poor should be put first as they have suffered so much in the past from the effects of poverty.*
● Develop your explanation with more detail/an example.	*This is following the teaching of Paul as he said, 'Let each of you look not to your own interests, but to the interests of others. Let the same mind be in you that was in Christ Jesus.' (Philippians 2:4–5).*
● **Explain a second belief.**	*The poor have a lot to teach the rich, as they share in the rejection and suffering of Jesus, so Christians who have wealth should listen to them, see Jesus in them, and speak up for them.*
● Develop your explanation with more detail/an example.	*This teaching is summed up by Pope Benedict XVI in the 'Evangelii Gaudium 198'.*
● Add a reference to scripture or another source of religious belief. If you prefer, you can add this reference to your first belief instead.	*'I want a Church which is poor and for the poor. They have much to teach us ... in their difficulties they know the suffering Christ'.*

TIP This quote from scripture supports the point well.

TIP This quote from another source of Christian belief is a good example to use in support of this point.

9 Explain **two** Christian beliefs about why human life is special and has dignity.

Refer to scripture or another source of Christian belief and teaching in your answer.

[5 marks]

● **Explain one belief.**	
● Develop your explanation with more detail/an example.	
● **Explain a second belief.**	
● Develop your explanation with more detail/an example.	
● Add a reference to scripture or another source of religious belief. If you prefer, you can add this reference to your first belief instead.	

10 Explain **two** Catholic beliefs about gender equality.

Refer to scripture or another source of Christian belief and teaching in your answer.

[5 marks]

Test the 12 mark question

11 'Applying Christian teachings on stewardship is the only way to remove world poverty.'

Evaluate this statement. In your answer you:

- should give reasoned arguments in support of this statement
- should give reasoned arguments to support a different point of view
- should refer to Christian arguments
- may refer to non-religious arguments
- should reach a justified conclusion.

[12 marks]
Plus SPaG 3 mar

REASONED ARGUMENTS IN SUPPORT OF THE STATEMENT ● **Explain why some people would agree with the statement.** ● Develop your explanation with more detail and examples. ● Refer to religious teaching. Use a quote or paraphrase or refer to a religious authority. ● **Evaluate the arguments.** Is this a good argument or not? Explain why you think this.	*I believe that applying Christian teaching on stewardship is the only way to remove world poverty. Stewardship means using wealth in a responsible way and avoiding exploiting the poor. The prophet Amos said, 'Let justice flow like rivers' and he condemned the way people were taking advantage of the poor in his day. It is an important point that poor people often can't stand up for themselves and their rights are ignored by multinational companies who force them to work for very little. Applying the principles of stewardship, fair trade is needed to help lift these people out of poverty. Furthermore, wealthy people need to be involved in stewardship by giving to organisations and charities that help the poor, as the poor cannot always help themselves. Jesus encouraged this approach in his parable of the Sheep and Goats when he stated that those who help the poor actually help him.*
REASONED ARGUMENTS SUPPORTING A DIFFERENT VIEW ● **Explain why some people would support a different view.** ● Develop your explanation with more detail and examples. ● Refer to religious teaching. Use a quote or paraphrase or refer to a religious authority. ● **Evaluate the arguments.** Is this a good argument or not? Explain why you think this.	*Others disagree because they say that a lot of world poverty is caused by the people themselves or by their lack of skills, and those who are lazy need to try to get employment and take a lesson from the story of the ants in Proverbs. Others argue that the best way to help get rid of world poverty is to have an amnesty and wipe out the debt that less economically developed countries have. Some owe millions and cannot afford to pay the money back, so with high interest rates the debt keeps growing. The strongest argument here is that what is needed is education so that people can help themselves. Just giving money helps on a temporary basis but what is needed is the provision of skills and materials so that people in poor countries can become self-sufficient.*
CONCLUSION ● **Give a justified conclusion.** ● Include your own opinion together with your own reasoning. ● **Include evaluation.** Explain why you think one viewpoint is stronger than the other or why you think they are equally strong. ● Do not just repeat arguments you have already used without explaining how they apply to your reasoned opinion/conclusion.	*I believe that if the rich of the world applied the principles of stewardship, all poverty could be wiped out. There are sufficient riches in the world to ensure that no one goes without. The problem is that the wealth isn't distributed evenly and many of those who have wealth are greedy and exploit the poor. Sharing is the answer so I strongly agree with the statement, as until people become less selfish world poverty will continue and people will continue to be exploited.*

TIP

Here there is good evaluation, showing chains of reasoning throughout, but the answer would have been even better if there had been some focus on 'the only way'.

12 'It is wrong for the Catholic Church to be so wealthy when so many people are poor.'

Evaluate this statement. In your answer you:

- should give reasoned arguments in support of this statement
- should give reasoned arguments to support a different point of view
- should refer to Christian arguments
- may refer to non-religious arguments
- should reach a justified conclusion.

[12 marks]
Plus SPaG 3 marks

REASONED ARGUMENTS IN SUPPORT OF THE STATEMENT ● **Explain why some people would agree with the statement.** ● Develop your explanation with more detail and examples. ● Refer to religious teaching. Use a quote or paraphrase or refer to a religious authority. ● **Evaluate the arguments.** Is this a good argument or not? Explain why you think this.	
REASONED ARGUMENTS SUPPORTING A DIFFERENT VIEW ● **Explain why some people would support a different view.** ● Develop your explanation with more detail and examples. ● Refer to religious teaching. Use a quote or paraphrase or refer to a religious authority. ● **Evaluate the arguments.** Is this a good argument or not? Explain why you think this.	
CONCLUSION ● **Give a justified conclusion.** ● Include your own opinion together with your own reasoning. ● **Include evaluation.** Explain why you think one viewpoint is stronger than the other or why you think they are equally strong. ● Do not just repeat arguments you have already used without explaining how they apply to your reasoned opinion/conclusion.	

13 'Women should be allowed to become ordained priests in the Catholic Church.'

Evaluate this statement. In your answer you:

- should give reasoned arguments in support of this statement
- should give reasoned arguments to support a different point of view
- should refer to Christian arguments
- may refer to non-religious arguments
- should reach a justified conclusion.

[12 marks]
Plus SPaG 3 marks

Check your answers using the mark scheme on page 238. How did you do?
To feel more secure in the content you need to remember, re-read pages 202–213.
To remind yourself of what the examiner is looking for in your answers, go to pages 8–13.

Apply answers

Please note that these are suggested answers to the Apply questions, designed to give you guidance, rather than being definitive answers.

1 Catholic Christianity

1.1 **A** In *Creation of Adam*, Adam is shown as the perfect man – someone full of strength and potential. This reflects the belief that God made creation to be good. **B** *Arguments for the statement could include:* Creation of Adam illustrates the Christian belief that humanity depends on God for life, shown by the fact that Adam is waiting for God's touch to bring him to life/ illustrates the Christian belief that humanity is made in the image of God, shown by the fact that God and Adam both look powerful and muscular/ are lying in similar positions/ illustrates the important Christian belief that there is a longing for a close relationship between God and humanity, shown in the way God and Adam are reaching out their hands to each other. *Arguments against the statement could include:* Creation of Adam suggests that God and humans are equal, because God and Adam are nearly the same size, but this is not a Christian belief.

1.2 **A** God's hand is large compared to the size of the cloud above it/ the lines from God's hand extend to the edge of the circle, showing that his power extends throughout the universe. **B** *A good answer would include an explanation of your opinion on the statement, which refers to specific details in Meière's mosaic and Creation of Adam. If you agree with the statement, points might include:* Meière's mosaic gives a better idea about God's role as creator because it shows God created everything in the universe, as shown by the lines extending from God's hand to the edge of the circle, whereas Creation of Adam only shows God creating humanity/ Meière's mosaic gives a greater sense that God is always creating, because it doesn't show a specific act or moment of creation, whereas Creation of Adam only deals with the moment when God created humanity. *If you disagree with the statement, points might include:* Creation of Adam gives a better idea about God's role as creator because it teaches more about God's creation of humanity, e.g. it makes it clear that humanity depends on God for life/ reflects the idea that God made humanity in his image/ reflects the idea that God made everything to be very good. None of these points is illustrated in Meière's mosaic. *Your answer should also explain why someone else might agree with the statement when you have disagreed with it, or vice versa, by referring to some of the points made above.*

1.3 **A** *For this question, you need to make two separate points and develop each one with some further explanation. Points could include the following:* Genesis 1 shows God is able to create the whole universe from nothing. All he needs to create the universe is his own word, which shows how powerful he must be/ Genesis 1 teaches everything God made is 'very good'. This shows God must be all-powerful, because he had the power to make everything exactly as he wanted it to be. **B** *Your answer should explain whether you think the statement is true or not, giving the reasons why. You should refer to specific knowledge of Christianity, and consider arguments for and against the statement. Your answer might include the following points:* Genesis 1 teaches Catholics that God is omnipotent, because he has the power to create the whole universe from nothing. This inspires Catholics to trust God because they know he has the power to do anything he wants/ it is vitally important for Catholics to trust God because this gives them the confidence to follow God/ however, Genesis 1 also teaches that God is the creator of everything. This teaches Catholics they should only worship one God. This is a fundamental belief in Christianity, so it could be argued that this is more important than trusting God/ Genesis 1 also teaches Catholics they should care and look after creation, because God created it. Some might argue this is just as important as trusting God, as if the world is not cared for then humanity will suffer/ humanity will be ignoring an important expectation from God.

1.4 **A** God commands Adam not to eat from the tree of the knowledge of good and evil, but doesn't actively prevent Adam from doing so. Adam is given the choice (free will) to eat from the tree or not. **B** *Arguments for the statement could include the following:* belief in free will has a huge influence because without free will people wouldn't have to worry about making the right choices or taking responsibility for their actions/ belief in free will means Catholics know they are able to take actions which displease God. This means they have to try to always make choices they believe will please God. This affects many of their decisions in their lives today. *Arguments against the statement could include the following:* the creation stories teach that humans are made in the image of God and share his Spirit. This means Catholics today should value all people and treat them equally, as they are equally made in the image of God/ this means Catholics today should show respect to everyone they meet, and work against practices that exploit people or promote inequality. Some might argue that this influences Catholics today in a more concrete way than a belief in free will.

1.5 **A** *Possible answers include:* belief in the sanctity of life means Catholics today are against abortion/ against euthanasia. **B** *Arguments for the statement could include the following:* Genesis 1:28 tells Adam and Eve to 'subdue' the earth and 'have dominion' over every living thing/ this suggests humans have been given power and authority over the world and everything in it/ humans should be able to use that power to do what they want with the world's resources/ the creation stories teach that humans are special, because they alone have been made in the image of God/ this means humans are more important than other animals, so should be able to use the world's resources in a way that is of most benefit to humans. *Arguments against the statement could include the following:* Genesis 2:15 tells how God put Adam and Eve in the Garden of Eden to 'till it and keep it'/ this suggests God has given humans the job of looking after the world with care and love/ the creation stories teach that the whole of creation is special because God created it, so the whole of creation should be looked after/ to do this, humans have to be careful about how they use the world's resources, and only use them in a way that doesn't cause long-term damage to the environment.

1.6 **A** *Your answer should include two of the following:* the law – tells how the Jews became the people of God/ contains the laws that God wanted the Jews to follow/ the history books – show how God guided the Jews and how they often refused to listen/ the wisdom books – contain a mixture of prayers, psalms, poems and books of advice/ the books of the prophets – contain advice from the prophets. **B** *Your answer could include the following points:* the Old Testament provides important context and background for the events in the New Testament/ helps Christians to understand why the incarnation was necessary/ helps Christians to understand important truths about God/ e.g. his role in creation (Genesis)/ helps Christians to understand their faith/ e.g. by providing advice in the wisdom books/ helps Christians to know how to live in a way that is pleasing to God/ e.g. by following the Ten Commandments.

1.7 **A** *For this question, you need to make two separate points and develop each one with some further explanation. Points could include two of the following:* God guided the writing of the Bible through the Holy Spirit. The Holy Spirit is God's presence and love in the world, who guides people to know the will of God/ the Bible contains the words of the prophets. These were early Christian teachers who were sent to earth by God to pass on his messages/ the Bible contains the actions and teachings of Jesus. Jesus is the Word of God made flesh, so God speaks to all people through him/ the Bible contains the writings of the apostles. The apostles were Jesus' closest followers and preached God's word. **B** *Your answer could include the following points:* Catholics believe the Magisterium is important for interpreting the teachings in the Bible/ the Bible was written almost 2000 years ago in a very different time and society. Catholics would say they need guidance from the Magisterium to know how to interpret the Bible correctly today/ the Magisterium is the teaching authority of the Catholic Church, which comes from the Pope and the bishops. It is guided by the Holy Spirit and given authority through apostolic succession. This means Catholics should trust and pay attention to the Magisterium's teachings, rather than just relying on the Bible. *Your answer should also explain why some Christians would agree with the statement. Points might include the following:* God guided the writing of the Bible, so it should contain everything Christians need to know to live good Christian lives/ the Bible contains the teachings and actions of Jesus. These tell Christians all they need to know to live in a way that is pleasing to God/ the Bible contains the writings of the apostles, which discuss how to apply Jesus' teachings to everyday life. Even if Jesus' teachings are not clear in themselves, the apostles' writings should make sure Christians understand how to live in a way that is pleasing to God.

1.8 **A** *Your answer should include two of the following:* God made everything/ everything God made was good/ humans are the high point of God's creation. **B** *Your answer should explain why fundamentalists agree with the statement. Points could include the following:* they believe the Bible is the word of God, so should be accurate in all respects/ they believe God loves them and wouldn't give them misleading information/ they believe people do not have the right to come up with their own interpretations of the Bible. *Your answer should also explain why Catholics disagree with the statement and what they believe instead. Points could include the following:* Catholics believe not everything in the Bible should be interpreted literally/ they believe the Genesis creation stories are myths: simple stories designed to convey a deeper message/ they believe everything in the universe formed over a much longer period of time.

1.9 **A** Genesis 1 describes how God made all creation to be 'good'. Humans are part of this creation, therefore they are also good/ Genesis 1 tells how humans are made in the image of God. This means they share some of his qualities, including the quality of being good. **B** *Reasons why the Catholic Church disagrees with the statement include the following:* the Church believes religion and science don't have to contradict each other/ believes science can help people to understand God's creation/ believes religion and science are trying to ask different questions, so it is ok if they sometimes come up with different answers. *Your answer should also explain why some Christians might agree with the statement. Points could include the following:* a literal interpretation of the Bible means it is not possible to believe in the theory of evolution/ Genesis 1 says everything in the universe was created in six days, but scientists believe it has taken billions of years for life to evolve.

1.10 **A** *Points could include two of the following:* All of creation should be valued because it was made by God/ God made humans stewards of the earth/ Jesus taught Christians to 'love your neighbour as yourself'. **B** *Your answer should begin with a paragraph that gives arguments to support the statement. Points could include the following:* the environment is essential for human life/ protecting the environment may not help people in a direct or immediate way, but it is very important for making sure people in the future will be able to live happily/ protecting the environment shows love to animals as well as people. *Your conclusion should explain whether you think the statement is true or not. You should refer to both sides of the argument and explain which you think is more persuasive/accurate.*

1.11 **A** *Your answer should give two examples of actions that Catholics can take to help look after the environment, e.g:* recycling more/ taking the bus instead of driving/ buying products from environment-friendly businesses. **B** *Your answer should explain why the Catholic Church is against the statement. Points could include the following:* the Church teaches that the actions of many people working towards the same goal can make a difference/ 'Everyone's talents and involvement are needed to redress the damage caused by human abuse of God's creation.' (Laudato Si 14)/ the Church believes individual Catholics should use their particular talents to help save the environment. Your answer should also explain whether you agree with the Catholic Church's viewpoint. *You should give reasoned arguments to explain your opinion, e.g. if you agree with the Church, you could explain why you believe individual people can make a difference by giving specific examples of how individual people have helped to protect the environment. If you disagree with the Church, you could explain why you believe individual people cannot make a difference, and how a difference can be made instead.*

1.12 **A** *Examples could include two of the following:* encouraging people in England and Wales to live more simply through the livesimply awards/ helping to create the Sustainable Development Goals by founding the Beyond 2015 campaign/ helping farmers to adopt sustainable farming methods with groups such as MONLAR/ supporting projects that use renewable energy. **B** *Arguments might include the following:* Catholics believe in stewardship, and that God has given them a responsibility to look after the earth/ they believe God made all of creation to be 'good' (Genesis 1), and all of God's creation should be valued/ these beliefs mean Catholics should take care of the environment/ CAFOD supports sustainable projects that help to protect the environment/ e.g. they support projects that use renewable energy/ Catholics believe it is important to love your neighbour as yourself (Mark 12:31)/ CAFOD aims to show love by helping people in poverty/ e.g. they help farmers to adopt effective, sustainable farming methods.

2 Incarnation

2.1/2.2 **A** *Points could include two of the following:* the incarnation shows how much God loves the human race/ means God can empathise better with humanity/ helps Christians to value God's love/ led to Jesus' resurrection and ascension, which saved humanity from sin. **B** *Arguments could include:* in Luke 1:26–38, Gabriel tells Mary she will give birth to the Son of God/ the accounts say Jesus is conceived by the Holy Spirit, so he is not just a normal human being/ in Matthew 1:18–24, the angel confirms Jesus is being sent to earth by God, which suggests he is not a normal human being/ in Matthew 1:18–24, Jesus is called 'Emmanuel', meaning 'God is with us'.

2.3 **A** The Word of God is eternal/ the Word of God is God/ the Word of God is distinct from God/ the Word of God is how God expresses his power and love/ Jesus is the Word of God/ the Word of God took on human nature to live on earth/ to guide people closer to God. **B** *Your answer should explain whether you think the statement is true or not, giving the reasons why. You should refer to specific knowledge of Christianity, and consider arguments for and against the statement. Your answer might include the following points:* the phrase 'The Word was God' shows the Word of God is God/ this is supported by Christian belief in the nature of the Trinity, which states that each person of the Trinity is fully God/ John 1:1–4 says the Word is eternal – so shares this same characteristic with God/ but the phrase 'The Word was with God' shows the Word and God are distinct from each other/ John 1:1–4 says God expresses his power and love through the Word – suggesting they have different purposes/ John 1:14 says the Word became Jesus, but God (the Father) did not, so this makes them different from each other.

2.4 **A** A general title a person uses to refer to themselves/a normal human being/ a title for someone who has been given power and authority by God. **B** *Points could include:* Christians would disagree with this statement because they would say there is evidence to support both claims/ 'the Son of Man must undergo great suffering' (Mark 8:13)/ Jesus knew his crucifixion would cause him agony because he was fully human/ Jesus was born normally and lived a full human life/ Jesus used the title 'Son of Man' to emphasise his humanity/ Jesus confirmed he was the Son of God at his trial (Mark 14)/ other accounts in the Bible confirm Jesus is the Son of God (e.g. Luke 1:26–38)/ Christians believe the Son of God is fully God.

2.5 **A** Alpha and Omega/ Ichthus/ Chi-Rho. **B** *Your arguments against the statement should include at least two specific examples of how symbols can be used. Points could include:* symbols are a useful way to summarise religious beliefs/ Symbols are an easy way for Christians to declare their faith/ e.g. the Ichthus symbol is a declaration of belief in Jesus Christ as the Son of God/ symbols are useful for persecuted Christians as they can be quickly drawn and erased to indicate belief/ the location of a meeting/ e.g. the Ichthus symbol was used in this way in early Christianity/ symbols are a simple way to remind people of religious beliefs/ e.g. the Chi-Rho symbol reminds Christians that Jesus died to save them from sin.

2.6 **A** *Points could include two of the following:* to inspire people/ as a focal point for prayer/ to remind or teach people about aspects of God's work. **B** *A good answer would include various arguments to support the statement, backed up by examples, with sentences linked to each other in a logical chain of reasoning. Points could include:* it is impossible to portray God accurately because no one knows what God looks like/ an infinite God cannot be represented using finite means/ art that portrays God therefore misleads people about what God is like/ e.g. Michelangelo's *Creation of Adam* might give people the idea that God is an ageing man/ the second commandment also forbids people to make statues or paintings of God/ it is important for Christians to obey the Ten Commandments.

2.7 **A** *For this question, you need to make two separate points and develop each one with some further explanation. Points could include:* the statue shows evidence of Jesus' crucifixion, e.g. holes in the hands/ a crown of thorns. This reminds Catholics that Jesus loves humanity so much he sacrificed his life for them/ Jesus is pointing to his heart, which has flames coming out of it. Jesus is drawing attention to the burning love he has for all people. **B** *A good answer would include an explanation of your opinion on the statement, which refers to specific knowledge of Christianity and is backed up by examples. If you agree with the statement, points might include:* images of Jesus help to remind/ teach Christians about Jesus' life and teachings/ Jesus is hugely important in Christianity as the Saviour of humanity, so it is good for Christians to be reminded about him through art/ art depicting Jesus can inspire people to do good things/ e.g. the Sacred Heart statue reminds Christians how much Jesus loves them. This might inspire them to show love to other people. *If you disagree with the statement, points might include:* God expects people to obey the Ten Commandments and it is not worth breaking them for the sake of showing Jesus in art/ portraying Jesus in art misleads people about his nature and what he looked like. This could lead people to have false beliefs about Jesus/ e.g. art showing Jesus as human could mislead people into thinking he is not fully God. *Your answer should also explain why someone else might agree with the statement when you have disagreed with it, or vice versa, by referring to some of the points made above.*

2.8 **A** The commandments and rules God gave to the Jews, which can be found in the Old Testament/ mainly focuses on the actions people should or should not do. **B** *Points could include:* Jesus taught it is more important to focus on attitudes than actions/ the main point of the parable of the Sheep and the Goats is that people should show love towards others/ by showing love, Christians will be rewarded with God's presence in heaven/ the Beatitudes confirm this in the phrase, 'Blessed are the pure in heart, for they will see God.'/ many other good qualities stem from having a loving attitude, e.g. forgiveness/mercy/calmness.

2.9 A *Points could include:* Jesus is the 'glory of God' and 'fully alive' because he was the perfect human being, e.g. he always displayed God's wishes/ by following Jesus' teachings, all people can become more 'fully alive' and share in God's glory. **B** *Arguments for the statement could include:* God is invisible/ transcendent, so it is hard to understand him without the help of Jesus/ Jesus is the Son of God and displays qualities of God/ this means Christians can understand God better through learning about Jesus/ 'Jesus revealed God to men' (*Adversus haereses*)/ God is better able to understand/empathise with humans because he experienced being human in Jesus. *Arguments against the statement could include:* Christians can get to understand God through the Old Testament/ through the way he works in the world/ God created humanity so he understands humanity/ God is omnipotent so knows everything, including what humanity is like.

2.10 **A** Beliefs that go against the teachings of the Church/ e.g. the belief that Jesus is not fully human or not fully God. **B** *Your answer should explain one quote each from Dei Verbum 4* and *Verbum Domini 12. Points could include:* 'For He sent His Son … so that He might dwell among men and tell them of the innermost being of God' (*Dei Verbum 4*)/ 'Dwell among men' suggests Jesus is human, as otherwise he would not be able to live among other humans without arousing suspicion/ 'He sent His Son' confirms Jesus is (the Son of) God/ Jesus would only be able to tell people about God's innermost being if he was God.

'Jesus Christ, therefore, the Word made flesh, was sent as 'a man to men'' (*Dei Verbum 4*)/ 'the Word' is another name for the Son of God, confirming Jesus is God/ the Word was 'made flesh' into a human/ the Word was sent as 'a man', meaning he was sent as a human.

'… the eternal word became small – small enough to fit into a manger. He became a child, so that the word could be grasped by us' (*Verbum Domini 12*)/ the 'word' refers to the Son of God/ 'eternal' stresses the divine nature of the Word/ The Word became a child, i.e. became human.

'In his perfect humanity [Jesus] does the will of the Father at all times … Jesus thus shows that he is the divine *Logos* … but at the same time the new Adam, the true man' (*Verbum Domini 12*)/ this quote refers to both Jesus' perfect humanity and also his divine nature.

2.11 **A** A free/unconditional gift of God's love to all people/ the love that unites the persons of the Trinity. **B** *Points could include:* to say reality is sacramental means to see the whole of reality as a sign of God's love. Catholics believe God's presence and love can be seen throughout the world/ the incarnation brought God's presence and love into the world, by bringing God to earth in Jesus (the incarnation)/ so the incarnation made reality sacramental.

2.12 **A** When a person confesses their sins: reconciliation. When a person becomes a member of the Church: baptism. When a person becomes a priest: ordination. **B** *Arguments for could include:* the sacraments give grace (God's love) to a person/ help to make a person's life more holy/ welcome Christ into a person's life/ baptism makes a person a child of God/ confirmation strengthens a person's faith/ in the Eucharist people receive the life of Christ and so become closer to God/ reconciliation restores a person's relationship with God. *Arguments against could include:* prayer is a better way for a Catholic to become closer to God because it helps them to develop a personal relationship with God/ studying the Bible is better because it helps Catholics to get to know God/ following Jesus' teachings is better because this is how Catholics are able to enter heaven when they die/ going on pilgrimage is better because it can inspire and strengthen faith in God.

2.13 **A** *Points could include:* by supporting a pro-life organisation that campaigns against abortion/ by supporting an organisation that cares for women who have decided not to abort. **B** *Your answer should explain whether you think the statement is true or not, giving the reasons why. You should refer to specific knowledge of Christianity, and consider arguments for and against the statement. Arguments in support of the statement could include:* life begins at conception/ this belief is supported by Luke 1:44/ the Catholic Church teaches that the whole person is present from the moment of conception/ *imago dei* means that all life is holy and sacred, including the unborn/ abortion is therefore killing life, which is the same as murder. *Arguments in support of other views could include:* life does not begin until birth or the earliest viability (when the foetus can survive outside of the womb)/ a new foetus is not conscious/ so abortion is not killing life/ Luke 1:44 should not be interpreted literally.

3 The Triune God

3.1 **A** *Reasons could include two of the following:* music unites people in praise/ increases the beauty of worship/ helps people to feel more involved in worship/ inspires people to praise God/ can make worship feel more joyous or solemn. **B** *Your paragraph to support the statement should ideally include various arguments that are backed up by examples, with sentences linked to each other in a logical chain of reasoning. Points could include:* worship and prayer can still happen without music/ the music is just decorative: it might help to heighten the meaning of the words, but isn't essential to understand their meaning/ the use of music can exclude people who are not very musical/ some churches do not have the resources to include much music in their services but this doesn't stop the services from being held. *In your paragraph against the statement, points could include:* fewer people might attend church if there was no music, and churches should try to attract as many people as possible to prevent the faith from dying out/ music allows people to join in with the worship, which is an important reason for attending church/ music unites Christians together, and having a strong community is important for the future of the faith/ the Catholic Church strongly approves of the use of music. *Your conclusion should explain whether you think the statement is true or not. You should refer to both sides of the argument and explain which you think is more persuasive/accurate.*

3.2 **A** Plainchant. **B** *Arguments to support the statement could include:* modernising the music in a church could help to make the services more accessible/engaging and attract younger people/ the upbeat nature of contemporary worship songs could help to attract people who feel church services are too solemn or serious/ all Christians have a duty to help spread the faith and this is one way that Catholic churches can do so/ if people can join in with the singing then they feel more involved in the worship/ this can make the worship more interesting and more meaningful for those attending church. *Arguments to support a different point of view could include:* it is more important to choose music that seems appropriate to the service rather than always only using more contemporary music/ some services might be best suited to more solemn traditional hymns, or complex music that can only be sung by a choir/ not everyone likes contemporary worship songs and some people think their upbeat nature is disrespectful/ plainchant is 'specially suited to the Roman liturgy' (*Sacrosanctum Concilium* 116) so churches should not disregard it/ traditional hymns have been proven to help the praise of God over many years, whereas contemporary worship songs haven't.

3.3 **A** The Gloria praises God's glory and goodness/ e.g. begins with the words 'Glory to God in the highest'/ whereas the Sanctus praises God's holiness/ as it is based on the angels in the Temple crying out 'Holy, holy, holy is the Lord of hosts'. **B** *A good answer would include an explanation of your opinion on the statement, which refers to specific knowledge of Christianity and is backed up by examples. If you agree with the statement, points might include:* music does not change the meaning of the acclamations/ the acclamations still praise God if they are said rather than sung. *If you disagree with the statement, points might include:* music helps to heighten the meaning of the words/ is a more powerful way to praise God/ e.g. a complex setting of the Gloria may help to reflect God's glory and greatness/ e.g. a reflective setting of the Sanctus can help to show the peace and harmony of heaven. *Your answer should also explain why someone else might agree with the statement when you have disagreed with it, or vice versa, by referring to some of the points made above.*

3.4 **A** *Your answer could include two of the following beliefs:* even though there are three separate Persons, there is only one God (Deuteronomy 6:4)/ the Trinity consists of three separate Persons who coexist with each other (Matthew 3:16–17)/ God the Father pours the Holy Spirit, which is the love that unites the Father and Son, into the hearts of all Christians (Galatians 4:6). **B** *Arguments for the statement could include:* Jesus' baptism is the passage in the Bible when God reveals himself as the Trinity/ this passage confirms there are three separate Persons who coexist at the same time/ it is important because it shows the Trinity consists of the Father (the voice from heaven), the Holy Spirit (the dove), and the Son. *Arguments against the statement could include:* Deuteronomy 6:4 is equally important because the fact there is only one God is just as important as knowing there are three Persons/ Deuteronomy 6:4 confirms this by saying 'the Lord alone'/ Galatians 4:6 is equally important because it explains the relationship between the Trinity and a Christian/ this makes the Trinity relevant to Christian's lives rather than being an abstract concept.

3.5 **A** Genesis 1:1–3 shows that God the Father created the universe ('In the beginning when God created the heavens and earth')/ it also shows the Holy Spirit was involved, as it refers to the 'wind from God', which can also be translated as 'spirit'/ it shows that God created the universe with the power of his word, which is a reference to the Son of God. **B** *Your answer should explain whether you think the statement is true or not, giving the reasons why. You should refer to specific knowledge of Christianity, and consider arguments for and against the statement. Arguments in support of the statement could include:* the Nicene Creed was written because the Bible didn't give enough information about the Trinity/ it teaches that the Son and the Father share the same nature ('consubstantial with the Father')/ and are both eternal ('born of the Father before all ages')/ it teaches that the Holy Spirit is also equal in majesty and power to the Father and Son ('who with the Father and the Son is adored and glorified')/ so confirms the Father, Son and Holy Spirit are all equal/ this equality is not made clear in the Bible. *Arguments in support of other views could include:* the Bible includes important beliefs about the Trinity/ the statements in the Nicene Creed stem from the teachings in the Bible/ e.g. there is only one God (Deuteronomy 6:4)/ e.g. the Trinity consists of three separate Persons who coexist with each other (Matthew 3:16–17)/ the Bible more clearly explains how the Trinity was involved in the creation of the universe (Genesis 1:1–3)/ the Bible more clearly explains the relationship between the Trinity and Christians (Galatians 4:6).

3.6 **A** *Points could include two of the following:* belief in the Trinity inspires Christians to share God's love through doing good actions (mission)/ by speaking publicly about their faith (evangelism)/ by donating to charities/ belief that Jesus is one of the three Persons of the Trinity and fully God influences Christians to take Jesus' teachings seriously. **B** *Arguments to support the statement could include:* mission involves taking practical action to help others so makes more of a concrete improvement to people's lives/ mission can be seen as a less pushy/obtrusive way of sharing God's love/ mission might involve more commitment and effort than evangelism (e.g. compare building and running a school to giving a public speech about God) so is a greater demonstration of love. *Arguments to support a different point of view could include:* helping someone to experience the joy and peace of being a Christian is the best gift of love a person could receive/ people can only really understand and appreciate God's love if others share their knowledge of it/ the more Christianity grows, the more God's love will be shared, and evangelism plays an important part of this.

3.7 **A** Mark 1:9–11 shows the three Persons of the Trinity coexisting/acting together at the same time/ the Holy Spirit descends 'like a dove' on Jesus/ while the voice from heaven is the Father/ who speaks to Jesus saying 'You are my Son'. **B** *Your answer should explain whether you think the statement is true or not, giving the reasons why. You should refer to specific knowledge of Christianity, and consider arguments for and against the statement. Arguments in support of the statement could include:* calling God 'Father' helps to strengthen a Christian's relationship with God/ reminds them that God will take care of them (like a Father)/ reminds them that they should obey God/ have responsibilities towards God (like children)/ reminds them that God is personal/ it is possible to have a personal relationship with God/ helps to strengthen the Christian community (as everyone shares the same Father). *Arguments against the statement could include:* by calling God 'Father' Christians may forget about some of his other characteristics/ e.g. God is transcendent, impersonal and eternal/ none of these characteristics is embodied by the word 'Father'/ it is not possible for Christians to have the same relationship with God that Jesus did/ as Jesus was God/ so they should use a different name for God.

3.8 **A** The Son came to earth as Jesus to bring redemption/ the Holy Spirit is continually guiding believers towards the Father, to complete the work of Jesus' redemption. **B** *Points could include the following:* St Augustine showed how the relationship within the Trinity can be understood through the concept of love/ he taught that love needs three things: a giver, a receiver, and the love between them/ the Trinity can be thought of as three Persons united in love/ 'True love is: a trinity of lover, beloved and the love that binds them together into one'/ LaCugna taught about the relationship between the Trinity and Christians, and how love is an important part of this/ she said the love that unites the Father and Son (the Holy Spirit) is shared with Christians to guide them back to the Father/ the Son also came to earth as Jesus to save humanity and guide them back to the Father/ love therefore underpins and powers the relationship of the Trinity with humanity.

3.9 **A** *Points could include two of the following:* the Son is eternal/ the Father and Son have always coexisted together/ the Father and Son are equal and of the same nature. **B** *A good answer would include an explanation of your opinion on the statement, which refers to specific knowledge of Christianity and is backed up by examples. If you agree with the statement, points might include:* without the Magisterium, Catholics would be relying primarily on the Bible, which can be interpreted in many different ways/ the Bible also doesn't give enough information about certain beliefs or theological concepts/ e.g. it gives little detail about the Trinity/ this is why there have been various disputes about the nature of the Trinity in the history of Christianity/ the Magisterium was needed to settle these disputes and confirm the correct beliefs that Catholics should follow. *If you disagree with the statement, points might include:* the Magisterium is not the source of Catholic beliefs/ the job of the Magisterium is to interpret the Bible, which would still exist without the Magisterium/ the Bible is the word of God and contains fundamental Christian beliefs/accounts of Jesus' work and teachings/ this is what Catholics should base their beliefs on/ Catholics are also guided to believe the right thing by the Holy Spirit, which happens regardless of whether the Magisterium exists or not. *Your answer should also explain why someone else might agree with the statement when you have disagreed with it, or vice versa, by referring to some of the points made above.*

3.10 **A** *Points could include:* a person shares in Jesus' death and resurrection/ by being submerged under water, a person joins Jesus in the tomb after he died/ by rising up out of the water, a person joins in with Jesus' resurrection/ a person is filled with the Holy Spirit/ which is the same Holy Spirit that filled Jesus during his baptism/ the person is baptised 'in the name of the Father and of the Son and of the Holy Spirit'. **B** *Arguments to support the statement could include:* the most important reason is for a person to become a member of the Church/ a child of God/ to join in with Jesus' death and resurrection/ to be cleansed from sin/ to be made a sharer in the life of the Trinity (not just the Holy Spirit)/ a person can receive the strength of the Holy Spirit in other ways (e.g. through grace/ Confirmation/ Sacrament of the sick)/ but baptism is the only way to become a member of the Church.

3.11 **A** *Reasons could include two of the following:* it helps to strengthen a person's relationship with God/ it allows a person to communicate with God/ it helps a person to know what God wants for them/ it encourages reflection in the middle of a busy life/ it can bring comfort. **B** *A good answer would include an explanation of your opinion on the statement, which refers to specific knowledge of Christianity and is backed up by examples. If you agree with the statement, points might include:* spontaneous prayer allows a person to say what they want to God/ open up to God about personal concerns and worries/ which helps to deepen their relationship with God/ feels like a more 'normal' conversation than using traditional prayer/ feels more sincere than traditional prayer/ means God knows how best to help a person. *If you disagree with the statement, points might include:* traditional prayers have stood the test of time/ proved over many years to be an effective way of communicating with God/ allow someone to communicate with God when they're not sure what to say/ allow the mind to go deeper than the words and open up to the presence of God. *Your answer should also explain why someone else might agree with the statement when you have disagreed with it, or vice versa, by referring to some of the points made above.*

3.12 **A** Prostrating/ standing with arms stretched out in front/ joined hands. **B** *Your answer should explain whether you think the statement is true or not, giving the reasons why. You should refer to specific knowledge of Christianity, and consider arguments for and against the statement. Arguments in support of the statement could include:* the intention behind the prayer is much more important than the posture of the person praying/ the posture doesn't affect the meaning of the prayer/ prayer is 'raising the heart and mind to God' – neither of which are affected by the position of the body/ if posture was important then Christian Churches would make a bigger deal about it. *Arguments in support of other views could include:* using different postures can help to distinguish/ separate the prayer from other activities/ so helping the person to focus on the prayer itself/ different postures can also help a person to remember the overall aim of the prayer/ e.g. using joined hands is a reminder that the prayer is meant to ask for help/ different postures can contribute to the feeling a person puts into a prayer/ help to make the prayer feel more sincere/ different postures can also help others to know when a person is praying/ which means they are less likely to be disturbed.

4 Redemption

4.1 **A** *Your answer could include two of the following:* churches face east towards Jerusalem/ are built in the shape of a cross/ have the altar against the east wall. **B** *Arguments for could include:* the Mass is the most important service in Catholic worship so providing a space for it is important/ Christians can pray anywhere but it is harder to celebrate the Mass anywhere, so it helps to have a purpose-built space to celebrate it. *Arguments against could include:* it is important that a church provides a space for Christians to meet and worship, but this involves more than just the Mass/ it is also important to provide a space for individual prayer/ it could be argued that the most important purpose is to inspire Christians to become closer to God.

4.2 **A** The consecrated Bread can be saved in the tabernacle so it can later be taken to people who can't get to Mass. **B** *Arguments could include:* Bible readings about Jesus are given from the lectern/ the lectern helps people to see the reader and clearly hear the Bible readings/ Christ is truly present when the Bible readings are given/ the altar reminds Christians of Jesus' sacrifice on the cross/ Christ is truly present on the altar during the consecration/ the crucifix is a cross with Jesus dying on it/ reminds Christians of the suffering Jesus went through to save humanity/ the tabernacle houses the Real Presence of Christ/ reminds Christians that Christ is still caring for them.

4.3 **A** *Points could include:* the altar is a place of sacrifice/ so reminds Christians about Jesus' sacrifice on the cross/ the altar is used at Mass to offer the Bread and Wine to God, as Jesus offered himself on the cross/ a table is where people eat from/ so it reminds Christians about the Last Supper. **B** *A good answer would include an explanation of your opinion on the statement, which refers to specific knowledge of Christianity and is backed up by examples. If you agree with the statement, points might include:* a crucifix is a reminder of the suffering Jesus endured out of his love for humanity/ reminds Christians how much Jesus loves them so is a good source of comfort/ could inspire people to find strength in their own suffering/ could inspire people to share Jesus' love with others. *If you disagree with the statement, points could include:* the crucifix is too gory/morbid to be a good source of comfort/ a cross or Risen Christ reminds Christians that Jesus was resurrected and ascended to heaven, and that they will hopefully join him there, which is a good source of comfort/ a cross or Risen Christ could inspire people to follow Jesus' teachings in order to join him in heaven. *Your answer should also explain why someone else might agree with the statement when you have disagreed with it, or vice versa, by referring to some of the points made above.*

4.4 **A** *Points could include:* 'restoration' means bringing things back to the way God intended them to be/ 'cosmic order' refers to the universe and everything in it/ 'The restoration of the cosmic order' means making the whole of creation as perfect as God intended it to be from the beginning/ this was partly achieved through Jesus' resurrection and ascension/ and will be completed at the end of time. **B** *Arguments could include:* sin exists because of free will/ the Catholic Church teaches that people are born with a tendency to sin, which is only possible because they have free will/ sin broke the relationship between God and humanity/ Jesus' death was necessary to restore this relationship/ if free will didn't exist then neither would sin, so Jesus would not need to die to save people from sin.

4.5 **A** *Resurrection:* when a person is raised back to life after they die/ may be physical or spiritual/ the event when Jesus rose back to life after dying on the cross. *Ascension:* when a person ascends/goes to heaven/ the event when Jesus returned to God the Father in heaven 40 days after his resurrection. **B** *Arguments for could include:* the resurrection destroyed the ultimate power of sin and death, and made life after death possible for everyone/ the resurrection gave meaning to Jesus' death/ without the resurrection, there could be no ascension/ 'If Christ has not been raised, your faith is futile and you are still in your sins' (1 Corinthians 15:17)/ without the resurrection there would be no Christianity. *Arguments against could include:* the ascension proves Jesus is now with the Father in heaven/ this gives Christians faith they will also be raised to heaven/ from heaven, Jesus continues to work in and through his believers, giving strength and courage to Christians today. *The paragraph giving your opinion on the statement should explain why you agree or disagree with it. A good answer would refer to some of the arguments above and explain how they back up your opinion/why you think the arguments are convincing or not.*

4.6 **A** *Points could include:* Jesus redeemed humanity by offering himself to the Father on the cross/ this is re-enacted in the Mass/ as the Body and Blood of Christ are offered to the Father on the altar/ through receiving Holy Communion, Catholics welcome Christ into their lives to give them grace and the strength to resist sin/ this helps them to accept Jesus' redemption and get closer to salvation. **B** *Points could include:* some Christians believe salvation is an ongoing process/ as although Jesus' death and resurrection defeated the ultimate power of sin, sin still exists/ people have to choose to accept Jesus' salvation by resisting the temptation to sin and accepting forgiveness when they do sin/ some Christians believe salvation will be completed at the end of time/ as this is when the power of sin and death will be completely destroyed/ and all believers will be able to share in the glory of Christ and experience the joy of heaven.

4.7 **A** Jesus is the example because through his total obedience to God, he set the example for all people to follow/ Jesus is the restorer because through his death, he restored the relationship between God and humanity/ Jesus is the victor because through his death and resurrection, he defeated the ultimate power of sin and death. **B** *Points could include:* the Bible helps to show that redemption is ongoing because even

though Jesus' death redeemed humanity, people still have to accept this redemption themselves/ so the ongoing evangelism of the Church helps more people to share in Jesus' redemption/ e.g. in Acts 1:6–11, Jesus tells his disciples they will be his witnesses 'to the ends of the earth'/ Jesus expects his disciples to continue to spread his teachings so everyone can accept his redemption/ e.g. in Acts 2:1–4, the apostles are filled with the power of the Holy Spirit/ giving them the courage and ability to spread Jesus' teachings, so more people can accept his redemption/ Acts 1:6–11 also describes how two angels told the disciples that Jesus would return in the future/ this reflects the teaching that Jesus will complete the redemption of the world at the end of time.

4.8 **A** Some Christians find the metaphor useful because it reflects the idea that they are slaves or servants of Christ/ as Christ 'paid a ransom' for the sins of all humans, so they no longer have to be slaves to sin/ some Christians find the metaphor unhelpful because it is not clear who the 'ransom' is paid to/ it implies there is someone greater than God. **B** *Your answer should explain whether you think the statement is true or not, giving the reasons why. You should refer to specific knowledge of Christianity, and consider arguments for and against the statement. Arguments in support of the statement could include:* metaphors help to explain why Jesus' death was necessary and what it achieved/ help to simplify/summarise a difficult concept/ by comparing it with something more understandable or accessible/ e.g. St Irenaeus' metaphor of a tree draws parallels between the fall of Adam and Eve and Jesus' salvation/ it reminds Christians that the original event which created the need for salvation was Adam and Eve's disobedience of God/ and that by obeying God, Jesus brought salvation/ e.g. St Anselm's metaphor compares Jesus' death with the idea of paying a ransom in the slave trade/ which helps Christians to understand that Jesus' death helped to free humanity from sin. *Arguments in support of other views could include:* metaphors could be interpreted wrongly/ e.g. St Anselm's metaphor could be interpreted to mean there is someone greater than God/ metaphors may be based on a particular understanding of the Bible that not everyone agrees with/ e.g. not everyone agrees with St Irenaeus' interpretation of Genesis 3/ metaphors might use ideas that are unfamiliar to people/ e.g. the idea of paying a ransom in the slave trade/ in which case they are not very helpful, as the metaphor itself has to be explained.

4.9 **A** *Points could include:* natural law means that people are born with an understanding of right and wrong/ this understanding guides a person's conscience/ for Christians, it means that everyone has a conscience that instinctively knows the difference between right and wrong. **B** *Your answer should explain whether you think the statement is true or not, giving the reasons why. You should refer to specific knowledge of Christianity, and consider arguments for and against the statement. Arguments in support of the statement could include:* Catholics believe a person's conscience is the voice of God in their heart and soul/ 'There he is alone with God, Whose voice echoes in his depths' (*Gaudium et Spes* 16)/ following your conscience therefore means following or being faithful to God/ conscience is guided by natural law/ an instinctive understanding of good and evil/ so following your conscience should mean doing good/ which is what God wants/ the Catholic Church teaches that people shouldn't ignore what they believe God is telling them in their hearts. *Arguments in support of other views could include:* the Catholic Church teaches that people shouldn't go against the teachings of the Church/ even if their conscience tells them otherwise/ 'Personal conscience and reason should not be set in opposition to the moral law or the Magisterium of the Church' (Catechism of the Catholic Church 2039)/ as the Church's teachings have been guided by the Holy Spirit over hundreds of years/ it is possible that a Catholic is interpreting their conscience incorrectly/ or a Catholic's conscience needs more development/education/ so sometimes they should listen to others or follow the teachings of the Church rather than following their conscience.

4.10 **A** Catholics apologise to God and each other for their sins/ this reminds them that God has forgiven and redeemed them/ Jesus is offered again to the Father in the consecration/ reminding Catholics that redemption is ongoing/ the priest repeats the words Jesus said at the Last Supper/ reminding Catholics they can share in Jesus' sacrifice/ receiving Communion reminds Catholics they are part of the new covenant, which was established when Jesus died on the cross. **B** *Arguments for might include:* during the Eucharistic Prayer, the Bread and Wine become the Body and Blood of Christ/ without this change, Jesus could not be offered up to God the Father on the altar, so making his sacrifice a present reality/ making his redemption ongoing/ the Eucharistic Prayer reminds believers of Jesus' words at the Last Supper/ which are the words that allow Christians to share in Jesus' offering of himself on the cross. *Arguments against might include:* the Gospel reading is more important as it reminds believers of Jesus' teachings/ shows how God loves all people/ the offering itself is more important as this means Jesus' redemption is ongoing/ Communion is more important as this is when believers receive God's grace/ which gives them strength and guidance.

4.11 **A** Catholics believe they receive the Body and Blood of Christ, whereas many Anglicans believe they receive the Spirit of Christ/ Catholics view the Eucharist as a re-enactment of the Last Supper, whereas Nonconformist Christians view the Eucharist as a memorial of the Last Supper. **B** *Your answer should explain whether you think the statement is true or not, giving the reasons why. You should refer to specific knowledge of Christianity, and consider arguments for and against the statement. Arguments in support of the statement could include:* Catholics believe the Eucharist is 'source' of Christian life because it gives life to their soul/ they receive God's grace through receiving the Body and Blood of Christ/ Christ is offered again to the Father/ many Christians might view the Eucharist as the 'summit' of Christian life because it celebrates the most important event in Christianity/ is the highest form of prayer a Christian can make. *Arguments against the statement could include:* the Eucharist is not important to all Christians/ e.g. it is not celebrated by the Quakers and Salvation Army/ Nonconformist Christians view the Eucharist as a memorial of the Last Supper/ instead of a re-enactment of Jesus' sacrifice on the cross/ this means they may not see it as the 'source and summit of Christian life'.

4.12 **A** Catholics believe that confessing and accepting God's forgiveness is important/ at the start of the Mass Catholics apologise to God and each other for their sins/ Catholics believe God sent his Son to earth out of love/ there is always a reading from the Gospel, which reinforces this belief/ Catholics believe the Bread and Wine become the Body and Blood of Christ/ so they are treated with great respect/ many Catholics receive Communion on their tongue. **B** *Your answer should explain whether you think the statement is true or not, giving the reasons why. You should refer to specific knowledge of Christianity, and consider arguments for and against the statement. Arguments in support of the statement could include:* it is not possible for the Bread and Wine to turn into the Body and Blood of Christ/ many Christians (e.g. many Anglicans) do not believe this/ the Bible is not always interpreted literally, so 'this is my body' does not necessarily mean the Bread becomes the Body of Christ. *Arguments against the statement could include:* 'this is my body' show that the Bread has become the Body of Christ/ the appearance of the Bread and Wine do not have to change to become the Body and Blood of Christ, as this would be physically impossible/ Christ is God, so he is able to transcend the laws of nature and become present in the Eucharist.

5 Church and the Kingdom of God

5.1 **A** *Points could include:* 'making the Stations of the Cross' involves walking between the 14 Stations (images that cover Jesus' journey from Pilate's house to the hill of Calvary), saying a prayer at each one/ this symbolises accompanying Jesus on his last journey and sharing in his suffering. **B** *Your answer should explain whether you think the statement is correct and why, by referring to specific knowledge of Christianity. Points might include:* going on a pilgrimage can involve a physical journey to a sacred place, such as a pilgrimage to Jerusalem or Lourdes/ but it can also be a spiritual journey/ e.g. Catholics believe life is a spiritual journey towards heaven/ the journey can also be symbolic/ e.g. making the Stations of the Cross is a type of pilgrimage of prayer where the person symbolically accompanies Jesus on his final journey towards God.

5.2 **A** *Your answer could include two of the following:* Jerusalem, because it is where Jesus died/ Rome, because it is the centre of Catholic faith/ where the Pope lives/ Lourdes, because of the healing power of the waters/ Walsingham, because it is the Catholic national shrine for England/ requires less travelling for Catholics living in England. **B** *Points could include:* Catholics can be inspired by holy places on pilgrimage/ they can meet other Catholics who they would not meet in their local church/ they can be healed by the waters at Lourdes/ they can show or renew their commitment to their faith in a way that might have more meaning than just going to their local church/ in Jerusalem and nearby they can see the places where Jesus lived and taught, which might help them to understand him better.

5.3 **A** *Points could include:* in *Les Miserables*, the Bishop of Digne forgives the thief Valjean after Valjean steals silver from him/ his act of kindness persuades Valjean to become a better person and set up a factory to help create jobs and wealth for other people/ this illustrates the power of forgiveness and its importance to Christians. **B** *A good answer would include an explanation of your opinion on the statement, which refers to specific knowledge of Christianity and is backed up by examples. If you agree with the statement, points might include:* films can help to illustrate Christian beliefs in an entertaining and accessible way/ films may reach a much wider audience than more direct methods of evangelism/ films can illustrate in an engaging/emotionally powerful way how Christian beliefs can improve individual people's lives, which helps people to appreciate these beliefs more. *If you disagree with the statement, points might include:* there are more direct ways of spreading Christian beliefs, e.g. evangelism/ non-Christians watching a film might not fully grasp or appreciate the Christian beliefs that are being illustrated/ people may focus too much on other aspects of a film. *Your answer should also explain why someone else might agree with the statement when you have disagreed with it, or vice versa, by referring to some of the points made above.*

5.4 **A** *Points could include:* belief in the Kingdom of God motivates Catholics to help spread the Kingdom of God on earth/ e.g. by showing Kingdom values in their own lives/ by trying to create peace and justice/ by showing forgiveness to others/ by resisting the temptation to sin/ by undertaking evangelism or missionary work/ belief in the Kingdom of God may give Catholics hope and courage during difficult times. **B** *Arguments could include:* the Lord's Prayer teaches Christians about the main ways to spread the Kingdom/ e.g. 'Hallowed be thy name' teaches that respecting and recognising God's holiness and majesty is important/ e.g. 'Thy will be done' teaches that accepting and following God's will is important/ e.g. 'Forgive us our trespasses' teaches that forgiving others, and accepting God's forgiveness, are important/ e.g. 'Deliver us from evil' teaches that resisting sin is important.

5.5 **A** *Peace:* a state of total trust and unity between people/ the absence of conflict and war. *Justice:* ensuring all people have access to basic human rights/ treating all people fairly and equally, regardless of their sex, race, religion/ respecting the dignity of every person. *Reconciliation:* bringing back together people who have fallen apart/ restoring damaged relationships between people. **B** *Your answer* should explain whether you think the statement is true or not, giving the reasons why. You should refer to specific knowledge of Christianity, and consider arguments for and against the statement. Arguments in support of the statement could include: fighting against injustice means creating a more equal society/ equality is one of the features of the Kingdom of God/ in a more equal society, there will be fewer reasons to engage in conflict/ so peace will also spread/ a more just society means fewer people living in poverty, therefore more people will be able to focus on God because they do not need to focus on finding basic necessities to live/ 'Give us this day our daily bread' (The Lord's Prayer). *Arguments in support of other views could include:* Christians also need to focus on creating peace/ injustice is not the only reason why conflict exists/ Christians also need to focus on reconciliation and forgiveness/ as this helps peace and justice to spread/ so perhaps should be tackled first/ Christians also need to focus on evangelism/ as the Kingdom of God will only be fully established when everyone chooses to do God's will.

5.6 **A** A meeting between the Pope and the bishops/ to discuss issues that affect the whole Church/ might be called to discuss difficult issues that require consultation/ to make sure the Pope is making the best decisions for the whole Church. **B** *Teachings might include:* the Bible should be taken seriously as the word of God but not interpreted literally/ all members of the Church have important roles to play, not just the Pope/ all people should be able to take a full part in the worship of God, e.g. by hearing Mass in their own language/ the Church should not be separate from modern society. *You should also explain your opinions on these teachings, for example:* 'It is good for the Church to say that Catholics do not have to interpret the Bible literally, as this means they are able to accept Catholic teachings and scientific theories such as the Big Bang theory, by reading Genesis 1 as a myth rather than a literal account of the creation of the universe'; 'I agree that people should be able hear the Mass in their own language because then they can understand what is happening and feel more involved in the worship.'

5.7 **A** There is a sense of revolution within the prayer/ some people thinks it supports those who are rebelling against their governments/ encourages the weak and poor to rise up against those in power/ 'He has brought down the powerful from their thrones, and lifted up the lowly'/ 'He has filled the hungry with good things, and sent the rich away empty.' **B** The Magnificat shows that Mary was humble/ as she recognised she was only special because of what God had done for her/ 'for he has looked with favour on the lowliness of his servant'/ Mary accepted God's will/ by willingly accepting the role of mother of Jesus, shown in her praise of God in the prayer/ 'My soul magnifies the Lord'/ Mary trusted God/ believing that God would help people who are weak and poor like her/ 'He has filled the hungry with good things'.

5.8 **A** One/ Catholic. **B** *A good answer would include an explanation of your opinion on the statement, which refers to specific knowledge of Christianity and is backed up by examples. If you agree with the statement, points might include:* apostolic means the authority of Jesus' closest followers has been passed to the Pope and bishops/ this means Catholics can trust the authority of the Church's teachings/ which is vitally important for maintaining the faith. *If you disagree with the statement, points might include:* 'one' is more important because Jesus prayed that the Church 'may all be one' (John 17:21)/ if the Church was not united, Catholics wouldn't know what to believe/ 'Holy' is more important because it means the Holy Spirit is guiding the Church in the right direction/ 'Catholic' is more important because it means the Church is united worldwide/ which strengthens the Church and gives authority to its teachings. *Your answer should also explain why someone else might agree with the statement when you have disagreed with it, or vice versa, by referring to some of the points made above.*

5.9 **A** 'Conciliar' refers to the authority of the Councils/ and the fact that decisions are made through Councils/ 'pontifical' refers to the authority of the Pope and his teachings/ the Church is both because it is led by the Pope/ who has the highest authority/ but Councils help the Pope to make important decisions/ and influence the direction of the Church. **B** The Catholic Church would agree because Jesus taught that people should help others/ e.g. the parable of the Good Samaritan/ there would be no Church without people to be a part of it/ the Church believes that everyone should help to support the weakest and poorest members of society/ 'The Church sincerely professes that all men … ought to work for the rightful betterment of this world in which all alike live' (*Gaudium et Spes* 21).

5.10 **A** Catholics try to show love to those in need/ e.g. by donating to charities such as CAFOD/ volunteering for charities such as SVP/ giving food or money to the homeless/ contributing to environmental projects that help to protect the earth for future generations/ Catholics may try to act with kindness towards everyone they meet/ show forgiveness towards people who have wronged them. **B** *If you agree with the statement, points might include:* providing practical help can make an immediate, direct difference to individual people's lives/ e.g. by providing food for the homeless (as SVP does)/ Jesus' teachings suggest practical help for individuals is a good way to show love/ e.g. the parable of the Sheep and the Goats/ although this type of help might reach fewer people, the people it helps are then in a better position to help others, so spreading love throughout a community. *If you disagree with the statement, points might include:* providing help on a local level does not solve the root causes of poverty or injustice/ so even though challenging international policies and laws might seem like a less direct way to show love, it can ultimately help more people/ e.g. campaigning against policies that contribute to inequality (as CAFOD does) shows love by helping to lift more people out of poverty.

5.11 **A** A call from God to take on a certain role in life/ for a person to use their talents for a particular reason. **B** *Arguments in support of the statement might include:* people who commit to a religious life are able to dedicate more time than others to developing the Kingdom values in their life/ take vows of poverty, chastity and obedience to show their commitment to God's values/ serve God in a way that people with other commitments such as jobs/families are not able to. *Arguments in support of other views might include:* all vocations allow people to live by the Kingdom values in different ways/ e.g. priests show commitment to God by taking a promise of celibacy/ parents can show the Kingdom values in their relationship with each other, and with their children.

5.12 **A** By washing the feet of 12 prisoners on Maundy Thursday/ by restoring relationships between Cuba and the USA/ by bringing together leaders of countries at war with each other, e.g. the Palestinian and Israeli presidents/ by helping to reconcile tensions between Muslims, Jews and Catholics/ by arranging services where Muslim and Jewish leaders could pray together with him. **B** *Arguments might include:* Pope Francis sets a good example for living by the Kingdom value of peace because he works to restore relationships between countries in conflict/ Christians can follow this example by trying to restore relationships in their own lives/ e.g. by reaching out to people of other religions/ as Pope Francis has done/ he also sets a good example by showing Christians they can help create justice by helping the poor/ living simply/ criticising policies that lead to inequality and exploitation.

6 Eschatology

6.1 **A** When a person is baptised, they are given a candle that is lit from the Paschal candle/ this shows they have been filled with the light of Christ/ the Paschal candle is also lit at funerals/ to show the deceased person has joined Christ in the resurrected life. **B** *Arguments might include:* the Alpha and Omega symbols show that Christ is eternal/ this is important because it reflects the belief that the Son of God shares the same nature with God the Father/ the three Persons of the Trinity are equal/ the five grains of incense represent the five wounds Christ received during his crucifixion/ this is important because it reminds Christians of the suffering that Jesus endured during his crucifixion, out of his love for humanity.

6.2 **A** At the end of time everyone will be resurrected and judged by Christ/ which confirms whether they spend the rest of eternity in heaven or hell. **B** *Arguments might include:* the saints in the painting have perfect bodies, despite having been tortured/ this shows that people who keep to their faith will be raised up to heaven/ in the painting Christ is raising those on his right up to heaven/ this reflects the parable of the Sheep and the Goats, which teaches that those who do good and try to become closer to God will be rewarded with heaven/ in the painting one of the angels is holding a small book with the names of those who will be raised to heaven, which is smaller than the book of those who are destined for hell/ this suggests it is not easy to get into heaven, so Christians should spend their lives trying to become closer to God if they want to make sure they can enter heaven when they die.

6.3 **A** *Tombstone:* a large carved stone that is placed over a person's grave, to indicate the location of the grave so it can be treated with respect. *Monument:* a structure that is built to remember an important person or event. *Remembrance garden:* a quiet outside space where the ashes of people who have been cremated can be kept. **B** *If you agree with the statement, points might include:* a tombstone is often inscribed with the letters 'R.I.P.' (rest in peace)/ which expresses the hope the person is now enjoying the peace of eternal life in heaven/ Catholic tombstones are often shaped like a cross/ which expresses the hope the person will be resurrected with Jesus to eternal life/ these reflect the fundamental Catholic belief that people who live good Christian lives will spend eternity in heaven with God when they die. *If you disagree with the statement, points might include:* monuments also reflect Catholic beliefs, e.g. the Chi-Rho symbol on a sarcophagus reflects the belief that Jesus died so everyone would be able to experience heaven/ skeletons on a monument reflect the belief that everyone is judged equally by God/ like a tombstone, a remembrance garden also reflects the hope that the person is now enjoying the peace and beauty of heaven.

6.4 **A** A resurrected body will live forever (it is imperishable)/ be sinless and perfect (it is raised in glory)/ be powerful and strong (it is raised in power). **B** *Arguments for might include:* Jesus' resurrection teaches Catholics that life continues after death/ that a resurrected body will be physical but different from an earthly body (e.g. John 20:19–29)/ that showing obedience to God can lead to an afterlife in the presence of God/ all Catholics really need to know about the afterlife is that if they obey God, they will be raised to heaven. *Arguments against might include:* because Jesus' resurrection might have been unique to him, it may not teach Catholics enough about how their own afterlife works/ Jesus' resurrection does not give Catholics enough guidance on how to make sure they earn their own place in heaven/ about how God's judgement works/ about what heaven and hell are like.

6.5 **A** Catholics believe some people may go to purgatory/ where their souls are cleansed from the effects of sin/ other Christians believe people will either go straight to heaven or hell/ some Christians believe judgement happens immediately after death/ others believe judgement happens at the end of time/ some Christians believe that everyone who has faith in God will go to heaven/ others believe that people also have to do good deeds to enter heaven. **B** *Arguments in support might include:* Christians believe death is not the end but a transition to a new phase of life/ the start of eternal life without the limitations of the earthly body/ the soul continues to live on/ God's judgement is fair and merciful/ Christians are likely to be judged favourably by God and enter heaven/ which is a state of eternal happiness. *Some Christians might disagree with the statement because:* death itself is likely to be painful/ they will be separated from people they love/ they believe they may be judged unfavourably by God/ which would lead to eternity in hell.

6.6 **A** Catholics might try to do more good deeds to result in a positive judgement/ e.g. they might volunteer for a charity/ Catholics might try to follow Jesus' teachings more carefully/ e.g. by showing love towards others/ Catholics might try not to sin/ make sure they confess to any sins/ participate in the sacrament of reconciliation on a regular basis. **B** *Example of an argument against the statement:* Christians do not need to enter purgatory when God has already forgiven their sins/ if God has forgiven their sins then they should accept this forgiveness and be happy to enter heaven. *Example of an argument for the statement:* everyone has done bad things of which they are ashamed/ they should want to enter purgatory and go through this cleansing process, as it will allow them to feel happier in the presence of God.

6.7 **A** Showing love and kindness to others is important for entering heaven/ in the parable, the rich man goes to hell as he does not show love and kindness towards Lazarus/ hell is a place of torment where people are cut off from a relationship with God/ the rich man is 'in agony in these flames'/ people in hell are conscious and aware of those in heaven/ the rich man is aware of Abraham and Lazarus in heaven/ it is not possible to move between heaven and hell/ Abraham says there is a 'great chasm' between heaven and hell/ having faith in God and following Jesus' teachings will lead people to heaven/ 'If they do not listen to Moses and the prophets, neither will they be convinced even if someone rises from the dead'. **B** Whether or not you agree with the statement might depend on your interpretation of it. You could agree with the statement by arguing that the parable teaches wealth should be used to help others, and having 'too much' of it suggests hoarding it rather than giving it to people in need. You could disagree with the statement by arguing that the parable does not teach

that having money in itself is bad, but that how it is used is important. The parable also teaches that showing love and kindness is important/ that a person's actions and choices during their lifetime determine where they will spend the afterlife (as it is not possible to move between heaven and hell)/ that having faith in God, and following Jesus' teachings, will lead people to heaven.

6.8 **A** Refers to the idea of reconciling the whole of creation to God/ bringing the whole of creation together in harmony with God/ a process that was started with Jesus' death and resurrection, and will be completed at the end of time. **B** *Your answer should explain whether you think the statement is true or not, giving the reasons why. You should refer to specific knowledge of Christianity, and consider arguments for and against the statement. Arguments in support of the statement could include:* the end of time suggests cosmic disasters/a failing universe when things will very much not be perfect/ Christians believe the end of time is when all people do God's will, but it is hard to imagine this happening/ it is difficult to believe Julian of Norwich's vision of Jesus was real. *Arguments against the statement could include:* Christians believe all things will be perfect at the end of time as they will be fully reconciled with God/ everyone will enjoy the eternal happiness of heaven/ this is supported by Church teachings, e.g. 'The Church … will attain its full perfection only in the glory of heaven, when there will come the time of the restoration of all things' (*Lumen Gentium* 48)/ supported by Julian of Norwich's vision of Jesus saying 'all shall be well'.

6.9 **A** God does not decide to send anyone to hell/ determine in advance that someone will go to hell/ people send themselves to hell by choosing to reject God/ this means a person's choices and actions during their lifetime will affect whether they go to hell or not. **B** *If you agree with the statement, points might include:* some Christians believe that faith alone is enough to enter heaven/ salvation was completed with Jesus' death and resurrection/ God does not want to send people to hell/ God is forgiving and merciful. *If you disagree with the statement, points might include:* faith alone is not enough – actions and behaviour also matter/ the Catholic Church teaches that performing good deeds and actions is important/ 'while we perform with hope in the future the work committed to us in this world by the Father, and thus work out our salvation' (*Lumen Gentium* 48)/ if Catholics commit mortal sins and do not confess/ apologise for them, they will go to hell/ Michelangelo's *The Last Judgement* suggests getting into heaven is not easy.

6.10 **A** *Anointing of the sick:* a sacrament for a person who is seriously ill/ centres around the action of anointing them with holy oil. *Commendation of the dying:* a short service for a person who is dying/ centres around the dying person receiving their last Holy Communion. **B** *Your answer should explain whether you think the statement is true or not, giving the reasons why. You should refer to specific knowledge of Christianity, and consider arguments for and against the statement. Arguments in support of the statement could include:* to receive a favourable judgement from God, it is more important that the Catholic person has faith and performed good deeds during their lifetime/ neither of these things are influenced by the last rites. *Arguments against the statement could include:* the last rites help a dying person to reaffirm their beliefs/ the anointing of the sick forgives a person's sins/ both these things may help a Catholic to enter heaven/ the last rites also help to give the dying person strength, courage, peace and comfort/ these things may be invaluable to the dying person and their family.

6.11 **A** At a funeral, the coffin is sprinkled with holy water, which is also used in baptism/ the Paschal candle (which represents the Risen Christ) is lit at both funerals and baptisms/ these actions show that the deceased person has joined in Christ's resurrection. **B** *If you agree with the statement, points might include:* a solemn funeral shows respect to the dead person/ death should not be treated lightly or frivolously/ it is very sad when a loved one dies/ people who do not think they will see their loved one again (as they do not believe in an afterlife), or who think their loved one may be in hell, will be unlikely to view funerals as happy occasions. *If you disagree with the statement, points might include:* Christians believe death is not the end but the transition to a new stage of life/ hopefully in the presence of God in heaven/ this means funerals should not be too solemn/ especially because separation from the dead person is only temporary.

6.12 **A** A belief in the sanctity of life means many Christians today are against abortion/ against euthanasia/ against the death penalty/ because these practices do not respect the belief that life is sacred and holy/ should only be taken by God/ Christians try to treat everyone with respect/ help people to maintain their dignity/ give the ill and elderly all the care and support they need. **B** *Your answer should explain whether you think the statement is true or not, giving the reasons why. You should refer to specific knowledge of Christianity, and consider arguments for and against the statement. Arguments in support of the statement could include:* euthanasia is considered to be murder/ so accepting it would break the sixth commandment/ 'You shall not murder' (Exodus 20:13)/ the sanctity of life is an important Catholic belief, and euthanasia goes against this as it does not respect life/ the Church teaches that only God has the right to take away life, so euthanasia goes against this belief as well. *Arguments against the statement could include:* in some situations euthanasia could be considered the most loving and compassionate action to take, allowing a person to die with dignity/ so from this point of view it could reflect Christian morals/ it should be accepted because it allows a person to end their suffering painlessly/ in order to survive the Church needs to move with the times, so there may be a situation in the future where the Church has to accept euthanasia because the rest of society does.

7 Islam: beliefs and teachings

7.1 **A** *Your answer could include two of the following beliefs:* 'He is God the One'/ there is only one God/ God is a unified, indivisible being/ God does not consist of different Persons/ 'God the eternal'/ God has always existed/ 'He begot no one nor was He begotten'/ God was not born or came into being out of something else/ God does not have any children/ 'No one is comparable to him'/ God is unique/ no other person or thing has God's qualities. **B** *Your answer should explain whether you think the* statement is true or not, giving the reasons why. You should refer to specific knowledge of Islam, and consider arguments for and against the statement. Arguments in support of the statement could include: Tawhid is the belief in one, indivisible God/ so Muslims should only worship one God/ it also means there is nothing comparable to God/ so Muslims should never make anything in their lives more important than God/ this influences Muslims to prioritise God in their lives/ e.g. by praying to God five times a day/ e.g. by putting God before their family or jobs/ it means everything they do should be centred around pleasing/obeying God. Arguments in support of other views could include: belief in the prophets is more important/ because this means accepting that God's revelations through the prophets are true/ and the Qur'an is the word of God/ the Qur'an is the source of authority for all matters of doctrine, practice and law/ so has a huge influence on the way Muslims live and worship/ belief in God's judgement is more important/ as this motivates Muslims to take responsibility for their actions/ and to live good lives/ avoid sin in their daily lives.

7.2 **A** God is immanent/ present everywhere in the world and the universe/ God is also transcendent/ beyond and outside the universe/ God can be both because he created the universe (so is outside it) but is also able to act within it/ God is merciful/ God shows compassion, mercy and forgiveness/ God is just/ God will punish people who act badly or make bad choices. **B** *A good answer would include an explanation of your opinion on the statement, which refers to specific knowledge of Islam and is backed up by examples. If you agree with the statement, points might include:* Sunni and Shi'a Muslims share the same fundamental beliefs/ e.g. they both believe in the same God/ and acknowledge the importance of the prophets/ so both groups agree with the core beliefs in the Shahadah ('There is no God but Allah and Muhammad is the Prophet of Allah')/ differences in leadership are not as important as differences in belief, and many of the beliefs are the same. *If you disagree with the statement, points might include:* tensions and conflict between Sunni and Shi'a Muslims in the world today suggest the differences are more important than the similarities/ who is the rightful leader of a religion is very important, as this is the person that everyone follows/ looks to for guidance and advice/ Sunni and Shi'a Muslims not only disagree about who the rightful leader is, but how much authority they should have/ Sunni and Shi'a Muslims also emphasise different beliefs/ e.g. Sunni Muslims are more likely to believe that God has already determined everything that will happen in the universe/ all of these differences are important enough to split Islam into two distinct groups.

7.3 **A** God is transcendent because he created the universe, so is beyond and outside it/ but he is also immanent because he is able to act within the universe, and is within all things. **B** *Your paragraphs could include the following points: Fairness and justice:* it is more important for Muslims to know that God will judge people fairly and equally on the Day of Judgement/ as this motivates them to do good during their lives/ accept responsibility for their actions/ accept God's judgement as being fair/ teaches them the importance of justice/ encourages them to act fairly and justly towards others. *Immanence:* it is more important to know that God is present in and involved with life on earth/ as this helps Muslims to form a closer relationship with God/ suggests that God cares about the world and what happens in it. *Omnipotence:* it is most important to know that God is all powerful/ as this explains how God is able to create and sustain the universe/ contributes to belief in the supremacy of God's will/ helps Muslims to accept God's will. *Your conclusion should explain whether or not you agree with the statement and why, by referring to some of the points above.*

7.4 **A** *Your answer could include two of the following:* angels serve God/ pass on God's words to people through the prophets/ take care of people throughout their lives/ record everything a person does during their lives/ take people's souls to God after they die/ escort people into paradise or hell/ send rain, thunder and lightning to earth. **B** *A good answer would include an explanation of your opinion on the statement, which refers to specific knowledge of Islam and is backed up by examples. If you agree with the statement, points might include:* angels are how God communicates with people/ by passing on his messages perfectly to the prophets/ the Qur'an is the source of authority for all matters of doctrine, practice and law/ without the angel Jibril this may not have been passed on to Muhammad, or passed on imperfectly/ so Islam would be very different/ if God was not able to communicate with Muslims, then they would not really know how to worship/obey/please him/ the existence of Islam is based on revelations to the prophets that have come through the angels. *If you disagree with the statement, points might include:* it is impossible to know how Islam would have developed without angels/ but if God wanted to communicate with people, he would have found a way regardless/ e.g. by speaking to them directly/ through visions or miracles/ there are examples of this in the history of Islam/ e.g. when Ibrahim had a dream in which God asked him to sacrifice his son.

7.5 **A** Many Muslims believe they will be judged by God for their actions on the Day of Judgement/ and rewarded or punished as a result/ so they have the responsibility to make sure their actions are good enough to be rewarded by God. **B** *Your answer should explain whether you think the statement is true or not, giving the reasons why. You should refer to specific knowledge of Islam, and consider arguments for and against the statement. Arguments in support of the statement could include:* some Muslims believe God has already determined everything that will happen in the universe/ has written down everything that will happen in a 'book of decrees'/ because God created people and because his will is so powerful, Muslims must act according to his will/ some Muslims believe they are not able to change their destiny or the overall plan that God has set for them as a result. *Arguments in support of other views could include:* even Muslims who believe they cannot change their overall destiny still believe they do have some choice over how they behave/ many Muslims believe predestination means God knows everything that is going to happen/ but does not decide everything that is going to happen/ so they have the free will to make their own choices/ which is why God's judgement is an important aspect in Islam/ 'God does not change the condition of a people [for the worse] unless they change what is in themselves' (Qur'an 13:11).

7.6 **A** Barzakh. **B** Some Muslims would agree with this statement because they believe where they spend the afterlife is determined by their actions and faith during their lifetime/ as God will judge all people on the Day of Judgement/ and send those who have kept their faith in God and done good deeds to heaven/ heaven is a state of eternal happiness in the presence of God/ this reward should encourage Muslims to live a good life through which they show their faith in God. Some people might disagree with the statement because they believe it is best to live in the present/ an approach to life should not be based on beliefs in something for which there is no proof/ faith in God should not be dependent on the reward of heaven/ there are other reasons for doing good deeds/ e.g. out of a sense of kindness and compassion.

7.7 **A** Prophets help Muslims to understand God's message/ to stay on the right path/ act as good role models/ teach Muslims how to live a good life in obedience to God. **B** *Reasons why Muslims would disagree with the statement might include:* Muhammad is more important because he received the final revelation of Islam/ received the Qur'an, which is the source of authority for all matters of doctrine, practice and law/ 'he is God's Messenger and the seal of the prophets' (Qur'an 33:40)/ he helped to fully establish Islam by conquering Makkah and converting the city to Islam. *Arguments to support the statement could include:* Adam is the father of the human race – all of the human race (including Muhammad) is descended from Adam/ God gave Adam knowledge and understanding, which Adam passed on to the rest of the human race/ so the knowledge of how to live a good life in obedience to God stems from Adam.

7.8 **A** The Ka'aba is a small, cube-shaped building in the centre of the Grand Mosque in Makkah/ it is important to Muslims because it is considered to be the house of God/ the holiest place in Islam. **B** *Your answer should explain whether you think the statement is true or not, giving the reasons why. You should refer to specific knowledge of Islam, and consider arguments for and against the statement. Arguments in support of the statement could include:* Ibrahim showed total dedication to God/ fulfilled all the tests and commands given to him by God/ e.g. he refused to worship idols and preached that there is only one God/ he followed God's command to rebuild the Ka'aba/ he was willing to sacrifice his son to God/ he left his wife and son in the desert on God's command/ these events show he had complete faith in God/ was willing to put God before his family. *Arguments in support of other views could include:* Ibrahim tried to stop idol worship by using an axe to destroy all the idols in his town temple/ some people might say this could encourage Muslims to respond with violence to something they think is wrong/ some people might say that Ibrahim should not have been so willing to sacrifice his own son/ so does not provide a good role model for Muslim families.

7.9 **A** The Imams are the leaders of Shi'a Islam/ descendants of Muhammad/ chosen by God/ able to interpret the Qur'an and Islamic law without fault/ important for helping to preserve and explain the law/ for guiding Muslims in how to live correctly/ the twelfth Imam will return in the future to bring justice and equality to all. **B** *Arguments to support the statement could include:* Muhammad received the Qur'an from God/ which has a huge influence on how Muslims live and worship God/ he converted the city of Makkah to Islam/ without which Islam might not exist today/ he agreed with God that Muslims should pray five times a day/ Sunni Muslims still follow this practice. *Arguments to support other views could include:* the knowledge of how to live a good life in obedience to God originally stems from Adam, so he has had a greater impact/ Ibrahim's actions influence Muslims when they go on Hajj, as the pilgrimage recounts events in his life/ so Ibrahim has a stronger impact on this pillar of Islam/ Ibrahim's willingness to sacrifice his son to God is a strong message to Muslims to put God first/ which may have significantly impacted individual Muslims in their lives and decision-making.

7.10 **A** The Psalms. **B** The Qur'an was revealed by the angel Jibril/ who directly/ perfectly passed on God's words to Muhammad/ Muhammad learned these words by heart and scribes wrote them down/ an official version of the Qur'an was compiled to make sure God's words were not distorted/ because the Qur'an contains accurate transcriptions of God's words, it is the highest authority in Islam/ other holy books do not have the same authority because they have been lost/distorted/corrupted over time.

8 Islam: practices

8.1 **A** *Your answer could include any two of the following:* salah – Muslims are expected to pray three or five times a day/ sawm – Muslims are expected to fast during the month of Ramadan/ Zakah – Muslims are expected to give 2.5% of their savings to charity every year/ Khums – a 20% tax, half of which goes to charity and half to religious leaders/ Hajj – Muslims are expected to undertake the Hajj pilgrimage once in their lifetime/ jihad – the struggle to maintain the faith and defend Islam/ amr-bil-maruf – encouraging people to do what is good/ nahi anil munkar – discouraging people from doing wrong/ tawallah – showing love for God and people who follow him/ tabarra – not associating with the enemies of God. **B** The Shahadah states there is only one God (Allah)/ Islam is founded on this belief/ it influences Muslims to worship God as the creator of everything/ to never make anything in their lives more important than God/ the Shahadah also states that 'Muhammad is the Prophet of Allah'/ this reflects how important Muhammad is as the person who received the final revelation of Islam/ belief in Muhammad means belief in the Qur'an as the word of God/ this influences Muslims to take the Qur'an seriously and follow its teachings/ e.g. by praying a number of times a day/ giving Zakah/ fasting/ going on pilgrimage.

8.2 **A** Muslims perform ritual washing (wudu)/ wash their faces, hands and feet under running water/ or sand or dust if water is not available/ to make themselves spiritually clean. **B** *Arguments for might include:* prayer has to be done three or five times a day, every day/ this means Muslims have to set aside time for prayer regardless of what else they are doing during the day/ they also have to get up before sunrise every day to pray, which is very early in the summer months. *Arguments against might include:* some Muslims might find fasting for a whole month harder/ as this requires more discipline and commitment/ some might find going on Hajj harder/ if they are physically weak or do not have the money to travel to Makkah.

8.3 **A** Sunni Muslims pray five times a day/ Shi'a Muslims pray three times a day/ by combining the midday and afternoon prayers, and sunset and night prayers/ unlike Sunni Muslims, Shi'a Muslims rest their foreheads on a clay tablet when prostrating in prayer/ because they believe in only using natural elements/ in a mosque the mihrab indicates the direction to pray/ outside the mosque Muslims may use a special compass to find the right direction/ in a mosque the prayers are led by an imam/ at home prayers may not be led by anyone. **B** *A good answer would include an explanation of your opinion on the statement, which refers to specific knowledge of Islam and is backed up by examples. If you agree with the statement, points might include:* structured prayers mean people know exactly what to do when they pray/ do not have to come up with the right words to use/ they unite a religious community/ provide comfort because of the familiarity. *If you disagree, points might include:* structured prayers are too restrictive/ spontaneous prayers allow a person to pray about their own personal concerns/ allow a person to develop a closer relationship with God/ are more meaningful.

8.4 **A** The Night of Power is when Jibril first appeared to Muhammad and started revealing the Qur'an/ Qur'an 96:1–5 contains the words that Jibril spoke/ Jibril instructed Muhammad to start reciting his words/ the Night of Power happened on one of the odd-numbered dates in the second half of Ramadan/ observing the Night of Power gives Muslims the benefits of worshipping for a thousand months/ 'The Night of Glory is better than a thousand months' (Qur'an 97:3). **B** *Your answer should explain whether you think the statement is true or not, giving the reasons why. You should refer to specific knowledge of Islam, and consider arguments for and against the statement. Arguments in support of the statement could include:* the Qur'an is the word of God/ the source of Muslim beliefs and practices/ so Muslims should know it as well as possible/ studying the Qur'an during Ramadan is a way of thanking God for revealing the Qur'an/ Muslims study the Qur'an during the Night of Power/ which is thought to give them the benefits of worshipping for a thousand months. *Arguments in support of other views could include:* fasting shows greater discipline and commitment/ this shows obedience and dedication to God/ Muslims are obligated to fast/ 'So any one of you who is present that month should fast' (Qur'an 2:18)/ fasting reminds Muslims why it is important to help those in poverty.

8.5 **A** Zakah is 2.5% of savings; Khums is 20% of savings/ Zakah goes to charity; Khums also goes to Shi'a religious leaders/ Zakah is given by Sunni and Shi'a Muslims; Khums is only given by Shi'a Muslims. **B** *A good answer would include an explanation of your opinion on the statement, which refers to specific knowledge of Islam and is backed up by examples. If you agree with the statement, points might include:* giving Zakah or Khums helps to remove selfishness and greed/ teaches Muslims to use their money to help others/ this pleases God/ if Muslims develop a good attitude towards money, this will have a lasting effect all year round, not just when Zakah or Khums is given. *If you disagree with the statement, points might include:* the most important reason is because it is a requirement for Muslims/ helps Muslims to purify their souls/ and so become closer to God/ helps those in need/ strengthens the Muslim community. *Your answer should also explain why someone else might agree with the statement when you have disagreed with it, or vice versa, by referring to some of the points made above.*

8.6 **A** It is the holiest place in Islam/ the house of God/ it was rebuilt by the prophet Ibrahim/ it is where Hajj begins. **B** *Arguments for might include:* Hajj requires Muslims to take at least five days out of work/ and to save up the money to travel to Makkah/ it is physically demanding/ e.g. requires Muslims to pray for a whole afternoon in the hot summer sun/ it shows commitment to Islam because it is centred around Muslim beliefs/ the actions of Muslim prophets. *Arguments against might include:* sincerely reciting the Shadahah in front of Muslim witnesses is the best way as this makes a person a Muslim/ expresses the core beliefs of Islam/ praying is the best way as this demonstrates commitment to God every day/ fasting is the best way as requires the most discipline.

8.7 **A** Pilgrims must enter a state of purity called ihram/ this involves ritual washing, praying and putting on ihram clothing/ it symbolises purity, unity and equality. **B** *A good answer would include an explanation of your opinion on the statement, which refers to specific knowledge of Islam and is backed up by examples. If you agree with the statement, points might include:* the main actions of Hajj recall the actions of the prophets/ e.g. walking between the two hills recalls Hajira's search for water after she was left in the desert by Ibrahim/ standing at Arafat recalls Muhammad's last sermon/ sacrificing an animal recalls Ibrahim's willingness to sacrifice his own son/ remembering the good examples set by the prophets is an important part of Hajj. *If you disagree with the statement, points might include:* there is more to Hajj that just remembering the actions of the prophets/ e.g. it is about showing dedication and commitment to God/ feeling a part of the Muslim community/ receiving forgiveness for sins/ rejecting evil and the temptation to sin.

8.8 **A** A belief in greater jihad motivates Muslims to live according to the teachings of Islam/ 'This is My path, leading straight, so follow it, and do not follow other ways' (Qur'an 6:153)/ e.g. by observing the Five Pillars/ studying the Qur'an/ putting God above all else/ avoiding temptations/ helping those in need/ a belief in greater jihad encourages Muslims to constantly try to improve themselves/ helps Muslims to acknowledge that this is sometimes a struggle. **B** *Arguments for might include:* greater jihad is a constant, daily struggle/ many Muslims today are unlikely to take part in lesser jihad in their lives/ greater jihad requires more from Muslims, e.g. observing the Five Pillars/ putting God above everything else/ avoiding temptations and negative traits. *Arguments against might include:* some Muslims who have pacifist leanings might struggle to take part in a war to defend the faith/ a Muslim might have to sacrifice their own life in combat/ other countries or faiths might be very resistant to a holy war and respond aggressively/ this would make following lesser jihad in today's world potentially devastating for those involved.

8.9 **A** The festivals were started by Muhammad in Madinah, after he fled from persecution in Makkah/ he told the people in Madinah that God had set aside two days for festivities. **B** *Points could include:* Id-ul-Fitr celebrates the end of a month of fasting, which requires huge amounts of discipline and commitment, so Muslims should be able to have fun/ Id-ul-Fitr allows Muslims to thank God/ Muslims pray and listen to a sermon as part of the festivals/ for Id-ul-Fitr, Muslims visit their local cemetery to remember the dead/ for Id-ul-Adha, Muslims donate money to the poor/ Ibrahim's willingness to sacrifice his son is relevant today as it reminds Muslims to show complete obedience to God/ festivals help to strengthen the Muslim community.

8.10 **A** By performing plays that tell the story of Husayn's death/ by taking part in public expressions of mourning/ by beating themselves on their chests/ by visiting Husayn's tomb. **B** *Points could include:* for Shi'a Muslims, Ashura is a solemn festival/ day of great sorrow/ as it commemorates the death of Husayn/ which is seen as a symbol of the struggle against injustice, tyranny and oppression/ it is observed with public expressions of grief and mourning/ Muslims might beat or even cut themselves to connect with Husayn's suffering.

9 Judaism: beliefs and teachings

9.1 **A** 'Hear, O Israel! The Lord is our God, the Lord alone. You shall love the Lord your God with all your heart and with all your soul and with all your might.' For Jews, this passage confirms the belief there is only one God/ a single, whole, indivisible being/ who they should show complete loyalty, love and dedication towards. **B** *Arguments could include:* The belief in God as One also means that God is a single, indivisible being (not three Persons, as in Christianity)/ that God is the source of all Jewish morality, beliefs and values/ that everything in the universe has been created and is sustained by God/ that God is always present in people's lives/ that everything Jews see and experience is a meeting with God.

9.2 **A** A more literal interpretation is that the events in Genesis actually happened about 6000 years ago/ i.e. God took six days to create the universe and everything in it/ a more liberal interpretation is that God is the creator of everything/ but the universe is much older and life has evolved over many years. **B** *Your answer should explain whether you think the statement is true or not, giving the reasons why. You should refer to specific knowledge of Judaism, and consider arguments for and against the statement. Arguments in support of the statement might include:* Jews believe that evil exists because God gave people free will/ if free will didn't exist, there would be no evil/ so Jews would not be able to do bad things that displease God/ so they would have a better relationship with God. *Arguments in support of other views might include:* if free will didn't exist, Jews would not be able to actively choose to do good/ actively choose God/ but choosing God is clearly important to God, otherwise he would not have created free will/ so without this choice, any relationship with God would be meaningless.

9.3 **A** On the journey through the wilderness to Canaan, e.g. when the Jews were led by a pillar of fire or a cloud/ in the Temple in Jerusalem, e.g. when Isaiah saw God 'seated on a high and lofty throne' (Isaiah 6:1). **B** *Arguments for the statement could include:* Jews believe God has given them many laws to follow (the mitzvot) and will judge them for how well they follow these laws/ this has a great impact on their lives today as they are expected to follow these laws in their daily lives/ particularly if they are Orthodox Jews/ the laws cover the worship of God but also other areas such as the types of food they can eat/ and how they should treat other people/ so affect almost every aspect of their lives. *Arguments in support of other views could include:* if God is the creator of the universe then he must also be omnipotent, omniscient and omnipresent/ which gives him the power to know if Jews are following his laws and to judge them accordingly/ which gives Jews motivation to follow his laws, so impacting on their lives today/ Jews celebrate God's role as the creator every week during Shabbat/ understanding God as the creator of free will and evil helps Jews to know why his laws are important in the first place/ knowing that God is the creator of everything means he is the only God that should be worshipped/ which is a fundamental belief in Judaism, and impacts upon how Jews worship and relate to God in their daily lives.

9.4 **A** Some Jews believe they will be judged by God as soon as they die/ others believe God will judge everyone on the Day of Judgement. **B** *You might finish the first paragraph as follows:* It matters if there are different beliefs about life after death within a religion because then believers don't know how to live their lives in a way that would guarantee them a good afterlife. For example, if there are different ideas about how to gain entry to heaven then believers might get confused or doubt which teachings are best to follow. In addition, if there is no clear idea about what heaven is like (as in Judaism), this could discourage believers from trying their hardest to please God to end up in heaven when they die. *You might finish the second paragraph as follows:* it doesn't matter if there are different beliefs about life after death within a religion because it is more important to focus on the present. For example, Jews are not too concerned with the afterlife because they think it is more important to focus on living in a way that pleases God, whereas focusing on the afterlife might mean believers don't make the most of their lives. And if it is impossible to know what happens in the afterlife, then there is not too much point in worrying about it – living in a way that pleases God should lead to the best afterlife possible, whatever it is.

9.5 **A** Reform Jews believe there will be a future Messianic age, but this will be achieved by everyone working together, rather than as the result of leadership from the Messiah/ whereas Orthodox Jews believe there is a descendent of King David in every generation who has the potential to become the Messiah, who will lead the Jews during the Messianic age. **B** *Arguments for the statement could include:* the idea of a Messianic age is not relevant because there are too many problems in the world today/ they could not be solved by the leadership of one person/ there are always wars somewhere in the world, so a time of perfect peace and harmony is impossible/ it is impractical to think that all Jews could be gathered back to the land of Israel/ the rebuilding of the Temple in Jerusalem would create conflict, not a peaceful age/ a leader from the Jews or any religious leader would not have sufficient authority in an increasingly atheist and materialistic world. *Arguments against the statement could include:* the idea of a Messianic age is relevant because it encourages Orthodox Jews to work towards being worthy of redemption/ encourages Reform Jews to work together to create world peace/ this is particularly important at a time when there is much division and conflict in the world/ the hope for a Messianic age provides comfort for Jews facing persecution and hardship/ it is important for all people to have an ideal to work towards/ all humanity and religious groups agree that there should be lasting justice and peace.

9.6 A 'I give all the land that you see to you and your offspring forever' (Genesis 13:15). **B** *Arguments could include:* Abraham tried to convince people in Ur to worship God rather than idols/ he travelled from Haran to Canaan after God told him to continue his journey/ he agreed to the covenant with God/ which required him to 'walk in [God's] ways and be blameless' (Genesis 17:1), i.e. to show dedication and obedience to God/ he accepted this by being circumcised himself and circumcising all the males in his household.

9.7 A *You could include any two of:* You shall have no other Gods besides Me/ you shall not make for yourself a sculptured image, or any likeness/ you shall not swear falsely by the name of the Lord your God/ remember the Sabbath day and keep it holy/ honour your father and your mother/ you shall not murder/ you shall not commit adultery/ you shall not steal/ you shall not bear false witness against your neighbour/ you shall not covet *(Simplified versions of these commandments would also be accepted).* **B** *In the paragraph arguing for the statement, points could include:* the covenant at Sinai requires Jews to follow God's laws/ including the Ten Commandments and all of the mitzvot/ which not only affect the worship of God but other areas of a Jew's life, such as what they eat/ while this means that in return, God will protect them and be their God/ some people might question whether it is possible or fair to ask Jews to obey all of the 613 mitzvot in the Torah. *In the paragraph arguing against the statement, points could include:* the covenant at Sinai means the Jews are God's chosen people/ that God will protect them from harm and be their God/ this is worth having to obey all of God's laws/ because God sustains the world/ brings Jews protection/meaning/happiness/the hope of an afterlife in heaven.

9.8 A A belief in healing the world motivates Jews to help achieve social justice/ volunteer for a charity such as World Jewish Relief/ help protect the environment/ obey the mitzvot/ try to become closer to God. **B** *Arguments could include:* justice requires treating the poor and vulnerable fairly/ which means showing them kindness/ healing the world involves taking actions to help God's work in sustaining the world/ for many Jews it means helping to make the world a better and more just place/ e.g. by volunteering for a charity that helps those living in poverty/ which contributes to social justice and shows kindness to others/ therefore creating justice and healing the world both reinforce each other/ and rely on showing kindness to others.

9.9 A Breaking Shabbat law by doing work that is not normally allowed during Shabbat/ e.g. rescuing a child from the sea/ putting out a fire/ driving a sick person to hospital/ performing a life-saving operation. **B** *In the paragraph arguing for the statement, points could include:* Jews believe in the sanctity of life/ which means life is sacred and holy because it has been created by God/ so only God has the right to take it away/ if God chooses to take away a person's life, he must have a reason for this/ God is omniscient/omnipotent/benevolent so knows what is best for a person and shouldn't be challenged/ belief in God should mean accepting all of his decisions for a person, including when to end their life. *In the paragraph arguing against the statement, points could include:* sometimes it is difficult to know what God's plan for a person is/ and whether trying to save a patient is interfering with his plan or not/ e.g. some Jews think the duty to preserve life means a patient should be kept alive at all costs/ whereas others think a patient's death shouldn't be prolonged if they are in great pain/ pikuach nefesh emphasises how valuable human life is/ so Jews should try to save lives because this may be part of God's plan/ as this is the most loving thing to do.

9.10 A Genesis 3 teaches that free will exists/ God has given humans free will/ which is shown in the fact that Adam and Eve are able to use their free will to disobey God and eat from the tree/ Genesis 3 also teaches that using free will to go against God has serious consequences/ which is shown in the fact that God banished Adam and Eve from the Garden of Eden as a result of their disobedience. **B** *A good answer would include an explanation of your opinion on the statement, which refers to specific knowledge of Judaism. If you agree with the statement, points might include:* it is very important for Jews to show love to their neighbour/ 'Love your fellow as yourself' (Leviticus 19:18)/ and to show kindness to others/ obeying the mitzvot between man and man makes other people happier as well/ and strengthens the Jewish community/ by showing love towards others, Jews are also showing love for God/ so obeying these mitzvot has two benefits: improving relationships with other people and pleasing God. *If you disagree with the statement, points might include:* a Jew's relationship with God is more important than their relationship with other people/ so they should focus on the mitzvot that are concerned with how to worship God/ this will help to ensure that God judges them favourably/ worshipping God correctly should be the most important thing in Judaism, as God is the most important thing to Jews. *Your answer should also explain why someone else might agree with the statement when you have disagreed with it, or vice versa, by referring to some of the points made above.*

10 Judaism: practices

10.1 A By the use of Jewish symbols such as a menorah (many-branched candlestick)/ Star of David (six-pointed star that represents King David). **B** *Your answer should explain whether you think the statement is true or not, giving the reasons why. You should refer to specific knowledge of Judaism, and consider arguments for and against the statement. Arguments in support of the statement might include:* the synagogue is sometimes called the 'house of prayer'/ Jews believe it is best to pray in a group/ certain prayers can only be said in the presence of a minyan (a group of at least 10 adults)/ so having a space for communal prayer is very important/ prayer brings Jews

closer to God than any other activity in the synagogue. *Arguments in support of other views might include:* the synagogue is also called the 'house of study' or 'school'/ it is possible for Jews to pray at home/ an equally important role is to strengthen the Jewish community/ e.g. through social activities/ another important role is to help educate Jews in their faith/ e.g. by providing classes in Hebrew for young Jews/ e.g. by giving Jews access to books and scriptures they might not be able to find elsewhere.

10.2 A The Ark (Aron Hakodesh) is the cabinet where the Torah scrolls are kept, and the holiest place in the synagogue/ the ner tamid (ever-burning light) is a light that sits above the Ark, which is kept on at all times to symbolise God's presence/ the bimah (reading platform) is the raised platform from where the Torah is read. **B** *Arguments could include:* the holiest place in the synagogue is the Ark, which represents the first Ark that held the Ten Commandments in the Temple/ when Jews face the Ark in the synagogue, they face Jerusalem (where the Temple was built)/ the ner tamid is a reminder of the menorah that was lit every night in the Temple/ the bimah is a reminder that the altar was the central feature of the courtyard in the Temple/ all of these features in the prayer hall are reminders of the Temple, which shows how important it is to Jews.

10.3 A Orthodox Jews believe the Torah was given directly to Moses by God/ so the laws in the Torah should be strictly followed, including laws about how to worship/ men and women should have different roles in worship/ Reform Jews believe the Torah was inspired by God but written by humans/ so it can be adapted for modern times/ this means there is more individual choice/freedom in how to worship/ and men and women are able to take on the same roles in worship. **B** *Points might include:* Reform services are in Hebrew and the country's own language, which makes them easier to understand for Jews who are not fluent in Hebrew/ however, Orthodox services in Hebrew are inclusive and accessible to all Orthodox Jews, whatever their language/ the person leading the service in Reform Judaism faces the congregation most of the time, which may help people to understand what is happening than if the person has their back to the congregation (as in Orthodox Judaism)/ Reform services are more structured, which may help people to understand what each part of the service means.

10.4 A *Your answer might include two of the following:* the opening prayers might consist of a series of prayers and psalms that praise and give thanks to God/ after this the Shema is recited and accompanied by blessings/ the Amidah (standing prayer) is prayed in silence while standing and facing Jerusalem; it consists of a series of blessings/ the Amidah is sometimes followed by a reading from the Torah/ the final prayers include the closing Aleinu prayer, which gives praise and thanks to God. **B** *Arguments in support of the statement might include:* prayer is vital for communicating with God/ and reminds Jews what their faith is all about/ this helps them to become closer to God/ it strengthens their relationship with God/ and with the rest of the Jewish community/ without prayer Jews would not be able to have a personal relationship with God. *Arguments in support of other views might include:* healing the world is also very important to Jews/ it also brings Jews closer to God, just through actions rather than prayer/ it is a practical way to help God sustain the world he created/ Jews should not just have faith in God, they should also live in a way that pleases God, which involves helping others/ Jews are only able to focus on prayer if they live in a safe environment.

10.5 A *Your answer could include two of the following actions (with explanations of their significance):* the congregation stands when the Ark is opened to reveal the Torah scrolls/ as a reminder of how the Jews stood at the bottom of Mount Sinai when Moses returned with the Ten Commandments/ the Torah is dressed with a cover and various ornaments/ as a reminder of the vestments worn by priests in early Judaism/ the Torah is paraded round the synagogue/ to represent the march through the wilderness, when the original Ark was carried from Mount Sinai to Jerusalem/ many Jews touch the Torah with their prayer book or prayer shawl, then touch their lips/ recalling that God's words should be on their lips and sweet like honey (Ezekiel 3:3). **B** *Points could include:* Jews believe Shabbat is a time to celebrate that God has kept his promises in the covenant between God and the Jews/ and to celebrate God's creation/ as it recalls the Genesis creation story, when God created everything in six days and rested on the seventh day/ God commanded the Jews to celebrate Shabbat in the fourth commandment (Exodus 20:8)/ the fact that no work is done on Shabbat gives Jews time to focus on God and all he has given them/ including their families, as Shabbat is a time when Jews should enjoy eating together and spending time with the rest of the family.

10.6 A *Your answer could include two of the following preparations (with explanations of their significance):* the house is cleaned/ made neat and presentable/ Jews change into smart clothes/ to welcome in Shabbat, which is seen as being like welcoming a special bride or queen into the home/ the food and house are prepared before Shabbat begins/ as most types of work are not allowed during Shabbat/ at least two candles are placed on the table/ to represent the two commandments to remember and observe Shabbat/ two loaves of challah bread are placed on the table/ to represent the food that God provided for the Jews when they were wandering in the wilderness/ wine is placed on the table/ to symbolise joy and celebration. **B** *Arguments for the statement could include:* most types of work are not allowed during Shabbat, as stated in the fourth commandment/ 'you shall not do any work' (Exodus 20:8–10)/ so Jews are expected to relax and enjoy the day/ the Friday evening meal is an important part of Shabbat celebrations/ which gives families time to enjoy eating a meal together/ and telling religious stories or singing songs/ families also spend time together on the Saturday, e.g. by sharing another special meal. *Arguments against the statement could include:* Shabbat is most important as a time to remember and worship God/ and give thanks for God's creation/ as Shabbat recalls the Genesis creation story, when God created everything in six days and rested on the seventh day/ the emphasis on worshipping God is why Jews attend the synagogue on Friday evening and Saturday morning/ why parents may study the Torah on Saturday afternoon/ why blessings/prayers/religious stories are a part of the Friday meal/ why Jews are reminded of God through the food they eat during Shabbat/ e.g. the challah bread reminds Jews of the food that God provided for them in the wilderness.

10.7 A *Your answer could include two of the following:* by praying in the home/ through Shabbat celebrations (e.g. the Friday evening meal/the Havdalah ceremony)/ by touching the mezuzah/ by following the Jewish dietary laws when cooking. **B** *Your answer should explain whether you think the statement is true or not, giving the reasons why. You should refer to specific knowledge of Judaism, and consider arguments for and against the statement. Arguments in support of the statement might include:* the Talmud explains how to interpret the Torah and apply its laws to everyday life/ e.g. it gives advice on how to follow the dietary laws or the laws of Shabbat/ so Jews should study it carefully to get a more complete understanding of the Torah/ be able to follow the laws in the Torah correctly/ Orthodox Jews believe studying the Talmud is important/ the authority of the early rabbis means their beliefs and thoughts should be respected/considered. *Arguments in support of other views might include:* the Torah is more important/ as it forms the basis of Jewish law/ the discussions and debates in the Talmud might just confuse interpretation of the Torah/ some Reform Jews do not believe the Talmud needs to be carefully studied/ as they do not believe the laws in the Torah have to be followed as closely as possible in order to please God/ Jews can learn how to please God in other ways/ e.g. from their parents/ from attending classes or services in the synagogueb.

10.8 A *Your answer might include two of the following:* the Orthodox naming ceremony usually happens on the first Shabbat after the baby's birth, whereas the Reform ceremony may be held at another time/ both parents take part in a Reform naming ceremony, whereas the father recites the Torah blessing and asks God for the good health of his wife and baby in an Orthodox ceremony/ some Orthodox Jews give a small amount of money 31 days after the birth of their firstborn son, but this is not a usual Reform practice. **B** *Arguments might include:* Brit Milah recalls the covenant God made with Abraham/ as circumcision 'would be a sign of the covenant between Me and you' (Genesis 17:11)/ it reminds Jews they are God's chosen people/ but to be God's chosen people, they are expected to follow his laws/ during the redemption of the firstborn son, prayers are said asking that the child may 'enter into Torah, into marriage, and into good deeds'/ this reminds Jews of the importance of following the laws in the Torah.

10.9 A *Your answer might include two of the following:* a Jew might read from the Torah/ lead part of the service/ say prayers/ make a short speech. **B** *You might finish the first paragraph as follows:* I agree with this statement because the Bar or Bat Mitzvah ceremony marks the point when a Jewish person has to take full responsibility for following Jewish law/ This may have a significant impact on their life, as they may have to start following new laws/ or think more carefully about the laws their parents are already helping them to follow./ It is also when a Jewish person is seen to become an adult,/ and when they are allowed to become part of the minyan./ Jews may view it as a significant moment as it helps to bring them closer to God. *You might finish the second paragraph as follows:* I disagree with this statement because there are other moments in a Jewish person's life that some might think are equally significant. For example, the Brit Milah ceremony is when a male Jew is circumcised as a reminder that they are one of God's chosen people./ This reminder stays with them for their whole life./ Some Jews might think their marriage is equally or more significant, because it is when they get to marry the person they love and this brings holiness into their everyday lives.

10.10 A In Judaism, 'betrothal' is a period of engagement/ which typically lasts for the year before a wedding/ which can only be broken by death or divorce/ when the couple do not live together, but prepare for their future lives together. **B** *Arguments for the statement might include:* both the bride and groom may fast before the wedding to cleanse themselves of sin/ the bride and groom both recite two blessings over wine/ In Reform weddings, the bride and groom exchange rings/ a Reform marriage contract usually describes mutual hopes for the marriage, which are the same for the bride and groom/ the rabbi blesses both the bride and groom. *Arguments against the statement might include:* in Orthodox weddings, the groom gives the bride a ring but the bride doesn't give the groom a ring/ an Orthodox marriage contract may suggest unequal expectations or treatment/ e.g. it may cover the husband's duties to his wife, but not the wife's duties to her husband/ the groom breaks a glass under his heel to show regret for the destruction of the Temple in Jerusalem, but the bride doesn't do this.

10.11 A They make a small tear in their clothes/ to follow the example of Jacob, who 'rent his clothes, put sackcloth on his loins, and observed mourning for his son many days' (Genesis 37:34)/ they say a blessing that refers to God as the true judge/ which shows they accept God's decision to take the person's life. **B** *A good answer would include an explanation of your opinion on the statement, which refers to specific knowledge of Judaism. If you agree with the statement, points might include:* in Judaism there are set periods of mourning that decrease in intensity over the period of a year/ these help to give structure to a person's mourning/ and give them enough time to grieve fully but also help them to get back to normal life/ during the first period of mourning, Jews do not have to worry about following certain Jewish laws/ during shiva (the second period of mourning), mourners stay at home to pray together and support each other/ mirrors are covered so they can't focus on their appearance, helping them to focus instead on coming to terms with a person's death. *If you disagree with the statement, points might include:* mourning/grieving is very personal and some people might find the structure or rigidity of Jewish mourning customs unhelpful/ e.g. they might need longer than 24 hours to mentally prepare themselves for the funeral/ they might need more than a week before returning to work/ they might want to mourn alone during shiva/ they might find that listening to music brings them solace, but are unable to do so during the third period of mourning/ they might find that going to parties helps to distract them after a person's death, but are unable to do so for the first year of mourning.

10.12 A *Your answer might explain one of the following passages from the Torah:* 'But make sure that you do not partake of the blood; for the blood is the life, and you must not consume the life with the flesh' (Deuteronomy 12:23)/ this means Jews should not eat food containing blood/ so they should only eat kosher meat (where the blood has been drained from it)/ 'You shall not boil a kid in its mother's milk' (Exodus 23:19)/ this means Jews should not eat meat and dairy products at the same time/ and several hours must pass between eating meat and anything containing milk/ which means Jews have to be very careful about preparing food. **B** *Your answer should explain whether you think the statement is true or not, giving the reasons why. You should refer to specific knowledge of Judaism, and consider arguments for and against the statement. Arguments in support of the statement might include:* the dietary laws mean Jews can only eat certain kosher foods/ and have to keep dairy products and meat separate/ which ideally means having a kitchen with two sets of utensils and crockery, two sinks and two food preparation areas/ some Jews may not be able to afford to have a special kitchen like this/ the dietary laws also make it hard to eat out at restaurants/ and to buy food in supermarkets/ Jews with busy lifestyles, allergies or those who live in non-Jewish communities may find it particularly hard/ the laws are outdated in modern society/ the original reasons for the laws may no longer apply/ there are more meaningful ways to show obedience to God/ some Reform Jews don't follow the dietary laws but still follow God. *Arguments in support of other views might include:* if Orthodox Jews manage to follow the laws then they can't be too difficult to follow/ Jews can buy meat from kosher butchers or foods with kosher labels on them, so they know they are buying the right food/ the laws test a person's self-control and obedience to God/ – if the laws were relaxed then that would defeat the point of them/ the laws remind Jews daily of their faith/ – if they were relaxed they would lose these reminders/ the laws mark Jewish people out as different from others and should be kept for this reason.

10.13 A *Your answer might include two of the following differences:* during Rosh Hashanah, Jews will try to take actions to improve their relationships with others – e.g. by making up for any harm they have caused other people – whereas Jews will spend much of Yom Kippur in the synagogue in order to improve their relationship with God/ Jews celebrate Rosh Hashanah with a festive meal, but fast during Yom Kippur/ Jews wear white during Yom Kippur, but wear any smart clothes for Rosh Hashanah. **B** *Points could include:* some Jews believe it is important to show kindness during Rosh Hashanah in particular because this may influence God's judgement/ and affect their fortunes for the coming year/ Rosh Hashanah is a particularly good time to mend or improve relationships with other people/ which involves showing them kindness/ but some Jews may argue it is important to show kindness all year round/ as instructed in Leviticus ('love your fellow as yourself')/ and suggesting this is more important during Rosh Hashanah suggests it is less important at other times, which is not true.

10.14 A To prepare for Pesach, Jews remove leaven from their homes/ this recalls how the Jews did not have time to let their bread rise when they escaped from Egypt/ some firstborn sons fast before Pesach starts/ in thanksgiving for the firstborns' escape from death in Egypt/ recalling the story of the final plague, which killed the firstborn children of the Egyptians but not the Jews/ during the Passover Seder, the story of the escape from Egypt is told from a book called the Haggadah/ the different foods symbolise different aspects of the Jews' escape from Egypt/ e.g. the green vegetable symbolises new life in the Promised Land. **B** *The following points could be included in the paragraph supporting the statement:* it is important for religious believers to understand the history of their faith/ knowing about the escape from slavery in Egypt might help Jewish children to appreciate God more/ feel more willing to obey God's laws, as they know what God has done for them/ passing on the history of a religion to the next generation is important for its continuity/ Pesach rituals do this in a fun way, e.g. by finding bread crumbs to burn. *The following points could be included in the paragraph supporting a different point of view:* Pesach rituals are important to older Jews as well/ help Jews to celebrate and give thanks to God/ are more than just an opportunity to teach Jewish history/ help Jews to feel empathy with those who are oppressed.

11 Theme A: religion, relationships and families

11.1 A *Your answer might include two of the following:* male and female were created in the image of God (Genesis 1:27)/ God takes Adam (humanity) and splits him into two complementary parts (Genesis 2)/ male and female may have different roles but they are of equal value to God. **B** *Your answer should include the following arguments, and you should say which of them you find most convincing:* the sacrament of marriage enables two people in love to commit themselves publically and exclusively to each other/ sex should be unitive (join people together)/ sex should be open to creating new life (procreative)/ sexual love in marriage deepens the couples love for each other/ sex outside of marriage is a sin and forbidden. *A non-religious person might give the following arguments:* there is nothing wrong with those who love each other having sex/ need to see if the couple are sexually compatible/ not everyone wants to commit to getting married.

11.2 A *Your answer might include two of the following examples:* God loves every human being/ both sexes have dignity and value/ the full meaning of the body and person can only be appreciated within a deep relationship with the opposite sex/ in marriage both partners give themselves to each other completely/ extramarital sex damages relationships/ sex should be open to creating new life/ Pope John Paul II wanted to clarify the Catholic's position on the body and relationships/ show the value and importance of respect and mutual love in marriage. **B** *Your arguments may centre on whether you agree or disagree with the following:* sex outside of marriage is a form of exploitation for personal pleasure/ casual sex makes people selfish, caring only for themselves and not their marriage partner/ adultery breaks the marriage vows and shows no commitment to a spouse/ is a sin and distorts God's original plan for human beings/ important to maintain control of thoughts to avoid seeing people as sex objects (Matthew 5:28).

11.3 A *Your answer might include two of the following:* sex should be saved for marriage as it should be an exclusive act shared only with the person you have pledged to spend your life with/ it is the final step of joining husband and wife together/ sex before marriage trivialises it/ if both partners wait until marriage there is no chance of sexually transmitted disease. **B** *Arguments in support of the statement could include:* although the law allows it the Catholic Church will not marry homosexuals/ does not accept physical homosexual relations/ says that sex should be open to the possibility of new life/ 'You shall not lie with a male as with a woman; it is an abomination.' (Leviticus 18:22) *Arguments against the statement could include:* Catholics show respect and love for all people regardless of their sexual orientation/ 'You shall love your neighbour as yourself.' (Matthew 22:39)

11.4 **A** *Your answer might include two of the following:* the consent binds the spouses to each other/ 'till death do us part'/ it finds its fulfilment in the two becoming one flesh/ important part of a valid marriage which if fulfilled cannot be annulled. **B** *Arguments in support of the statement could include:* Genesis states that God's intention is for a man and a woman to be joined as one/ the Bible teaches that homosexual relations are not God's intention e.g. Romans 1:26-28/ same sex couples cannot have children naturally and lovingly from God, so cannot meet the requirements for a valid marriage. *Arguments against the statement could include:* modern society as a whole accepts homosexual relations/ homosexuals should have the same rights as heterosexuals/ should be integrated into society and not marginalised/ being able to have children isn't an essential part of marriage/ what matters is the love for each other.

11.5 **A** *Your answer might include two of the following:* the Catholic Church opposes the idea of people in a relationship living together because it breaks the sanctity of marriage and removes any sense of commitment from the sexual union/ however many young couples choose to cohabit to begin with to see if they are compatible or because they cannot afford to get married; they can still be committed to each other. **B** *Your argument may include the following points:* the marriage promise is made before a priest who represents God/ stresses that marriage is serious and is for life/ 'to have and to hold from this day forward, for better and for worse, for richer for poorer, in sickness and in health, to love and to cherish, till death do us part/ shows total commitment to each other until one partner dies/ Catholics believe that a valid marriage cannot be annulled or a divorce take place.

11.6 **A** Your answer might include two of the following: an annulment might take place if one partner doesn't take the exclusiveness of marriage seriously and has affairs/ if a partner or both refuse to have sex or always insist on using contraception/ if they were forced into marriage or if there wasn't a proper marriage in the first place. **B** *Your arguments in support of the statement might include:* sometimes marriages turn out to be a mistake/ sometimes a partner is abusive/unfaithful/ may be a hostile atmosphere in the home/ Jesus did not totally rule out divorce/ divorce might be the compassionate thing to do. *Your arguments against the statement might include:* couples should stick to their promises/ they knew what they were committing to/ they need to try to find help to improve the relationship.

11.7 **A** Natural family planning means not using unnatural methods to prevent a pregnancy taking place, instead using the woman's monthly cycle/ the Catholic Church does not support the use of a condom or the pill as it prevents God's will from being done regarding whether or not the couple should have children. **B** *Your arguments in support of the statement might include:* the world is already overpopulated and there is enormous pressure on resources/ contraceptives stop the spread of sexually transmitted infections (STIs)/ families should only have the number of children they can support/ contraception prevents unwanted pregnancies e.g. some people have sex outside of marriage. *Your arguments against the statement might include:* Genesis 1:22 says, 'Be fruitful and multiply'/ it is wrong to stop God's gift, lovingly intended for a married couple/ contraception encourages the exclusiveness of marriage. *Your conclusion should explain whether you think the statement is true or not. You should refer to both sides of the argument and explain which you think is more persuasive/accurate.*

11.8 **A** *Your answer might include the following:* Catholic families form a community/ purpose of family is to help one another develop including spiritually/ family encourages participation in the wider community including the life of the church/ provides environment for love/stability/security/education/ is where everyone is valued. **B** *Your arguments in support of the statement might include: families provide safety, support and security/ where people can be themselves and develop accordingly/ people can make mistakes without fear. Your arguments against the statement might include:* other important purposes include providing love/care/a nurturing environment/education/stability/moral guidance/religious teaching.

11.9 **A** Traditionally Catholics believe that a mother's major role was in looking after the home and children/ this role is to be respected/ husbands should fully support their wives in this important role/ nowadays many mothers work part- or full-time/ this is often necessary in order to help provide for the family financially/ increasing gender equality has meant that roles traditionally reserved for women and men are being shared or switched. **B** *Your arguments in support of the statement might include:* there is a growing acceptance of same-sex parents in British society/ it is the love between parents and children that really matters. *Your arguments against the statement might include:* the Catholic Church teaches that procreation should take place between a man and woman who have married/ many Catholics believe children need a mother and a father.

11.10 **A** *Your answer include might two of the following:* men and women were created in the image of God (Genesis 1:27)/ 'there is no longer male and female; for all … are one in Christ Jesus' (Galatians 3:28)/ women have important roles in the Bible e.g. Mary, the mother of Jesus. **B** *Arguments that could be used in a debate could include:* early Christians lived in a male dominated world/ travelling women preachers would not be accepted/ some denominations have women leaders or priests/ women have played an important role in the history of Christianity, including the New Testament/ Jesus' disciples were male/ Catholic priests are male/ most of the events in the Bible were about men/ leaders in the Church have mostly been men.

11.11 **A** Catholics believe that men and women are of equal importance as they are made in God's image but have different roles/ equality is not the same as uniformity/ men and women have equal roles in supporting each other. **B** *Points could include:* Catholics only allow men to become priests/ traditionally women were expected to look after the home and the children/ men and women should be treated equally with equal opportunities/ are equally capable of fulfilling the same roles including roles in the home/ other denominations allow women to be priests and church leaders.

11.12 **A** *Your answer might include two of the following examples:* in some jobs women are paid less than men although this is against the law/ there are more men in leadership roles/ only men can be priests in the Catholic Church. **B** *Points could include:* some men will always think that they are superior to women/ some will always think that women should just look after the home/children/ the 1975 Sex Discrimination Act was designed to prevent gender discrimination/ many follow the biblical teachings which promote equality.

12 Theme B: religion, peace and conflict

12.1 **A** *Your answer might include:* James meant that the tongue can become uncontrollable/ it can be used to bless God or spread poison/ it is therefore vitally important to control what is said or great harm can be caused. **B** *Arguments could include:* importance of not letting seeds of bitterness, anger and jealousy grow in one's thoughts/ Cain failed to control his thoughts and it led to him murdering his brother (Genesis 4)/ Jesus warned that it is wrong to harbour hatred as it can lead to violence and murder/ wrong thoughts can result in a person experiencing the fire of hell/ Matthew 5:21–22.

12.2 **A** *Your answer might include two of the following:* reconciliation restores harmony after relationships have broken down/ Matthew 2:24 explains how people should be reconciled as a priority before bringing a gift to God/ God wants to be reconciled to humans through his plan for salvation. **B** *Points could include:* hatred if it isn't returned doesn't grow/ it takes the heat out of the situation to turn the other cheek/ however some people are so full of hate that it will continue even if forgiveness and the hand of friendship is extended to them/ some find it impossible to forgive acts of terror and murder that ruin lives. *Your conclusion should explain whether you think the statement is true or not. You should refer to both sides of the argument and explain which you think is more persuasive/accurate.*

12.3 **A** Your answer might include: Jesus used righteous anger in the temple (John 2:13–17)/ righteous anger can be controlled and channelled into positive action to improve a situation. **B** *Points could include:* protest against injustice can be done peacefully/ Christians believe that it doesn't break the law to take part in a peaceful march or procession/ violent protest can be ineffective, causing more opposition and is a damaging way to create change/ may cause loss of life/ however some Christians may take part in protests which might lead to violence if they feel it is the only way to get a government to take notice and end an injustice.

12.4 **A** *Your answer might include two of the following:* just cause/ reasonable chance of winning/ declared by the state or sovereign/ only proportional force is used/ innocent civilians are protected/ must be the last resort/ environment should be protected. **B** *Points could include:* war causes extreme devastation and destruction/ no war meets all the just war theory criteria/ modern warfare is indiscriminate/ causes huge suffering/ however the Catholic Church teaches that sometimes it is better to go to war than allow injustice to continue/ can be the lesser of two evils/ Catechism of the Catholic Church 2309.

12.5 **A** *Your answer might include:* they are indiscriminate/ have long term effects/ are disproportionate/ there are no victors, only victims/ they are tremendously expensive/ possession increases tension and fear. **B** *Points could include:* might get into the hands of a madman or terrorist/ could be set off accidentally or if wrong information is received/ situations can escalate out of control/ however they can act as a deterrent/ may stop attacks because of fear.

12.6 **A** Your answer might include two of the following: massive number of casualties/ civilians get hurt as well as armed forces/ many refugees/ environment destroyed for generations. **B** *Points in your first paragraph could include:* other countries are taking hundreds of thousands of refugees/ need to love our neighbours/ need to show compassion to desperate people/ refugees can make a significant contribution to society and the economy. *Points in your second paragraph could include:* Britain is already over populated/ funding is already stretched to provide services and homes/ fear that some many come to cause trouble and terrorism. *Your conclusion should explain whether you think the statement is true or not. You should refer to both sides of the argument and explain which you think is more persuasive/accurate.*

12.7 **A** *Your answer might include two of the following:* Old Testament tells of the Israelites in many wars/ fighting to establish themselves in the Promised Land/ defending their country/ Exodus 21:24/ however the Ten Commandments include 'Do not murder'/ wish for peace (Isaiah 2:4). **B** *Points in your first paragraph could include:* religion sometimes used as an excuse for violence/ religions all preach peace so believers should follow their teachings. *Points in your second paragraph could include:* religious minorities often persecuted/ need to fight to defend themselves and their right to religious freedom/ some believe they will gain spiritual rewards for defending their faith.

12.8 **A** *Your answer might include two of the following:* some Christians believe that Jesus was a pacifist/ Jesus taught that it is better to bring peace than violence/ Matthew 5:39/ Matthew 5:9/ Matthew 26:53/ oppose causing suffering/ Ten Commandments include 'Do not murder'. **B** *Points could include:* Christians are taught to turn the other cheek/ early Christians refused to fight/ Martin of Tours thought it wrong to fight/ Martin Luther King Jr achieved a lot without supporting violence/ Society of Friends (Quakers) believe all violence is wrong/ peacemakers will be called children of God/ however perhaps some circumstances are so horrific they need to be stopped by violence e.g. genocide/holocaust/ can be lesser of two evils.

12.9 **A** *Your answer might include two of the following:* CAFOD/ Aid to the Church in Need/ Caritas International. **B** *Points could include:* leaders of countries don't have to listen to religious leaders/ wars are started for many complex reasons and may have nothing to do with religion/ Pope Francis has tried to bring peace in the Ukraine and Middle East/ brought leaders together e.g. presidents of Israel and Palestine/ can help to create atmosphere for peace. Your conclusion should explain whether you think the statement is true or not. You should refer to both sides of the argument and explain which you think is more persuasive/accurate.

12.10 **A** *Your answer might include two of the following:* IRA attacks in Warrington/ London/Manchester/Omagh/ Islamist extremist attacks in London/ Glasgow/ Manchester. **B** *Your arguments in support of the statement might include:* violence is usually against innocent civilians/ usually designed to undermine governments (against teaching in Romans)/ aim of frightening people/ Catechism of the Catholic Church 2297/ morally wrong. *Your arguments used to disagree with the statement might include:* perhaps violence is the only way to defend religious beliefs and practices/ Jewish Maccabees (1 Maccabees 2:44–48)/ without it Judaism might not have survived.

12.11 **A** *Your answer might include two of the following:* it is illegal/ not allowed by international law even in war/ denies victim basic human rights/ barbaric/ wrong and inhumane/ Catechism of the Catholic Church 2297. **B** *Points in your first paragraph could include:* very serious threat as if leads to terrorism and violence/ radicalised people believe that they are right and everyone else is wrong/ could bring about the disintegration of British society/ real threat to human rights and freedom of belief. Points in your second paragraph could include: other major threats including the widening divide between rich and poor/ proliferation of nuclear weapons/ growing individual and national debt.

12.12 **A** *Your answer might include two of the following:* Bible says to live in peace and harmony/ 2 Corinthians 13:11/ be reconciled (Philippians 4:2–3)/ blessed are the peacemakers/ vision for future peace (Isaiah 2:4)/ Luke 6:27–28. **B** *Points could include:* Christians encouraged by biblical teaching to work for peace/ don't hold things against others (Matthew 5)/ Catholics support peace organisations/ Pax Christi/ Justice and Peace Commission/ actions of Pope Francis/ however some Christians might not be able to do anything to prevent conflict/ should be up to everyone to try and help overcome disputes.

13 Theme C: religion, human rights and social justice

13.1 **A** *Your answer might include two of the following:* humans are created in the image of God (Genesis 1:27)/ everyone is in Christ (Colossians 3:11)/ love your neighbour as you love yourself (Mark 12:31/ do justice, love kindness, walk humbly with God (Micah 6:8). **B** *Points could include:* 'everyone should have the right to freedom of thought, conscience and religion' (International Covenant on Civil and Political Rights 18)/ 'no one is to be forced to act in a manner contrary to his own beliefs' (*Dignitatis Humanae* 2)/ believers and non-believers should be allowed freedom of speech and expression/ however with the right to freedom of speech should come the responsibility to not be offensive/ not stir up hatred/ not encourage persecution.

13.2 **A** *Your answer might include two of the following:* involves rights and duties with respect for everyone/ every social group should be considered/ everyone should have dignity/ should be respected and protected/ rights should be given to everyone e.g. food/clothing/shelter/education/employment/freedom of conscience and religion/ society should be built on truth and justice and be motivated by love. **B** *Points could include:* UN Declaration of Human Rights should be followed by all countries/ parable of Sheep and Goats shows that helping people get basic human rights means helping Jesus/ still many parts of the world where people do not have these human rights so still a lot more needs to be done/ however Catholic Church is already involved in campaigning for people to receive human rights through teachings/ speeches of Popes/ duty of all to campaign – not just Catholics.

13.3 **A** *Your answer might include two of the following:* people who want rights must accept that others should have them too/ the right to freedom of speech should be used responsibility e.g. not to encourage violence and hatred/ the right to education includes the student having the responsibility to want to learn/ people shouldn't just claim rights for themselves but also for the weak and vulnerable. **B** *Points could include:* governments might not take any notice of what the Catholic Church says/ particularly if there is a different majority religion in those countries/ governments may resent foreigners trying to interfere in their countries/ however people pressure is powerful/ use of media can make governments think again/ someone has to stand up for justice – this is a moral duty of Christians. *Your conclusion should explain whether you think the statement is true or not. You should refer to both sides of the argument and explain which you think is more persuasive/accurate.*

13.4 **A** *Your answer might include two of the following:* 'for the love of money is the root of all kinds of evil' (1 Timothy 6:10)/ Jesus told his disciples to take no money with them (Mark 6:8–9)/ wealth is God given but should be used wisely to help others (1 John 3:17)/ Parable of the Rich Man and Lazarus (don't ignore the poor). **B** *Points could include:* wealth is a gift from God/ can be used to do an enormous amount of good/ God made people stewards to use money wisely and responsibly/ Christians aren't expected to make themselves poor (2 Corinthians 8:12)/ however wealth can lead to being greedy/ can make people lose focus on God in order to get rich/ people may get rich by depriving the poor.

13.5 **A** *Your answer might include two of the following:* need to work to create money to buy food/ work stops people being idle and gossiping (2 Thessalonians 3:10–11)/ need to create savings for difficult times (Genesis 41). **B** *Points could include:* the Catholic Church has huge wealth which could be used to feed people/ take millions out of poverty/ the Church has vast amount of land/buildings/art works which could be sold to help the poor/ however if the Church gave away all its wealth it would not be able to fulfil its functions of providing places of worship/pay staff including priests/ run schools/operate hospitals/ the Church is gradually selling off works of art to help those in need/ already gives a lot to the poor.

13.6 **A** *Your answer might include two of the following:* greed makes people ignore spiritual things/ motivates people to want more and more/ is one of the deadly sins/ goes against the teaching to 'love your neighbour'/ makes people selfish/ destroys a person's relationship with God/ Jesus taught against it (Luke 12:15). **B** *Arguments in support of the statement could include:* wealth can be used to do an enormous amount of good/ sharing offerings and tithes can support not only the Church but many charities who are helping the poor/ families have to be looked after/ people who work hard should be entitled to a reward/ parable of the Sheep and Goats. *Arguments against the statement could include:* wealth causes a distraction to a person's spiritual life/ if people really want to devote their lives to God they shouldn't be hindered by possessions and the need to possess them/ 'You cannot serve God and wealth.' (Matthew 6:24)/ 'If you wish to be perfect, go, sell your possessions, and give the money to the poor, and you will have treasure in heaven; then come, follow me.' (Matthew 19:21)/ 'it is easier for a camel to go through the eye of a needle than for someone who is rich to enter the Kingdom of God' (Matthew 19:24).

13.7 **A** *Your answer might include two of the following:* he said that poverty is a scandal/ there is enough wealth to take everyone out of poverty/ there are enough resources to feed everyone/ there shouldn't be so many hungry children or children without education/ need to find a way to provide justice, fairness and respect for everyone. **B** *Arguments in support of the statement could include:* the poor deserve preferential treatment because they have suffered from not having had basic requirements/ Philippians 2:4/ the poor are the first to receive the mercy of God/ caring for the poor is a demand on all Christians/ Jesus showed compassion to the needy/ exploitation needs to end. *Arguments against the statement could include:* non-believers may argue if people have earned their money they deserve to spend it as they wish/ there will always be poor people/ there is only so much the Church or anyone can do/ people can help the poor in other ways e.g. by providing education and skills.

13.8 **A** *Your answer might include two of the following:* give money to the homeless/ support the work of organisations like the Salvation Army and St Vincent de Paul Society/ give practical help like the Good Samaritan/ show compassion and kindness by offering direct help/ encourage education and skills training/ campaign for justice. **B** *Points could include:* it is wrong for poor people to just be satisfied with living on handouts/ people should try to improve things for themselves e.g. by getting a job/ people should strive to improve their education/skills/ however sometimes poverty isn't the fault of the person/ it may be a result of where they live in the world/natural disasters/extreme weather/exploitation (unfair wages)/illness/ the situation is such that it not possible to break out of poverty without help/ e.g. e.g. parable of Rich man and Lazarus (Luke 16:19-31)/ and James 2:15–17.

13.9 **A** *Your answer might include two of the following:* campaigns for the government to give more aid/ provides short-term aid/ supports Fairtrade/ helps with education/ improves health care/ challenges exploitation/ campaigns for fair wages/ provides access to clean water. **B** *Points in support of the statement could include:* Christian Aid helps to overcome poverty regardless of faith/ unites Christians of all denominations in its work/ responds quickly to disasters/ gives short-term and long-term aid/ helps refugees/ helps local organisations/ Christians accept the need to be Good Samaritans (Luke 10:29–37)/ Genesis 4:9/ *Evangelii Gaudium* 191. *Points against the statement could include:* there are many different Christian and non-Christians charities that Christians may wish to contribute to/ all are good causes and promote human rights/ some Christians may have personal reasons or knowledge of situations which make them want to support particular charities. *Your conclusion should explain whether you think the statement is true or not. You should refer to both sides of the argument and explain which you think is more persuasive/accurate.*

13.10 **A** *Your answer might include two of the following:* due to their upbringing – family may be prejudiced/ media bias/ ignorance of people of other races/ fear that other races might take their jobs/ fear of those who look different/ they had a bad experience with someone of a different race/ historical reasons. **B** *Points could include:* so many people are racially prejudiced/ people want to support their own race at the expense of others/ however Christians are taught that God loves every race equally/ all are created by God (Genesis 1:27/ all are children of God/ racial discrimination is against the law/ the law may not be able to stop prejudiced thoughts but can prevent them being translated into actions/ Christians are taught to treat everyone equally as discrimination causes great harm e.g. *Evangelium Vitae* 34.

13.11 **A** *Your answer might include two of the following:* sexual union should be open to God blessing the couple by creating new life/ creation of new life is impossible for people of the same sex/ purpose of homosexual sex is distorted and so is seen as sinful. **B** *Arguments in support of the statement could include:* times have changed – most people now believe in equal opportunities/ most Protestant Churches have female leaders/ the Catholic attitude is sexist and out of date/ the Bible teaches equality/ women, just like men, can be called by God to the priesthood. *Arguments in support of other views could include:* Jesus only had male apostles/ he ordained only men as priests at the Last Supper/ having female priests would break with tradition/ Catholics believe men and women are equal but that women have a different role from men including looking after the home and children.

13.12 **A** *Your answer might include two of the following:* children of all races and religions are welcome to attend Catholic schools/ Catholics and non-Catholics mix together to promote understanding and tolerance/ recent popes have been from many different countries/ the College of Cardinals represents every continent/ many priests in the UK are from different countries/ Catechism of the Catholic Church 842. **B** *Arguments in support of the statement could include:* it is the responsibility of all Catholics to follow the Church's teaching/ Youcat 377/ Catholics should treat everyone fairly (Youcat 302)/ should take part in campaigns to promote equality and justice/ should encourage mixed groups and education. *Arguments against the statement could include:* some Catholics are not in a position to help/ it is difficult to stop thoughts and attitudes/ it is not just Catholics but everyone who should stop racial prejudice.

Exam practice answers

1 Catholic Christianity

Test the 1 mark question

1.   C) Transcendent

2.   A) Do good and avoid evil

Test the 2 mark question

Suggested answers, other relevant answers would be credited. 1 mark for each correct point:

3.   The Genesis creation stories show that God has the power to create everything in the universe from nothing/ show that God is powerful enough to make everything exactly the way he wants it to be ('it was very good', Genesis 1:31).

4.   The books in the New Testament were backed by the authority of the apostles or someone close to the apostles/ were written early on (mostly before the end of the first century)/ agreed with other teachings and accounts of Christian beliefs/ were accepted by all Christian Churches at the time.

Test the 4 mark question

Suggested answers, other relevant answers would be credited. 1 mark for each simple contrasting or similar point, another mark for developing each point, so a maximum of 4 marks for two developed points:

6.   The belief that humans are made in God's image means all people are worthy of honour and respect/ this means everyone should respect their own dignity and the dignity of other people/ the belief that humans have been created and blessed by God means human life is sacred and holy/ every stage of life should be treated with care and respect/ this in turn means Catholics are against euthanasia and abortion.

7.   Christians believe God has given them free will/ the story of Adam and Eve in Genesis 2 shows this/ God gives Adam the choice of whether or not to eat from the tree of the knowledge of good and evil/ free will is why evil exists in the world/ using free will to sin results in turning away from God/ using free will to do good results in becoming closer to God.

Test the 5 mark question

Suggested answers, other relevant answers would be credited. 1 mark for each simple contrasting or similar point, another mark for developing each point, so 4 marks for two developed points, 1 extra mark for a correct reference to a source of Christian belief or teaching:

9.   Genesis 1 tells how God created the universe and everything in it in six days/ Catholics believe 'day' means a much longer period of time/ so the universe might be as old as scientists suggest it is/ whereas some fundamentalist Christians believe the universe and all life in it were literally created in six days/ in Genesis 2 God creates the first woman from the rib of the first man/ Catholics think this is a myth designed to help teach how men and women relate to each other/ some fundamentalists would take this story literally/ the Genesis creation stories describe how God created humans/ Catholics do not interpret this literally and believe God created humans through the process of evolution/ fundamentalists do interpret this literally and believe God made humans separately (rather than them evolving from other species).

10.   If the Genesis creation stories are not interpreted literally then they do not have to contradict the theory of evolution/ Catholics believe science can help people to understand God's creation/ e.g. the Big Bang theory explains how God created the universe/ the Church believes religion and science are asking slightly different questions so it is acceptable if they come up with slightly different answers/ religion tries to explain why things happen while science tries to explain how things happen/ 'If methodical investigation … is carried out in a genuinely scientific manner … it never truly conflicts with faith' (*Gaudium et Spes* 36).

Test the 12 mark question

Suggested answers shown here, but see page 12 for guidance on levels of response.

12.   **Arguments in support:**

•   The Bible was written almost 2000 years ago by people living in a very different time and society/ so Catholics need guidance on how to interpret the Bible in the modern world/ e.g. the Bible does not include guidance on issues such as the use of modern technology or nuclear weapons.

•   The Church helps Catholics to know how to keep the word of God 'pure' while also making it relevant for the modern world/ 'Sacred scripture is the word of God […] while sacred tradition takes the word of God […] and hands it on to their successors in its full purity' (Dei Verbum 9).

•   It is a bad idea just to rely on the Bible alone because it can be interpreted in very different ways, and without extra guidance it is difficult to know which interpretations are best/ e.g. the Genesis creation stories can be read figuratively or

literally, which gives very different understandings of how the universe and life were created/ the fact that there is sometimes a wide variety of Christian views on the same topic shows how difficult interpretation of the Bible can be/ e.g. some Christians are against artificial contraception while others accept it.

Arguments in support of other views:

•   The Bible gives Catholics everything they need to know how to live in a way that pleases God/ God guided the writing of the Bible through the Holy Spirit, so would have made sure it contained accurate information about how to live as a good Christian/ the Bible contains the teachings and actions of Jesus, which is all Christians really need to know about to live in a way that is pleasing to God.

•   Christian principles such as 'love your neighbour as yourself', showing forgiveness, and helping others are easy to apply to everyday life in any society/ these can all be found in the Bible and do not need to be elaborated on by the Church.

•   Catholics can also get to know God and how to live in a way that pleases him through other methods, e.g. through prayer, revelations, studying Christian works of art (such as Michelangelo's *The Last Judgement*), and talking to other Christians.

•   Catholics are guided by the Holy Spirit and God's grace to do the right thing/ this would happen with or without the Church, as God's grace is a free and unconditional gift.

13.   **Arguments in support:**

•   *Creation of Adam* illustrates a number of different Christian beliefs about creation, and is particularly good for reflecting beliefs about the creation of humanity.

•   The painting clearly reflects the belief that humanity is made in the image of God (Genesis 1:27) in a number of ways: God and Adam are lying in similar positions, and they also both look powerful.

•   God is shown bringing a human to life rather than any other type of species, clearly showing that humans are special to God/ specially created by God.

•   The painting clearly shows that humanity depends on God for life by the fact that Adam is waiting for God's touch to bring him to life.

•   The painting also reflects the belief that God made everything 'very good' (Genesis 1:31) through the fact that Adam is shown as the perfect man, full of strength and potential.

Arguments in support of other views:

•   *Creation of Adam* could mislead some people about certain Christian beliefs about creation/ e.g. the painting suggests Adam was brought to life by God touching him, but Genesis 2:7 says that God breathed into his nostrils to bring him to life/ e.g. in the painting God and Adam are nearly the same size, suggesting God made humans to be equal to him, but this goes against Christian beliefs.

•   *Creation of Adam* focuses on the act of God creating humanity but doesn't reflect the Christian belief that God created the whole universe and all life in it/ Meière's mosaic in St Bartholomew's Church in New York is one example of a work of art that shows God created everything in the universe (illustrated by the lines extending out from God's hand to the edge of the circle, which represents the universe).

•   Another work of art studied better illustrates Christian beliefs about creation, e.g. Capronnier's stained glass window of Adam and Eve or Kastav's fifteenth-century fresco depicting the creation of the sun and moon, giving reasons why.

2 Incarnation

Test the 1 mark question

1.   B) Eucharist

2.   C) The world and everything in it is a sign of God's love

Test the 2 mark question

Suggested answers, other relevant answers would be credited. 1 mark for each correct point:

3.   The sacraments sanctify a person's life by giving them grace/ baptism makes the person a child of God/ confirmation renews the power of the Holy Spirit in a person's life/ reconciliation restores a person's relationship with God/ the sacrament of the sick forgives a person's sins.

4.   In both accounts an angel imparts information about Jesus and Mary's role in his birth/ both accounts make it clear that Mary is a virgin/ both accounts teach that Jesus is conceived by the power of the Holy Spirit/ both accounts confirm that Jesus is the Son of God.

Test the 4 mark question

Suggested answers, other relevant answers would be credited. 1 mark for each simple contrasting or similar point, another mark for developing each point, so a maximum of 4 marks for two developed points:

6.   Christian symbols are used as a declaration of faith/ e.g. in the early days of Christianity, Christians used the Ichthus symbol to declare their faith in Jesus Christ as the Son of God and the Saviour/ Christian symbols are used as reminders of Christian beliefs/ e.g. the Chi-Rho symbol reminds Christians that Jesus was sent by God to save humanity through his death/ Christian symbols are used as decoration in churches, on vestments, and in Christian art/ e.g. the Alpha and Omega symbols are used as decoration on the Paschal candle.

7. The incarnation is when God took on the human condition to become Jesus/ the annunciation is when God's plan for the incarnation was announced/ Jesus was conceived by the Holy Spirit/ his mother Mary was a virgin/ the Son of God came to earth to guide people closer to God/ to save humanity from its sins/ the incarnation shows how much God loves the human race/ Jesus was fully human and fully God/ the Catholic Church believes the incarnation makes it acceptable to show God and Jesus in a human form in art/ Christianity would not exist without the incarnation and Jesus' resurrection/ which made eternal life in heaven possible.

Test the 5 mark question

Suggested answers, other relevant answers would be credited. 1 mark for each simple contrasting or similar point, another mark for developing each point, so 4 marks for two developed points, 1 extra mark for a correct reference to a source of Christian belief or teaching:

9. The Word of God is eternal/ like God the Father, the Word has always existed/ 'In the beginning was the Word' (John 1:1)/ the Word of God is God/ the Word comes from inside God and is God's self-expression/ 'The Word was God' (John 1:1)/ the Word of God is separate to God/ the Word is one of the three Persons of the Trinity, who are all distinct and co-exist with each other/ 'The Word was with God' (John 1:1)/ the Word became flesh in Jesus/ the Incarnation is when the Word took on human nature to live on earth/ 'And the Word became flesh and lived among us' (John 1:14).

10. Both Luke and Matthew's accounts of the annunciation confirm that Jesus is the Son of God/ in both accounts an angel visits Mary or Joseph and tells them that Jesus is God's Son/ these accounts are given in Luke 1:26–38 and Matthew 1:18–24/ when Jesus was arrested he was the Son of God/ he admitted to being the Son of God even though he knew this would lead to his death/ the high priest asked 'Are you the Messiah, the Son of the Blessed One?' and Jesus said 'I am' (Mark 14)/ Jesus was able to perform various miracles that he could only have done as the Son of God/ e.g. Jesus turned water into wine at the wedding in Cana/ this story is given in John 2:1–11 in the Bible.

Test the 12 mark question

Suggested answers shown here, but see page 12 for guidance on levels of response.

12. Arguments in support:

• As we are humans, focusing on Jesus' humanity makes him more relatable/ helps to make Jesus' teachings and examples seem more achievable/ e.g. if Jesus was able to always treat others kindly when he was human then we should be able to as well.

• Focusing on Jesus' humanity helps to remind people that Jesus made mistakes and had normal human weaknesses/ but God still took him up to heaven after he died/ this reminds Christians that God will forgive their own mistakes and weaknesses/ and inspires them to keep following Jesus' teachings so they will hopefully also be raised to heaven.

• Jesus' humanity gives more meaning to his crucifixion, because his suffering was greater because of his human nature/ but Jesus still went through this suffering to save humanity/ so this is a good reminder of God's love for people.

• The fact that God fully experienced being human means God can empathise better with the human race/ this gives Christians the confidence that God knows what is best for them/ so it is useful to remember Jesus' humanity for this reason.

Arguments in support of other views:

• By focusing too much on Jesus' humanity, people might forget he is also divine.

• Jesus is special because of his divinity/ if Jesus was just a normal human being, he probably wouldn't have been able to live his whole life in total obedience to God/ so he may not have been able to save humanity through his death/ so some might argue that without Jesus' divinity there would be no Christianity.

• Jesus' divinity helps to give credibility to his teachings/ Jesus is better able to teach people about God and what God wants because he is God.

13. Arguments in support:

• Depicting God in art goes against the second commandment/ 'You shall not make for yourself an idol' (Exodus 20:4)/ approving of art that depicts God or Jesus suggests that the Church thinks it is acceptable to break the Ten Commandments.

• Art can mislead people about what God and Jesus are really like/ e.g. art that depicts Jesus as human can make people forget about his divinity/ e.g. art that depicts God as a person can make God seem less powerful than he really is/ by approving such art, the Church is contributing to the spread of misinformation about God and Jesus.

• No one knows what Jesus looked like so it is wrong to guess this in art/ similarly it is impossible to portray an infinite, transcendent God in art/ art that portrays God and Jesus will always be inaccurate so it should not be approved by the Church.

Arguments in support of other views:

• Jesus was fully human, so it should be acceptable to show Jesus in a human form.

• God revealed himself on earth in the form of a human (Jesus), so it should be acceptable to show God as a human.

• Jesus died to save all of humanity, so it should be acceptable to show him as a member of any ethnicity.

• The benefits of portraying God and Jesus in art outweigh the negatives/ art portraying God and Jesus can help people to learn about them in an accessible, visual way/ it can also inspire people and give them something to focus on as they pray/ it can also remind people about important Christian beliefs/ e.g. the Sacred Heart statue can remind Christians how much God loves them.

3 The Triune God

Test the 1 mark question

1. D) Sanctus

2. A) Magisterium

Test the 2 mark question

Suggested answers, other relevant answers would be credited. 1 mark for each correct point:

3. Plainchant is sometimes used to sing the Latin parts of the Mass/ traditional hymns or contemporary worship songs are sometimes sung by the whole congregation/ music is sometimes used to sing the acclamations/ Alleluia is sometimes sung to introduce the Gospel reading/ the Sanctus is sometimes sung just before the Eucharistic Prayer.

4. The Father created the universe/ through the Son/Word, by using his word to create/ through the power of the Holy Spirit/ a 'wind' (spirit) swept over the face of the water.

Test the 4 mark question

Suggested answers, other relevant answers would be credited. 1 mark for each simple contrasting or similar point, another mark for developing each point, so a maximum of 4 marks for two developed points:

6. The Magisterium is led by the Pope who is the successor to St Peter/ who was chosen by Jesus to lead the apostles/ the apostolic authority has been passed on to the bishops through the laying on of hands/ this means the bishops (who form part of the Magisterium) have the authority of Jesus' closest followers/ the Magisterium is guided by the Holy Spirit/ which means that official declarations of faith are infallible (without error).

7. The Father is the creator of all things/ the Father and Son are both eternal/ share the same nature/ the Son took on the limitations of human nature to become Jesus/ to save humanity from sin/ was conceived by the Holy Spirit/ rose into heaven after he died to take his place as God/ the Holy Spirit comes from both the Father and Son, uniting them in love/ gives life to all things/ is equal in majesty and power to the Father and Son/ inspires prophets to let them know the will of God.

Test the 5 mark question

Suggested answers, other relevant answers would be credited. 1 mark for each simple contrasting or similar point, another mark for developing each point, so 4 marks for two developed points, 1 extra mark for a correct reference to a source of Christian belief or teaching:

9. Prayer is a way for a Christian to communicate with God/ e.g. by using spontaneous prayer to share their concerns and worries with God/ communal prayer can help to strengthen the Christian community/ e.g. by saying a traditional prayer with other members of the congregation/ prayer can provide time for reflection in the middle of a busy life/ comfort Christians when they feel upset/ help Christians to develop their relationship with God/ 'When a person prays, he enters into a living relationship with God' (Youcat 469).

10. Christians are God's children/ and brothers or sisters to Jesus/ God the Father pours out the Holy Spirit into a Christian's heart/ which fills the person with grace/ 'And because you are children, God has sent the Spirit of his Son into our hearts, crying, 'Abba! Father!' (Galatians 4:6)/ the Holy Spirit inspires people to know the will of God/ 'who has spoken through the prophets' (the Nicene Creed)/ the love of the Trinity inspires Christians to help others/ 'The entire activity of the Church is a love that seeks the integral good of man' (Deus Caritas Est 19)/ the Son came to earth to bring people back to a relationship with the Father/ the Holy Spirit is continually guiding believers towards the Father.

Test the 12 mark question

Suggested answers shown here, but see page 12 for guidance on levels of response.

12. Arguments in support:

• Baptism is a sign of initiation into the Church/ how a person becomes a member of the Church and a child of God.

• Jesus ordered his apostles to baptise all his followers (Matthew 28:19)/ and was baptised himself by John the Baptist/ so all Christians should be baptised.

• Through baptism, a person enters into the life of the Trinity/ joins in with Jesus' death and resurrection/ so they are able to share in Christ's victory over the power of sin and death/ is filled with the Holy Spirit/ who helps to sustain their faith and commitment to God/ is cleansed of their sins.

Arguments in support of other views:

• A significant number of Christians are not baptised/ e.g. the Quakers and Salvation Army do not practise baptism, but are still Christians.

• Baptism of babies and small children is meaningless as they are too young to understand what is happening/ too young to make their own commitment to God/ it would be better to say that anyone who wants to call themselves a Christian should first be confirmed/ or baptised when they are older.

• Being a Christian involves having faith in God and Jesus/ following Jesus' teachings/ but it is possible to do this without being baptised.

• All believers are filled with the Holy Spirit/ all believers are able to share in Jesus' redemption if they wish to accept it/ not just those who are baptised.

13. **Arguments in support:**

• Understanding the relationship within the Trinity is important for understanding how love is a vital part of God's nature/ helps to explain how 'God is love' (1 John 4:16)/ as the Trinity can be thought of as three Persons united in love/ 'True love is: a trinity of lover, beloved and the love that binds them together into one' (St Augustine).

• Understanding the relationship within the Trinity helps to explain how God's love is shared with people/ is important for understanding how God relates to people/ as the Holy Spirit is the love that unites the Father and the Son/ which pours out into the hearts and lives of believers/ so sharing God's love with them.

• Understanding the fact that the Father and Son are equal/ share the same nature/ and the Son took on the human form in Jesus/ helps Christians to accept Jesus as fully God/ which is important for accepting Jesus' teachings.

Arguments in support of other views:

• The best way to understand God is through his actions in the world and people's lives/ to understand the outward effects of the Trinity/ e.g. God the Father sent his Son to earth to save humanity/ the Son sacrificed himself to save humanity/ this helps Christians to understand how great God's love is.

• Christians can understand God without thinking of him as the Trinity/ but learning about his other characteristics/ e.g. as the omnipotent creator, as a fair and merciful judge, etc.

• The best way to understand God is to understand Jesus' teachings and actions/ as Jesus was God/ displayed qualities of God/ but made these qualities relatable/ understandable as Jesus was also fully human.

4 Redemption

Test the 1 mark question

1. C) St Anselm

2. D) Quakers

Test the 2 mark question

Suggested answers, other relevant answers would be credited. 1 mark for each correct point:

3. The lectern allows people to clearly hear the word of God/ Christ is present when the word of God is proclaimed/ the altar is where Christ is offered to the Father/ as it is a place of sacrifice, it reminds Christians that Jesus' sacrifice is being made again/ the tabernacle houses the Real Presence of Christ/ images of Jesus (e.g. a crucifix) remind Christians that Christ is present in the church.

4. God gave humans free will/ as he wants humans to be able to actively choose him/ Adam and Eve's misuse of free will brought sin into the world/ the Catholic Church teaches that all people are born with the tendency to misuse their free will and sin/ Jesus' teachings help people to use their free will correctly, in a way that would please God/ Jesus' death was necessary to restore the relationship between God and humanity that had been broken through the misuse of free will.

Test the 4 mark question

Suggested answers, other relevant answers would be credited. 1 mark for each simple contrasting or similar point, another mark for developing each point, so a maximum of 4 marks for two developed points:

6. Belief that salvation is ongoing motivates Catholics to resist the temptation to sin/ to accept forgiveness when they do sin/ as they believe this is how they accept salvation/ motivates Catholics to attend Mass/ to receive the Body and Blood of Christ/ as this gives them grace and the strength to resist sin/ motivates Catholics to live by Kingdom values/ help to spread the Kingdom of God on earth/ as salvation will be completed when the Kingdom of God is fully established.

7. The offering of Christ on the cross is the highest form of prayer to God/ the Mass re-enacts this sacrifice, so it is the highest form of prayer for a Christian/ the Mass celebrates the most important event in Christianity/ Christ's Body and Blood give life to the soul/ Christians receive God's grace during the Mass, which gives them strength and guidance.

Test the 5 mark question

Suggested answers, other relevant answers would be credited. 1 mark for each simple contrasting or similar point, another mark for developing each point, so 4 marks for two developed points, 1 extra mark for a correct reference to a source of Christian belief or teaching:

9. The crucifix reminds Christians of Jesus' death, whereas the cross and Risen Christ remind Christians of Jesus' resurrection/ some Christians prefer to focus on Jesus' death as a reminder of his love for humanity, while others prefer to focus on his resurrection as a reminder that the resurrection transformed everything/ 'If Christ has not been raised, your faith is futile and you are still in your sins' (1 Corinthians 15:17)/ some Christians do not agree with portraying Jesus through art/ because they believe this goes against the second commandment/ 'You shall not make for yourself an idol' (Exodus 20:4)/ so they prefer to use a cross.

10. Jesus is the example because through his total obedience to God, he set the example for all people to follow/ Mark 14–15 tells how Jesus knew how much suffering his crucifixion would cause, but he still went through with it/ Jesus is the restorer because through his death, he restored the relationship between God and humanity/ which had been broken by sin/ this is symbolised by the veil in the temple tearing in two/ 'And the curtain of the temple was torn in two, from top to bottom' (Mark 15: 38)/

Jesus is the victor because he was victorious over suffering and death/ through his death and resurrection, he destroyed the ultimate power of sin and death.

Test the 12 mark question

Suggested answers shown here, but see page 12 for guidance on levels of response.

12. **Arguments in support:**

• Christians believe conscience is the voice of God in their heart and soul, guiding them to make the right choices/ 'There he is alone with God, Whose voice echoes in his depths' (*Gaudium et Spes* 16)/ following the voice of God will bring a Christian closer to God.

• Conscience is guided by natural law/ an instinctive understanding of good and evil/ so if a person follows their conscience then they should do good, which is what God wants.

• The Catholic Church teaches that people shouldn't ignore what they believe God is telling them in their hearts.

Arguments in support of other views:

• The Catholic Church teaches that people shouldn't go against the teachings of the Church/ even if their conscience tells them otherwise/ 'Personal conscience and reason should not be set in opposition to the moral law or the Magisterium of the Church' (Catechism of the Catholic Church 2039)/ as the Church's teachings have been guided by the Holy Spirit over hundreds of years.

• Conscience needs to be educated/ Christians can only do the right thing when they have enough knowledge to make the right decision/ this means a Christian should balance following their conscience with following Church teachings.

13. **Arguments in support:**

• Jesus' resurrection made life after death possible/ by destroying the ultimate power of sin and death/ this means Christians are now able to overcome sin to spend afterlife in the eternal presence of God in heaven/ so Christians no longer have to fear death because of the resurrection.

• The resurrection gave meaning to Jesus' death.

• Without the resurrection there would be no Christian faith/ 'If Christ has not been raised, your faith is futile and you are still in your sins' (1 Corinthians 15:17).

Arguments in support of other views:

• The resurrection would not have been possible without the sacrifice of Jesus' death/ through which Jesus showed complete obedience to God/ therefore Jesus' death is more important.

• Jesus' death redeemed humanity/ made up for the sins of Adam and Eve/ making salvation possible/ so this is more important.

• It is not really possible to separate Jesus' resurrection from his death and ascension/ they are all part of one event that redeemed and saved humanity.

• It could be argued that Jesus' birth and life are more important, as without these the resurrection could not have happened/ Christians would not have all of Jesus' teachings to follow today/ would not understand God as well as they do today.

5 Church and the Kingdom of God

Test the 1 mark question

1. B) Lourdes

2. A) Bringing back together people who have fallen apart

Test the 2 mark question

Suggested answers, other relevant answers would be credited. 1 mark for each correct point:

3. Helps the person to feel more involved in the meaning of the prayer/ is a way to accompany Jesus on his last journey/ is a way to share in Jesus' sufferings as a sign of gratitude and thanks/ helps the person to stay focused on their prayers.

4. The Pope is the leader of the Church/ has the highest authority/ is the representative of Christ on earth/ the Pope's teachings must be taken very seriously/ can be declared infallible/ the decisions of a Council have no authority until approved by the Pope.

Test the 4 mark question

Suggested answers, other relevant answers would be credited. 1 mark for each simple contrasting or similar point, another mark for developing each point, so a maximum of 4 marks for two developed points:

6. The Bible should be taken seriously as the word of God but not read in a literal way/ e.g. the Genesis creation stories should be read as myths rather than literal accounts of how the universe was created/ all members of the Church have important roles to play, not just the Pope/ e.g. all people in the Church are important in helping to spread the Kingdom of God on earth/ people should be able to take a full part in the worship of God/ e.g. hear the Mass in their own language/ the Church should guide people on how to live in the modern world/ e.g. by providing guidance on issues such as contraception/pollution/the use of technology.

7. Christians will try to show Kingdom values in their everyday lives/ by following the teachings of Jesus/ e.g. by showing love to others/ by displaying gentleness and mercy/ Christians may try to teach others about the importance of showing Kingdom values/ e.g. by educating their children/ Christians may take on a religious vocation/ e.g. priesthood or religious life/ take vows to show their commitment to the Kingdom values.

Test the 5 mark question

Suggested answers, other relevant answers would be credited. 1 mark for each simple contrasting or similar point, another mark for developing each point, so 4 marks for two developed points, 1 extra mark for a correct reference to a source of Christian belief or teaching:

9. The Magnificat shows that Mary was humble/ as she recognised she was only special because of what God had done for her/ 'for he has looked with favour on the lowliness of his servant'/ the Magnificat shows that Mary accepted God's will/ by willingly accepting the role of mother of Jesus, shown in her praise of God in the prayer/ 'My soul magnifies the Lord'/ the Magnificat shows that Mary trusted God/ believing that God would help people who are weak and poor like her/ 'He has filled the hungry with good things'.

10. The Church teaches that everyone should help to support the weakest and poorest members of society/ contribute to justice/ to help create equality for all/ for example by donating to charities/ 'The Church sincerely professes that all men … ought to work for the rightful betterment of this world in which all alike live (*Gaudium et Spes* 1)/ the Church teaches that exploitation and greed should be overcome/ as these lead to inequality and suffering/ 'Today we … have to say "thou shalt not" to an economy of exclusion and inequality' (*Evangelii Gaudium* 53).

Test the 12 mark question

Suggested answers shown here, but see page 12 for guidance on levels of response.

12. **Arguments in support:**

• A pilgrimage is a unique experience that can provide great spiritual inspiration/ bring a person closer to God.

• A pilgrimage is one of the best ways to meet other Christians from around the world/ to feel a part of the worldwide Christian community/ to learn about how Christianity is practised in other countries.

• A pilgrimage shows commitment and dedication to God/ so Christians should aim to go on at least one pilgrimage if they are serious about their faith.

• A pilgrimage allows Christians to visit important sites such as the Via Dolorosa or the Vatican/ which may help them to understand their faith better.

Arguments in support of other views:

• Some Christians do not have the time or money to go on pilgrimage.

• Catholics believe that the whole of life is a pilgrimage towards heaven/ 'Christians, on pilgrimage toward the heavenly city, should seek and think of these things which are above' (*Gaudium et Spes* 57).

• There are other ways that Christians can feel part of the Christian community/ e.g. by attending church/ there are other ways that Christians can show their commitment to God/ e.g. by following Jesus' teachings/ there are other ways that Christians can feel spiritually inspired/ e.g. by attending talks by Christian speakers.

13. **Arguments in support:**

• If people have the basics needed to survive, they will be more able to focus on God and help the Kingdom to spread/ 'Give us this day our daily bread' (The Lord's Prayer)/ doing charity work helps provide these basic needs.

• Doing charity work contributes to justice/ justice helps to create peace/ both of these are important elements of the Kingdom.

• Doing charity work expresses Kingdom values such as love, generosity and compassion, which help the Kingdom to spread.

Arguments in support of other views:

• The Kingdom of God will come when all people accept the rule of God in their hearts/ so it is better for Christians to focus on evangelism, to increase the number of people who accept God's will.

• Forgiveness is also important for helping to spread the Kingdom/ both in showing forgiveness to others and in accepting God's forgiveness.

• Peace and reconciliation are important elements of the Kingdom/ so Christians should focus on acting as peacemakers.

• Kingdom values can be expressed through vocations such as family life or priesthood/ not just through charity work.

6 Eschatology

Test the 1 mark question

1. D) The wounds Jesus received during his crucifixion

2. C) Particular judgement

Test the 2 mark question

Suggested answers, other relevant answers would be credited. 1 mark for each correct point:

3. Lit in the Easter Vigil to represent the light of Christ coming into the world/ used in the Easter Vigil to light the candles of the congregation/ used in the Easter Vigil to represent the wounds Christ received during his crucifixion/ lit at funerals to show the deceased has joined Christ in the resurrected life/ used at baptisms to light the candle given to the person being baptised.

4. People should be constantly preparing for the end of time/ by following Jesus' teachings/ by keeping faith in God/ by performing good deeds and actions/ by not committing mortal sins/ by confessing and being truly sorry after committing a mortal sin.

Test the 4 mark question

Suggested answers, other relevant answers would be credited. 1 mark for each simple contrasting or similar point, another mark for developing each point, so a maximum of 4 marks for two developed points:

6. If people are judged favourably by God, they will enter heaven/ if they are judged unfavourably by God, they will enter hell/ heaven is the state of eternal happiness in the presence of God/ where God's love removes all cares and worries/ hell is the state of eternal separation from God/ where people are aware of the happiness of those in heaven/ it is not possible to move between heaven and hell/ people have to choose to accept God in order to enter heaven/ God does not send people to hell/ people choose hell by rejecting God.

7. Final judgement is when Christ comes in glory to judge the whole of creation/ Christ is the central figure in *The Last Judgement*, raising his right hand in judgement/ the Book of Revelation says that final judgement will happen after seven angels blow trumpets to bring about the end of the world/ these angels are shown in *The Last Judgement*/ after the final judgement, those who have been judged favourably by God will stay with him forever/ in *The Last Judgement*, those on Christ's right are being raised up to heaven to stay in the presence of God.

Test the 5 mark question

Suggested answers, other relevant answers would be credited. 1 mark for each simple contrasting or similar point, another mark for developing each point, so 4 marks for two developed points, 1 extra mark for a correct reference to a source of Christian belief or teaching:

9. People will be judged favourably by God if they perform good deeds and actions/ show love and kindness to others/ e.g. by helping the poor/ in the parable, the rich man does not help Lazarus and so goes to hell/ hell is a place of torment where people are cut off from any relationship with God/ are aware of the happiness of those in heaven/ in the parable, the rich man is aware that Abraham and Lazarus are in heaven/ 'I am in agony in these flames' (Luke 16:24)/ it is not possible to move between heaven and hell/ a person's actions during their lifetime determine where they spend the afterlife/ 'between you and us a great chasm has been fixed' (Luke 16:26)/ having faith in God, and following Jesus' teachings, will lead people to heaven/ 'If they do not listen to Moses and the prophets, neither will they be convinced even if someone rises from the dead' (Luke 16: 31).

10. Cosmic reconciliation refers to the idea of bringing the whole of creation together in harmony with God/ when God created the universe he made all things perfectly balanced in harmony/ 'God saw everything that he had made, and indeed, it was very good' (Genesis 1:31)/ sin broke this harmony/ through his death and resurrection, Jesus destroyed the power of sin and death and helped to restore harmony to the world/ 'through him God was pleased to reconcile to himself all things, whether on earth or in heaven, by making peace through the blood of his cross' (Colossians 1:20)/ the whole of creation will be fully restored and reconciled with God at the end of time/ 'and all manner of thing shall be well' (Revelations of Divine Love 32).

Test the 12 mark question

Suggested answers shown here, but see page 12 for guidance on levels of response.

12. **Arguments in support:**

• Some Christians believe that performing good deeds and actions is necessary to enter heaven/ salvation is an ongoing process/ 'faith apart from works is barren' (James 2:20).

• Showing kindness to others is an important part of this/ a central Christian teaching/ 'love your neighbour' is the second greatest commandment (Matthew 22:39).

• It is important for Christians to focus on doing what they can to ensure they enter heaven when they die/ as this is the difference between eternal happiness in the presence of God versus eternal separation from God/ eternal torment and agony.

Arguments in support of other views:

• Some Christians believe faith alone is enough to enter heaven/ salvation was completed with Jesus' death and resurrection/ faith is more important than good works/ what is important is what is in the heart – not gaining good points by mechanically doing good deeds.

• The main reason for Christians to show kindness to others is because it is the right/moral/loving thing to do/ it creates happiness both for the person showing kindness and the person receiving it/ Jesus taught it is important/ 'love your neighbour'.

13. **Arguments in support:**

• The sanctity of life means life is sacred/ because it is created by God/ so every life should treasured and valued/ and therefore extended as long as possible.

• The sanctity of life means all lives are equal/ because everyone is created in the image of God/ so very ill and dying patients are still worth just as much as anyone else/ and should be kept alive wherever possible.

• Not trying to keep very ill patients alive disrespects the sanctity of life/ devalues life/ is equivalent to murder.

Arguments in support of other views:

• The Catholic Church believes that a person who is close to death should not receive treatment that will only prolong their suffering.

• The sanctity of life means only God has the right to take away life/ God's plans for a person's life should not be interfered with/ not allowing a person to die a natural death could be seen as interfering with God's plan.

- The sanctity of life means life should be valued and respected/ a person's dignity is important/ allowing a person to die naturally rather than prolonging their suffering could be seen as respecting a person's dignity.

7 Islam: beliefs and teachings

Test the 1 mark question

1. D) The Torah
2. C) Jibril

Test the 2 mark question

Suggested answers, other relevant answers would be credited. 1 mark for each correct point:

3. Sunni Muslims believe their leader should be elected, whereas Shi'a Muslims believe their leader should be a descendant of Muhammad and chosen by God/ Shi'a Muslims believe their leader has the authority to provide religious guidance, whereas Sunni Muslims don't/ Sunni Muslims believe Abu Bakr was the rightful leader after Muhammad died; Shi'a Muslims believe Ali was/ Sunni Muslims follow the six articles of faith; Shi'a Muslims follow the five roots of 'Usul ad-Din/ Sunni Muslims pray five times a day; Shi'a Muslims three times a day/ Sunni Muslims give Zakah; Shi'a Muslims also give Khums.

4. Tawhid/ angels/ the holy books/ the prophets/ the Day of Judgement/ the supremacy of God's will.

Test the 4 mark question

Suggested answers, other relevant answers would be credited. 1 mark for each simple contrasting or similar point, another mark for developing each point, so a maximum of 4 marks for two developed points:

6. God is immanent/ present everywhere in the world and the universe/ involved with life on earth/ God is transcendent/ beyond and outside the universe/ God is beneficent/ all-loving and all-good/ seen in his gift to humans of everything they need to live on earth/ God is fair and just/ will judge all people equally on the Day of Judgement/ God is merciful/ cares for people and understands their suffering/ forgives people who are truly sorry/ God is omnipotent/ has the power to create and sustain everything in the universe/ is aware of all human actions and thoughts.

7. Encourages Muslims to take responsibility for their actions/ because they know God will hold them accountable and reward or punish them accordingly/ motivates Muslims to follow the teachings in the Qur'an and dedicate their lives to God/ e.g. by following the Five Pillars or Ten Obligatory Acts/ helps Muslims to accept unjust situations/ as they know God will provide justice in the afterlife.

Test the 5 mark question

Suggested answers, other relevant answers would be credited. 1 mark for each simple contrasting or similar point, another mark for developing each point, so 4 marks for two developed points, 1 extra mark for a correct reference to a source of Muslim belief or teaching:

9. Muhammad received the final revelation of Islam/the Qur'an from God/ which is the highest source of authority for all matters relating to Islamic teaching, practice and law/ 'he is God's messenger and the seal of the prophets' (Qur'an 33:40)/ helped to fully establish Islam/ by conquering Makkah and converting the city to Islam/ travelled to heaven and met God/ agreed with God that Muslims should pray five times a day.

10. There is only one God/ God is a unified, indivisible being who cannot be divided into different persons/ God is eternal/ has always existed/ God was not born or came into being out of something else/ God does not have any children/ God is unique/ no other person or thing has God's qualities/ 'Say, "He is God the One, God the eternal. He begot no one nor was He begotten. No one is comparable to Him."' (Qur'an 112:1–4).

Test the 12 mark question

Suggested answers shown here, but see page 12 for guidance on levels of response.

12. **Arguments in support:**

- The Qur'an is God's word/ as passed on by the angel Jibril to Muhammad/ so must include everything God wants Muslims to know about how to live a good life in obedience to him.

- The Qur'an is accepted as the highest authority in Islam/ e.g. the authority of the holy books is one of the six articles of faith in Sunni Islam/ so Muslims should always look to the Qur'an for guidance on how to live a perfect Muslim life.

- The Qur'an includes stories about the lives of the prophets/ who were sent to earth to help make sure people followed God's path/ act as good role models to Muslims.

- Major Islamic practices stem from the Qur'an, such as fasting during Ramadan (Qur'an 2:18)/ giving Zakah (Qur'an 2:215)/ undertaking Hajj (Qur'an 3:97).

Arguments in support of other views:

- Shi'a Muslims believe the Imams are necessary to help explain the teachings in the Qur'an/ as the Qur'an was written hundreds of years ago so needs interpreting for the modern world/ as the Qur'an can be interpreted in different ways.

- The Sunnah (Muhammad's teachings and actions) also have the authority to provide religious guidance/ help Muslims to live a perfect Muslim life.

- Some Islamic practices are not detailed in the Qur'an/ e.g. giving to charity is mentioned in the Qur'an, but the exact amount that should be given as Zakah is not/ this was worked out at a later date by Muslim scholars.

13. **Arguments in support:**

- God sends prophets to earth to help convey his desires for humanity/ they do this by conveying God's words and setting good examples for how to live a life in obedience to God/ so Muslims should pay attention to the prophets as role models.

- Ibrahim showed total dedication to God/ fulfilled all the tests and commands given to him by God/ e.g. he was willing to sacrifice his son to God/ he left his wife and son in the desert on God's command/ these events show he had complete faith in God/ was willing to put God before his family/ which gives Muslims a strong example of how they should put God before everything else.

- Muhammad dedicated his life to preaching God's word and proclaiming that God is One/ challenged the people of Makkah to give up habits that went against God's word, despite facing persecution as a result/ provides a good example of how Muslims should dedicate their lives to God.

Arguments in support of other views:

- Angels are pure and sinless/ do not ever displease God/ ceaselessly praise and worship God/ always obey God's commands/ these are all traits that Muslims should aspire to.

- Angels take care of people throughout their lives/ this could inspire Muslims to show kindness to others.

- The prophets showed violence in some of their actions/ e.g. Ibrahim smashed the idols in the temple with an axe/ e.g. Muhammad marched on the city of Makkah/ so it could be said they are not good role models from this point of view.

8 Islam: practices

Test the 1 mark question

1. C) Shahadah
2. B) Husayn

Test the 2 mark question

Suggested answers, other relevant answers would be credited. 1 mark for each correct point:

3. Compass/ mihrab/ qiblah wall.

4. By donating directly to a charity/ by giving to a mosque.

Test the 4 mark question

Suggested answers, other relevant answers would be credited. 1 mark for each simple contrasting or similar point, another mark for developing each point, so a maximum of 4 marks for two developed points:

6. Muslims circle the Ka'aba/ remembering the shrine God told Ibrahim to build/ Muslims walk seven times between the hills of Safa and Marwah/ this recalls Hajira's search for water/ Muslims collect water from the well of Zamzam/ this recalls when Ishmael struck his foot on the ground and water gushed up from the earth/ Muslims throw pebbles at the Jamarat/ this recalls when Ibrahim threw stones at the devil/ Muslims sacrifice an animal/ this recalls Ibrahim's willingness to sacrifice his own son.

7. It is important to fast during Ramadan because this is a command from God/ revealed to Muhammad via the angel Jibril/ 'So any one of you who is present that month should fast' (Qur'an 2:18)/ it is important to fast because it develops self-discipline/ shows obedience and dedication to God/ reminds Muslims to help those in poverty.

Test the 5 mark question

Suggested answers, other relevant answers would be credited. 1 mark for each simple contrasting or similar point, another mark for developing each point, so 4 marks for two developed points, 1 extra mark for a correct reference to a source of Muslim belief or teaching:

9. It is one of the Five Pillars and Ten Obligatory Acts/ Muslims are expected to take part in Hajj at least once during their lifetime/ 'Pilgrimage to the House is a duty owed to God by people who are able to undertake it' (Qur'an 3:97)/ to show commitment to God/ to become closer to God/ to be reminded of the good examples set by the prophets/ e.g. Ibrahim's willingness to sacrifice his own son/ 'Who could be better in religion than those who […] follow the religion of Abraham, who was true in faith?' (Qur'an 4:125)/ to feel part of the Muslim community.

10. Jihad is the struggle against evil/ greater jihad is the inward, personal struggle to follow the teachings of Islam/ '… this is My path, leading straight, so follow it, and do not follow other ways' (Qur'an 6:153)/ it is more important than lesser jihad/ requires Muslims to put God above everything else/ to observe the Five Pillars and study the Qur'an/ lesser jihad is the outward, collective struggle to defend Islam from threat/ it is acceptable to fight in self-defence if all other peaceful methods have been tried first/ it cannot be used to justify terrorist attacks.

Test the 12 mark question

Suggested answers shown here, but see page 12 for guidance on levels of response.

12. **Arguments in support:**

- Giving to charity helps the poorest and most vulnerable members of the Muslim community/ e.g. by providing them with food and shelter/ this gives them strength/ it also brings the whole community together, by making the wealthy more aware of the poor.

- Giving Khums helps to fund religious education/ this increases knowledge and understanding in the Muslim community, so making it stronger.

• A strong community is important because this protects the faith from attack/ giving to charity provides support for Muslims/ thus making it easier for Muslims to follow Islamic teachings (e.g. prevents stealing to feed a family)/ so any practice that strengthens the community is important.

Arguments in support of other views:

• Other practices also strengthen the Muslim community/ e.g. prayer connects Muslims together (as they all pray facing Makkah/ all use the same prayers and rak'ah)/ Hajj brings Muslims together and creates a strong sense of community/ particularly as Muslims all wear similar ihram clothing (usually white)/ celebrating festivals brings Muslims together.

• Other things are more important than strengthening the Muslim community/ e.g. showing obedience to God/ following the examples of the prophets/ putting God above everything else/ so other practices are more important for these reasons/ e.g. prayer and studying the Qur'an.

13.　Arguments in support:

• Christian festivals (such as Easter and Christmas) are official public holidays in Britain, so the festivals of other predominant religions should be recognised in the same way.

• Making Id-ul-Fitr an official public holiday would give Muslims time off work to attend special prayers in mosques or large outdoor areas/ visit their local cemetery to pray for the dead/ celebrate with family and friends.

• Id-ul-Fitr allows Muslims to celebrate the end of a month of fasting/ it is an important reward for a difficult month requiring great self-discipline/ this should be recognised officially.

• Id-ul-Fitr allows Muslims to thank God for giving his wisdom and guidance in the Qur'an/ many Muslims would say this is the most important part of their history to remember, as without the Qur'an Islam would not exist in the same way today/ making Id-ul-Fitr an official public holiday would help with this.

Arguments in support of other views:

• Christianity is the main religious tradition in Britain/ so only Christian festivals should be recognised as official public holidays/ if Muslim festivals were made official public holidays, Hindu/Sikh/Buddhist festivals would have to be made official public holidays as well.

• If Id-ul-Fitr was made an official public holiday this would dilute the meaning and significance of the festival/ in the same way that Christmas has become commercialised and is celebrated by non-Christians as well as Christians.

• Instead it would be better for businesses to give Muslims time off to celebrate/ some Islamic businesses in Britain already do this.

9 Judaism: beliefs and teachings

Test the 1 mark question

1.　A) Do not cause harm to anyone

2.　A) Abraham

Test the 2 mark question

Suggested answers, other relevant answers would be credited. 1 mark for each correct point:

3.　God created the universe and everything in it/ in six days/ about 6000 years ago/ God took four days to make the universe fit to support life/ and two days to create all living creatures/ God created the universe but it developed/evolved over a much longer period of time.

4.　During Rosh Hashanah/ during Yom Kippur/ on the Day of Atonement/ as soon as they die/ on the Day of Judgement.

Test the 4 mark question

Suggested answers, other relevant answers would be credited. 1 mark for each simple contrasting or similar point, another mark for developing each point, so a maximum of 4 marks for two developed points:

6.　The covenant at Sinai means Jews today have to obey God's laws/ including the Ten Commandments and the mitzvot in the Torah/ this influences how they worship God/ how they celebrate Shabbat and Jewish festivals/ the food they eat/ the covenant at Sinai also means Jews are considered to be the chosen people of God/ that God is the God of the Jews/ which inspires Jews to centre their lives around God/ e.g. by showing dedication and commitment to God in the way they live and worship.

7.　Many Jews believe they will go to heaven/paradise/Gan Eden when they die/ if they follow their faith correctly/ heaven is where people are with God/ some Jews believe people who do not go to heaven go to Sheol/ a place of waiting where souls are cleansed/ some Jews believe they will be judged by God as soon as they die/ supported by Ecclesiastes 12:7/ others believe God will judge everyone on the Day of Judgement/ supported by Daniel 12:2/ some Jews believe in physical or spiritual resurrection/ but many do not.

Test the 5 mark question

Suggested answers, other relevant answers would be credited. 1 mark for each simple contrasting or similar point, another mark for developing each point, so 4 marks for two developed points, 1 extra mark for a correct reference to a source of Jewish belief or teaching:

9.　Justice means bringing about what is right and fair, according to the law, or making up for a wrong that has been committed/ pursuing justice is a sacred duty for Jews/ 'to do justice and love goodness' (Micah 6:8)/ the laws in the Torah give guidance to Jews on how to treat the poor and vulnerable, to help achieve justice/ healing the world means taking actions to help God's work in sustaining the world/ it may involve contributing to social justice or helping to protect the environment/ e.g. volunteering for a charity such as World Jewish Relief/ some Jews believe it also involves obeying the mitzvot and trying to become closer to God/ showing kindness to others means showing positive, caring actions towards all living things/ the Torah teaches that Jews should love others as they loves themselves/ 'love your fellow as yourself' (Leviticus 19:18).

10.　God is a single, whole, indivisible being/ not three Persons, as in Christianity/ God is the only being who should be praised and worshipped/ everything in the universe has been created and is sustained by God/ 'when God began to create the heaven and earth' (Genesis 1:1)/ God is the source of all Jewish morality, beliefs and values/ including all of the laws Jews should follow (the mitzvot)/ Jews should show total loyalty, love and dedication towards God/ 'You shall love the Lord your God with all your heart and with all your soul and with all your might' (Deuteronomy 6:5).

Test the 12 mark question

Suggested answers shown here, but see page 12 for guidance on levels of response.

12.　Arguments in support:

• Orthodox Jews believe there will be a future leader of the Jews (called the Messiah)/ who will bring about world peace and unite humanity together/ by ruling over humanity with kindness and justice/ and upholding and teaching the law in the Torah.

• The Messiah will bring about the Messianic age/ when war will end and people will live in peace and harmony/ 'Nation shall not take up sword against nation; They shall never again know war' (Micah 4:3).

• Global peace will not be achieved until the Messiah comes/ Jews will not be able to achieve this on their own/ so there is little point in trying to create world peace before then.

Arguments in support of other views:

• Reform Jews believe everyone should work together to achieve world peace/ and this will bring about the Messianic age/ rather than the leadership of one person.

• Orthodox Jews believe the Messiah will come if God deems the Jews to be worthy of redemption/ but perhaps Jews will only be worthy of redemption if they first try to make the world a better place.

• The moral principles of pursuing justice/ healing the world/ showing kindness to others all require Jews to help create a more peaceful, just society.

13.　Arguments in support:

• Jews believe that God will judge them for how well they follow his laws/ both once a year during Rosh Hashanah, to determine their fortunes for the coming year/ and after they die, to determine how they spend their afterlife.

• This encourages and motivates Jews to obey God's laws/ including the 613 mitzvot in the Torah/ which has a large influence on how they live their lives/ e.g. what food they eat, how they worship God, how they celebrate Shabbat, how they treat others.

• Focusing on God's role as judge emphasises the importance of living in a good way and following God's laws/ which might be helpful for Jews who struggle to follow all of the laws, or do not see the importance of following all of the laws.

• It may also help Jews who feel wronged/ because they know God's judgement will be fair.

Arguments in support of other views:

• It is hard to understand God as the judge without also understanding God as the lawgiver/ as Jews need to know what they are being judged on.

• It is equally/more important to understand God as the creator/ who created everything in the universe, including human life/ as this influences belief in the sanctity of life/ the obligation to save a life (pikuach nefesh)/ means that everything Jews see and experience is a meeting with God.

• Understanding God as the creator of free will helps Jews to understand the need for God's laws/ because the laws help Jews to use their free will correctly/ without this knowledge Jews might question the necessity of the laws.

• Understanding God as the creator and sustainer encourages Jews to help improve society and protect the world/ to fulfil God's plan for the world he created/ helps to explain the importance of healing the world.

10 Judaism: practices

Test the 1 mark question

1.　C) Ner tamid

2.　B) Amidah

Test the 2 mark question

Suggested answers, other relevant answers would be credited. 1 mark for each correct point:

3.　By holding a Bar Mitzvah ceremony/ the boy reads from the Torah at a service in the synagogue/ wears a tallit for the first time/ may lead part of the service/ makes a short speech/ his father gives a speech thanking God/ there is a meal or party/ the boy receives gifts.

4.　Orthodox synagogues usually hold daily services; Reform ones often don't/ Orthodox services are in Hebrew; Reform ones are in Hebrew and the country's own language/ in Orthodox services the leader has their back to the congregation; in Reform services they mostly face the congregation/ in Orthodox services men and women sit separately; in Reform ones they sit together/ Reform services tend to be shorter than Orthodox ones/ but more rigidly structured/ Orthodox men and married women always cover their heads, Reform men and women might not/ the singing is unaccompanied in Orthodox services but may be accompanied in Reform ones.

Test the 4 mark question

Suggested answers, other relevant answers would be credited. 1 mark for each simple contrasting or similar point, another mark for developing each point, so a maximum of 4 marks for two developed points:

6. To learn more about the history of Judaism/ e.g. the Tenakh contains accounts about the early history of the Jews, such as the escape from Egypt/ to learn more about God's laws/ as obeying these correctly is an important part of the Jewish faith (particularly for Orthodox Jews)/ to learn how to apply God's laws to everyday life/ the Talmud helps Jews to interpret the Torah and apply it to their lives today.

7. By doing good actions such as charity work/ as Jews believe this will improve God's judgement/ by sharing a special meal with their families/ this includes symbolic foods, e.g. apples dipped in honey to symbolise hope for a sweet new year/ by attending services in the synagogue/ where prayers are said asking God to continue to be the king of the world for the coming year.

Test the 5 mark question

Suggested answers, other relevant answers would be credited. 1 mark for each simple contrasting or similar point, another mark for developing each point, so 4 marks for two developed points, 1 extra mark for a correct reference to a source of Jewish belief or teaching:

9. In the naming ceremony the baby is formally introduced to the community and God/ Orthodox babies are blessed in the synagogue on the first Shabbat after their birth/ the father recites the Torah blessing and asks God for the good health of his wife and baby/ a baby girl's name is announced/ both Reform parents take part in the ceremony/ in the Brit Milah ceremony a baby boy is circumcised/ when he is eight days old/ placed on a chair that symbolises the presence of the prophet Elijah/ placed on the knee of the companion of the child/ blessed by his father/ formally named/ there is a festive meal/ recalls the covenant God made with Abraham/ circumcision 'would be a sign of the covenant between Me and you' (Genesis 17:11)/ in the redemption of the firstborn son, some Orthodox Jews give money to redeem their firstborn son from Temple service/ five silver coins are given to a kohen/ prayers are said asking for the child to 'enter into Torah, into marriage, and into good deeds'/ 'but you shall have the first-born of man redeemed ... Take as their redemption price ... the money equivalent of five shekels' (Numbers 18:15–16).

10. Kosher food is acceptable to eat, trefah food is not/ it is not acceptable to eat food containing blood/ 'But make sure that you do not partake of the blood; for the blood is the life, and you must not consume the life with the flesh' (Deuteronomy 12:23)/ dairy products and meat cannot be eaten together/ several hours must pass between eating meat and anything containing milk/ 'You shall not boil a kid in its mother's milk' (Exodus 23:19)/ for this reason many Orthodox homes have kitchens with two sinks and two food preparation areas.

Test the 12 mark question

Suggested answers shown here, but see page 12 for guidance on levels of response.

12. Arguments in support:

• In Reform Judaism women and men can take on the same roles in worship/ e.g. both can become rabbis or be part of the minyan.

• Reform Jewish men and women can choose whether or not to wear a tallit and tefillin for prayer.

• Jewish men and women can attend the same services in the synagogue, or choose to pray at home.

• Both boys and girls may celebrate their coming of age in Reform Judaism.

• At Reform weddings, the marriage contract usually focuses on mutual hopes for the marriage that are the same for the husband and wife.

• In Orthodox Judaism both men and women follow the dietary laws.

Arguments in support of other views:

• In Orthodox Judaism women are not allowed to be rabbis.

• Orthodox Jewish men wear a tallit and tefillin for prayers but women do not.

• Orthodox boys celebrate their coming of age with a Bar Mitzvah ceremony but girls do not celebrate with a Bat Mitzvah ceremony/ in Reform Judaism, boys celebrate their coming of age at 13 and girls at 12.

• At Orthodox weddings, the marriage contract may detail aspects such as the husband's duties to his wife, and how he will provide for his wife if they get divorced, but not vice versa.

• During the third period of mourning after a death, male mourners say the kaddish daily in the synagogue but women do not.

13. Arguments in support:

• The set periods of time help to give structure to a person's mourning/ give them enough time to grieve fully but also help them to get back to normal life.

• When they first hear of the death Jews say a blessing that refers to God as the true judge/ this helps them to accept God's decision to take the person's life.

• During the first period of mourning, Jews do not have to worry about following certain Jewish laws

• During shiva (the second period of mourning), mourners stay at home to pray together and support each other/ mirrors are covered so mourners cannot focus on their appearance, helping them to focus instead on coming to terms with a person's death.

Arguments in support of other views:

• Mourning/grieving is very personal and some people might find the structure or rigidity of Jewish mourning customs unhelpful.

• Most Jews are buried as soon after death as possible/ but mourners might need longer than 24 hours to mentally prepare themselves for the funeral.

• The second period of mourning lasts for seven days/ when Jews stay at home and mourn together/ do not work/ but they might need more than a week before returning to work/ might want to mourn alone.

• During the third period of mourning Jews are not allowed to listen to music/ but they might find that listening to music brings them solace.

• During the first year after a person's death Jews are not allowed to go to parties/ but they might find that going to parties helps to distract them after a person's death.

11 Theme A: religion, relationships and families

Test the 1 mark question

1. C) Adultery

2. D) Homosexual

Test the 2 mark question

Suggested answers, other relevant answers would be credited. 1 mark for each correct point:

3. The Catholic Church believes that marriage should be between a man and a woman/ described in Genesis 2:24/ do not think that it is part of God's plan for human beings for same-sex couples to be married/ sex should be open to the possibility of new life – impossible for same-sex couples/ sex between same-sex couples is regarded as a sin.

4. Many Christians are against cohabitation (a couple living together and having a sexual relationship without being married)/ some Christians who oppose sex before marriage think it is sinful/ the Catholic Church teaches that a sexual relationship should only take place within marriage/ it breaks the sanctity of marriage and the sexual union/ doesn't have the same sense of commitment and faithfulness as marriage/ some Protestant Christians accept that although marriage is best, people may live together in a faithful, loving, committed way without being married.

Test the 4 mark question

Suggested answers, other relevant answers would be credited. 1 mark for each simple contrasting or similar point, another mark for developing each point, so a maximum of 4 marks for two developed points:

6. The Catholic Church and most Christians teach that sex should take place only within marriage/ sex expresses a deep, loving, lifelong union/ it is one of God's gifts at creation/ 'Therefore a man leaves his father and his mother and clings to his wife, and they become one flesh.' (Genesis 2:24)/ 'The sexual act must take place exclusively within marriage. Outside of marriage it always constitutes a grave sin.' (Catechism 2390).

Society has changed/ many people do not see sex as requiring commitment/ contraception has reduced the risk of pregnancy/ many people engage in casual sexual relationships/ some liberal Christians accept that for some people sex before marriage is a valid expression of their love for each other/ atheists and humanists do not see marriage as a sacrament so do not think it is necessarily wrong to have sex before marriage.

7. The Catholic Church teaches that having an affair breaks the vows made in marriage, 'To have and to hold from this day forward, for better, for worse'/ other Christian denominations also agree that adultery is wrong as it breaks the promise to exclusively 'love and cherish' their partner in their marriage/ Catholics believe that it betrays the innocent partner and causes harm and a feeling of rejection/ other Christians agree as it brings distress, suffering and tensions into the home, and affects any children/ many non-religious people would also agree as it destroys the trust between the married couple and can cause the break-up of the marriage.

Test the 5 mark question

Suggested answers, other relevant answers would be credited. 1 mark for each simple contrasting or similar point, another mark for developing each point, so 4 marks for two developed points, 1 extra mark for a correct reference to a source of Christian belief or teaching:

9. Marriage is seen as an exclusive union of a man and woman/ vows are made before God and witnesses/ 'I call upon these persons here present to witness that I, (full name), take you (full name) to be my lawful wedded husband/wife, to have and to hold from this day forward, for better for worse, for richer for poorer, in sickness and in health, to love and to cherish, till death do us part.'/ a sacrament through which God's love and blessing is given to a couple/ 'Therefore a man leaves his father and his mother and clings to his wife, and they become one flesh.' (Genesis 2:24)/ provides the loving relationship and atmosphere through which children can grow and flourish/ is a sign of the love of Christ for the Church.

10. The Creation stories show that God made man and woman of equal value/ 'in the image of God he created them, male and female he created them.' (Genesis 1:27)/ Genesis 2:23–24 says that woman was created from the bone of a man so they originate from one flesh and are equal in value/ together they are the full form of a human being/ Paul taught that 'There is no longer Jew or Greek, there is no longer slave or free, there is no longer male and female; for all of you are one in Christ Jesus.' (Galatians 3:28)/ men and women complement each other in support in marriage/ although the genders are equal they have different roles/ traditionally a woman looks after the home and children although many do go out to work in Britain today/ the man's role includes providing protection, discipline and an income/ some roles are seen as exclusive for men in the Catholic Church e.g. being priests (not in most Protestant churches)/ should have equal rights e.g. equal pay for doing equal work/ 'Love your neighbour' applies to everyone equally.

Test the 12 mark question

Suggested answers shown here, but see page 12 for guidance on levels of response.

12. Arguments in support:

• If the marriage is valid then a divorce is breaking vows made in front of a priest or deacon who acts as a witness for God and the Church.

• These same vows were made by the couple who for whatever reason are seeking an annulment/ if their consent was made (the moment of marriage) – 'I take you to be my wife/husband' – then that binds the spouses to each other 'till death do us part'.

• An annulment may be used an excuse for a divorce/ so if a divorce is wrong an annulment should be too as really there is no difference between them/ they have been living together as man and wife.

Arguments in support of other views:

• The Catholic Church opposes the idea of divorce but supports an annulment if the 'marriage' was not valid in the first place/ Catholics believe that there is nothing wrong with an annulment, so the couple could find happiness in a future valid marriage.

• The big difference between a divorce and an annulment is that with a divorce the couple have been properly married/ this is not the case with an annulment.

• Catholics would agree that a proper marriage hasn't taken place if one partner continues to have affairs after a marriage has taken place – it is unfair for the other partner and they should be allowed to end the 'marriage' (Matthew 5:32)/ they obviously haven't taken the vow of exclusiveness seriously.

• If a partner refuses to have sexual intercourse or always insists on using contraception then they are not prepared to live by the promise that they would accept children lovingly from God/ this would be unfair on a partner who wishes to start a family and enjoy a sexual relationship within marriage.

• If the couple were forced to marry e.g. by parents, they would not have been married freely and willingly/ so it is only right that the marriage can be annulled.

13. Arguments in support:

• If a person has divorced and their original partner is still alive, the Catholic Church will not allow a remarriage in their church, as it is breaking the original marriage vows made before a priest or deacon and before God.

• Unless their original partner is no longer alive, remarriage is encouraging the committing of adultery/ Jesus said that adultery is wrong (Mark 10:11–12).

• Those who divorce and get remarried despite their original partner being still alive will not be allowed to receive Communion in a Catholic church/ it would break the sanctity of (valid) marriage.

• A civil marriage could take place instead of one in church before God.

Arguments in support of other views:

• Society has changed/ many people get divorced and remarried in Britain today/ why shouldn't people be given a second chance and be allowed to remarry in church.

• Some Christian churches, for example Methodists and Anglicans, sometimes will marry divorcees and will not stop them from receiving Communion.

• If the first marriage turned out to be a serious mistake should it prevent people from trying again and remarrying/ if in church it would demonstrate that they are taking their new commitment seriously.

• The couple might feel that it isn't a proper and valid wedding unless it takes place in a church.

12 Theme B: religion, peace and conflict

Test the 1 mark question

1. A) Reconciliation
2. C) Pax Christi

Test the 2 mark question

Suggested answers, other relevant answers would be credited. 1 mark for each correct point:

3. Jesus showed righteous anger when he drove the money changers out of the Temple/ if there is injustice, righteous anger can be channelled towards changing the situation and restoring justice.

4. Just cause/ reasonable chance of winning/ declared by the state or sovereign/ only proportional force used/ innocent civilians protected/ must be the last resort/ environment should be protected.

Test the 4 mark question

Suggested answers, other relevant answers would be credited. 1 mark for each simple contrasting or similar point, another mark for developing each point, so a maximum of 4 marks for two developed points:

6. Catholic Christians believe that use of weapons of mass destruction is wrong as it causes the indiscriminate death of many innocent civilians (this includes chemical and biological weapons and nuclear weapons)/ the devastating effects are long-lasting/ other Christians also believe that they should not be used because of financial reasons/ they cost millions in research, building and maintenance/ the money could be much better spent on hospitals, education, and other things which improve peoples' lives.

7. The Catholic Church believes that refugees who have had to flee from war should be welcomed and protected by all countries/ Populorium Progressio 67 states that it is the duty of all to help/ 'Love your neighbour as you love yourself'/ it is the humane thing to help.

Some people in Britain argue that there are not enough resources to support taking in large numbers of refugees/ some people in Britain also need help and it is impossible to help everyone.

Test the 5 mark question

Suggested answers, other relevant answers would be credited. 1 mark for each simple contrasting or similar point, another mark for developing each point, so 4 marks for two developed points, 1 extra mark for a correct reference to a source of Christian belief or teaching:

9. Christians should follow the example of Jesus/ Jesus forgave those who crucified him (Luke 23:34)/ Jesus forgave Peter for his denial of him (John 21:15–17)/ Jesus taught that we should always forgive/ Jesus told Peter we should forgive 'seventy-seven times' (Matthew 18:21–22/ Christians must forgive if they want God to forgive them/ Lord's Prayer – Matthew 6:12/ parable of the Unforgiving Servant (Matthew 18:23 – 35)/ forgiveness can lead to reconciliation and an end to conflict.

10. Some believe that Jesus was a pacifist/ Jesus taught to 'turn the other cheek' (Matthew 5:39)/ 'Blessed are the peacemakers, for they will be called children of God' (Matthew 5: 9)/ Jesus refused to use force when he was arrested (Matthew 26:51–53)/ the Ten Commandments teach that it is wrong to kill/ the early Christians were pacifists e.g. Martin of Tours/ the Religious Society of Friends (Quakers) refuse to kill but will help the ambulance services/ Catholics are taught to work for reconciliation e.g. Pax Christi.

Test the 12 mark question

Suggested answers shown here, but see page 12 for guidance on levels of response.

12. Arguments in support:

• Teaching about the sanctity of life – the belief that it is wrong to take life, and that by doing so a believer is disobeying religious commands.

• Arguments in favour of pacifism (both religious and non-religious) – violence breeds violence and does not bring about peace and stability.

• Modern warfare targets innocent civilians through use of weapons of mass destruction. Modern warfare is therefore morally wrong.

• Jesus taught, 'But if anyone strikes you on the right cheek, turn the other also.' (Matthew 5:39)

• 'Blessed are the peacemakers, for they will be called the children of God.' (Matthew 5:9).

Arguments in support of other views:

• Idea of just war – criteria include: started and controlled by a properly instituted authority/ just cause/ last resort/ not to involve suffering to innocent civilians/ protect trees, crops, animals/ not an act of aggression or to gain territory/ aim to restore peace and freedom/ enable release of prisoners of war/ must be winnable/ proportionality.

• War can be the lesser of two evils: it can be justified if its purpose is to: stop atrocities/ depose a dictator/ defeat terrorists/ stop the spread of weapons of mass destruction/ if the consequences of war are better than the consequences of not fighting, then war is justified.

• People have a right to self-defence/ 'Love your neighbour'.

• Jesus used force in the temple because it had become 'a den of thieves.'

13. Arguments in support:

• Nuclear weapons could destroy the whole world.

• They could get into the wrong hands e.g. terrorists/ those who have them could bully those who do not/ unless countries get rid of them other countries will want them and there will be more danger of a rogue state getting them.

• Nuclear bombs dropped to end the Second World War had the effect of killing people for years to come because of radiation.

• They do not meet the just war criteria e.g. of proportionality or not killing innocent civilians/ religions should support the destruction of nuclear weapons as they go against religious teachings of peace/ 'those who take the sword will die by the sword'.

Arguments in support of other views:

- Nuclear weapons may be a deterrent/ could result in maintaining the peace and preventing war as people are too frightened to use them.

- If others have them they may be needed for defence to maintain a balance of power/ need to protect their people from attack.

- Nuclear weapons have been invented/ technology cannot be undone.

- The industry provides employment for those who make them.

- Jesus said, 'The one who has no sword must sell his cloak and buy one.' (Luke 22:36).

13 Theme C: religion, human rights and social justice

Test the 1 mark question

1. D) CAFOD

2. B) Promoting tolerance

Test the 2 mark question

Suggested answers, other relevant answers would be credited. 1 mark for each correct point:

3. Everyone's rights and duties (worldwide) need to be considered/ careful thought must be given to the needs and ambitions of every group of people including the wellbeing of everyone/ it is right to give dignity to every person because humans are superior to all other living beings/ people are the same all over the world and should not be ignored/ every person should receive the necessities of life e.g. food/ clothing/shelter/ other rights include to have children/an education/employment/ respect/freedom of conscience and religion/privacy/ society must be built on truth and justice, and motivated by love.

4. Take personal responsibility and work to end injustice and the denial of human rights/ support Catholic agencies who work to bring about changes e.g. the Justice and Peace Commission and Caritas International/ support practical action e.g. provide shelter and food/ work with agencies of all religions.

Test the 4 mark question

Suggested answers, other relevant answers would be credited. 1 mark for each simple contrasting or similar point, another mark for developing each point, so a maximum of 4 marks for two developed points:

6. Most Christians believe that people with different racial backgrounds are all equal to each other/ created in the image of God (Genesis)/ every individual should be judged as a child of God/ since God loves every person into existence, each person has infinite value in God's eyes/ God values individuality and everyone should be respected.

A minority have a more insular attitude/ wrongly believe that only one racial group historically belongs to the British Isles/ despite it being against the law they may cause racial abuse e.g. at football matches.

7. Catholic teaching about homosexuality is based around its teaching on the meaning and purpose of sex/ through a sexual union God can bless the couple by creating new life/ this cannot happen when the two people are of the same sex/ so the Catholic Church believes that any sexual union that is not open to new life is sinful as it distorts the purpose of sex/ Catechism of the Catholic Church 2357/ calls on homosexuals to live chaste lives.

The Church of England supports the idea of same-sex civil partnerships/ does not teach that homosexuals should be celibate/ many non-believers are not against homosexuality because of the belief that everyone should be treated equally with equal rights/ therefore they agree with same-sex marriage.

Test the 5 mark question

Suggested answers, other relevant answers would be credited. 1 mark for each simple contrasting or similar point, another mark for developing each point, so 4 marks for two developed points, 1 extra mark for a correct reference to a source of Christian belief or teaching:

9. Christians believe that humans are created in the image of God which gives them a sense of dignity (Genesis 1:27)/ humans share in the qualities of God and are superior to other living beings/ the sanctity of life/ Colossians 3:11 says that there should be no divisions between people because all people have dignity/ Christians should be caring and do what is good/ this means following God's commands which means striving for justice and equality (Micah 6:8)/ God loves humans so much that God became man in Jesus and died to save all human beings.

10. Genesis 2 stresses that men and women are complementary to each other/ each have a different role to play/ are made in the image of God and so are equal, but that does not mean uniformity/ 'equal dignity and equal rights do not mean uniformity' (Youcat 401)/ role of the woman within the home is irreplaceable but doesn't stop women going out to work/ leadership role of men in the Church/ everyone is equal in Christ (Colossians 3:11, Galatians 3:28).

Test the 12 mark question

Suggested answers shown here, but see page 12 for guidance on levels of response.

12. **Arguments in support:**

- The Catholic Church owns property to the value of billions of pounds; this includes land, churches, schools, hospitals and art treasures.

- If this property was sold, the money could be given to those struggling in poverty.

- 'Riches should be stored up in heaven, not on earth' (Sermon on the Mount).

- 'You cannot serve both God and money' (Matthew 6:24).

- Parables of the Rich Man and Lazarus/ Sheep and Goats/ it is morally wrong to have all this wealth while people are poor.

Arguments in support of other views:

- The Church has to operate successfully providing all the services it does.

- People need places for worship, schools for education, and hospitals for the sick.

- Some of the art treasures are gradually being sold off – can't flood the market or the value would decrease.

- There has to be a balance between helping the poor and providing for peoples' spiritual needs.

- The Church does a lot through giving and supporting charities such as CAFOD and Christian Aid/ also campaigns to get governments to help and to stop exploitation.

13. **Arguments in support:**

- The Church of England has allowed women to become priests since 1993 and bishops since 2014 e.g. Libby Lane.

- Many Protestant Churches have had women leaders for decades/ many women had important roles in the Bible.

- The Catholic Church needs to move with the times and give equal opportunities to women/ current situation is a form of sexism.

- Ordination should be based on 'calling', not on gender.

- In Christ all are one, male and female (Colossians 3:11, Galatians 3:28).

Arguments in support of other views:

- Tradition is important in the Catholic Church.

- Jesus ordained his male followers, the apostles, as priests during the Last Supper.

- This is not seen as diminishing the role or status of women.

- There are examples of how men and women are equal but different/ Youcat 330.